Public Relations Cases

Public Relations Cases

EIGHTH EDITION

JERRY A. HENDRIX
American University

DARRELL C. HAYES
American University

Australia • Brazil • Japan • Korea • Mexico • Singapore • Spain • United Kingdom • United States

WADSWORTH
CENGAGE Learning™

Public Relations Cases: Eighth Edition
Jerry A. Hendrix, Darrell C. Hayes

Senior Publisher: Lyn Uhl

Publisher in Humanities: Michael Rosenberg

Assistant Editors: Megan Garvey and Rebekah Matthews

Editorial Assistant: Erin Pass

Technology Project Manager: Jessica Badiner

Marketing Manager: Erin Mitchell

Marketing Assistant: Ryan Ahern

Marketing Communications Manager: Christine Dobberpuhl

Content Project Manager: Tiffany Kayes

Art Director: Linda Helcher

Print Buyer: Elizabeth Donaghey

Permissions Editor: Roberta Broyer

Production Service/Compositor: Macmillan Publishing Solutions

Photo Manager: Don Schlotman

Photo Researcher: Sarah Evertson

Cover Designer: Lou Ann Thesing and Laura Brown

Cover Image: Courtesy Thrivent Financial (first and second images); Courtesy Oceana; Courtesy Convention & Visitors Bureau of Greater Cleveland and Rock and Roll Hall of Fame; Courtesy General Dynamics Armament and Technical Products

For product information and technology assistance, contact us at
Cengage Learning Academic Resource Center, 1-800-354-9706.
For permission to use material from this text or product, submit all requests online at
www.cengage.com/permissions.
Further permissions questions can be e-mailed to
permissionrequest@cengage.com.

Library of Congress Control Number: 2008943751

International Edition:

ISBN-13: 978-0-495-56782-0

ISBN-10: 0-495-56782-5

Wadsworth Cengage Learning
20 Channel Center
Boston, MA 02210
USA

Cengage Learning products are represented in Canada by Nelson Education, Ltd.

For your course and learning solutions, visit **academic.cengage.com**.

Purchase any of our products at your local college store or at our preferred online store **www.ichapters.com**.

Printed in Canada
1 2 3 4 5 6 7 12 11 10 09 08

Brief Contents

Contents

Preface

We continue to believe that readers of a public relations textbook should be provided with a clear set of guiding public relations principles accompanied by cases that generally illustrate those principles in a positive light and thus serve as models of effective management and practice. In order to give students the most current examples of award-winning communication campaigns, all but two of the 30 cases are new to this edition. Most of the cases were winners of the Public Relations Society of America's prestigious Silver Anvil Award contest, and therefore constitute some of the finest examples of public relations practices available.

The book is divided into four sections: Solving Public Relations Problems, Reaching Major Audiences, Emergency Public Relations, and Integrated Marketing Communications.

In Part 1, the introductory chapter begins with a philosophy we have held for a long time—that the best public relations is characterized by interaction, or better still, interactive participation among sources and receivers of communication. This philosophy is based on the underlying premise that public relations is mostly persuasion. Some years ago, communication researchers discovered that the most effective means of persuasion is self-persuasion. Audience involvement thus becomes a crucial ingredient of successful public relations.

Chapter 1 also includes a section on new technology and ethics in public relations. As in previous editions, we have included the Public Relations Society of America (PRSA) Member Code of Ethics in Appendix II, but you will also find some additional dimensions of ethics in this opening chapter.

In Chapter 2, you will encounter the "Hendrix process model," which involves initial research, the setting of objectives, programming, and evaluation. (The elements of this process model form a convenient mnemonic device, the acronym ROPE.) This model focuses special attention on the significance of objectives and their arrangement in a hierarchical order of output and impact functions. Another feature of this process model, reflecting a training and background in speech communication, is special emphasis on the role of interpersonal communication, including speeches, speakers bureaus, small-group and one-on-one formats, and nonverbal aspects of communication. In a word, the ROPE process model is interactive.

Part 2 consists of audience-centered applications of the process, with accompanying illustrative cases. The audience-centered forms of public relations included are media relations, employee and member relations, community relations, public affairs and government relations, investor relations, international public relations, and relations with special publics. Most of the cases were winners of the Silver Anvil Award contest, conducted annually by the PRSA. The cases follow the Silver Anvil entry format, which is somewhat different from the format of the ROPE model. The major difference is that the ROPE model sets objectives apart as a separate category, and the Silver Anvil format does not. The ROPE programming phase includes planning and communication (execution), and both Silver Anvil and ROPE models begin and end with research and evaluation. Thus, the two models have a difference mainly in format, not substance.

Part 3 includes both theory and illustrative cases for emergency or crisis public relations. This field of PR is not oriented to a particular audience, so we have set it apart in a separate section of the book.

Also set apart is the section on integrated marketing communications (IMC), the newest area of public relations. IMC is a combination of public relations and marketing techniques, so it is not really new. Though some practitioners, scholars, and the PRSA itself omit the word "marketing" and call it "integrated communications," our preference is to use the widely accepted term "integrated marketing communications."

Finally, the appendixes contain questions for class discussion and the PRSA Member Code of Ethics 2000, which contains guidelines for the ethical practice of public relations.

The Instructor's Manual for the eighth edition has been expanded with additional material from many of the cases and updated scenarios for class exercises and discussions. Instructors who adopt the book will have access to the online edition of the Instructor's Manual and may request a copy of the video material from the publisher.

ACKNOWLEDGMENTS

Many public relations practitioners have helped by granting permission to use their cases. We hope they will accept our gratitude and understand that space does not permit a list of all their names.

As with previous editions, we are indebted to the students and administrators in the American University School of Communication for their encouragement and support. We would particularly like to acknowledge graduate assistants Colleen Lerro, Erika Eckstrom, and Lisa Rassenti for helping us with the eighth edition.

Many professionals at Cengage Learning contributed to the publication and success of our book. We'd like to thank development editor Cheryl Forman and publisher Michael Rosenberg for their leadership, guidance, and patience on this edition. Authors work closely with their production editors, and it is a pleasure to thank content project manager Tiffany Kayes for her outstanding work on this edition. Assistant editor Megan Garvey and media editor Jessica Badiner worked with us on the Instructor's Manual and DVD and assistant editor Rebekah Matthews conducted the peer review that helped inform the plan for the new edition.

Finally, we gratefully acknowledge the following reviewers, whose constructive comments helped in the development of this eighth edition: Christine Apel, Loras College; Lois Boynton, University of North Carolina at Chapel Hill; Mary Frances Casper, Boise State University; Eddie Downes, Boston University; Jim Eggensperger, Iona College; Alison Feldman, University of Southern Queensland; Donyale Griffin, Wayne State University; Tricia Hansen-Horn, University of Central Missouri; Kirk Hazlett, Curry College; Christine Helsel, Eastern Illinois University; Alison Henderson, University of Waikato; Debbie Menger, University of Texas, San Antonio; Kathy Menzie, Washburn University; Marjorie Nadler, Miami University; Brent Northup, Carroll College of Montana; Richard Parker, University of Arkansas at Little Rock; Pamela Parry, Belmont University; Phillip Powell, Valparaiso University; Richard Robinson, University of Tennessee at Martin; Danielle Smalley, University of Technology, Sydney; Michael Smith, La Salle University; Steve Wiegenstein, Culver-Stockton College; Kelly Wolfe, Webber International University.

About the Authors

Jerry A. Hendrix, Ph.D., is professor emeritus of communication at American University in Washington, D.C., where he taught for 37 years. He is an accredited member of the Public Relations Society of America.

Darrell C. Hayes is an assistant professor at American University's School of Communication, Washington, D.C. Before joining the faculty, he had more than 15 years of experience in public relations with technology firms, with nonprofit associations, and as a government communication manager. He has also worked with a marketing research firm and been the managing director of the Aerospace Education Foundation. He is an accredited member of the Public Relations Society of America.

Solving Public Relations Problems

1

Public Relations in Action

One of the best ways to learn about public relations is through the study of contemporary examples of its practice. Such case studies can bring public relations to life in a way that theoretical textbooks and classroom lectures cannot. Here we will first examine the nature of public relations through its definition and a process model. Then we will look at various forms of public relations along with several cases to illustrate each form.

One way of defining public relations has been simply to invert the term, so it becomes "relations with publics." An improved modification of this definition is "*interrelationships* with publics." This better reflects the nature of contemporary public relations as an *interactive* form of communication in which the targeted audiences yield information to the organization through its research efforts and often *participate* in the public relations programming itself. This interactive or mutual dimension of public relations is seen in the comprehensive description adopted by the Public Relations Society of America (PRSA) in 1982 (see Exhibit 1-A).

In helping to define and implement policy, the public relations practitioner utilizes a variety of professional communication skills and plays an integrative role both within the organization and between the organization and the external environment.

PROCESS

The public relations process is a method for solving problems. It has four phases: research, objectives, programming, and evaluation. Each element may be modified by the demands of different audiences or publics, including employees, members, customers, local communities, shareholders, and, usually, the news media.

E X H I B I T   1-A   PRSA's Official Statement on Public Relations*

Public relations helps our complex, pluralistic society to reach decisions and function more effectively by contributing to mutual understanding among groups and institutions. It serves to bring private and public policies into harmony.

Public relations serves a wide variety of institutions in society such as businesses, trade unions, government agencies, voluntary associations, foundations, hospitals, and educational and religious institutions. To achieve their goals, these institutions must develop effective relationships with many different audiences or publics such as employees, members, customers, local communities, shareholders, and other institutions, and with society at large.

The managements of institutions need to understand the attitudes and values of their publics in order to achieve institutional goals. The goals themselves are shaped by the external environment. The public relations practitioner acts as a counselor to management, and as a mediator, helping to translate private aims into reasonable, publicly acceptable policy and action.

As a management function, public relations encompasses the following:

- Anticipating, analyzing, and interpreting public opinion, attitudes, and issues that might impact, for good or ill, the operations and plans of the organization.
- Counseling management at all levels in the organization with regard to policy decisions, courses of action, and communication, taking into account their public ramifications and the organization's social or citizenship responsibilities.
- Researching, conducting, and evaluating, on a continuing basis, programs of action and communication to achieve informed public understanding necessary to the success of an organization's aims. These may include marketing, financial, fund-raising, employee, community, or government relations, and other programs.
- Planning and implementing the organization's efforts to influence or change public policy.
- Setting objectives, planning, budgeting, recruiting and training staff, developing facilities—in short, *managing* the resources needed to perform all of the above.
- Examples of the knowledge that may be required in the professional practice of public relations include communication arts, psychology, social psychology, sociology, political science, economics, and the principles of management and ethics. Technical knowledge and skills are required for opinion research, public issues analysis, media relations, direct mail, institutional advertising, publications, film/video productions, special events, speeches, and presentations.

---

* Formally adopted by the PRSA Assembly on November 6, 1982. Reprinted courtesy PRSA.

The *research* phase of the process involves identifying and learning about three key elements: (1) a *client* or organization that has (2) a *problem* or potential problem to be solved that involves (3) one or more of its *audiences*, or publics.

The second phase of the public relations process involves the setting of *objectives* for a program to solve the problem. These objectives may include the kind of influence the client hopes to exert with the audiences, such as informing them or modifying their attitudes or behaviors. The objectives may also include statements about the program itself, such as its composition or how it will operate.

The third phase of the process consists of planning and executing a *program* to accomplish the objectives. The program comprises a central theme, messages, and various forms of communication aimed at reaching the audiences.

Finally, *evaluation*, as defined in this process, consists of two parts. First, it includes an ongoing procedure of program monitoring and adjustment. Second, evaluation refers back specifically to the objectives that were set in the second phase of the process and examines the practitioner's degree of success in achieving them.

CASES

The illustrations of this process in action—the cases—are grouped in this text according to the various audiences that public relations practitioners reach. Each audience calls for some modifications in the overall four-step process, and the cases illustrate the modified process in action.

Cases are presented to illustrate relations with the media, with internal audiences, with the community, with the government, with investors, with consumers, with international audiences, and with special groups.

Effective public relations cases serve as models for students and practitioners alike. They enhance public relations theory, making it come alive with illustrations and examples of the PR process in action. Moreover, audience-centered cases exemplify the constraints involved in conducting research, setting objectives, designing and executing a program, and evaluating what has been done. In sum, cases, especially audience-centered cases, effectively illustrate public relations principles and management and test theoretical applications in real situations and environments.

NEW TECHNOLOGY

The most striking aspect of the cases included here is the pervasiveness of new technology, most notably the use of the Internet.

First-generation "brochure-ware" Web sites are becoming more interactive. The Internet is regularly used to conduct relations with a variety of publics. Organizations keep their media kits on the Web site in the form of news releases, background information, photographs, executive speeches, quarterly and annual reports to shareholders, position papers, interviews, and so forth. The sites provide means for e-mail feedback and allow discussion boards and even online collaboration through wikis where a group can meet at a Web site and individually provide content and update or change the contributions of others. The most famous is "Wikipedia," an online encyclopedia with millions of users able to update and correct an entry.

Discussions about Web 2.0 suggest the new technology has not only brought new channels of communication but also changed the fabric of interaction and even the very culture of society. Web 2.0 involves an interconnectedness of communities with people engaged in mutually beneficial conversations at sites such as Wikipedia, health discussion boards, or eBay to sell stuff. Social media is one expression of this trend where everyone has the ability to publish and share information on the Web. Instead of passive recipients of the traditional "mass media," such as newspapers, books, and movies, individuals may post information on blogs; develop MySpace pages where they link to "friends" to update each other on their lives; establish social news sites such as Digg and Mixx; post video narratives on YouTube; or show their photos on Flickr and Zooomr. In November 2007, the American Society of Association Executives (ASAE) published a special edition of *Association Now* called "Everything Is Connected" to help associations understand the trends and to adapt their communication practices. *The New York Times* columnist Thomas L. Friedman suggested the convergence of new technologies has made this a "horizontal world" where global collaboration has become the skill that differentiates the best in their businesses.

E-mail has become the dominant form of communication both internally and externally. E-mail has virtually replaced internal print materials, such as newsletters, written memos, and some face-to-face communication. Externally, e-mail has become the major means of communicating news releases, media alerts, and other forms of media relations. E-mail also provides instant communication with consumers, investors, and a variety of other targeted publics. Text messaging involves the migration of e-mail to the cell phone. It has become the standard for communicating quickly with friends and family and is the system of choice for emergency notifications on college campuses. The ability to deliver messages, video, and news via the cell phone has become the next technological frontier for communication campaigns.

Many organizations have created *intranets*—internal Internets—to handle large volumes of internal communication with employees and members. Some organizations also have created *extranets*—selective external Internets—to reach targeted external groups, such as investors, journalists, consumers, and others. CD-ROMs, DVDs, and digital audio and video files also have become a major public relations tool, with vast storage and the potential for interaction with targeted groups. Instant messaging has made online collaboration immediate, speeding both the flow of information and decision-making loops in organizations. Cell phone text messaging made computer e-mail portable and has even led to the rapid mobilization of street protests in many countries. Viral messaging uses the natural propensity of people to share information with others to spread organizational information. Many newspapers have dropped their film critics because text messages and online postings became the preferred recommendations on whether or not young people view a film.

Web logs, or blogs, allow anyone to become a publisher and to share personal opinions or their own "news." This has blurred the distinction between traditional journalism and other information sources. Some senior managers in organizations have established their own blogs to make sure the organization's positions are posted on this wider tableau of public opinion. Podcasting emerged as another tool for reaching audiences. With the popularity of "personal on-demand" players, podcasts became another way to share news, special events, or personal opinions via the Internet. Individuals, institutions, and corporations have established a presence in virtual worlds such as Second Life to further interact and connect with their publics who populate these sites. The rapid exchange of information and messages in this digital universe not only affects the way organizations must more quickly respond to an emergency but has also impacted the practice of public relations in a major, ever-expanding way. It has both cluttered the message channels and yet opened new avenues for connecting with publics.

The emphasis on technology comes with a caveat. Even as PR agencies and corporations rush to establish digital practices and social media specialties, this trend often assumes new technology that provides all communication to all publics. All audiences are not equally technologically engaged. A Pew Internet & American Life Project study found 41 percent of Americans rarely used tech assets or were completely off the network.[1] Solid strategic communication, no matter the technology used to communicate, still stands as the foundation principle of this book.

ETHICS

The PRSA Member Code of Ethics (see Appendix II), adopted by the Public Relations Society of America Assembly in 2000, provides a way that each member "can daily reaffirm a commitment to ethical professional activities and decisions." The code of ethics first presents a set of core professional values that should guide all ethical practitioners of public relations. These values include responsible advocacy; honesty; expertise; independence (objective and responsible counsel to clients); loyalty to clients while serving the public interest; and fairness in dealing with clients, employers, competitors, the media, and the general public.

The second part of the code consists of such ethical principles of conduct as "protecting and advancing the free flow of accurate and truthful information," "promoting healthy and fair competition" among professional public relations practitioners, disclosing honest and accurate information in all communications, protecting "the privacy of clients, organizations, and individuals by safeguarding confidential information," "avoiding real, potential, or perceived conflicts of interest," and working constantly to "strengthen the public's trust in the profession." All students of public relations, as well as long-time practitioners, should read the entire code.

This commitment to ethical practices on the part of the PRSA is intended to counter the image of public relations practitioners as "hired guns" who will say or do whatever it takes to accomplish the goals of their clients. There is some basis for this negative public perception of the profession. The following is a discussion of some of the practices that have earned public relations a sometimes-less-than-savory reputation.

On a continuum going from bad to worse, we might begin with the relatively innocuous practice of *lowballing*. This consists of downplaying expectations for a program or project that may not be especially successful in its outcome. The mass media frequently accuse the White House of "lowballing" a presidential visit abroad, a peace initiative in some part of the world, or some other effort that may not yield much tangible results.

Closely related to lowballing is the ubiquitous *spin* that is used by governmental and corporate public relations practitioners to make their programs look good. The "spin" actually consists of the one-sided use of facts or data to create a desired impression. These practitioners are often referred to by the mass media as *spin doctors*. By selectively using only positive aspects of a program or a political campaign, practitioners can portray their clients' activities in a favorable light. Conversely, the endeavors of an opponent may be selectively portrayed only in the negative.

Next we might examine six types of *distortion* sometimes found in the practice of public relations. The first of these is commonly called *hype*. Hype is the use of hyperbole or magnification, sometimes referred to as the "blowing out of proportion" of the attributes of a person, event, or product. The mass media are fond of portraying various criminal acts as "the crime of the century." Advertising constantly uses hype in its exaggerated claims for products and services, and public relations practitioners have been known to "stretch the truth" about clients and their programs.

A second type of distortion is *minimizing*, the exact opposite of hype. Sometimes practitioners will play down the seriousness of a failure or the negative aspects of a product or other problems experienced by a client.

A third type of frequently used distortion is *overgeneralization*, or drawing sweeping conclusions based on one isolated case or example. If a candidate for the presidential nomination of a political party loses the New Hampshire primary, for example, the mass media, along with the candidate's opposition, usually conclude that the nomination is lost, based on the results of that one primary election. Similarly, singular successes have been used to draw sweeping positive conclusions. One case study should never be the sole basis for such generalizations.

Categorization is a fourth type of distortion sometimes found in the practice of public relations. An example of categorization may involve the portrayal of a person, event, or product as "good" or "bad" with no middle ground or shades of gray. Other frequently used categories include "successful," "unsuccessful," "useful," "useless," and the like.

Closely related to categorization is the practice of *labeling*. An individual or program may be labeled either a "winner" or a "loser," often on the basis of sketchy or nonexistent evidence. History is replete with the use of such labels as "witch," "communist," "limousine liberal," and "right-wing conservative." The list could go on endlessly.

A final form of distortion may be called *image transfer*. This involves the deliberate shifting of image from one person, event, or product to another, but dissimilar, person, event, or product. Such advertising techniques as the identification of a product with an attractive or sexy model are perhaps the most frequent use of image transfer. Public relations practitioners also seek to transfer the high-credibility images of popular paid spokespersons to low-credibility or unknown programs, causes, or events.

In addition to lowballing, spinning, and a variety of distortions, we should consider the even more offensive practices of using outright *lies* and *coverups*. One example of these practices is the manufacturer that knows its product is defective and potentially dangerous. Instead of making this information public, the company blames accidents on improper consumer use and handles the resulting litigation on a case-by-case basis. These case-by-case settlements are usually substantially less expensive than staging a product recall. Meanwhile, the company's public relations office is busy denying product fault, issuing statements blaming the consumer. In regard to coverups, the defining event *that has become generic* in its field was the Watergate affair, a major turning point in American political history and the coverup by which all subsequent coverups have been measured.

This is by no means an exhaustive list of unethical public relations practices. The PRSA Member Code of Ethics cites other activities such as corruption of communication channels and other deceptive practices. For an understanding of the ethical practice of public relations, the student of public relations should carefully study the Member Code of Ethics in Appendix II, along with the unethical practices discussed here.

In the public relations workplace, the best argument for ethical practices is that they are "good business." The positive side is that the company or organization can point with pride to its ethical practices. The negative side is that, if an organization or client is caught by the ubiquitous mass media in an unethical practice, this will become a headline news story and perhaps blot out all previous positive accomplishments. This study of applied ethics should therefore become an overriding concern in the education of public relations practitioners.

THE OVERALL PLAN OF THIS BOOK

Part I introduces you to public relations, with special emphasis on the process outlined above. The elements of this process are eclectic, but the arrangement of those elements forms the acronym ROPE (research, objectives, programming, evaluation). A major feature is a new emphasis on and a new way of classifying public relations objectives. Objectives are viewed as the central and guiding element in the process, and they are arranged in a hierarchical order.

Another feature of this public relations process, consistent with its interactive nature, is a heightened emphasis on interpersonal interaction as a form of controlled communication. The importance of speeches and speakers' bureaus as methods of public relations communication is recognized, but this book also advocates the extensive use of small-group and dyadic (one-on-one) interpersonal formats, along with a treatment of nonverbal communication. A recurring theme is that in truly effective communication there can be no substitute for direct interaction.

Part II explores how public relations reaches major audiences. It looks at media relations; internal communication, including employee and member relations; community relations; public affairs, or government relations; investor and financial relations; consumer relations; international public relations; and relations with special publics. Following a conceptual treatment of each form of relations are several example cases. Most of these illustrative cases have won Silver Anvil Awards from the PRSA. As such, they represent the very best among models of public relations.

Part III concentrates on emergency public relations, an important area in contemporary practice. Both students and professionals need to be reminded of the need to study crisis PR procedures. Unlike such audience-centered forms as media relations or community relations, emergency PR is an area in which no one specializes. Yet all practitioners need to be prepared for it.

Part IV focuses on the newest development in the field: Integrated Marketing Communications, the combination of both public relations and advertising to accomplish essentially marketing objectives.

Finally, the appendixes include the PRSA Member Code of Ethics.

ENDNOTE

1. Horrigan, John B. "A Typology of Information and Communication Technology Users," Pew Internet & American Life Project (May 2007), www.pewinternet.org.

GENERAL PUBLIC RELATIONS READINGS

Austin, Erica Weintraub, and Bruce E. Pinkleton. *Strategic Public Relations Management.* Mahwah, NJ: Erlbaum, 2001.

Botan, Carl H., and Maureen Taylor. "Public Relations: State of the Field," *Journal of Communication* 54 (December 1, 2004): 645–661.

Bruning, Stephen D., Melissa Dials, and Amanda Shirka. "Using Dialogue to Build Organization-Public Relationships, Engage Publics, and Positively Affect Organizational Outcomes," *Public Relations Review* 34 (March 2008): 25–31.

Center, Allen H., Patrick Jackson, Stacey Smith, and Frank Stansberry. *Public Relations Practice: Managerial Case Studies and Practice*, 7th ed. Englewood Cliffs, NJ: Prentice-Hall, 2007.

Cutlip, Scott M., Allen H. Center, and Glen M. Broom. *Effective Public Relations*, 9th ed. Englewood Cliffs, NJ: Prentice-Hall, 2006.

Gower, Karla A. *Legal and Ethical Considerations for Public Relations*, 2d ed. Long Grove, IL: Waveland Press, 2008.

Grunig, Larissa A., James E. Grunig, and David M. Dozier. *Excellent Public Relations and Effective Organizations.* Mahwah, NJ: Erlbaum, 2002.

Guth, David W., and Charles Marsh. *Public Relations: A Values-Driven Approach*, 4th ed. Boston: Allyn & Bacon, 2008.

Heath, Robert L. *Handbook of Public Relations*. Thousand Oaks, CA: Sage Publications, 2000.

Lamb, Lawrence F., and Kathy Brittain McKee. *Applied Public Relations*. Mahwah, NJ: Erlbaum, 2005.

Ledingham, John A., and Stephen D. Bruning. *Public Relations as Relationship Management*. Mahwah, NJ: Erlbaum, 2001.

Lesly, Philip, ed. *Lesly's Handbook of Public Relations and Communications*, 5th ed. New York: AMACOM, 1998.

Mickey, Thomas J. *Deconstructing Public Relations*. Mahwah, NJ: Erlbaum, 2002.

Mogel, Leonard. *Making It in Public Relations*. Mahwah, NJ: Erlbaum, 2002.

Newsom, Doug, Judy VanSlyke Turk, and Dean Kruckeberg. *This Is PR: The Realities of Public Relations*, 9th ed. Belmont, CA: Wadsworth, 2006.

Seitel, Fraser P. *The Practice of Public Relations*, 10th ed. Englewood Cliffs, NJ: Prentice-Hall, 2006.

Smith, Ronald D. *Strategic Planning for Public Relations*, 2d ed. Mahwah, NJ: Erlbaum, 2005.

Thomsen, Steven R. "Public Relations in the New Millennium: Understanding the Forces That Are Reshaping the Profession," *Public Relations Quarterly* 42 (spring 1997): 11–17.

Toth, Elizabeth L. *Public Relations Values in the New Millennium*. Mahwah, NJ: Erlbaum, 2000.

Wilcox, Dennis L. *Public Relations Writing and Media Techniques*, 5th ed. Boston: Allyn & Bacon, 2005.

Wilcox, Dennis L., Glen T. Cameron, Phillip H. Ault, and Warren K. Agee. *Public Relations: Strategies and Tactics*, 9th ed. Boston: Allyn & Bacon, 2008.

Zappala, Joseph M., and Ann R. Carden. *Public Relations Worktext*, 2d ed. Mahwah, NJ: Erlbaum, 2004.

2

A Public Relations Process

As we saw in Chapter 1, the public relations problem-solving process involves four procedures. First, initial research is performed to establish the basic elements of the communication transaction. Second, objectives for the transaction are established. Third, programming, including all the methods of communication used, is planned and executed to carry out the objectives. Finally, ongoing and follow-up evaluation is conducted both to monitor and to measure how well the program accomplished its objectives.

Now for a detailed look at each of the elements in this process.

RESEARCH

Research consists of investigating three aspects of the overall public relations procedure: the client or organization for whom the program is being prepared, the opportunity or problem that accounts for the program at this time, and all audiences to be targeted for communication in the PR program.

Client Research

First, public relations practitioners must be thoroughly familiar with their clients. If the practitioner is working in an in-house PR department, the client will be the organization housing the department. An employee of a PR firm will obviously be independent of the client. In either case, background data about the client or organization—its financial status, reputation, past and present public relations practices, and public relations strengths, weaknesses, and opportunities—are an essential starting point for any program. A communication audit, whether formal or informal, can reveal much about an organization's distinctive style of culture, communication practices, and relationships with its publics.

If the organization is a business, the practitioner needs to be familiar with its products and services as well as the overall competitive environment. The practitioner should also know about the marketing, legal, and financial functions of the organization in order to coordinate them with the public relations efforts. Interviews with key management personnel and documents such as annual and quarterly reports can provide this information. The location of the organization, whether in a single city or in multiple branches, the delivery system for the products or services (such as the use of a dealer network), the organization's major suppliers, and, of course, the identity and demographics of the customers are all necessary to understand the client.

If the organization is nonprofit, the practitioner must become acquainted with the services provided and the organization's clientele, including major donors.

Other important background information includes the precise mission of the organization, its management's goals, priorities, and problems, and how this proposed public relations program might help accomplish these overall objectives.

Along with this background information, the practitioner needs a good working knowledge of the organization's personnel—its total workforce, both management and nonmanagement. Special attention must be given to key management people, not just the director of public relations, if there is one. How does top management view the role of public relations? Are PR people regarded as problem solvers and decision makers, or are they simply "hired guns"?

The financial status of a publicly owned corporation is easy to determine. Financial data for such organizations must be reported to the U.S. Securities and Exchange Commission (SEC), and this information is always available in the company's annual report or other financial publications.

Finally, the practitioner needs to raise questions that directly relate to public relations. What is the client's reputation in its field and with its customers or clientele? In marketing, this often refers to brand identity and brand equity. The answers to these questions constitute the organization's public image, an area of primary concern to PR practitioners. What image liabilities or assets does the organization possess? What are its present and past public relations practices? Does the organization have particular PR strengths, that is, practices or programs that would enhance its public image? What are its PR weaknesses, the practices or programs that might create an unfavorable image or negative public opinion? What opportunities exist for promoting favorable public opinion or behavior toward the organization?

Thus, the first requisite for effective research in the public relations process is an in-depth understanding of the client for whom the program is prepared.

Opportunity or Problem Research

The second aspect of research, a logical outgrowth of knowledge of the client, consists of clearly determining why the organization should conduct a particular PR program at a particular time. Is it because of a unique opportunity to favorably influence public opinion or behavior toward the client, or is it in response to the development of unfavorable opinion or behavior toward the client? If it is the latter, extensive research must be done on the source of the problem, whether it be an individual or an organization.

Public relations programs that arise out of opportunities are called proactive programs. In the short run, effective proactive programming may seem extravagantly expensive to management, but these programs often head off the need to respond to problems with even more expensive reactive programs. The proactive program is like preventive medicine, or the concept of "wellness" now being widely promoted by health maintenance organizations. Preventive medicine is far more desirable than surgery in response to a severe illness. Similarly, an organization should keep close tabs on its ongoing relations with its constituent audiences to avoid PR problems.

This is not to argue that proactive programs are good and reactive programs are bad. In spite of all efforts to avert them, problems may develop. The reactive program then becomes necessary and perhaps beneficial. When a fire breaks out, we must call the fire department. Public relations practitioners must be ready to extinguish "fires," but they should also be skilled in "fire prevention."

Proactive programs are generally long range and strategic in nature. The organization cannot afford to let its guard down in maintaining good relations with important audiences. Reactive programs, on the other hand, are usually short range, often ending as soon as the immediate problem is cleared up. But a good, ongoing, proactive program with the same audience may prevent the recurrence of similar problems.

Thus, an investigation of why a public relations program is necessary, whether it should be proactive or reactive, and whether it should be ongoing or short range is the second aspect of research in the public relations process.

Audience Research

The third aspect of research in the public relations process involves investigating the target audiences, or "publics." This part of the research process includes identifying the particular groups that should be targeted, determining appropriate research data that will be useful in communicating with these publics, and compiling or processing the data using appropriate research procedures.

Audience Identification.   All organizations have long-range, and sometimes short-term, "relations" or communications, with certain "standard" publics. The publics of principal concern to most organizations include the media, internal employees or members, the organization's home community, and the national, state, and local governments. A business that provides a product or service for customers is concerned with consumers as an important public. A publicly owned business has the additional, significant audience of its shareowners and the financial community. Finally, all organizations have unique groups of constituent audiences, or special publics. Nonprofit organizations are concerned with donors as a special public. Schools are interested in maintaining communications with parents. Large corporations may need to communicate regularly with their dealers and suppliers.

To address publics most effectively, we should segment each public into its diverse components, so each component may become a separate public to be targeted for special messages. The media, for example, should be segmented into mass and specialized groups. Of the two internal publics, employees can be segmented into management and nonmanagement, and members should be divided into organization employees, officers, members, prospective members, state or local chapters, and related or allied organizations (see Chapter 4). The organization's home community should be segmented into community media, community leaders, and community organizations. Government publics should be subdivided into federal, state, county, and city levels; then each of these levels should be further segmented into legislative and executive branches. Consumer publics can be subdivided into groupings that include company employees, customers, activist consumer groups, consumer publications, community media, and community leaders and organizations (see Chapter 8). Investor publics for financial relations should be segmented into shareowners and potential shareowners, security analysts and investment counselors, the financial press, and the SEC. (See Exhibit 2-a for suggested segmentation of these major publics.)

Targeting.   Once the publics have been identified and segmented into their components, the practitioner is ready for the more difficult task of targeting the most important publics on a priority basis. This prioritizing calls for a situational assessment of the significance to the client or organization of each potential public. The importance of a potential public is determined by its degree of influence, prestige, power, or perhaps need, and by its level of involvement with the client or organization. Four key questions to consider in targeting and prioritizing publics are:

- Who is this public (demographics, psychographics, and so on)?
- Why is it important to us?
- How active or involved is this public, relative to our interests?
- Which publics are most important to us, in priority rank order?

Desired Data.   Once target publics have been segmented into their key components, the practitioner is ready to assess informational needs for each public. Typically, the practitioner will want to know each targeted public's level of information about the organization; the image and other relevant attitudes held about the organization and its product or service; and past and present audience behaviors relevant to the client or organization. Researching the demographics, media habits, and levels of media use of each targeted audience will tell the practitioner how best to reach it. All these data are used to formulate objectives for the public relations program.

Research Methods

With this general framework of informational needs in mind, the practitioner must next decide which research procedures will yield the necessary data.

E X H I B I T 2-a   Major Publics

Media Publics

Mass media

Local
> Print publications
>> Newspapers
>>
>> Magazines
>
> TV stations
>
> Radio stations

National
> Print publications
>
> Broadcast networks
>
> Wire services

Specialized media

Local
> Trade, industry, and association publications
>
> Organizational house and membership publications
>
> Ethnic publications
>
> Publications of special groups
>
> Specialized broadcast programs and stations

National/International
> General business publications
>
> Trade, industry, and association publications
>
> Organizational house and membership publications
>
> Ethnic publications
>
> Publications of national special groups
>
> Specialized broadcast programs and networks

Employee Publics

Management

> Upper-level administrators
>
> Mid-level administrators
>
> Lower-level administrators

Nonmanagement (staff)

> Specialists
>
> Clerical personnel
>
> Secretarial personnel

Uniformed personnel
   Equipment operators
   Drivers
   Security personnel
   Other uniformed personnel
Union representatives
Other nonmanagement personnel

Member Publics

Organization employees

Headquarters management
Headquarters nonmanagement (staff)
Other headquarters personnel

Organization officers

Elected officers
Appointed officers
Legislative groups
Boards, committees

Organization members

Regular members
Members in special categories—sustaining, emeritus, student members
Honorary members or groups

Prospective organization members

State or local chapters
Organization employees
Organization officers
Organization members
Prospective organization members

Related or other allied organizations

Community Publics

Community media

Mass
Specialized

Community leaders

Public officials
Educators

Religious leaders
Professionals
Executives
Bankers/Financial leaders
Union leaders
Ethnic leaders
Neighborhood leaders

Community organizations

Civic
Service
Social
Business
Cultural
Religious
Youth
Political
Special interest groups
Online interest groups
Other

Government Publics

Federal

Legislative branch
Representatives, staff, committee personnel
Senators, staff, committee personnel
Executive branch
President
White House staff, advisers, committees
Cabinet officers, departments, agencies, commissions

State

Legislative branch
Representatives, delegates, staff, committee personnel
Senators, staff, committee personnel
Executive branch
Governor
Governor's staff, advisers, committees
Cabinet officers, departments, agencies, commissions

County

County executive
Other county officials, commissions, departments

City

    Mayor or city manager

    City council

    Other city officials, commissions, departments

International

    Official delegations

    Nongovernmental organizations

Investor Publics

Shareowners and potential shareowners

Security analysts and investment counselors

Financial press

    Major wire services: Dow Jones & Co., Reuters Economic Service, AP, UPI, Bloomberg

    Major business magazines: Business Week, Fortune, and the like—mass circulation and specialized

    Major newspapers: New York Times, Wall Street Journal, USA Today

    Statistical services: Standard & Poor's Corp., Moody's Investor Service, and the like

    Private wire services: PR Newswire, Business Wire

    Securities and Exchange Commission (SEC), for publicly owned companies

Consumer Publics

Company employees

Customers

    Professionals

    Middle class

    Working class

    Minorities

    Other

Activist consumer groups

Consumer publications

Community media, mass, and specialized

Community leaders and organizations

International Publics

Host country media

    Mass

    Specialized

Host country leaders

Public officials
Educators
Social leaders
Cultural leaders
Religious leaders
Political leaders
Professionals
Executives

Host country organizations

Business
Service
Social
Cultural
Religious
Political
Special interests
Other

Special Publics

Media consumed by this public

Mass
Specialized

Leaders of this public

Public officials
Professional leaders
Ethnic leaders
Neighborhood leaders

Organizations composing this public

Civic
Political
Service
Business
Cultural
Religious
Youth
Other

Integrated Marketing Communications

Customers

     New customers
     Old customers
     Potential customers

Employees

     Management
     Nonmanagement

Media

     Mass
     Specialized

Investors

     Shareowners and potential shareowners
     Financial analysts
     Financial press

Suppliers

Competitors

Government Regulators

Public relations people use two general methods of research: nonquantitative and quantitative.

Nonquantitative Research. One source of nonquantitative data is organization or client records (business reports, statistics, financial reports, past public relations records) and communications (speeches and personal blogs by executives, newsletters, news releases, memorandums, pamphlets, brochures).

A second source of nonquantitative data is published materials. These include news articles from mass media and trade publications, published surveys or polls, library references, government documents, directories, Internet discussion groups, social media dialogues, and published trade association data.

Third, nonquantitative research can be conducted through interviews or conversations with key members of targeted publics. Important civic leaders, elected officials, business leaders, religious leaders, educators, influential editors, reporters, and other key individuals in the community can provide invaluable background information for a public relations program.

Fourth, feedback from the client's customers or clientele can be helpful as a means of nonquantitative research. Customer responses may come via telephone, mail, e-mail, comments posted on interactive forums, or face-to-face interactions.

Fifth, talking with organized groups with an interest in the client can be useful. These groups may include the organization's formal advisory boards, committees, commissions, or panels from inside or outside the organization.

Finally, groups created especially for research purposes can provide valuable insight. The most popular form of this procedure is the focus group, usually consisting of 8 to 12 people who are representative of the audience the client wishes to reach. A moderator who is skilled in interviewing and group-process management encourages the participants of the focus group to consider the client's image, products, services, and communication proposals, or other issues affecting the client. The focus-group meetings are usually videotaped and carefully studied to identify and analyze participants' reactions and comments.

Throughout this process, the World Wide Web has become an essential source of information for public relations practitioners. Whether using popular search sites such as Google or Yahoo!, specialized meta-search engines or news aggregators, there seems to be an ever-evolving source of data mining sites.

Some researchers are experimenting with ways to conduct surveys and focus groups using the Internet. For example, chat rooms provide a way to bring diverse audiences into a focus-group setting.

It should be emphasized that although these six methods of nonquantitative research may yield useful data regarding all areas of concern in the research process, the data will not be scientifically reliable. For a scientific level of reliability, statistical research methods must be used.

Quantitative Research.   Three methods of quantitative research are widely used in public relations: sample surveys, experiments, and content analysis. The key to each is the use of statistical methods.

The sample survey is the most frequently used quantitative research method in the public relations process. It is most useful in determining audience information levels, attitudes, behaviors, and media habits. Surveys can be conducted by mail, by telephone, or in person, with cost increasing in that order.

Mail questionnaires (both regular and e-mail) are the least expensive survey method because of lower staffing requirements. They can yield more data because length is no problem and respondents can give thorough answers. The major problem with such questionnaires is the low response rate. Unless the intended respondents have a high level of interest in the subject, mail questionnaires can be a big waste of the researcher's time and money.

Telephone interviews have become the most popular means of conducting surveys. Sampling can be done using the random digit dialing technique and an ordinary telephone directory. Although more expensive than mail questionnaires, telephone interviews provide a more economical use of staff time. The limitations of communicating by voice alone may hamper the rapport between interviewer and respondent since the interviewer cannot make judgments about accuracy and sincerity based on nonverbal cues. Nonetheless, telephone interviewing has become the first choice in the conduct of sample surveys. With many young people relying strictly on wireless cell phones, there are concerns about the ability to reach an appropriate cross section of the public when using phone interviews.

Personal interviews remain an important, though expensive and time-consuming, survey method. The interviewer can make judgments based on the respondent's nonverbal as well as verbal cues, so no survey method is more accurate. Getting a good sample, however, is much more difficult than with the random digit dialing technique used for telephone interviews. Many people are reluctant to consent to a personal interview because of the time and inconvenience involved. As with mail questionnaires, personal interviews are most effective with respondents who are truly interested in the subject and willing to sacrifice their time.

With all their limitations, and with the onus of being considered "quick and dirty" by most social and behavioral scientists, surveys remain the most popular of quantitative research methods used in public relations.

Controlled experiments have been gaining in popularity. Conducted either in laboratory settings or in the field, experiments are the most accurate indicator of causality in the behavioral sciences. Experiments are often used in advertising or public relations to determine which forms of communication or messages may be most effective with selected audiences. In the experimental method, two groups of subjects are randomly chosen. One group is exposed to the communication media, and the other is not. Both groups are tested before and after the communication exposure. If the responses of the exposed group change significantly after the communication, then these responses can be attributed causally to the messages.

A third quantitative method of research often used in public relations is content analysis. This systematic procedure is used in analyzing themes or trends in the message content of selected media. Content analysis can be used to learn how the media are treating clients—their public image as reflected in the media, negative or positive coverage, and the like. This research procedure is also useful in issues management, in which practitioners identify and analyze the impact of public issues on a client's corporate or organizational interests. Thus, content analysis can be helpful in the evaluation of media treatment in the publicity process and in tracking social, economic, or political trends or issues that may affect clients.

Quantitative research should be conducted only by professional firms with good reputations in their field or by staff members who are trained and experienced researchers. Public relations staff members who have not received formal training in research techniques will waste the client's time and money. Worse, their work will probably be inaccurate and misleading.

With the public relations program's informational needs satisfied through nonquantitative or quantitative research methods, the practitioner is ready to attend to the second phase of the process—that of formulating objectives.

OBJECTIVES

Objectives are the single most important element in this public relations process. They represent the practitioner's desired outcomes in communicating with the targeted publics. They are the raison d'être for PR programs. Some writers draw a distinction between "goals" as more general outcomes and "objectives" as specific, immediate results. Here we avoid that confusion by consistently using one term to signify desired program outcomes, and that term is objectives. Whether they are to be broad or narrow, long-range or short-range, they should be stipulated in the statement of the objective itself. Before we discuss the types of objectives used in public relations, we should examine the method used in formulating such objectives.

Many organizations are now using management by objectives (MBO) or similar strategic planning processes to align general organizational objectives with those for individual work units, such as the public relations department. MBO involves cooperative goal setting by groups of superiors and subordinates in the employee hierarchy. For example, the director of public relations and the assistant director may represent management, and various writers, graphics specialists, and other staff members may represent the "subordinates" in the MBO process. Together they devise short-term and long-range objectives and evaluation procedures for the work unit and for its particular programs. Then, using these procedures, both groups cooperatively evaluate their work at agreed-on times. They also periodically review and revise their objectives and evaluation procedures.

Our concern here is with objectives for individual PR programs. Regardless of whether such objectives are determined using MBO, a creative collaborative process or more traditional authoritarian means, two criteria apply to all program objectives.

First, objectives should be stated in the form of infinitive phrases, each containing one infinitive and each being a specific and separately measurable desired outcome. An infinitive phrase consists of a verb plus the complement, or receiver of the verb's action. For example, a practitioner may hope that, after the PR program is executed, the audience will be informed that a special event is taking place and will attend the event. The phrasing of the objectives in infinitive form could be:

- To publicize special event X
- To stimulate attendance at special event X

These objectives could be combined—to publicize and stimulate attendance at special event X—but this compound phrasing would complicate the measurement or evaluation of both objectives.

Second, public relations objectives should be verifiable. To be verifiable, the desired outcome should be stated in quantified, measurable terms, and a time frame or target date should be set for its accomplishment. Although the objectives just stated meet our infinitive test, they are not stated specifically in quantitative or chronological terms. Thus, they can be reworded as:

- To publicize special event X through the community's daily newspaper, its TV station, and its three radio stations during the month of October

- To stimulate an attendance of at least 1,500 persons at special event X on May 15

We can measure the first objective by determining, by using a clipping service and a broadcast media monitoring service, how many media outlets actually used the announcement of the special event. We can measure the second objective by checking actual attendance figures or ticket sales at the event itself.

Two basic types of objectives are used in public relations programs: impact objectives and output objectives. Together, they can be viewed as a hierarchy in ascending order of importance (see Exhibit 2-b). Within each category, however, there is no performance hierarchy or order of importance. For example, informational objectives need not be completed before attitudinal or behavioral objectives, and the importance of each of these subsets of impact objectives is purely situational.

E X H I B I T 2-b   A Hierarchy of Public Relations Objectives

Impact Objectives

Informational objectives

    Message exposure
    Message comprehension
    Message retention

Attitudinal objectives

    Attitude creation
    Attitude reinforcement
    Attitude change

Behavioral objectives

    Behavior creation
    Behavior reinforcement
    Behavior change

Output Objectives

Distribution of uncontrolled media

Distribution or execution of controlled media

Output Objectives

Output objectives, the lower category in the hierarchy, represent the work to be produced, that is, the distribution or execution of program materials. Some writers refer to these activities as "process objectives," "support objectives," or "program effort." Whatever the terminology, these activities should not be confused with desired program impacts. Output objectives, as discussed here, refer to stated intentions regarding program production and effort (or output). They are classified as a form of objective because they describe a type of desired outcome often stated in public relations programs. In fact, the PRSA's Silver Anvil winners use a much higher percentage of output objectives than impact objectives. In the best of all possible worlds, PR directors would use only impact objectives. But here it seems appropriate to deal with PR objectives as they actually exist in the real world. Such objectives can easily be made specific and quantitative. For example:

- To send one news release to each of the community's major media outlets: its daily newspaper, its TV station, and its three radio stations by May 10

- To make an oral presentation to an important conference of security analysts in each of the following five cities: New York, Los Angeles, Chicago, Houston, and Denver, before December 15

These objectives can then be measured easily by counting the number of news releases actually sent to the media outlets and the number of oral presentations actually made to security analysts. Time frames can be added if desired.

Some practitioners use only output objectives in their public relations programs. The advantage of such usage is that output objectives set definite, specific, and attainable goals, which can be measured quantitatively. Once these goals have been met, the practitioner can claim success. Unfortunately, output objectives are unrelated to the actual impact the program may have on its intended audiences, and for this we must move to the top, and more significant, category in our hierarchy of public relations objectives.

Impact Objectives

There are three kinds of impact objectives: informational, attitudinal, and behavioral. These are called impact objectives because they represent specific intended effects of public relations programs on their audiences.

Informational Objectives.   Informational objectives include message exposure to, message comprehension by, and/or message retention by the target public. Such objectives are appropriate when the practitioner wishes to publicize an action or event; seeks to communicate instructions, operating procedures, or other forms of information; or wants to educate an audience about a noncontroversial subject. Two examples of informational objectives are:

- To increase awareness of the company's open house (by 10 percent) among all segments of the community (during the month of May)

- To increase employee awareness of new plant safety procedures (by 50 percent during our three-month safety campaign)

Attitudinal Objectives.   Attitudinal objectives aim at modifying the way an audience feels about the client or organization and its work, products, or services. Attitude modification may consist of forming new attitudes where none exists, reinforcing existing attitudes, or changing existing attitudes.

There will probably be no public attitudes toward a completely new organization. The task of public relations, then, will be the creation of favorable attitudes toward the organization. Two examples of such objectives are:

- To create favorable public attitudes toward a new department store (among 25 percent of mall shoppers during the grand opening celebration)
- To promote favorable attitudes toward a company's new retirement policy (among 80 percent of current employees during the current fiscal year)

It should be stressed that this type of attitudinal objective (forming new attitudes) applies only to organizations and actions that are not controversial and therefore have not generated prior audience attitudes. Some new organizations or actions immediately create reactions among affected groups. In these cases, objectives that seek to reinforce or change existing attitudes are more appropriate.

The second form of attitudinal objective has as its goal the reinforcement, enhancement, or intensification of existing attitudes. A given audience may have moderately favorable, but weak, attitudes toward an organization. In this case, public relations may seek to strengthen these attitudes through a variety of actions, events, or communications. An example of this might be:

- To reinforce favorable public opinion toward a nonprofit organization (among 80 percent of its past donors during March and April)

The final form of attitudinal objective is the changing, or reversing, of (usually negative) existing attitudes. In this case, the practitioner must be careful not to take on a "Mission Impossible." The reversal of attitudes is, of course, the most difficult of all tasks in public relations, so the old military adage "Don't fight a losing battle" may serve as a useful guideline here. Attitude or behavior reversal takes time and, as a rule, it cannot be accomplished with one short-range PR campaign. When Ivy Lee attempted to reverse the public image of John D. Rockefeller, Sr., the task took years. Little by little, Lee was successful in converting Rockefeller's image from that of the ogre responsible for the deaths of Colorado miners and their families to the image of a beloved philanthropist. Many practitioners would rightly have regarded such an enormous task as a "losing battle," given the resources of most individuals or organizations. But with unlimited Rockefeller money, the task was finally accomplished.

Sometimes the practitioner will seek to reverse existing positive attitudes. For example, some Republicans in Congress (and in the White House) have attempted to portray many of the government's social programs in a negative light, although most of these programs have enjoyed great popularity since their inception during President Franklin D. Roosevelt's New Deal era.

Two examples of objectives that seek attitude change are:

- To reverse (within a period of one year) the negative attitudes and ill will now being expressed toward the manufacturer of a defective product (among 20 percent of the manufacturer's former and current customers)

- To change the favorable attitudes that exist regarding the proposed program (among 10 percent of the members of the U.S. Congress before the vote on the bill)

Attitudinal objectives, then, may involve any of three goals: formation of new attitudes where none exist, reinforcement of existing attitudes, or change in existing attitudes.

Behavioral Objectives. Behavioral objectives involve the modification of behavior toward the client or organization. Like attitude modification, behavior modification may consist of the creation or stimulation of new behavior, the enhancement or intensification of existing favorable behavior, or the reversal of negative behavior on the part of an audience toward the practitioner's client or organization.

Examples of the creation of new behavior might include:

- To accomplish adoption of new safety procedures (among 75 percent of the organization's employees by September 15)

- To persuade (60 percent of) persons over the age of 50 to regularly take a colon cancer test (during the next two years)

- To stimulate new diet procedures (among 70 percent) of children in the city school system (during the current school year)

Enhancement or intensification of existing positive behaviors might involve such objectives as:

- To encourage (30 percent) greater usage of seat belts in automobiles (this year)

- To stimulate (50 percent) higher attendance at meetings by association members (during the next national convention)

The reversal of negative behaviors could include:

- To discourage defacement of public monuments (by 20 percent) in a city park (over a period of eight months)

- To discourage smoking (by 80 percent) in the east wing of the restaurant (during the next three months)

Objectives, as presented here, result from and are shaped by the findings revealed in the research phase. As mentioned earlier, research data should be sought in the area of audience information levels, attitudes, behaviors, and media habits. If information levels about the client or related matters are low, then informational objectives are called for in the public relations program. If audience attitudes toward the client are nonexistent, weak, or negative, then the practitioner will know the kinds of attitudinal objectives to formulate. Finally, if desired audience behaviors are nonexistent, weak, or negative, the practitioner will have a framework for developing appropriate behavioral objectives. Data regarding audience media habits may not contribute directly to the formulation of program objectives, but these findings are useful in determining appropriate media usage in the programming phase of the process.

In addition to impact objectives, the practitioner may devise output objectives for each PR program. These objectives are of less significance because they represent outcomes that have nothing to do with program effects on target audiences.

In the public relations process, objectives precede and govern programming decisions. The degree of influence these objectives exert can best be seen in the programming phase itself.

PROGRAMMING

Public relations programming, as presented in this process, includes the following elements of planning and execution:

1. Stating a theme, if applicable, and the messages to be communicated to the audiences
2. Planning the action or special event(s) sponsored by the client
3. Planning the use of the media, either uncontrolled or controlled
4. Effectively communicating the program

Theme and Messages

The first element of a program, its theme and messages, should encompass the program's entire scope and must be carefully planned in conjunction with the action or special event central to the program.

The program theme should be catchy and memorable. The best themes are in the form of short slogans consisting of no more than five words. Not all programs require themes or slogans, but a brief, creative theme can become the most memorable part of the entire public relations effort. Often, extensive research is conducted to evaluate the effectiveness of different potential messages. "Framing" a message involves crafting appropriate language that influences perceptions and subsequent judgments about a campaign.

Most PR programs will have one central message epitomized in such a slogan or theme. In some cases, programs may have several messages, possibly one for each separate audience. The practitioner should work out as concisely as possible just what is to be communicated to each audience during the entire program.

Action(s) or Special Event(s)

A central action or a special event to be sponsored by the client should be considered along with the program's theme and message. The client's actions or events will usually be the focal point of the theme and messages, although some PR programs omit this element and concentrate on theme and messages alone. However, it is highly recommended that programs be action oriented. A central action or event can make most programs more newsworthy, interesting, and effective. To best advance the public image of the client, this action or event should be substantive, usually serious, and in the public interest. It will be most effective if the event involves large numbers of people and includes the presence of at least one celebrity. Shallow "pseudoevents" should be avoided; they sometimes do more harm than good by damaging the client's credibility. For the most part, gimmicks and stunts are best left to carnivals and circuses. There are exceptions, of course. Sometimes carnivals, circuses, beauty pageants, and similar activities can be presented as a means of raising funds for worthy causes. If these events can be seen as serving the public interest, they may enhance the client's credibility. Typical public relations actions and special events are included in Exhibit 2-c.

E X H I B I T 2-c   Actions and Special Events

Special days, nights, weeks, months

Displays and exhibits

Trade shows and exhibitions

Fairs, festivals, expositions

Meetings, conferences, conventions, congresses, rallies

Anniversaries, memorial events

Special awards, retirements, salutes

Open houses, plant tours

Town meetings, public debates, parties

Coffee hours, teas

Contests

Parades, pageants, beauty contests, fashion shows

Sponsoring community events

Sponsoring organizations (community youth organizations, Little League, Junior Achievement Organization)

Sponsoring scholarships, contributions

Creating charitable and educational foundations

Receptions

Concert tours, theatrical tours

Performing and graphic arts tours

Visits, pleasure tours for selected publics and groups

Picnics, outings, cookouts, barbecues

Nature trails, flower shows

Groundbreaking ceremonies, cornerstone layings, safety programs

Product demonstrations

Traveling demonstrations, home demonstrations

Visits by dignitaries, celebrities

Guest lectures, kickoffs, farewells, going-aways, welcome-backs, welcoming ceremonies

Elections of officers

Issuing reports or statistics

Announcing results of polls or surveys

Grand openings

Announcing an appointment

Announcing a new policy or policy change

Announcing a new program, product, or service

Announcing important news about the client or organization

Public relations personalities (Miss America, celebrity spokespersons/ambassadors)

Dedications

School commencements, assemblies, events, convocations

Fetes, galas, proms, dances, balls, disco parties

Banquets, luncheons, breakfasts, dinners, buffets

Art shows, openings, exhibits

Concerts, plays, ballets

Film festivals, fashion shows

Animal shows (dogs, cats, birds)

Sporting events, ski trips, ocean cruises, pack trips, hikes, marathons, bike-a-thons, swim-a-thons, miscellaneous-a-thons, races

Celebrity sporting events, cruises

Museum tours, home tours

Embassy tours

Celebrity appearances, autograph-signing ceremonies

Car washes, neighborhood cleanups, services for the elderly

Health screening tests

Committee hearings

Training programs

Opinion-leader meetings and conferences

Special education programs: thrift education, health education, conservation education

Leadership programs

Participation in community events

Celebrations of national holidays

Theme events and celebrations: "Roaring Twenties," "Old New Orleans," "Colonial New England," "Ancient Greece"

Events honoring other nations or cultures

Uncontrolled and Controlled Media

The two forms of communication used in public relations are usually classified as uncontrolled and controlled media.

The use of uncontrolled media involves the communication of news about the client or organization to the mass media and to specialized media outlets. Specifically, the decision-making editors of these outlets become the target audiences for uncontrolled media. The objective of this form of communication is favorable news coverage of the client's actions and events. The standard formats used to communicate client news to the media include news releases, feature stories, captioned photographs or photo opportunities, and news conferences. A more complete listing of these formats can be found in Exhibit 2-d. They are called uncontrolled media because the practitioner loses control of these materials at the media outlet itself. An editor may choose to use the practitioner's release or feature story in its entirety, partially, or not at all; or editors may send reporters who will write or videotape their own stories about the client, ignoring the practitioner's efforts. Because the client or practitioner does not pay the media outlet to use the story as advertising, the use of the material is at the complete discretion of the media outlet. Similarly, conversations about organizations and campaigns on Social Media sites, such as FaceBook, are easily influenced by factors and people outside the influence of the organization.

The use of controlled media, on the other hand, involves communication about the client that is paid for by the client. The wording of the material, its format, and its placement in the media are all at the discretion of the client. The formats for controlled media include print materials such as brochures, newsletters, and reports; audiovisual materials such as films, slide shows, and PowerPoint (a program for providing a kind of slide show on a laptop computer); and interpersonal communication such as speeches, meetings, and interviews. Also included in controlled media are institutional advertising aimed at enhancing the client's image, advocacy advertising that communicates the client's stand on a controversial issue, and other forms of nonproduct advertising. Increasingly indispensable are the ubiquitous Web pages and Web sites, which can contain large amounts of information about the client. Exhibit 2-d includes a more detailed listing of the forms of controlled media.

Effective Communication

The final aspect of programming is the effective communication of the program. Thus, the factors of source, message, channel, receivers, and feedback will be useful in our examination of communication principles. That is, effective communication depends on:

1. Source credibility
2. Salient information (message)
3. Effective nonverbal cues (message)
4. Effective verbal cues (message)

E X H I B I T 2-d **Uncontrolled and Controlled Media**

Uncontrolled Media

News releases—print and video news releases (VNRs)

Feature stories

Photographs with cutlines (captions) or photo opportunities

News conferences

Media kits—paper or digital (DVD or CD-ROM) or online format

Radio/TV public service announcements (PSAs) (nonprofit organizations only)

Interviews

> Print media
> Broadcast media
> Alternative online media

Teleconferences

Personal appearances on broadcast media

News audio files for radio

News images and video for TV

Special programs for radio and TV

Recorded telephone news capsules and updates from an institution

Informing and influencing editors, broadcast news and public service directors, columnists, and reporters (phone calls, e-mail, tip sheets, newsletters with story leads, media advisories)

Business feature articles

Financial publicity

Product publicity

Pictorial publicity

Background editorial material (backgrounders and fact sheets)

Letters to the editor

Op-ed pieces

Controlled Media

Print communication methods

> House publications
> Brochures, information pieces
> Handbooks, manuals, books
> Letters, bulletins, memos
> Podcasts and online streaming video

Bulletin boards, posters, flyers

Information racks

E-mail

External periodicals: opinion-leader periodicals, corporate general public periodicals, distributor-dealer periodicals, stockholder periodicals, supplier periodicals, periodicals for special publics

Annual reports

Commemorative stamps

Exhibits and displays

Mobile libraries, bookmobiles

Mobile displays

Attitude or information surveys

Suggestion boxes, systems

Instructions and orders

Pay inserts

Written reports

Billing inserts

Financial statement inserts

Training kits, aids, manuals

Consumer information kits

Legislative information kits

Teacher kits, student games

Teacher aids

Print window displays

Audiovisual communication methods

Institutional videos

Easel pad presentations

Transparencies for overhead projectors

Telephone calls, phone banks, dial-a-somethings, recorded messages

Multimedia exhibits and displays

Audio files, MP3s, CD-ROMs, and DVDs

Video DVDs

Visual and multimedia window displays

Oral presentations with visuals

Multimedia training aids

> PowerPoint (or similar presentation software)

> Teacher aids, student games

Specially equipped vans, trains, buses, boats, airplanes, blimps

Interpersonal communication methods

Formal speeches, lectures, seminars

Online discussion forums

Teleconferences

Roundtable conferences

Panel discussions

Question-and-answer discussions

Oral testimony

Employee counseling

Legal, medical, birth control, miscellaneous counseling

Committee meetings

Staff meetings

Informal conversations

Demonstrations

Speakers bureaus: recruiting and training speakers, speech preparation, clearance of materials with management, list of subjects, speakers' guide, engagements and bookings, visual aids, follow-up correspondence

Training programs

Interviews

Personal instructions

Social affairs

Face-to-face reports

Public relations advertising (not designed to stimulate product sales)

Print and broadcast advertising

Institutional advertising—image building

Public affairs (advocacy) advertising: institutional or organizational statements on controversial issues

Direct mail institutional advertising

Outdoor advertising: billboards, signs

Yellow Pages institutional advertising

Transit advertising, skywriting, fly-by advertising

Specialty items: calendars, ashtrays, pens, matchbooks, emery boards, memo pads

Online banner ads

Web sites

5. Two-way communication (channel and feedback)
6. Opinion leaders (receivers)
7. Group influence (receivers)
8. Selective exposure (receivers)
9. Audience participation (feedback)

Source Credibility.   The success or failure of the entire public relations trans-action can hinge on how the source of communication, the spokesperson for the client or organization, is perceived by the intended audience. Credibility involves a set of perceptions about sources held by receivers or audiences. The personal characteristics of believable sources that continually appear in communication research are trustworthiness, expertise, dynamism, physical attractiveness, and perceived similarities between the source and receivers.[1] These characteristics should serve the PR practitioner as guidelines for selecting individuals to represent the client or organization. Communication coming from high-credibility sources will clearly be in the best interests of the PR program.

Salient Information.   A second principle of effective communication involves the use of salient information in the client's messages addressed to target audiences. Members of audiences can be viewed as information processors whose attitudes and behaviors are influenced by their integration of significant new information into their preexisting beliefs.[2] This is another way of saying that the message content must be motivational for the intended audiences—it must strike responsive chords in their minds. Information that is not salient to a given audience in a given context should be discarded.

Nonverbal Cues.   A third principle of effective communication involves the use of appropriate nonverbal cues in the PR program's messages. Countless volumes have been published on a variety of aspects of nonverbal communication. But for purposes of effective programming, the PR practitioner should closely examine the nature of the client's actions or special events that are to serve as a basis for the overall effort. Choosing appropriate symbols to represent the client or the cause can be the most important aspect of nonverbal communication. Questions involving the mood, or atmosphere, desired at the event, the personnel to be used, the guests to be invited, the setting, the forms of interpersonal interaction, and the scheduling should be raised. These are essential details that can make the difference between success and failure for the client. Exhibit 2-e provides more details useful in planning effective nonverbal communication for the client.

Verbal Cues.   The use of effective verbal message cues, or the actual wording of the client's messages, is the fourth principle of communication considered here. The two most important characteristics of effective language usage are clarity and appropriateness.

To be clear, language must be accurate. The forms of communication used in a PR program should use words precisely, so the practitioner may need to consult a dictionary or thesaurus. Messages should be tested with a small audience to eliminate ambiguity before their actual use in a PR program. In addition to accuracy, simplicity of word choice contributes to language clarity. Why use big words when simple ones will do? Audiences will relate to such words as try better than endeavor, help better than facilitate, explain better than explicate, tell better than indicate, and learn better than ascertain. Finally, coherence is an important factor in clear language. The words in a message should be logically connected—they should hang together well. The use of simple sentences rather than compound or complex ones contributes to coherence. Clear transitions and summaries in messages also aid coherence. Accuracy, simplicity, and coherence, then, are the major factors in constructing clear messages.

EXHIBIT 2-e   Nonverbal Communication

Appropriate symbols

Mood or atmosphere desired: excitement, quiet dignity

Organizational personnel involved, including spokesperson(s) to be used

> Demographics of the audience: white/anglo, African American, Hispanic, Jewish, Asian, Arab (if applicable)
>
> Appearance, dress, actions/interactions expected

Guests: appearance and dress expected setting

> buildings, rooms, or exterior environment desired
>
> Colors
>
> Background: banner, logo
>
> Lighting
>
> Sound system
>
> Nature and use of space
>
> Types and arrangement of furniture, seating arrangements
>
> Other artifacts to be used: paintings, wall tapestries, sports banners, colored balloons
>
> Nature of central presentation appropriate for setting (vice versa)
>
> Music: type, volume
>
> Entertainment (if any)
>
> Food, beverages, refreshments (if any)

Forms of interpersonal interaction: sit-down dinner, stand-up cocktail party, reception

Use of time: where will emphasis be placed; will activity build to climax?

Messages should also be appropriate to the client, the audience, and the occasion. If the client is the city's leading bank, some levels of language may be inappropriate. Language used by a fast-food chain is different from that used in the messages of a funeral home. Similarly, language must be appropriate to the demographic level of the audience. Teenagers will obviously respond to a different use of language than senior citizens. The occasion for the use of the message also influences the level and type of language to be used. A diplomatic function held in a Washington embassy requires a different level of language from that used at a locker room gathering of an athletic team. Thus, appropriateness and clarity are the two major requisites for effectiveness in the use of verbal message cues.

Two-Way Communication.   The fifth principle of effective communication involves two-way interaction. Communication was once considered a linear process involving the transmission of a message from a source through a channel to a receiver. On receipt of the message at its destination, the communication transaction was considered complete. Today, however, the PR practitioner must program two-way communication activities that permit audience response—or feedback—in brief, the interactive aspects discussed earlier. For example, comments and ratings of an organization's video posted on YouTube.com constitute a form of two-way interaction.

Traditionally, a variety of print-oriented response mechanisms are available, such as the suggestion box for employee communication, response cards to be returned to the source of communication, and letters to the editors of publications. The most effective means of two-way interaction, however, is interpersonal communication activities: speeches with question-and-answer sessions, small-group meetings, and one-on-one communication. It is usually possible to divide target audiences into small groups that provide excellent opportunities for interpersonal communication. This is the most effective form of persuasion because of the high level of source-receiver engagement.

Opinion Leaders.   The sixth principle of effective communication involves the identification and targeting of opinion leaders as receivers of communication. Sometimes communication operates efficiently in a direct, one-step flow from source to receiver. On many occasions, however, communication is more effective when staged in a two-step or multiple-step flow. In these cases, the practitioner should seek opinion leaders, or "influentials," who in turn will communicate with their followers or cohorts. One simple way to identify opinion leaders is to catalog the leadership of all important groups in a given community or institution. These may include elected political leaders and others who hold formal positions in the community. In some cases, opinion leaders may hold no formal positions, but their advice is nonetheless sought and respected within given groups, institutions, or communities. Practitioners should create a list of opinion-leader contacts, much like their media contacts list, including all relevant data about the leaders, their positions, their availability, and their influence on other audiences.

Group Influence.   A seventh effective communication principle involves the use of group influence. People belong to a variety of formal and informal groups, whether through personal face-to-face interaction or via online affinity groups. The most valued groups, which exert the greatest influence on their members, are known as reference groups. Members feel a sense of cohesiveness, of belonging together; have mutual, face-to-face interactions and influence each other; and share a set of norms and roles that structure and enforce a degree of conformity by each member. When newspapers list the most popular or most e-mailed stories of the day, they attract additional viewers due to group influence.

The practitioner's task is to identify and target for communication key groups that can be most useful to the client or organization. Special effort should go into the preparation of a group contacts list, similar to the media and opinion-leader lists. Groups should be reached through interpersonal communication (speeches or presentations) as well as other appropriate methods. It is especially important to contact a formal group's program chairperson to schedule a speech or other presentation on behalf of the client. Acceptance of the client's message or position by key group leaders will then effectively engage the essential nature of group influence: acceptance by all members because of the group's operative cohesiveness and conformity.

Selective Exposure. An eighth principle of effective communication that should be observed by the public relations practitioner is selective exposure. Because the objectives of public relations include attitude and behavior modification, the temptation is always present to take on the most difficult of all tasks: changing existing attitudes or behaviors. Why is this the toughest task? The principle of selective exposure holds that people will accept and even seek out communication supporting their beliefs. However, communication researchers have also found that people will not necessarily avoid information incompatible with their views, as was once thought to be the case.[3] Moreover, other communication research indicates that when a persuasive message falls within the region (latitude) of personal acceptance, opinion or attitude will change in the direction of the advocated position. But when it falls within the region of rejection, attitudes will not change.[4] These communication research findings send a clear message to the PR practitioner—the easiest task in persuasion is reinforcement of existing attitudes or behaviors.

Clearly, trying to change attitudes or behavior is difficult and counterproductive, particularly in the face of strong resistance. Always avoid fighting a losing battle. When controversial messages are necessary, audiences or individual receivers should always be categorized on the basis of their agreement or disagreement with the message in question. Using terms that coincide with the Likert scale often used in attitude surveys, audiences can be categorized as "positive" (those who strongly agree with the message); "somewhat positive" (those who agree with the message); "undecided"; "somewhat negative" (those who disagree with the message); and "negative" (those who strongly disagree with the message).

The principle of selective exposure dictates that the practitioner first target the "positives," then the "somewhat positives," next the "undecideds," and last, if at all, the "somewhat negatives." The pure "negatives," those strongly opposed or in disagreement with the program's message, should usually be written off. If their attitudes are hardened, and especially if they have publicly expressed their disagreement, they are highly unlikely to change their minds. Given a long period of time, along with perhaps unlimited funds, the hard-core negatives may be slowly changed; but for most practical and immediate situations requiring persuasion, conversion of the negatives is not worth the time, effort, or money.

Audience Participation. A final principle of effective communication, observed whenever possible, is the use of audience participation. This is the only means of communication that encourages audience self-persuasion through direct experience or involvement with the client's services or products. Communication researchers have found that self-persuasion is more effective, by far, than any other means of influence.[5] Therefore, the practitioner should constantly seek opportunities to include audience participation in PR programs.

In summary, public relations programming consists of planning, including attention to theme and message, the use of an action or special event, the use of uncontrolled and controlled media, and program execution following the principles of effective communication.

EVALUATION

Evaluation as discussed here is an ongoing process of monitoring and, when appropriate, final assessment of the stated objectives of the PR program. It is usually inadvisable to wait until the execution of the program has been completed to begin the evaluation process. Instead, the practices described here should be engaged in at stipulated intervals during the execution, with program adjustments made as deemed appropriate.

Evaluating Informational Objectives

The measurement of informational objectives includes three dimensions: message exposure, message comprehension, and message retention.

Message exposure is most commonly determined by publicity placement through national or local clipping and media monitoring services. It can also be measured through the circulation figures and audience-size data readily available for publications and broadcast media. Attendance figures for events or meetings also provide an index of message exposure. Finally, exposure is measured by computerized tracking systems that have been developed by some public relations firms for monitoring their effectiveness in delivering messages to audiences.

Message comprehension, or at least the potential for comprehension, is most frequently determined by the application of readability formulas to the messages used in PR programs. The most often used are the Flesch Reading Ease Formula, the Gunning Fog Index, the Dale-Chall Formula, the Fry Formula, and the Farr-Jenkins-Patterson Formula.[6] These predict ease of comprehension based on measuring the difficulty of the words and the length of the sentences used in messages, but surveys must be used to measure actual message comprehension.

Message retention is usually tested by asking appropriate questions designed to check target audiences' knowledge of the client's message. Although message retention can be measured by the nonquantitative research methods discussed earlier, retention questions are usually administered in the form of sample surveys.

Thus, the key to determining the effectiveness of informational objectives lies in the assessment of message exposure, comprehension, and retention. The more of these measurements used, the more accurate the evaluation of effectiveness is likely to be.

Evaluating Attitudinal Objectives

Attitudinal objectives can be measured by several well-established survey research instruments, the most frequently used being Likert scales and the Semantic Differential.[7] Both of these instruments measure attitude intensity and direction; thus, they are useful in assessing whether new attitudes have been formed or whether existing attitudes have been reinforced or changed. These measurements require both pretesting and posttesting of target audiences to determine the degree of influence on attitudes attributable to the PR program. To be of any value at all, attitude measurement must be done by competent professionals, well-schooled and experienced in quantitative research methods.

Evaluating Behavioral Objectives

Finally, behavioral objectives can be measured in two ways. First, target audiences can be asked what their behaviors have been since exposure to the PR program. Like attitude measurement, assessment of audience behaviors requires testing before and after program exposure. However, the questions used will be different from those used in attitude research. Closed-end multiple-choice questions or checklists designed to determine audience behaviors are commonly used for this measurement.

A second means of assessing audience behavior is simply observing the behaviors of target audiences. In some cases, these can be counted, as in attendance at special events, numbers of telephone calls received, Web site "hits," or e-mail received. And in many situations, audiences may be small enough to observe before, during, and after exposure to the PR program.

Nonquantitative research methods can provide useful information both in asking audiences about their behaviors and in observing these behaviors. To obtain the most reliable evaluations of all three types of impact, however, competent professionals with established reputations in research should be retained.

Evaluating Output Objectives

In addition to measuring impact objectives, the PR practitioner must be concerned with assessing the effectiveness of output objectives, which involves the distribution of uncontrolled and controlled media. This effectiveness can be evaluated by keeping records of the number of news releases sent to publications and broadcast stations, the number of contacts made with journalists, the number of speeches given to targeted audiences, the number of publications distributed to each public, and the number of meetings held with key audiences. In the realm of output objectives, practitioners accomplish their goals by distributing appropriate quantities of media according to their original plans. Although these are easily achievable objectives, it should be reiterated that they have no bearing whatever on the PR program's priority goal—audience impact.

Evaluation of the two general forms of program objectives—impact and output—constitutes an ongoing dimension of this public relations process model. The process will not be completed, however, when the program objectives are evaluated. These evaluative data are recycled as part of a continuing procedure. They are useful in adjusting ongoing relations with various audiences, and they can be helpful when planning the client's next short-term PR program with similar audiences.

SUMMARY

The public relations problem-solving process includes four parts: research, determination of objectives, programming, and evaluation. The following outline provides a useful summary and review of the whole process.

Outline of the Public Relations Process

I. Research
    A. Client/organization: background data about your client or organization
        —its personnel, financial status, reputation, past and present PR prac-
        tices, PR strengths and weaknesses, opportunities
    B. Opportunity/problem: proactive or reactive PR program; long-range or
        short-range campaign
    C. Audiences (publics): identification of key groups to be targeted for
        communication
        1. Desired research data: each targeted audience's level of information
            about your client/organization; image and other relevant attitudes
            held about your client/organization and its products or services;
            audience behaviors relevant to your client/organization; demo-
            graphics, media habits, and media-use levels of each targeted
            audience
        2. Research procedures: nonquantitative and quantitative
II. Objectives
    A. Impact objectives
        1. Informational objectives: message exposure, comprehension,
            retention
        2. Attitudinal objectives: formation of new attitudes, reinforcement of
            existing attitudes, change in existing attitudes
        3. Behavioral objectives: creation of new behavior, reinforcement of
            existing behavior, change in existing behavior
    B. Output objectives: distribution or execution of uncontrolled and con-
        trolled media
III. Programming—planning and execution of:
    A. Theme (if applicable) and message(s)
    B. Action or special event(s)
    C. Uncontrolled media: news releases, feature stories, photos; controlled
        media: print, audiovisual, interpersonal communication, PR advertising
    D. Effective communication using principles of: source credibility, salient
        information, effective nonverbal and verbal cues, two-way communi-
        cation, opinion leaders, group influence, selective exposure, and audi-
        ence participation
IV. Evaluation—ongoing monitoring and final assessment of:
    A. Impact objectives
        1. Informational objectives: measured by publicity placement, surveys
        2. Attitudinal objectives: measured by attitude surveys
        3. Behavioral objectives: measured by surveys and observation of
            behaviors
    B. Output objectives: measured quantitatively by simply counting the
        actual output

ENDNOTES

1. For a summary of this research, see Daniel J. O'Keefe, *Persuasion: Theory and Research*, 2d ed. (Thousand Oaks, CA: Sage Publications, 2002), and Mary John Smith, *Persuasion and Human Action* (Belmont, CA: Wadsworth, 1982): 219ff, the latter a classic in its field.

2. For a detailed discussion of the information integration approach to persuasion, see Smith, *Persuasion and Human Action*, pp. 243–261.

3. The best discussion of selective exposure is David O. Sears and Jonathan L. Freedman, "Selective Exposure to Information: A Critical Review," *Public Opinion Quarterly* 31 (summer 1967): 194–213. Also a classic in the field.

4. For a good explanation of this research, called social judgment theory, see Nan Lin, *The Study of Human Communication* (Indianapolis, IN: Bobbs-Merrill, 1977), pp. 118–122. Also see Smith, *Persuasion and Human Action*, pp. 264–274.

5. For a review of this research, see Smith, *Persuasion and Human Action*, pp. 191–207.

6. For the Flesch Formula, see Rudolf Flesch, *How to Test Readability* (New York: Harper & Row, 1951); Gunning's Fog Index is found in Robert Gunning, *The Technique of Clear Writing*, rev. ed. (New York: McGraw-Hill, 1968); for the Dale-Chall Formula, see Edgar Dale and Jeanne Chall, "A Formula for Predicting Readability," *Educational Research Bulletin* 27 (January and February 1948); the Fry Formula is found in Edward Fry, "A Readability Formula that Saves Time," *Journal of Reading* 11 (1968): 513–516, 575–578; for a review of readability research, see Werner J. Severin and James W. Tankard, Jr., *Communication Theories: Origins, Methods, Uses* (New York: Hastings House, 1979), Chap. 6.

7. For a discussion of these and other research instruments used in attitude measurement, see O'Keefe, *Persuasion: Theory and Research*.

READINGS ON THE PUBLIC RELATIONS PROCESS

Research

Alreck, Pamela L., and Robert B. Settle. *The Survey Research Handbook*, 3d ed. Burr Ridge, IL: Irwin, 2003.

Beaulaurier, Bob. "Avoiding Pitfalls in Web-based Research," *Public Relations Tactics* 10 (November 2003): 17.

Broom, Glen M., and David M. Dozier. *Using Research in Public Relations: Applications to Program Management*. Englewood Cliffs, NJ: Prentice-Hall, 1996.

Buddenbaum, Judith M., and Katherine B. Novak. *Applied Communication Research*. Ames: Iowa State University Press, 2001.

Clary, Sandy. "You Are What You Know: Research for Campaign Success," *Public Relations Tactics* 15 (January 2008): 10.

Greely, Andrew. "In Defense of Surveys," *Transaction Social Science and Modern Society* 33 (May–June 1996): 26ff.

Hamelink, Cees J. *Mass Communication Research: Problems and Policies*. Norwood, NJ: Ablex, 1993.

Hocking, John E., Don W. Stacks, and Steven T. McDermott. *Communication Research*, 3d ed. Boston: Allyn & Bacon, 2003.

Holloway, Immy. *Qualitative Research Methods in Public Relations and Marketing Communications*. London: Taylor & Francis, 2007.

Karlberg, Michael. "Remembering the Public in Public Relations Research: From Theoretical to Operational Symmetry," *Journal of Public Relations Research* 8 (fall 1996): 263–278.

Profolio: Research and Evaluation. New York: Public Relations Society of America, 1997.

Stacks, Don W. *Primer of Public Relations Research*. New York: Guilford Publications, 2002.

Stone, Gerald C. "Public Relations Telephone Surveys: Avoiding Methodological Debacles," *Public Relations Review* 2 (winter 1996): 327–339.

Objectives

Brock, Timothy C., and Melanie C. Green, eds. *Persuasion: Psychological Insights and Perspectives*, 2d ed. Thousand Oaks, CA: Sage Publications, 2005.

Broom, Glen M., and David M. Dozier. "Writing Program Goals and Objectives." In *Using Research in Public Relations: Applications to Program Management*. Englewood Cliffs, NJ: Prentice-Hall, 1996, pp. 39–44.

Cutlip, Scott M., Allen H. Center, and Glen M. Broom. *Effective Public Relations*, 9th ed. Englewood Cliffs, NJ: Prentice-Hall, 2006.

Frederico, Richard F. "What Are Your Core Communication Values?" *Communication World* 11 (October 1994): 14 ff.

Hauss, Deborah. "Setting Benchmarks Leads to Effective Programs," *Public Relations Journal* 49 (February 1993): 16–17.

Jaques, Tony. "Systematic Objective Setting for Effective Issue Management," *Journal of Public Affairs* 5 (February 2005): 33–42.

Shelby, Annette Neven. "Organization, Business, Management, Communication and Corporate Communication: An Analysis of Boundaries and Relationships," *Journal of Business Communication* 30 (July 1993): 241–268.

Winokur, Dena, and Robert W. Kinkead. "How Public Relations Fits into Corporate Strategy," *Public Relations Journal* 49 (May 1993): 16–23.

Programming

Cutlip, Scott M., Allen H. Center, and Glen M. Broom. *Effective Public Relations*, 9th ed. Englewood Cliffs, NJ: Prentice-Hall, 2006.

Grunig, James E., ed. *Excellence in Public Relations and Communication Management*. Hillsdale, NJ: Erlbaum, 1992.

Guth, David, and Charles Marsh. *Public Relations: A Values-Driven Approach*, 3d ed. Boston: Allyn & Bacon, 2008.

Hunt, Todd, and James E. Grunig. *Public Relations Techniques*, 2d ed. Fort Worth, TX: Harcourt Brace, 1997.

Lesly, Philip, ed. *Lesly's Handbook of Public Relations and Communications*, 7th ed. New York: AMACOM, 1998.

Newsom, Doug, Judy VanSlyke Turk, and Dean Kruckeberg. *This Is PR: The Realities of Public Relations*, 9th ed. Belmont, CA: Wadsworth, 2006.

Okigbo, Charles, and Sonya Nelson. "Precision Public Relations: Facing the Demographic Challenge," *Public Relations Quarterly* 48 (summer 2003): 29–35.

Pratt, Cornelius B. "Crafting Key Messages and Talking Points—or Grounding Them in What Research Tells Us," *Public Relations Quarterly* 49 (fall 2004): 15–21.

Seitel, Fraser P. *The Practice of Public Relations*, 9th ed. Englewood Cliffs, NJ: Prentice-Hall, 2006.

Smith, Ronald D. *Strategic Planning for Public Relations*. Mahwah, NJ: Erlbaum, 2002.

Wilcox, Dennis L., Glen T. Cameron, Philip H. Ault, and Warren K. Agee. *Public Relations: Strategies and Tactics*, 9th ed. Boston: Allyn & Bacon, 2008.

Evaluation

Broom, Glen M., and David M. Dozier. "Using Research to Evaluate Programs." In *Using Research in Public Relations: Applications to Program Management*. Englewood Cliffs, NJ: Prentice-Hall, 1996, pp. 71–88.

Charland, Bernie. "The Mantra of Metrics: A Realistic and Relevant Approach to Measuring the Impact of Employee Communications," *Public Relations Strategist* 10 (fall 2004): 30–32.

Cutlip, Scott M., Allen H. Center, and Glen M. Broom. "Step Four: Evaluating the Program." In *Effective Public Relations*, 9th ed. Englewood Cliffs, NJ: Prentice-Hall, 2006.

Coffman, Julia. Public Communication Campaign Evaluation: an Environmental Scan of Challenges, Criticisms, Practice, and Opportunities. Communications Consortium Media Center, Harvard Family Research Project (May 2002).

Freitag, Alan R. "How to Measure What We Do," *Public Relations Quarterly* 43 (summer 1998): 42–47.

González, Ana Rita. "Grassroots Approaches to Reach the Hispanic Audience: Nontraditional Approaches to Measure ROI," *Public Relations Tactics* 12 (July 2005): 24.

Hauss, Deborah. "Measuring the Impact of Public Relations: Electronic Techniques Improve Campaign Evaluation," *Public Relations Journal* 49 (February 1993): 14–21.

Holloway, Deborah. "How to Select a Measurement System That's Right for You," *Public Relations Quarterly* 37 (fall 1992): 15–19.

Leinemann, Ralf, and Elena Baikaltseva. *Media Relations Measurement: Determining The Value of PR to Your Company's Success*. Aldershot, United Kingdom: Gower Publishing Company, 2004.

Lindemann, Walter K. "An 'Effectiveness Yardstick' to Measure Public Relations Success," *Public Relations Quarterly* 38 (spring 1993): 7–9.

Paine, Katie Delahaye. How to Measure Social Media Relations: The More Things Change, the More They Remain the Same. Institute for Public Relations (April 2007).

Pilmer, John. "Small Business? Small Budget? How to Measure for Success," *Public Relations Tactics* 12 (July 2005): 23.

Pratt, Cornelius B., and George Lennon. "What's wrong with outcomes Evaluation?" *Public Relations Quarterly* 46 (winter 2001): 40–44.

Richter, Lisa, and Steve Drake. "Apply Measurement Mindset to Programs," *Public Relations Journal* 49 (January 1993): 32.

Rossi, Peter H., and Howard E. Freeman. *Evaluation: A Systematic Approach*, 7th ed. Beverly Hills, CA: Russell Sage Foundation, 2003.

Stacks, Don W. *Primer of Public Relations Research*. New York: Guilford Publications, 2002.

Reaching Major Audiences

3

Media Relations

Journalists representing the mass and specialized media usually make up the external audience of highest priority for public relations practitioners. Media relations consists essentially of obtaining appropriate publicity, or news coverage, for the activities of the practitioner's client or organization. The field of public relations began as publicity and for many years was called that. Indeed, this process remains the basis for the burgeoning disciplines of public relations, public affairs, and corporate communications.

Media relations involves targeting the "gatekeepers" of the mass and specialized media for communication about the client or organization. However, the media are actually intermediate audiences. The ultimate targeted audiences in media relations are the consumers of the media.

RESEARCH

The research process for media relations includes investigation of the practitioner's client or organization, of the opportunity or problem that accounts for communication with the media, and of the various audiences themselves to be targeted for the PR effort.

Client Research

First, the practitioner should be familiar with background data about the client or organization, including its personnel, financial status, and reputation. Special attention must be given to past and present relations with media representatives. Has the client had negative or positive news coverage in the past? Has there been little or no coverage? Does the client have any particular media coverage strengths, such as unusual or glamorous products or a newsworthy chief executive officer? On the other hand, what are the client's publicity "negatives"? In what areas is the client vulnerable? Finally, the practitioner should assess the client's publicity opportunities. What special events can be most profitably staged for the client? What can be done to tie the client in with ongoing community or national special events? With information of this kind, the practitioner will be better prepared to serve the client's publicity or media relations needs.

Opportunity or Problem Research

The second aspect of research in preparation for media relations involves determining the reason for the program. Is it because an opportunity has presented itself for good news coverage, or has some problem arisen that will bring media representatives to the client's doorstep? This chapter is concerned more with the former situation, the publicity *opportunity*. For information on managing the media when a problem or crisis develops, see Chapter 11, "Emergency Public Relations."

Audience Research

The final aspect of research for media relations is thought by most practitioners to be the most important—identifying the appropriate media and *their* audiences to target for communication. These media fall into two broad categories, mass and specialized, each of which can be further subdivided (see Exhibit 3-a).

With these media categories, the practitioner's task is to prepare a comprehensive list of media contacts. Appropriate *media directories*, such as those listed in the suggested readings in this chapter, should be consulted in preparing such a list. Practitioners may find that much of their work has already been done for them by these directories. The national, regional, state, and city directories are thorough, but in some cases more information must be gathered. To be of optimal use, the media contact list should include:

1. The type and size of the audience reached by each media outlet
2. The type of material used by the media outlet—spot news, feature material, interviews, photos
3. The name and title of the appropriate editor, director, producer, reporter, or staff writer who handles news of organizations such as the client's
4. The deadlines for that media contact—monthly, weekly, daily, morning, afternoon, evening, date, day, or hour

The best advice for the practitioner in media relations is simply to *know the media outlet*. Each outlet has its own unique set of departments and editorial staffing, with particular requirements for submitting material. If in doubt, call the media outlet to obtain the necessary guidelines, along with the name and address of the person who holds the editorial position. It is usually best not to ask to speak with journalists themselves. They may be very busy and resent intrusions for routine information. As a rule, news releases for newspapers should be addressed to the city editor if they are general in nature or to the appropriate

---

E X H I B I T 3-A   Media Publics

Mass media

Local

    Print publications

    Newspapers

    Magazines

    TV stations

    Radio stations

National

    Print publications

    Broadcast networks

    Wire services

Specialized media

Local

    Trade, industry, and association publications

    Organizational house and membership publications

    Ethnic publications

    Publications of special groups

    Specialized broadcast programs and stations

National

    General business publications

    National trade, industry, and association publications

    National organizational house and membership publications

    National ethnic publications

    Publications of national special groups

    National specialized broadcast programs and networks

---

section editor if they are of special interest. For broadcast stations, news releases should usually be addressed to the news director or, in some cases, to the public service director.

Practitioners should never feel that their media contact lists are complete when they have compiled necessary information about the mass media alone. Each client or organization will be operating in a special field. Automobile manufacturers, fashion designers, dentists, and rock music groups—all have their own organizations or associations. And all are served by their own specialized publications. Public relations practitioners must be aware of all such publications that serve their client's field. The process of compiling a list of specialized media contacts begins with consulting a media directory. For comprehensive listings in a great variety of fields, look at publications or online services such are Cision (formerly Bacon's) and BurrellesLuce media directories. Later in this chapter, other directories and services are listed for medical, scientific, military, and minority media contacts.

Among the finished products of the practitioner's audience research, then, will be two media contact lists: one for mass media and the other for specialized media. News releases, photos, and feature stories directed to and published in specialized publications can often be of greater value to the client than similar exposure in the mass media. It should be emphasized that the purpose of compiling these *two* media contact lists is communication with the consumers of both the mass and specialized media—the client's ultimate intended audiences.

In the cases included later in this chapter, these audiences are sometimes specialized and sometimes mass in character.

Thus, the research process in media relations involves a thorough understanding of the practitioner's client or organization; the reason—opportunity or problem—for communicating with the media; and, most important, knowledge of the targeted media themselves—the nature of the media outlets, audiences reached, types of material used, specific names and titles of staff contacts, and their deadlines.

OBJECTIVES

Media relations uses both impact and output objectives. Some typical examples of both types are examined here, along with a sampling of the objectives used in the media relations cases included in this chapter.

Impact Objectives

Impact objectives represent the desired outcomes of modifying the attitudes and behaviors of target audiences. In media relations, they usually include such statements as:

1. To increase knowledge of news about the client among community media representatives

2. To enhance the client's credibility among media people

3. To reinforce favorable attitudes toward the client on the part of media representatives

4. To increase favorable client news coverage

Note that in each of these statements, percentages and time frames can be added as desired. The first statement could be rephrased to read: to increase knowledge of news about the client by 30 percent among community media representatives during the period June 1 to December 1. However, a majority of the award-winning cases in this book do *not* quantify their objectives or set time frames.

Almost invariably the objectives used in our sample cases targeted the client's ultimate audiences, rather than the media audiences, for desired impact. It is understood in each case, however, that the media must be the intermediate target audience. Perhaps the objectives would have been clearer and easier to measure if they had targeted *both* the desired media and the ultimate audiences.

Output Objectives

Output objectives in media relations refer to the efforts made by the practitioner on behalf of the client. These statements have nothing to do with the client's desired influence on audiences. Output objectives may include:

1. To be of service to the media—both proactively and reactively
    a. Proactively, to provide *newsworthy* stories about the client or organization
    b. Reactively, to be available for responses to media inquiries
2. To coordinate media interviews with client or organizational officers and personnel
3. To distribute feature story ideas to trade publications

PROGRAMMING

Programming for media relations includes the same planning and execution elements used in other forms of public relations: (1) theme and messages, (2) action or special event(s), (3) uncontrolled or controlled media, and (4) principles of effective communication.

Theme and Messages

Program themes, especially in connection with special events, should be included in the messages sent to media outlets. In media relations, the messages themselves should always be governed by the requirements for newsworthiness applicable to the targeted media outlets. Since media relations essentially involves the communication of client news to media outlets or the stimulation of news coverage of the client, the practitioner must understand the nature of news and the criteria for newsworthiness.

Some practitioners believe there are two kinds of news: "hard" and "soft." It is more accurate, however, to think of *spot news* and *feature material* as the two kinds of news.

Spot news is temporal, or time-bound, in nature. Within the rubric of spot news are two subcategories: hard and soft. *Hard spot news* is normally found on prominent pages of major metropolitan dailies. It affects large numbers of people and is of great and immediate interest to the audiences of most mass media outlets. Unfortunately, most hard spot news handled by PR practitioners is *bad news* about the client, such as disasters, plant closings, or layoffs. *Good* news about clients can usually be classified as *soft spot news*. It may not be of much interest outside the organization itself, in which case it should be printed in a house publication and not sent to a mass media outlet. A major challenge to the practitioner is to create special events or *make* good news about the client that will receive favorable coverage in the media.

Feature material, on the other hand, is not time-bound but may be used as "filler" for print and broadcast media. Feature stories for both kinds of media usually focus on human interest topics. Types of feature stories include "a day in the life of …"; profiles of personalities; interviews; descriptions of events that emphasize human interest factors and the personalities involved; and sidebars, or feature stories designed to accompany spot news stories in newspapers.

Keeping in mind the differences between spot news and feature material, the practitioner should also be sensitive to the general criteria used by journalists to determine what is newsworthy. The usual characteristics of news include what is new or novel, involves famous persons, is important to large numbers of people, involves conflict or mystery, may be considered confidential, will have significant consequences, is funny, is romantic, or involves sex.

News has also been defined as anything a media outlet chooses to print, broadcast, or film as "news." Since the selection is always the outlet's choice, the public relations practitioner must become familiar with the criteria used by that particular group of editors. This is simply another way of saying *Know the media outlet*.

Like other aspects of programming, theme and messages should be governed by the practitioner's understanding of what is news and both the general and particular newsworthiness criteria in use at individual media outlets.

Action(s) or Special Event(s)

The use of actions on the part of the client and the staging of special events assume special importance in media relations. They provide the basis for news coverage. They *are* the news about the client. Thus, the PR practitioner should review the list of actions and special events included in Exhibit 2-c. These can serve as methods of *making* news for the client. Each action or special event should be carefully planned and orchestrated for its maximum news value. If possible, celebrities should be present, and as many other news criteria should be incorporated as is feasible.

Uncontrolled Media

Uncontrolled media are the major vehicles for reporting client news to media representatives. The most commonly used forms are:

1. News releases—print/online and video
2. Photographs and photo opportunities
3. News conferences
4. Media interviews

News Releases—Print/Online and Video.   Of these four frequently used formats, news releases are the most popular with public relations practitioners. News releases provide a quick, economical means of communicating client spot news or feature material to appropriate media outlets. *Print news releases* are delivered by hand courier, mailed, faxed, or e-mailed. Corporations and other organizations often place current news releases on their Web sites or use online distribution services to reach audiences.

Online and e-mailed releases may be customized to include links to additional sources of information and even links to social media sites. Through the online links, the journalist may quickly retrieve other background information about an organization or see what the CEO is saying in a personal blog.

Search engine optimization further customizes the language in a news release through the use of key words that are relevant to current news issues. The news release may then gain higher exposure and rankings on search engines such as Google and Yahoo! Unfortunately, print news releases have become overused in major markets throughout the United States. Each morning, editors may be confronted with a stack of 70 to 100 or more releases from practitioners seeking news coverage for their clients or organizations. A prominent Washington bureau chief confided to one of our classes that, faced with his daily pile of news releases, he simply pulls a large, desktop-high wastebasket over to the edge of the desk and "files" most of the morning mail.

How, then, can practitioners expect to break through the blizzard of print news releases to call attention to their own client's news? The "secret" of successful news releases lies in the first word of the term itself—*news*. A really newsworthy story about a client can easily be telephoned to a city editor. The editor, if interested in the story, will assign a reporter to cover it. Major metropolitan editors or broadcast news directors rarely use news releases verbatim or even partially. If a story is there, the news release may alert them to it; but they invariably prefer to assign their own staff to do the actual news gathering and writing. Be prepared to provide additional information and interviews to flesh out the story. Expect the reporter to contact both your friends and your critics.

The news release may be used to initiate a relationship with a journalist, but the relationship must be cultivated through personal contacts such as phone calls and e-mail. Your goal is to become a credible and valued source of information about your organization for the journalist. Successful variations on the basic news release include briefer *media alerts*, *media advisories*, and *fact sheets*. All media outlets, in markets large or small, depend on PR practitioners for *information* about news events in their market areas. Print news releases and their shorter variations, despite their overuse, remain the major method of transmitting information from the client to the journalist.

The *video news release* (VNR) became a popular form of client news in the past, but its popularity has waned because of the stigma broadcast journalists have attached to "fake news" designed to flatter a public relations client. Like its print counterpart, the successful VNR must focus on *news* rather than on promotional pap about the client. VNRs are most frequently used in medium or small markets rather than major metropolitan markets. They should be produced by a reputable firm specializing in VNRs, and, ideally, the firm should be equipped to handle the entire task, including scripting, production, and satellite distribution. Most VNRs today, if produced at all, include accompanying B-roll and sound bites[1] that might better be interspersed in television newscasts than the complete VNR.

Photographs and Photo Opportunities.   Photographs are a second widely used form of uncontrolled media. As with news releases, public relations photographs are seldom used by major metropolitan daily newspapers. But, like news releases, they may serve to attract the attention of major editors to client news that might otherwise be overlooked. Public relations photographs have a better chance of being used by smaller publications in smaller markets. They are important enough to warrant attention to the details of their proper composition and preparation for PR purposes.

Good public relations photographs should be creative and imaginative in composition, avoiding the clichés a client may request, such as a speaker standing at a podium, one person handing something to another, a group shot of 10 or more people, or one person sitting at a desk. Photographs of this kind usually find their way into house publications. A good public relations photograph depicts something a newspaper photographer cannot duplicate or restage. Unique and interesting photographs may be used because of their creativity and news value.

A frequently used contemporary technique is the staging of a "photo opportunity," especially in markets where the major dailies or magazines are likely to assign their own photographers to a story. The photo opportunity should be carefully planned in advance and staged in a natural—not theatrical—way, so that it becomes an integral or necessary part of the news story and not something that can be missed by the assigned journalists and photographers.

News Conferences.   A third frequently used form of uncontrolled media is the news conference. News conferences should be used sparingly since they are usually inconvenient for journalists. If staged, the conference must live up to its descriptive adjective, *news*. Even on their very best days, metropolitan journalists are easily annoyed. They can resent being summoned to a news conference to hear a routine announcement that could have been faxed to the city desk or reported in a written release.

Many organizations use news conferences for significant announcements, such as major corporate changes, takeovers, mergers, introductions of new product lines, or responses to false accusations of wrongdoing. Other than for major government agencies, news conferences should never be routine. They should be reserved for truly newsworthy occasions that call for a personal presentation by the organization's CEO or by a visiting celebrity or dignitary. Video and audio recordings of the news conference may be posted on your Web site to increase exposure to your news. Don't forget to invite alternative media/bloggers to a news conference or teleconference as they may also generate coverage of the event.

News conferences can be conducted profitably, but the practitioner should always keep the preceding reservations in mind and usually resist the urge to hold one.

Media Interviews.   Media interviews are a fourth frequently used form of uncontrolled media. Whether given to print or broadcast journalists, interviews provide the most direct contact between the client and the media. The practitioner's role in this situation is that of a link, or coordinator, and sometimes also that of a trainer or coach for the client. The interview is not just to answer the reporter's questions, but to accent the themes and messages as outlined in the campaign.

In the case of print interviews, clients may have the options of declaring beforehand that their comments will be for background, not for attribution, or completely off the record. In these cases the client's name cannot be used; and in off-the-record interviews the content of the interview cannot be used in the media. Aside from interviews with high government officials in sensitive positions, however, most clients want to be both quoted and identified in the media as a means of promoting their organizations' interests.

Broadcast interviews do not permit the luxury of being off the record. If clients consent to broadcast interviews, they do so with the knowledge that while on camera (or microphone), they may be put through a "third degree" by an enterprising journalist. Moreover, the client loses control of the editing function. For this reason, many organizations insist on bringing their own video-taping equipment and crew in order to have an independent record of the interview. Increasingly, organizations are paying specialized consultants for "media training" for their executives who can then significantly influence favorable public opinion about their organizations.

Print and broadcast interviews, then, are one of the four most frequently used forms of uncontrolled media in the client's communication with journalists. In addition to news releases, photographs, news conferences, and interviews, the practitioner should consider the other communication vehicles listed in Exhibit 2-d.

Controlled Media

A variety of forms of controlled media can be used to provide journalists with background information. For example, practitioners usually prepare a media kit for news conferences. These kits include the opening statement made at the conference, a basic news release, backgrounder, fact sheet, photos with cutlines (captions), and such printed materials as brochures, folders, annual reports, speeches, and other information pieces. Increasingly, paper media kits are being supplemented or replaced by CD-ROMs/DVDs, which can cover much more information, along with graphics, video, and sound. Additionally, media kit materials are made available on corporate and organizational Web sites. In the true sense of the term, however, controlled media are not used in media relations. When journalists are given controlled communications, they make their own uses (or nonuses) of them. Thus, the client or practitioner has no control over how such materials will be used by journalists.

A case can be made that public relations advertising constitutes the use of controlled communications in media relations. The practitioner *does* deal with media outlets in such cases, but not with journalists. Advertising is purchased directly from the media outlet's advertising department.

The exhibits included with the cases in this chapter demonstrate the scope of both uncontrolled and controlled communications used in media relations.

Effective Communication

In media relations, the communication process can be aptly described as a two-step flow. The traditional two-stage model depicts a stream of messages from a mass media source to opinion leaders and then to the colleagues of the opinion leaders. In media relations, this process is partially reversed. Communication flows from the practitioner's client to the media and then in turn to the media audience.

Because of the special nature of media relations, not all of the nine principles of effective communication discussed in Chapter 2 apply.

Source credibility clearly is applicable in the case of media relations. Media representatives must perceive the client or organization and its spokesperson as trustworthy and reliable. Salient information, on the other hand, must be redefined for media relations. Information that meets the criteria of newsworthiness constitutes the salience for journalists. Both nonverbal and verbal cues contribute to communication effectiveness in media relations, just as they do in other forms of public relations. The use of two-way communication, however, plays a less important role in media relations than in other forms unless a journalist is wishing to check the accuracy of information used in a story. Journalists generally resent inquiries from practitioners to see if a client's news releases are going to be used. The feedback that practitioners really want in media relations is the use of their materials in the media.

The use of opinion leaders in the usual sense is not a part of media relations. In media relations, practitioners communicate directly with journalists. In some instances, journalists are regarded as community opinion leaders, but this principle applies more directly to community relations. The selective exposure principle may apply in some cases to media relations but, in general, journalists are more open-minded and often seek information that they may personally disagree with. Finally, the audience participation principle is valid and useful in media relations. When introducing new product lines, for example, many companies invite journalists to use the product on an introductory basis. Journalist participation at news conferences and other meetings arranged by PR practitioners provides other instances of effective audience participation in media relations.

Thus, most of the principles of effective communication apply to media relations to some degree. However, the group-influence principle is rarely used in media relations since journalists pride themselves on their independence of thought and action. But, on the whole, principles of effective communication should be a priority concern of the public relations practitioner in media relations.

EVALUATION

The evaluation process in all forms of public relations always refers to the program's stated objectives. In media relations, as in all of public relations, impact objectives are of the highest priority.

Evaluating Impact Objectives

The impact objective of informing the media about the client is generally measured by assessing the exposure of the message in the media, or publicity placement. National or local clipping and media monitoring services are usually retained to take this measure of effectiveness. Message exposure can also be measured by the circulation figures and audience-size data available from the publications and broadcast media themselves. Additionally, some public relations firms use sophisticated computerized tracking systems to evaluate effectiveness in delivering messages to audiences. Publicity placement, however, remains the predominant method for evaluating the success of message exposure.

Attitude objectives in most forms of public relations are measured by conducting sample surveys of the target audiences, but this may not be feasible with journalists targeted for communication. Some might react negatively to such an intrusion from a PR practitioner. Content analyses of media placement, however, can yield the desired measurements. A scientific assessment of attitudes is therefore possible and relatively easily obtained.

This same procedure is also useful in measuring favorable client news coverage. This objective is the ultimate goal of all media relations.

Evaluating Output Objectives

Along with the measurement of impact objectives, practitioners want to determine the effectiveness of their media relations output objectives. These consist essentially of distributing uncontrolled media to outlets, being responsive to media inquiries, and coordinating media interviews. They can be evaluated by keeping records of all such transactions. Although these objectives are easily accomplished, the practitioner should be reminded that these goals may have little bearing on media relations impact.

Evaluation of media relations, then, is heavily concentrated on successful and favorable placement of the practitioner's uncontrolled media. Other objectives are useful, but successful media relations ultimately boils down to the matter of placement. This is clearly visible in the priority given to placement in the evaluations of the cases in this chapter.

SUMMARY

With some modifications, the four-stage process is as useful in media relations as it is in other forms of public relations. Essentially, media relations involves establishing a favorable working relationship between PR practitioners and journalists representing appropriate mass and specialized media.

The most important aspect of research for media relations is the preparation of up-to-date lists of media contacts for both mass and specialized outlets. Objectives in media relations usually emphasize the desired behavioral impact of obtaining favorable news coverage for the client. An absolute essential for media relations programming is an understanding of the particular media outlets' audiences and the media's definitions of news for those audiences. This information should provide criteria for the development of newsworthy, client-centered special events, news releases, photographs, news conferences, interviews, and/or other forms of uncontrolled media used in reaching journalists.

Evaluation of media relations always refers back to the program's stated objectives. Impact objectives are generally measured through publicity placement, circulation and audience data, computer tracking of messages, or content analysis. The accomplishment of output objectives can be simply determined by counting or otherwise observing the desired outputs as they are set in motion. In essence, however, the effectiveness of media relations always comes down to media placement, that is, obtaining the desired publicity for the client.

ENDNOTE

1. The VNR itself is "A-roll." Most news directors prefer the unedited "B-roll" and sound bites to create their own news stories.

READINGS ON MEDIA RELATIONS

Alterman, Eric. "Better Red Than Dead?" *Nation* 280 (February 2005): 11.

Anderson, Rebecca B. "Thinning Out Your Target List: When Less Is More in Media Relations," *Public Relations Tactics* 13 (May 2006): 21–22.

Barbaro, Michael. "Wal-Mart Begins Quest for Generals in P.R. War," *New York Times* (March 30, 2006): C3.

Barstow, David, and Robin Stein. "Under Bush, a New Age of Prepackaged TV News," *New York Times* (March 13, 2005): A1.

Beasley, David. "Traditional Media Relations Finesse: The Power of the Phone Pitch in the Age of 'Click to Open," *Public Relations Tactics* 15 (May 2008): 21.

Beckman, Carol. "Nine Things to Remember When Talking to a Reporter," *Public Relations Tactics* 3 (September 1996): 13ff.

Beres, George. "A Major Distinction," *Editor & Publisher* 138 (July 2005): 70.

Bergman, Eric. "The Ethics of Not Answering," *Communication World* 22 (September–October 2005): 16–142.

Bush, Lee. "Focusing on Strategy: Moving Beyond Media Relations and Getting to the New Brand Marketing Table," *Public Relations Strategist* 13 (Spring 2007): 30–33.

Catuthers, Dewey. "Media Placement: An Art That Gets No Respect," *Public Relations Tactics* 5 (October 1998): 23ff.

Chermak, Steven, and Alexander Weiss. "Maintaining Legitimacy Using External Communication Strategies for Police-Media Relations," *Journal of Criminal Justice* 33 (September 2005): 501–512.

Collins, David. "Ten Rules of Editorial Etiquette," *Public Relations Quarterly* 39 (fall 1994): 8.

Davis, Ellen. "Push Your Luck: Successful Media Relations Often a Function of Chance, Timing," *Public Relations Tactics* 15 (May 2008): 23.

Deigh, Robert. "Be Part of the Media Mix: Tips for Becoming a News Source Journalists Seek," *Public Relations Tactics* 15 (May 2008): 22.

Erjavec, Karmen. "Hybrid Public Relations News Discourse," *European Journal of Communication* 20 (June 2005): 155–179.

Eveland, William P., and Douglas M. McLeod. "The Effect of Social Desirability on Perceived Media Impact: Implications for Third-Person Perceptions," *International Journal of Public Opinion Research* 11 (winter 1999): 315–333.

Feldman, Charles, and Suzanne Spurgeon. "After Deep Throat: How to Respond to Anonymously Sourced News Stories," *Public Relations Tactics* 12 (July 2005): 14.

Goldberg, Betsy. "That Other Broadcast Medium: Tuning in to the Power of Radio," *Public Relations Tactics* 12 (July 2005): 13–15.

Greve, Frank. "Journalism in the Age of Pseudoreporting," *Nieman Reports* 69 (summer 2005): 11–13.

Guiniven, John. "PR Professional, Not Telemarketer: The Do's and Don'ts of Pitching," *Public Relations Tactics* 12 (July 2005): 6.

Hallett, Josh. "In Through the Back Door: Using Blogs to Reach Traditional Media," *Public Relations Tactics* 15 (May 2008): 25.

Howard, Carole M. "10 Media Lessons Learned the Hard Way," *Public Relations Strategist* 2 (summer 1996): 45ff.

Howard, Carole M., and Wilma K. Mathews. *On Deadline: Managing Media Relations*, 2d ed. Prospect Heights, IL: Waveland, 1998.

"How to Manage Media Relations When the 'Journalist' Is a Blogger," *PR News* 63 (January 2007): 1.

"How to Optimize a Press Release for Search," *PR News* 63 (September 25, 2006): 36.

"How to Sell…the Media," *PR News* 63 (November 2007).

Levy, Ronald N. "Media Opportunity: Use Your Head," *Public Relations Quarterly* 48 (summer 2003): 27–28.

Levy, Sue. "Media Expansion Tests PR Tracking," *Marketing* (February 24, 2000): 39ff.

Lubove, Seth. "Get Smart: A Reporter's Take on Good PR Practices," *Public Relations Tactics* 5 (October 1998): 20.

Macaluso, Susan. "The Media World in Transition: What Is the VNR's Role in This New Landscape?" *Public Relations Tactics* 12 (June 2005): 21.

"Mapping Your Message: The Key to Telling a Media Relations Success Story," *PR News* 63 (June 2007).

Miklya, Liz. "Making Your Message More Memorable for the Media—Plus, How to Bridge Difficult Questions," *Public Relations Tactics* 12 (May 2005): 21.

Murray, William P. "Running a Multifaceted Health Care Campaign During a Time of Increased Media Scrutiny," *Public Relations Tactics* 12 (July 2005): 10.

Reese, Stephen D., Oscar H. Gandy, Jr., and August E. Grant. *Framing Public Life: Perspectives on Media and Our Understanding of the Social World*. Mahwah, NJ: Erlbaum, 2001.

Robe, Karl. "Get Smart: Steps To Develop On-Strategy, On-Message, Value-Producing Media Pitches," *Public Relations Tactics* 15 (May 2008): 20.

Sallot, Lynne M., Thomas M. Steinfatt, and Michael B. Salwen. "Journalists' and Public Relations Practitioners' News Values: Perceptions and Cross Perceptions," *Journalism and Mass Communication Quarterly* 75 (summer 1998): 366ff.

Salzman, Jason. *Making the News*. New York: Perseus Books Group, 2003.

Sayres, Scott. "Reporters Do the Darnedest Things!: An Explanation of Some of Their Actions," *Public Relations Tactics* 12 (May 2005): 28.

Spaeth, Merrie. "Presidential Politics and Public Relations in 2004," *Journalism Studies* 6 (May 2005): 237–240.

Stoff, Rick. "Taking Back the Message," *St. Louis Journalism Review* 35 (April 2005): 6–7.

———. "Trust Us," *St. Louis Journalism Review* 35 (July–August 2005): 11–27.

Sweeney, Katie. "Fuzzy Picture for VNRs, SMTs—Both Vehicles Come Under Scrutiny, and Congress Gets into the Act," *Public Relations Tactics* 12 (June 2005): 18.

Thompson, Mike. "Step into a Reporter's Shoes to Fine-Tune Your Media Relations," *Public Management* 89 (September 2007): 25–29.

Trufelman, Lloyd P. "Consumer-Generated Media—Challenges and Opportunities for Public Relations," *Public Relations Tactics* 12 (May 2005): 17–19.

Wallack, Lawrence M., Katie Woodruff, Lori E. Dorfman, and Iris Diaz. *News for a Change: An Advocate's Guide to Working with the Media*. Thousand Oaks, CA: Sage Publications, 1999.

Warneke, Kevin. "Keeping Tabs at the Ronald McDonald House in Omaha: How a Nonprofit Garnered Press Attention," *Public Relations Tactics* 12 (August 2005): 19.

Wright, Donald K. "We Have Rights Too: Examining the Existence of Professional Prejudice and Discrimination Against Public Relations," *Public Relations Review* 31 (March 2005): 101–119.

Ziegler, Todd. "Eight Ways for Organizations to Employ New Media," *Public Relations Tactics* 13 (December 2006): 20–21.

Media Directories

Bacon's Media Directories. Chicago: Bacon's.

Broadcasting/Cablecasting Yearbook. Washington, DC: Broadcasting Publications.

Burrelle's Media Directories. Livingston, NJ: Burrelle's.

Burrelle's Special Directories: Black Media /Hispanic Media/Women's Media. Livingston, NJ: Burrelle's.

Editor and Publisher International Yearbook. New York: Editor and Publisher.

Gale Directory of Publications. Farmington Hills, MI: Cengage.

Gebbie Press. New Paltz, NY.

Guide to U.S. Business, Financial and Economic News Correspondents and Contacts. New York: Larriston Communications.

Guide to U.S. Medical and Science News Correspondents and Contacts. New York: Larriston Communications.

Harrison's Guide to the Top National TV Talk & Interview Shows. Lansdowne, PA: Bradley Communications.

Hudson's Washington News Media Contacts Directory. Rhinebeck, NY: Hudson's.

Military Publications. New York: Richard Weiner.

Media Services

BurrellesLuce, Livingston, NJ.

Cision (formerly Bacons') Information, Inc., Chicago.

Business Wire, San Francisco.

MarketWire, Toronto.

Media Distribution Services, Abington, MA.

Medialink, New York.

PRIMEZONE Media Network, Los Angeles.

PR Newswire, New York.

Vocus, Lanham, MD.

Media Relations Cases

Case 3-1

Generating "buzz" defines many campaigns. In the world of social media, both traditional media and online viral marketing complement and support efforts to promote an event. Exhibit 3-1a is a sidewalk "chalk flyer," Exhibit 3-1b is a "landing page," and Exhibit 3-1c is a tear-off sheet posted in traffic areas to promote the music festival.

Setting the Stage:
2005 CMJ Rock Hall Music Fest

Convention & Visitors Bureau of Greater Cleveland and Rock and Roll Hall of Fame with Marcus Thomas LLC

SUMMARY

The Convention & Visitors Bureau of Greater Cleveland (CVB) and the Rock and Roll Hall of Fame set out to reclaim Cleveland's rightful position as the rock and roll capital of the world by establishing an annual music fest. With a modest budget and six weeks to generate a buzz, Marcus Thomas was brought on board to drive up attendance numbers. The agency dispatched guerilla street teams and engaged in viral marketing to spread word-of-mouth excitement. All campaign objectives regarding attendance and word-of-mouth buzz were exceeded, as determined by evaluation research, and the event generated $3 million for Cleveland.

SITUATION ANALYSIS

While Cleveland beat out New York and other tourism giants to become the home to the Rock and Roll Hall of Fame in 1986, most of the celebrity and fanfare around rock music remained in New York. Cleveland sought to change that, last year, when it approached the College Music Journal (CMJ) Network about holding a music festival in Cleveland that would rival New York's 25-year-old and still-running CMJ Music Marathon. Bobby Haber, CEO of CMJ Network Inc. in Manhattan, admitted he was skeptical. Would Cleveland

Courtesy Convention & Visitors Bureau of Greater Cleveland and Rock and Roll Hall of Fame

clubs pull together and put aside their individual interests for the greater good of the city? More importantly, could Cleveland get the audiences?

Goals

In addition to claiming Cleveland's rightful position as the rock and roll capital of the world, the CVB and the Rock and Roll Hall of Fame had other lofty goals. To reach their economic goals, we would have to attract at least 10,000 (ideally 20,000) young rockers to concerts over a three-day period. Additionally, the two organizations wanted to attract out-of-town visitors for overnight stays that would have a positive impact on the local economy. The Rock Hall and the CVB retained Marcus Thomas just six weeks before the Music Fest.

RESEARCH

Audience Analysis

Marcus Thomas evaluated target audience data from prior CMJ concerts held in New York City. Through primary qualitative research and secondary psychographic research, we further studied our audience's lifestyle and interest data rather than rely solely on demographic information. We wanted to identify precisely where our audience lived, worked, and played.

Market Research

In addition, the agency conducted research in eight specific markets—Athens, Chicago, Cincinnati, Columbus, Detroit, Pittsburgh, Syracuse, and Toledo—chosen because they offered the college and/or urban settings in which our audience was likely to reside. We then identified preferred gathering places and entertainment venues where we would be most likely to find and engage our audience.

Primary Research

A third means of fulfilling information needs included an e-mail campaign to members of our target audience in all eight markets. While somewhat informal, the effort provided invaluable insights and data about our audience members, as well as where and how best to reach them.

PLANNING

Because of the exceptionally short time frame, we employed our agency planning model, The Equation, in an expedited fashion. PowerPoint planning outlines, brainstorming sessions with and without our clients, conference calls, and e-mails were our planning tools. We were admittedly working on the fly but in a strategic, thoughtful, and measured way.

Objectives and Strategies

To reach stated Music Fest goals, we knew our communications needed to:

- Conserve precious resources by targeting only the most receptive audience members and reaching them in locations where they would be most likely to hear and relate to our messages

- Reach 400,000 audience members in order to "close" on 10,000–20,000

- Create a "buzz" as well as an experience in which our audience could choose to actively participate, since we knew this would be the best way to engage our target and drive out-of-town traffic to Cleveland

EXECUTION

Word of Mouth

To reach the advertising-resistant young underground music lovers, the agency engaged in a five-week marketing campaign.

Guerilla Marketing

The hard-to-miss guerilla street teams traveled in cars covered with Music Fest magnets and stencils as they plastered hundreds of underground clubs/bars, alternative music stores, coffee shops, universities, and so forth, with posters, postcards, and flyers. The teams also distributed T-shirts, Festival Village tickets, and Music Fest guitar picks to anyone jazzed up about attending the concerts. Further, the teams spray-chalked the sidewalks and exteriors of venues they visited with a large Music Fest stencil design, which attracted a lot of attention.

Marcus Thomas also printed and posted very rustic "I need a ride" sheets with phone number tear-offs. When would-be concert-goers called the local number, a recording advised that the "fan" already had a ride but encouraged the caller to attend the concerts. Hundreds of callers dialed the numbers. In addition, in Pittsburgh, the teams partnered with a radio station that was promoting the Music Fest, "105.9 the X." And, in Syracuse, one of the Music Fest bands, Gym Class Heroes, performed at a club and used the designed collateral to promote the Music Fest.

Viral Marketing

Marcus Thomas created e-mails linked to the CVB's Web site, travelcleveland. com, where visitors could download songs from Music Fest bands and test their knowledge about CMJ trivia. The e-mails were distributed to fans of performing bands, CVB and Rock Hall contacts, and to College 360, a network of 120,000 college students. Hundreds of visitors to the link have downloaded songs and thousands have visited the Web site. In addition, Marcus Thomas provided each of the 100 bands performing at the Music Fest with online kits to help promote attendance with their fan base for the Music Fest.

Marcus Thomas recorded a podcast with Warren Zane, musicologist at the Rock Hall, about the Music Fest that also featured music from participating bands (www.podcastalley.com). In addition, Marcus Thomas posted information about the Music Fest on more than 50 music blogging sites. Hundreds of visitors have viewed and/or responded to the blogs posted about the concerts.

EVALUATION

Reach 400,000 audience members in order to "close" on 10,000–20,000.

- Attendance records were met with nearly 18,000 concert-goers. The attendance significantly outpaced the original launch attendance for other leading annual events such as the CMJ Music Festival in New York City and the South by Southwest Music Festival. The guerilla campaign's total impressions were more than 546,000. "The CMJ Rock Hall Music Fest exceeded all my expectations. It took New York five to seven years to get to the point the Cleveland event reached in its first year," said Bobby Haber, CEO of CMJ Network Inc.

Conserve precious resources by targeting only the most receptive audience members and reaching them in locations where they would be most likely to hear and relate to our messages.

- Marcus Thomas and Rock Hall staffers conducted intercept interviews with Music Fest attendees at concerts to track where they traveled from and how they heard about the concerts. Based on survey data, the cities visited by the guerilla street teams had high representation, and more than 50 percent of the 18,000 Music Fest attendees traveled from outside of Northeast Ohio.

Create a "buzz" as well as an experience in which our audience could choose to actively participate, since we knew this would be the best way to engage our target and drive out-of-town traffic to Cleveland.

- According to economic impact data released by the CVB, the first year of this planned-to-be-annual, collaborative event generated more than $3 million in "economic impact" for Cleveland. Because of the great and overall success of the concerts, the CMJ Rock Hall Music Fest will return to Cleveland in 2006.

Courtesy Convention & Visitors Bureau of Greater Cleveland and Rock and Roll Hall of Fame

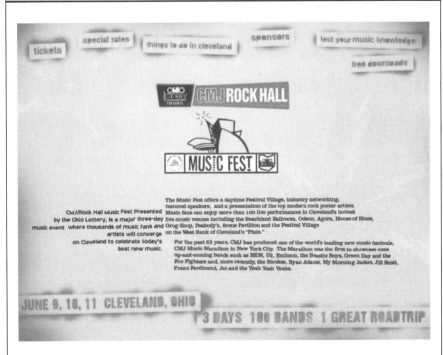

Courtesy Convention & Visitors Bureau of Greater Cleveland and Rock and Roll Hall of Fame

EXHIBIT 3-1c "Tear-Off Promotion Sheet"

Courtesy Convention & Visitors Bureau of Greater Cleveland and Rock and Roll Hall of Fame

Case 3-2

Museums not only provide historical perspectives but also fuel tourism and economic growth for a region. If a sign along the main highway between Chicago and St. Louis wasn't going to be sufficient, then a national and international media campaign was in order. Exhibit 3-2a is a news release about the new museum, and Exhibit 3-2b is a release announcing the four-day public celebration.

The Abraham Lincoln Presidential Museum Opening
Illinois Bureau of Tourism with Edelman Public Relations Worldwide

SUMMARY

Illinois, the "Land of Lincoln," had never been successful in creating a high-profile Lincoln destination that attracted significant numbers of visitors to the state. The Abraham Lincoln Presidential Library and Museum (ALPLM) aimed to be the first of its kind. Edelman was hired to promote the museum's April 2005 opening to help achieve that goal. Focusing on its state-of-the-art exhibits, Edelman helped turn a history museum—debuting in a small Illinois city—into an international tourist destination and media sensation. Despite a cluttered media environment, coverage 10 times greater than anticipated has driven museum attendance to surpass its goal by 500 percent the first year.

SITUATION ANALYSIS

Abraham Lincoln spent more than 30 years in Illinois before becoming president, and Springfield, Ill., is the town he called home. Yet despite the state's myriad Lincoln historic sites and promotional efforts, Illinois had never successfully capitalized upon this rich legacy. The state hoped to remedy that with the completion of the ALPLM in Springfield. The client wanted coverage equal to that of the 2002 opening of the library portion of the ALPLM complex, which generated nearly 144 million media impressions and was attended by more than 120 journalists. However, to succeed in attracting national and international

Courtesy Illinois Bureau of Tourism

media to this event and pushing the museum to the forefront of public consciousness, several challenges needed to be overcome:

- Coordinating four different state agencies, the museum, exhibit designers, and the White House
- Persuading media to travel to Springfield
- Securing coveted artifacts for media use
- Navigating a cluttered media environment following the death of Pope John Paul II

RESEARCH

Edelman used secondary research to assess the awareness of, and interest levels in, Lincoln, and to determine the best strategy, messaging and tactics to reach our audience. Research indicated that:

- Illinois is the seventh-ranked state in visits by historic and cultural travelers; 81 percent of U.S. adults are considered historic and cultural travelers, and spend more per trip than average travelers (Travel Industry Association of America—TIA).
- Illinois typically follows a regional marketing strategy, but anecdotal research showed that the ALPLM would be a national and international tourist attraction.
- Two of the top-10 projected planned travel activities for Americans in the United States for 2005 were visiting small towns or rural areas (64 percent) and visiting historic sites (41 percent) (TIA).
- About 30.2 million adults have taken an educational trip in the past three years (TIA).
- The definition of "museum" is changing as consumers clamor for experiences that both tell a story and educate (BRC Imagination Arts).

PLANNING

Planning for the opening was a nine-month process, and we recognized early on, based on the research about Lincoln, that a museum celebrating the life and times of our 16th president was a story in and of itself.

Based on these findings, we needed to craft messages that would resonate with various audience segments, including families, the scholarly community, Lincoln enthusiasts, domestic travelers, and international travelers in Illinois' strongest overseas markets—the UK and Germany.

Objectives

- Build national and international awareness of the museum among consumer and travel trade audiences.

- Drive visitors to the museum and to Springfield.

- Generate significant media coverage at local, state, regional, national, and international levels.

- Meet or exceed client expectations of attaining media coverage equal to that achieved by the opening of the Abraham Lincoln Presidential Library in 2002.

Strategies

- Generate interest in the museum before it opens.

- Capitalize on the wealth of events and the dignitaries (including President George W. Bush) attending the museum's dedication.

- Enlist a cross section of museum and political spokespersons to appeal to diverse demographic and geographic audiences.

- Capitalize on Lincoln's political stature, his ties to Illinois, the current patriotic sentiment, and the fact that Lincoln had not had an official presidential library and museum dedicated in his honor.

- Highlight scholarship and showmanship to bring the controversy and authenticity of Lincoln's story to life for a twenty-first-century audience.

- Use Lincoln's birthday (February 12) to seed momentum for April events.

- Establish an overseas presence in key markets to drive international interest.

To heighten interest in the launch event, the team capitalized on President Bush's attendance, as well as that of other prominent dignitaries, such as Speaker of the House Dennis Hastert, U.S. Senator Richard Durbin, U.S. Senator Barack Obama, U.S. Representative Ray LaHood, and Illinois Governor Rod Blagojevich.

Messages

- The ALPLM reinvents the concept of the presidential library and museum by employing twenty-first-century technology to make the nineteenth century live again.

- The ALPLM is a not-to-be missed, engaging educational tourism experience for all ages.

- For the first time, the complete story of Lincoln is now being told under one roof.

EXECUTION/TACTICS

Edelman worked with four different state agencies, the museum, exhibit designers, and the White House to maximize exposure of the ALPLM opening on April 16–19, 2005. Edelman executed the media plan using the following tactics both leading up to and during the opening:

Pre-event

- Ensured unified messaging by media training 20 people from various constituencies, including the museum's executive director and exhibit designer, the Illinois state governor, the Illinois state historian, and the Illinois tourism director

- Waged an aggressive media relations campaign and news bureau campaign, including an audio news release and B-roll of artifacts and of the museum in development, distributed on Lincoln's birthday

- Promoted opening events through outreach to local, state, national, and international media

- Coordinated dozens of press visits as well as an official media preview day attended by 100 journalists

- Developed a crisis plan for national and international security reasons

- Exhibited at key German and UK trade shows, with IBOT Deputy Director Jan Kostner in attendance

- Created a documentary with Chicago NBC affiliate WMAQ airing week before the launch event

Event

- Hosted and managed more than 300 media in attendance over four days of opening events

- Liaised with the White House advance team; counseled on logistics, media placement, processes

- Organized a satellite media tour the morning of the opening, B-roll following the event

- Capitalized on President Bush and other dignitaries' attendance at the dedication to enhance local and national media coverage frequency and depth

EVALUATION

The press attention Edelman generated has successfully driven traffic to the museum, which has already exceeded initial projections by 500 percent, drawing more than 500,000 visitors in its first 11 months. We achieved 10 times the media impressions of the 2002 library dedication, achieving more than 1.4 billion media impressions and 3,138 placements, most of which reflected the museum's key messages. The event's dedication ceremony drew an estimated 15,000 people to Springfield's Union Square, and Edelman hosted more than 300 media attendees during the opening ceremonies.

Our event and pre-event efforts resulted in these major media placements:

- National broadcast: Segments on all national television networks, including the "Today Show," "Good Morning America," "CBS Sunday Morning News," and "CBS Early Show"

- Print: Multiple articles in The Associated Press, *The New York Times*, *USA Today*, *Time*, *U.S. News & World Report*, and *National Geographic Traveler*

- Statewide: Coverage on all five major Chicago television networks; local print and broadcast coverage throughout Illinois

- International: Coverage in *The Guardian* and *Independent* on Sunday in the UK, with future coverage expected in BBC History. Coverage in *Die Welt* and the German newswire in Germany

- Awards: WMAQ's special won a 2005 Chicago/Midwest Emmy® Award in the Documentary Programs category

EXHIBIT 3-2a News Release on Museum

ABRAHAM LINCOLN PRESIDENTIAL LIBRARY & MUSEUM

For Immediate Release: April 1, 2005

New Abraham Lincoln Presidential Museum Marries Traditional Scholarship With 21st Century Showmanship

Interactive, state-of-the art technology brings Lincoln and his legacy brilliantly to life

SPRINGFIELD, Ill. - On April 19, 2005, Illinois Gov. Rod Blagojevich will officially open the Abraham Lincoln Presidential Museum, which reinvents the concept of the presidential museum with state-of-the-art, immersive exhibits that create history that feels like real life. With 40,000 square feet of permanent exhibits that double the size of any existing presidential museum, the museum offers a fitting tribute to the man most consider to be America's greatest president. The museum joins the already-open Abraham Lincoln Presidential Library as part of the Abraham Lincoln Presidential Library and Museum complex in Springfield.

The governor invites the public to celebrate the museum's arrival by attending a series of opening events beginning April 16 and culminating in a public dedication ceremony on Tuesday, April 19 at 11 a.m., which will be led by the governor and attended by other prominent state and national leaders.

"This world-class institution will help us all learn about and appreciate Illinois' most famous son and our shared national history," said Blagojevich. "The new museum will inform, engage, and inspire the state's residents and visitors alikeóand raise the national profile of both Springfield and Illinois."

To ensure that Lincoln's life and teachings remain a part of our lives, the Illinois Historic Preservation Agency (IHPA) teamed with design firm BRC Imagination Arts and a distinguished panel of renowned historians to develop the new 100,000-square-foot museum. Employing 21st-century technology to make the 19th century live again, the museum design combines scholarship with showmanship that will both inform and astound.

Courtesy Illinois Bureau of Tourism

E X H I B I T 3-2a   (Continued)

The New Museum Experience

Visitors to the museum complex will enter the museum's two state-of-the-art "exhibit journeys" off a 4,700-square-foot central plaza. Each journey makes a different time and aspect of Lincoln's life come alive, from his modest beginnings to his assassination and funeral, deepening our appreciation and understanding for the man Henry Cabot Lodge called one of the "best great men and the greatest good men whom history can show."

Journey One portrays Lincoln's childhood up to his election as 16th president. It re-creates his boyhood home as well as a harrowing New Orleans slave auction, his Springfield law office, the fiery Lincoln-Douglas debates and his departure for Washington in February, 1861.

Journey Two begins in a towering reproduction of the White House as Lincoln would have known it. It includes scenes depicting Lincoln and First Lady Mary Todd at the deathbed of their son, Willie; Lincoln in the War Department Telegraph Office as he receives the daily casualty counts of the Civil War; the White House Kitchen where black servants are gossiping about the possibility of emancipation; the presidential box at Ford's Theater; and, finally, a 95 percent scale reproduction of the House Chamber in the Old State Capitol where Lincoln's ornately draped casket lay in state before his interment in Springfield.

This is more than you-are-there-history, experiences include:

- **Ghosts of the Library**—This spectacular Holavision℀ show weaves an enchanting tale about the mystery and discovery awaiting the scholar in a great historical archive such as the Abraham Lincoln Presidential Library. During the presentation, high-tech special effects create misty, ghost-like visions of historical figures that share the stage with a live actor as viewers become part of a detective's journey into the past.

- **Campaign 1860**—This contemporary portrayal of the presidential race of 1860 features 30-second campaign commercials promoting each of that year's four candidates.

- **The Whispering Gallery**—Negative campaigning is nothing new! This is a twisted, unsettling hallway where visitors hear brutally unkind things said about Mr. and Mrs. Lincoln during their early months in Washington. Cruel caricatures and harsh political cartoons attacking the presidential couple cover the walls of the gallery.

- **The Emancipation Proclamation**—A special effects "illusion corridor," this exhibit features a gauntlet of dream-like images of people telling Lincoln what he should do. The compilation of varying, sometimes racist, opinions reminds visitors that Lincoln was leading a deeply divided nation. It also showcases the extraordinary courage it took to issue the Proclamation.

- **Treasures Gallery**—A soaring exhibit space that showcases many actual items that were a part of Lincoln's life; the gallery offers visitors close-up views of Lincoln's original handwritten Gettysburg Address, a signed copy of the Emancipation Proclamation, and personal effects such as Lincoln's shaving mirror, Mary Todd's music box and a recently donated presidential "briefcase," among other treasures.

- **Lincoln's Eyes**—In this dazzling special-effects theater presentation, an artist commissioned to create a portrait of Lincoln struggles to understand all the things he sees in Lincoln's eyes, sorrow, resolve, hope, vision, forgiveness and

---

EXHIBIT 3-2a   (Continued)

more. The presentation wraps around the audience with special effects and multiple layered screens of digital projection.

- **Ask Mr. Lincoln**—This unique interactive theater is a chance to ask our 16th president a question and receive the answer in his own words.

In addition to these permanent exhibits, 3,000 square feet of temporary exhibit space will feature Smithsonian-caliber changing exhibits on topics as diverse as America's First Ladies, Chicago's gangster era, the architectural genius of Frank Lloyd Wright and other topics illustrating the rich history of Illinois and America. The first temporary exhibit, "Blood on the Moon," commemorates the 140th anniversary of Lincoln's assassination. "Blood on the Moon" will be at the museum April 19 through October 16 and will feature Lincoln artifacts such as the bed he died in, which is on loan from the Chicago Historical Society; the carriage in which Abraham and Mary Lincoln rode to Ford's Theater, courtesy of the Studebaker National Museum; pieces of Lincoln's jacket, blood-stained shirt and gloves, Mary's dress and a fan from Ford's Theater, courtesy of Louise and Barry Taper; plus dozens of other historic artifacts, documents and images.

Elsewhere in the museum visitors will find a children's area called "Mrs. Lincoln's Attic," a restaurant, museum store and administrative offices. Both the library and museum have space available to rent for public or private events.

For more information, visit alplm.org.

# # #

EXHIBIT 3-2b   News Release on Opening Events

 ABRAHAM LINCOLN PRESIDENTIAL LIBRARY & MUSEUM

For Immediate Release: April 5, 2005

Abraham Lincoln Presidential Museum Opens with Four-Day Public Celebration

New attraction reinvents the presidential museum with unparalleled size, originality and educational promise

SPRINGFIELD, Ill. - Illinois Governor Rod Blagojevich today announced the schedule of activities for the grand opening of the Abraham Lincoln Presidential Museum, which compellingly recreates "The Great American Story" of Abraham Lincoln's life through immersive exhibits that employ state-of-the-art technology never seen before in a presidential museum.

Four days of activities will mark the museum's arrival, culminating in a public dedication April 19 attended by the Governor and other prominent state and national figures.

"The debut of this new world-class institution and the exploration of our shared national history give Springfield and Illinois ample reason to celebrate," said Gov. Blagojevich. "These festivities offer a tremendous opportunity to showcase the new museum for a national audience and to raise the Land of Lincoln's profile in the process."

The museum joins the already-open library as part of the Abraham Lincoln Presidential Library and Museum (ALPLM) complex in Springfield. Museum opening events begin on April 16 with "Looking for Lincoln," a two-day historical block party in downtown Springfield. The celebration will feature Lincoln era re-enactors, music, theater troupes, church choirs, folk dancers and artists from throughout Illinois. Most events are free to the public; the full schedule is available at www.alplm.org.

Some of the other major activities planned for the grand opening include:

- **Scholarly Conference "Lincoln in the Twenty-First Century"**–(April 17 and 18 at the Abraham Lincoln Presidential Library) A two-day Lincoln Scholarly Conference will examine Lincoln, from his attitude toward race and his domestic life to his wartime leadership and assassination. The conference will conclude on the 18th with a panel hosted by C-SPAN founder and CEO Brian Lamb and will

EXHIBIT 3-2b   (Continued)

feature three generations of the world's foremost Lincoln scholars, David Herbert Donald, Harold Holzer and Matthew Pinsker.

- **Interfaith Service of Thanksgiving for the Life of Abraham Lincoln**–(April 17, 11 a.m. at Union Square Park) The community will come together and find strength in the celebration of religious diversity in a public service led by various community religious leaders.

- **Recreation of Lincoln's Farewell Address and Torchlight Parade**–(April 17, 6:30 p.m. from the Old Train Depot to Union Square Park /ALPLM).

- **Outdoor Concert, Fireworks and Laser Spectacular**–(April 17, 8 p.m. at Union Square Park) A public concert by the 312th Army Band.

- **Recreated Lincoln White House State Dinner**–(April 18, 7:30 p.m. at the Springfield Renaissance Hotel) This fundraiser for the Abraham Lincoln Presidential Library Foundation will feature a Lincoln-era menu and 19th-century music courtesy of the 312th Army Band. The first David Herbert Donald Prize for Excellence in Lincoln Studies will be presented to its namesake, the author of the definitive one-volume Lincoln biography.

- **Public Dedication**–(April 19, 11 a.m. at Union Square Park) Gov. Blagojevich and other prominent leaders will speak at this hour-long event signaling the official opening of the museum, with music provided by the 312th Army Band. In addition, the winner of a student essay contest sponsored by the Abraham Lincoln Presidential Library and Museum and C-SPAN will read his or her modern-day version of the Gettysburg address to the crowd.

The museum invites visitors to experience 40,000 square feet of permanent exhibits, twice the size of any other presidential museum. The galleries, which employ 21st-century technology to make the 19th century live again, are the result of collaboration among the State of Illinois, the Illinois Historic Preservation Agency (IHPA), Burbank, Calif.-based BRC Imagination Arts, and a distinguished panel of renowned historians.

"The opening of the Abraham Lincoln Presidential Museum will be a popular celebration of public history at its best," said Richard Norton Smith, the museum's executive director. "Just as the exhibits inside invite visitor participation, so will the events outside. Like the Museum, they will recreate another time, even as they remind us of what is timeless. It will be, literally, a time to remember."

The museum will be open to the public Saturday, April 16 and Sunday, April 17 from 10 a.m. to 4 p.m. The museum will be closed on Monday, April 18 but will reopen to the public immediately following the dedication ceremony on Tuesday, April 19.

For more information about the Abraham Lincoln Presidential Library and Museum, or about the slate of opening activities, visit www.alplm.org.

# # #

Case 3-3

Some special events such as museum openings must reach a wide audience and require a very long lead time to establish articles in appropriate publications. Exhibit 3-3a is a news release, and Exhibit 3-3b is a fact sheet.

Dinosphere: Now You're in Their World Media Relations Campaign

The Children's Museum of Indianapolis with Borshoff Johnson Matthews

OVERVIEW

In summer 2001, The Children's Museum of Indianapolis selected Borshoff Johnson Matthews (BJM) to lead local, regional, national, and international media relations for a new $25 million dinosaur exhibit. Called "Dinosphere: Now You're in Their World," this one-of-a-kind dinosaur experience features one of the largest displays of juvenile and family dinosaur fossils in the nation. BJM's overall goal was to further enhance the reputation of The Children's Museum of Indianapolis at the national and international levels by reaching strategically selected audiences, primarily through news media.

RESEARCH

Before developing a three-year media relations plan and identifying key audiences, BJM conducted the following extensive primary and secondary research to provide a solid foundation for the plan's strategies and tactics:

- Investigated hundreds of print/broadcast news media to determine the best approach.

- Interviewed the Chicago Field Museum's public relations coordinator who assisted with the announcement of "Sue," the most complete *Tyrannosaurus rex* ever found and exhibited, to share best practices.

- Brainstormed with IPREX, a worldwide public relations alliance. BJM spoke with firms across the country with extensive travel/tourism experience.

- Contacted the Midwest Travel Writers Association to determine effective ways to create interest among travel writers.

- Reviewed all internal museum demographics and psychographics research reports, and all conceptualization- and planning-related Dinosphere documents, such as the museum's Economic Impact Report and internal consumer surveys.

- Interviewed nationally recognized scientists serving on the museum's paleontology advisory board.

- Met with the Indiana Convention and Visitors Association to find partnerships in media outreach.

PLANNING

The research (1) defined the museum's target audience demographic and psychographic; (2) provided a foundation of previously successful "museum opening" media relations strategies from which to create our own plan; (3) gave a clear understanding of the unique world of paleontology and successful science-related media strategies; and (4) resulted in a massive database of individual media targets in nine vertical markets with several subset markets.

Armed with solid marketing data and media research, BJM partnered with the museum to develop a momentum-building, annual media plan (adapted quarterly or as needed) that identified Dinosphere's differentiating factors; outlined strategies, key messages, and tactics; and detailed media pitching timelines.

Objectives

Measurable objectives after Dinosphere's grand opening in June 2004 are the following:

- Increase museum attendance by 20 percent annually.
- Increase museum household memberships by 10 percent.
- Increase museum store sales and merchandising opportunities.

Target Audiences

Target audiences are families/parents/children; frequent travelers; educators; dinosaur enthusiasts; science enthusiasts/scientists; toy collectors; museum administrators; art collectors; architecture enthusiasts; community leaders; museum members; and the general public.

EXECUTION

BJM pitched local, regional, trade, national, and international news media. Targeted news media included:

- National, top 10 markets, regional, and local media (print, evening and morning television and radio news, science radio and television, etc.)
- National and city-specific children and parenting magazines
- Travel publications and travel freelancers
- Airline publications
- Architecture publications
- Audiovisual magazines
- Philanthropy publications
- Science publications
- Sunday magazines
- Women's publications

As Dinosphere developed over time, BJM provided media contacts with evergreen stories and trigger events to keep the exhibit top of mind throughout its three-year development. A sampling of the most prominent media triggers leading up to Dinosphere's opening include:

2001–2002

(Significant Relationship Building among Key Media Outlets Took Place.)

- Dinosphere's initial announcement—Pitched to local, regional, and national print and broadcast media
- Acquisition of Lanzendorf art collection—Pitched to art and museum trade pubs and local, regional, and national media
- Groundbreaking for Dinosphere—Pitched to all local, regional, and national print and broadcast media

2003

- Furcula (wishbone) discovery—National, regional, and local print, broadcast, and Internet media received information regarding a wishbone larger than the one found in most Thanksgiving turkeys.
- Gorgosaurus brain tumor—In conjunction with the annual Society of Vertebrate Paleontologists conference, BJM announced the first-of-its-kind pathology discovery to national, regional, and local media.

2004

- Summer travel—Touted as the family summer travel destination, this pitch was sent to national travel and airline publications; children's, women's, and parenting publications; and more than 1,000 freelancers.

- *T. rex*'s arrival at the museum—The uncrating of "Bucky," the first juvenile *T. rex* fossil to ever be placed in a museum's permanent exhibit, was pitched to national, regional, and local print and broadcast outlets.

- Dinosphere's grand opening announcement—International, national, regional, and local print, broadcast, and Internet media were contacted with the grand opening's date and expert interview opportunities.

- In addition to frequent, targeted media relations pitching during our three-year campaign, BJM:
    - Developed foundation materials, construction images, and specimen and exhibit fact sheets
    - Monitored media trends/interests with dinosaur, education, travel, and other topics
    - Contacted all targeted news media on an ongoing basis
    - Flew select news media to dinosaur dig sites where the fossils were being unearthed and cleaned
    - Coordinated national news media meetings with the museum's CEO
    - Provided overall strategic and creative direction for the grand opening VIP parties

Challenges

The timing of world events significantly impacted our media campaign. The original 2001 announcement of the creation of Dinosphere was planned for mid-September but moved back to October after the tragic events of September 11. During October, the United States invaded Afghanistan. Furthermore, when Dinosphere was completed, the grand opening was planned for June 11, the same date on which President Ronald Reagan's funeral was unexpectedly scheduled. Therefore, Dinosphere's grand opening ceremonies were respectfully postponed to Saturday morning with a soft opening to the public on Friday. This allowed media to cover both opportunities, and Dinosphere's opening garnered much of the media coverage originally planned.

Nontraditional Tactics

Advertising, provided by another firm, complemented the media relations campaign closer to the grand opening.

EVALUATION

While feedback by museum visitors to Dinosphere has been overwhelmingly positive, BJM measured its success by quantitative methods since Dinosphere opened on June 11:

- Museum attendance has increased 30 percent, far surpassing the goal of 20 percent.

- Museum household memberships have risen 57 percent.

- Household membership revenues are above projected plans by 18.4 percent.

- Museum store sales have increased by 31 percent from August 2003.

- Ongoing media relations efforts resulted in more than 83 million impressions during the three-year Dinosphere campaign, including placements in *The New York Times*, *USA Today*, *Time for Kids*, *U.S. News & World Report*, CNN radio, ABC radio, CBS radio, NBC radio, NPR, National Geographic online, and many more.

Highlights of the 83,041,563 impressions created are the following:

- Dinosphere's initial public announcement resulted in about 5 million impressions nationally. From inception through completion, significant media coverage was achieved, including:

  - Gorgosaurus brain tumor announcement—27.6 million impressions worldwide

  - Furcula (wishbone at Thanksgiving)—2.4 million impressions nationally

  - Bucky, the teenage *T. rex*'s arrival at the museum announcement—4.1 million impressions nationally

- Dinosphere's grand opening on June 11, 2004, earned 43.8 million impressions from media worldwide.

E X H I B I T 3-3a   News Release

FOR IMMEDIATE RELEASE
Media kit (and electronic images) available at: http://www.blmpr.com/tern/

Satellite Feeds:

Friday, June 11:	**Saturday, June 12:**
Dedicated Window 2:30–2:45 PM ET	Dedicated Window 2:30–2:45 PM ET
Telstar 6/Transponder 15 (c) band	Telstar 6/Transponder 15 (c) band
Downlink: 4000(v)	Downlink: 4000 (v)

Nation's largest display of real juvenile and family dinosaur fossils Official opening ceremonies Saturday, June 12 at The Children's Museum of Indianapolis

Dinosphere: Now You're In Their World is the most immersive, scientifically-accurate dinosaur exhibit ever created

INDIANAPOLIS - The largest display of real juvenile and family dinosaur fossils in the United States opens its doors - and jaws - to visitors with official opening ceremonies tomorrow at The Children's Museum of Indianapolis. The new **Dinosphere: Now You're In *Their* World** exhibit transports children and families back in time 65 million years to the Cretaceous Period via a multi-level, multi-sensory, immersive environment. Visitors will experience the sights, sounds and smells of the Cretaceous period - when dinosaurs last roamed the earth.

Courtesy The Children's Museum of Indianapolis

EXHIBIT 3-3a   (Continued)

The Children's Museum of Indianapolis will be open today, as usual, and will welcome all of the families and children with timed Dinosphere tickets to visit the Dinosphere exhibit as planned. The official ceremonies were rescheduled to respect the National Day of Mourning.

"As one of the most comprehensive interactive, educational and research-oriented exhibits of its kind, Dinosphere provides a one-of-a-kind educational experience for children and families that they'll remember for the rest of their lives," said Dr. Jeffrey H. Patchen, Children's Museum president and CEO.

According to world-renowned paleontologist Dr. Robert Bakker, the $25 million Dinosphere "is one of the biggest things to happen to museums in about 50 years" and will be "the most exciting new addition on the list of real-bone dinosaur exhibits."

The Dinosaurs of Dinosphere

The star of Dinosphere is **"Bucky," the teenage** *Tyrannosaurus rex* **-a** *T. rex* **with an attitude!** Bucky will be the first juvenile *T. rex* ever placed on permanent exhibition in a museum and was discovered by a then-20-year-old Bucky Derflinger - the youngest person to ever find a *T. rex*.

The exhibit will feature a new species of *Gorgosaurus,* an older cousin of the *T. rex*. This one-of-a-kind specimen contains **the first evidence of a brain tumor** ever found in a dinosaur.

Visitors will also have the opportunity to see "Baby Louie," the only fully-articulated (complete) dinosaur embryo fossil ever discovered. Baby Louie, an *Oviraptor,* was discovered in the Xixia Basin in Central China.

Other specimens include "Kelsey", one of the most complete *Triceratops* skeletons known to science; a family of *Hypacrosaurs* –"Caroline," "Lauren," "Shiny" and "Abagail"; a *Leptoceratops*–"Frannie"; a *Maiasaura'*, and a *Didelphodon,* an early pouched mammal distantly related to the modern opossum.

The Dinosphere Immersive Experience

As visitors tour Dinosphere, they can stop to experiment and explore at interactive learning stations. These learning stations include **touching real fossils, piecing together dinosaur anatomy, and serving the appropriate dinner to a cast of hungry creatures.** Visitors also will conduct experiments and research via selected Web sites, the Museum's library and an interactive computer globe. A Dinosphere Question Lab and computer animation program brings the past to the present by encouraging families to discuss why dinosaurs became extinct and what people can do today to preserve the environment and prevent future animal and plant extinction.

Dinosphere Is One of Top Educational And Scientific Exhibits

Dinosphere offers the rare combination of serious paleontology research and highly interactive, educational programming for children and families. **No other museum in the United States has such a wide range of sizes and ages of dinosaurs available for research.** The Museum anticipates that paleontologists from around the world will come to Indianapolis to study the specimens. And, the exhibit is one of the first in which all of the dinosaurs are mounted so individual fossils can easily be removed by paleontologists for further scientific study.

"Dinosphere is a wonderful combination of original research, field work, specimen acquisition, laboratory preparation, exhibit construction and public programming. Paleontology needs more museums with active field-lab-education programs

EXHIBIT 3-3a (Continued)

like this one - **what The Children's Museum has accomplished is extraordinary," said Dr. Bakker.**

Bakker and several other prominent paleontologists, dinosaur and education experts worked with the Children's Museum to assure that Dinosphere is a lifelike and truthful exhibition of how dinosaurs lived. Advisory board members include:

- **Dr. Robert Bakker,** world-renowned paleontologist and *T. rex* expert; Dinosphere advisory board member. Dr. Bakker has been interviewed on *The Tonight Show, Good Morning America, The Today Show* and *Entertainment Tonight* to discuss breaking stories about dinosaurs and to explain the science behind "Jurassic Park," for which he was an advisor.

- **Phil Currie, Ph.D., and Eva (Currie) Koppelhaus, Ph.D.,** dinosaur researchers, Royal Tyrrell Museum of Paleontology in Alberta, Canada.

- **John Falk, Ph.D., and Lynn Dierking, Ph.D.,** directors of the Institute for Learning Innovation in Annapolis, Maryland and renowned experts on learning research and development in museum settings.

- **John Lanzendorf,** Chicago, Ill., world renowned paleo art collector and aficionado.

- **Pete and Neal Larson,** Founders of the Black Hills Institute of Geologic Research, Hill City, S.D. Pete Larson was on the team that discovered the *T. rex* "Sue," on display at the Chicago Field Museum.

- **Leona Schauble, Ph.D.,** University of Wisconsin - Madison, professor of educational psychology known for her work in constructivist learning and science education. **Michael Skrepnick,** world-famous paleo artist.

- **Dong Zhiming, Ph.D.,** research professor, Institute for Vertebrate Paleontology and Paleoanthropology, China Academy of Science.

Built from the Ground up to Encourage New "Family Learning" Model

Dinosphere is one of the first exhibits in the nation based on the concept of "family learning." Family learning focuses on cooperative exploration and interaction among children and adults, resulting in enhanced learning. The Children's Museum of Indianapolis is one of the first museums to fully incorporate the concept of family learning into all aspects of an exhibit, in keeping with the Museum's mission statement "creating extraordinary experiences that have the power to transform the lives of children and families."

Dinosphere Engages Children in the World of Science

Dinosphere strives to engage children in science - a skill of which development is key at an early age. Dr. Patchen said, "By introducing children to the world of dinosaurs, the Museum compels children to explore the world of science. The notion of extinction 65 million years ago and what extinction for endangered animals and plants means today plays a major part of the exhibit."

National test results show that less than five percent of fourth graders have advanced science proficiency, while 33 percent are below the basic level. This exciting interactive paleontology experience will help draw children into the world of science and research. To complement the educational aspects of the exhibit, The Children's Museum has developed units of study (grades K-2 and 3-6) for educators to use in the classroom, as well as other professional development opportunities and research workshops

E X H I B I T 3-3a   (Continued)

Other Dinosphere Highlights

Paleo Prep Lab:
In addition to being immersed in the world of dinosaurs and exploring Dinosphere's interactive activities, children and families can interact with professional preparators in Dinosphere's Polly H. Mix Paleo Prep Lab, where real specimens are being prepared. Special in-depth educational programs for older youth allow them to work side-by-side with the Museum's full-time paleontology and preparatory staff.

Lanzendorf Gallery of Dinosaur Imagery:
Another feature of Dinosphere is the "Gallery of Dinosaur Imagery featuring the John Lanzendorf Collection," named for John Lanzendorf, world-renowned paleo art collector and hair-dresser to the stars. The unique gallery displays the finest paintings, drawings and sculptures of dinosaur specimens in the world.

A rotating display that, in total, consists of 1,000 dinosaur toys and collectibles will also be on display in Dinosphere. Considered to be one of the top 10 and largest collections of its kind in the world, the compilation of toys spans more than 80 years, with many of the pieces originating in the 1950s and 1960s.

Dinosphere Tickets
Timed tickets will be required to enter Dinosphere, and are included in the price of Museum admission at no extra charge. To request tickets, call (317) 334-4000 or (800) 820-6214. E-tickets are available online at www.dinosphere.org.

Children's Museum Background:
With more than 450,000 square feet of space, The Children's Museum of Indianapolis is the largest children's museum in the United States. Situated on 13 acres of land in Indianapolis, it features 11 major galleries and hosts almost 1 million visitors annually.

The Children's Museum owes a great deal of gratitude to the foresight and vision of our Dinosphere donors - a $15 million gift from Lilly Endowment, a $3 million pledge from The Scott A. Jones Foundation and $4 million from the Enid Goodrich Educational Initiatives Fund of The Children's Museum and significant contributions from others, including Polly Morton Hix.

# # #

EXHIBIT 3-3b   Fact Sheet

Dinosphere:
Now You're In *Their* World!

What is Dinosphere?

The $25 million "Dinosphere" is a one-of-a-kind juvenile and family dinosaur experience for children and families at The Children's Museum of Indianapolis. Opened in June 2004, Dinosphere is the largest, most immersive display of real juvenile and family dinosaur fossils in the United States. According to world-renowned paleontologist Dr. Robert Bakker, Dinosphere will quickly earn its place "among the top dozen dinosaur exhibits in the world" and will be "the most exciting new addition on the list of real-bone dinosaur exhibits." Dinosphere will feature a unique combination of education-oriented and scientific-focused learning.

Where is Dinosphere?

Dinosphere is located at The Children's Museum of Indianapolis, the largest children's museum in the United States. Situated on 13 acres of land in Indianapolis, the Children's Museum features 11 major galleries and hosts almost 1 million visitors annually. The Children's Museum was recently rated the #1 children's museum in the nation by *Child Magazine* and *Family Fun Magazine*.

When Did Dinosphere Open?

Dinosphere opened to the public Friday, June 11, 2004.

What Specimens Are in Dinosphere?

The centerpiece of Dinosphere is 'Bucky,' a teenage Tyrannosaurus rex - the first juvenile *T. rex* on permanent display in a museum. A *T. rex* with an attitude! Bucky also is the first *T. rex* in which a "furcula" or wishbone has been discovered. Other specimens include:

- A nearly complete Gorgosaurus skeleton. A cousin of the *T. rex*, this Gorgosaurus is one of the most complete ever found. In 2003, paleontologists and scientists from Eli Lilly and Company discovered the first recognized evidence of a brain tumor ever found in a dinosaur in the Gorgosaurus specimen.
- Baby Louie, the only articulated dinosaur embryo fossil ever found in the world, featured on the cover of *National Geographic*.
- Kelsey, one of the most complete Triceratops skeletons known to science.
- Emily, a rare Leptoceratops - a small dinosaur with a razor-sharp, parrot-like beak that is a cousin to the Triceratops.
- Maiasaura, a plant-eating duckbill dinosaur.

Courtesy The Children's Museum of Indianapolis

EXHIBIT 3-3b   (Continued)

- A Hypacrosaur family - which includes an adult–"Shiny," a juvenile–"Lauren," and two infants–"Abagail" and "Caroline," give Museum visitors the unique opportunity of experiencing dinosaur family dynamics from the Cretaceous Period.
- A Didelphodon, an early marsupial - or pouched mammal - that is distantly related to the modern opossum.

How Did The Children's Museum Making Dinosphere Scientifically Accurate and Realistic?

The Children's Museum assembled a scientific advisory board of world-famous paleontologists and dinosaur experts to assure that Dinosphere reflects current theories of how these animals lived and what the Cretaceous world was like. These scientists are also actively leading ongoing studies of Dinosphere's rare and one-of-a-kind specimens. Advisory board members include:

- Robert Bakker, Ph.D., Boulder, Colo., one of the most noteworthy dinosaur paleontologists in the U.S.
- Phil Currie, Ph.D., and Eva (Currie) Koppelhus, Ph.D., Royal Tyrrell Museum of Paleontology in Alberta, Canada, which boasts one of the world's largest collections of paleontological materials.
- John Falk, Ph.D., and Lynn Dierking, Ph.D., renowned experts on learning research and development in museum settings.
- John Lanzendorf, Chicago, Ill., world renowned paleo art collector and aficionado.
- Pete and Neal Larson, founders of the Black Hills Institute of Geologic Research, Hill City, South Dakota. Pete Larson was on the team that discovered "Sue" the *T. rex*, now on display at the Chicago Field Museum.
- Leona Schauble, Ph.D., University of Wisconsin - Madison, professor of educational psychology known for her work in constructivist learning and science education.
- Michael Skrepnick, world-famous artist whose paintings and drawings of dinosaurs have illustrated articles, books and presentations by top paleontologists.
- Dong Zhiming, Ph.D., renowned Chinese paleontologist.

Why Did The Children's Museum Creating Dinosphere?

National test results show that only three percent of fourth graders have advanced science proficiency, while 33 percent are below the basic level. By introducing children to the world of dinosaurs, The Children's Museum also compels children to explore the world of science. To complement the educational aspects of the exhibit, the Museum has developed units of study for educators to use in the classroom, as well as other professional development opportunities and research workshops.

What Is a Visit to Dinosphere Like?

Visitors to Dinosphere are transported back in time as they enter a multi-level, multi-sensory immersive environment. Along the way, families can stop to experiment and explore at interactive learning stations. These learning stations, designed to encourage an interest in science, may include touching real fossils, piecing together dinosaur anatomy, and serving the appropriate dinner to a cast of hungry creatures.

E X H I B I T 3-3b   (Continued)

Visitors also conduct experiments and research via selected Web sites, the Museum's library and an interactive computer globe. A Dinosphere Question Lab and computer animation program brings the past to the present by encouraging families to discuss why dinosaurs became extinct and what people can do today to preserve the environment and prevent future animal and plant extinction.

How is Dinosphere Funded?

The Children's Museum owes a great deal of gratitude to the foresight and vision of our Dinosphere donors - a $15 million gift from Lilly Endowment, a $3 million pledge from The Scott A. Jones Foundation and $4 million from the Enid Goodrich Educational Initiatives Fund of The Children's Museum and significant contributions from others, including Polly Horton Hix.

4

Internal Communications

P ublic relations conducted inside organizations falls into two general categories: employee relations and member relations. Employee relations includes
all communications between the management of an organization and its personnel. Member relations refers to communications inside a membership organization between the officers, staff, and members.

EMPLOYEE RELATIONS

Research, objectives, programming, and evaluation are useful problem-solving
tools in employee relations. Good management of an organization is often measured by the quality of communication within the organization. Senior leaders
also understand that well-informed employees form the basis for many strategic
communication initiatives with external publics.

RESEARCH

Research for employee relations concentrates on client research, studying the reason for communication, and identifying the employee audiences to be targeted
for communication.

Client Research

Client research for employee relations focuses on *information* about the organization's personnel. What is the size and nature of the workforce? What reputation
does the organization have with its workforce? How satisfied are the employees?
What employee communications does the organization regularly use? Are any
special forms of communication used? How credible and effective are the

organization's internal communications? Has the organization conducted special employee relations programs in the past? If so, what were the results of such programs? What are the organization's strengths, weaknesses, and opportunities regarding its workforce? These questions might guide the initial research in preparation for an employee relations program.

Opportunity or Problem Research

A second focal point for research is the *reason* for conducting an employee relations program. Is a new program really necessary? Most organizations have regular and ongoing channels of internal communications that are used to convey management information, so this question should be answered with care because it justifies the necessary expenditure for a program. Would the program be reactive—in response to a problem that has arisen in employee relations, or would it be proactive— taking advantage of an opportunity to improve existing employee relations?

A survey of employee attitudes may reveal a variety of issues, including low levels of satisfaction and morale, dislike of the physical surroundings, and/or frustration with internal policies. The survey results may thus demonstrate a strong need for a reactive employee relations program.

Audience Research

The final area of research involves precisely defining the *employee audiences* to be targeted for communication. These audiences can be identified using the following terms:

Management
> Upper-level administrators
> Mid-level administrators
> Lower-level administrators

Nonmanagement (staff)
> Specialists
> Clerical personnel
> Executive assistants

Uniformed personnel
> Equipment operators
> Drivers
> Security personnel
> Other uniformed personnel

Union representatives
Other nonmanagement personnel

Effective research on employee relations is built on an understanding of the client's personnel, the opportunity or problem that serves as a reason for communication with the workforce, and the specific identification of the employee audiences to be targeted for communication.

OBJECTIVES

Objectives for employee relations include the two major categories of impact and output. Employee relations objectives may be specific and quantitative to facilitate accurate measurement. Optional percentages and time frames are included here in parentheses.

Impact Objectives

Impact objectives for employee relations include informing employees or modifying their attitudes or behaviors. Some typical impact objectives are:

1. To increase employee knowledge of significant organizational policies, activities, and developments (by 60 percent during March and April)
2. To enhance favorable employee attitudes toward a new organization program (by 40 percent during the current fiscal year)
3. To accomplish (50 percent) greater employee adoption of behaviors desired by management (in a three-month period)
4. To make (60 percent of) the employee force organizational spokespersons in the community (during the next two years)
5. To receive (50 percent) more employee feedback from organizational communications (during the coming year)

Behavioral, informational, and attitudinal impact objectives may be used in any combination in a public relations plan. The chosen objectives should be carefully determined so they demonstrate the program's goals.

Output Objectives

Output objectives in employee relations constitute the efforts made by the practitioner to accomplish such desired outcomes as employee recognition and regular employee communication. Some examples include:

1. To recognize employee accomplishments and contributions in (80 percent of) employee communications (during the current year)
2. To prepare and distribute employee communications on a weekly basis
3. To schedule interpersonal communication between management and a specific employee group each month (specify groups and months)

PROGRAMMING

Programming for employee relations should include the careful planning of theme and messages, action(s) or special event(s), uncontrolled and controlled media, and execution, using the principles of effective communication.

Theme and Messages

The theme and messages for employee relations depend on the reason for conducting the campaign or program. Both of these elements should grow out of the opportunity or problem that accounts for the particular program. That is, themes and messages usually grow out of the problems faced by companies and the methods chosen to solve them. For example, a practitioner working for a company that is moving its facilities and offices to a new building could produce a brochure entitled "A Company on the Move."

Action(s) or Special Event(s)

Action and special events used in employee relations programs include:

1. Training seminars
2. Special programs on safety or new technology
3. An open house for employees and their families
4. Parties, receptions, and other social affairs
5. Other employee special events related to organizational developments

A bank, for example, could sponsor a surprise Dividend Day for participants in the employee stock program, and a company moving into a new facility could arrange an employee open house and party. The CEO (chief executive officer) can host a company-wide town meeting to signal an important announcement.

Uncontrolled and Controlled Media

The use of uncontrolled media in employee relations is usually limited to sending news releases or announcements about employees' accomplishments to outside mass and specialized media as warranted. Actually, this is media relations, not employee relations, but it is often considered part of the employee relations program, as a news report is often perceived by employees as a most credible source of information about the organization.

Controlled media, on the other hand, are used extensively in employee relations programs. The most frequently used controlled media are e-mail, voice mail, Web sites, and memoranda. Also often used are employee publications such as magazines, newspapers, and newsletters addressed to particular groups or levels of employees in larger organizations. These publications are often highly professional and creative, both in writing and in design.

In addition to e-mail, voice mail, Web sites, and house publications, employee relations programs use a variety of other forms of controlled media, such as:

1. Bulletin boards
2. Displays and exhibits
3. Telephone hot lines or news lines
4. Inserts accompanying paychecks
5. Internal television/video
6. Executive blogs
7. Meetings
8. Teleconferences
9. Audiovisual presentations
10. Booklets, pamphlets, brochures
11. Speakers' bureaus (employees address community groups)

The use of media in employee relations differs from that in other forms of public relations because of the heavy emphasis on controlled media.

Effective Communication

Principles of effective communication are virtually the same for employee relations as for most other forms of public relations, although two-way communication and audience participation should be stressed. Special events are an excellent way to use these elements in employee relations.

EVALUATION

Impact and output objectives in employee relations can be evaluated using the same tools of measurement as in other forms of public relations (see Chapter 2). In addition, a variety of research techniques have been developed to deal exclusively with internal organizational communication.

Follow-up surveys were used in most of the case studies in this chapter. These yield quantitative measures of the stated objectives. Objectives were also assessed through publicity placement and employee participation in the programs.

Again, remember that to be effective and useful to the organization, research—both initial and evaluative—should be conducted by trained, experienced professionals who work for reputable research firms.

SUMMARY

The ROPE process provides a useful approach to the planning and execution of employee relations programs.

Research for employee relations concentrates on demographic data about the organization's workforce, existing levels of employee satisfaction, the state of relations between management and employees, and the effectiveness of employee communication. The uniqueness of research in this form of PR is, of course, the focus on information gathering about the workforce itself.

Both impact and output objectives are generally used in employee relations programs. Impact objectives include such desired outcomes as increasing employee knowledge of organizational matters and eliciting favorable employee attitudes and behaviors toward the organization. Output objectives are the efforts of practitioners to recognize employee contributions, distribute employee communications effectively, and otherwise enhance the impact objectives.

Programming for employee relations may include catchy themes; special events such as training seminars, special employee campaigns or programs, or social events for employees; and controlled media such as e-mail, voice mail, Web sites, memoranda, house publications, bulletin boards, displays, meetings, and a variety of electronic means of communication.

Evaluation of employee communication should refer back to each stated objective. Follow-up surveys are a popular means of evaluating attitudinal and behavioral objectives.

Each element of the ROPE process should be tailored for the particular situation, as we will see in this chapter's cases.

READINGS ON EMPLOYEE RELATIONS

Barkow, Tim. "Blogging for Business," *Public Relations Strategist* 10 (fall 2004): 40–43.

Bishop, Larry A. "Merging with Employees in Mind," *Public Relations Strategist* 4 (spring 1994): 46–48.

Buffington, Jody. "Can Human Resources and Internal Communications Peacefully Coexist?" *Public Relations Strategist* 10 (fall 2004): 33–36.

———. "A Tremendous Opportunity: Communicating During a Merger," *Public Relations Tactics* 11 (August 2004): 10.

Charland, Bernie. "The Mantra of Metrics: A Realistic and Relevant Approach to Measuring the Impact of Employee Communications," *Public Relations Strategist* 10 (fall 2004): 30–33.

Charles, Melissa. "Lessons from the Best in Fortune: Changing the Way You Look at Employee Publications," *Public Relations Tactics* 12 (January 2005): 21.

Corman, Steven R., and Marshall Scott Poole, eds. *Perspectives on Organizational Communication.* New York: Guilford Publications, 2001.

Crescenzo, Steve. "What Is the Role of the Corporate Editor?" *Communication World* 22 (September–October 2005): 12–142.

———. "Employees: PR Ambassadors, or Your Worst Nightmare?" *Communication World* 22 (May–June 2005): 10–11.

Cutlip, Scott M., Allen H. Center, and Glen M. Broom. "The Practice: Nonprofits, Trade Associations, and Nongovernmental Organizations." In *Effective Public Relations*, 9th ed. Englewood Cliffs, NJ: Prentice-Hall, 2006.

Deetz, Stanley A., Sarah J. Tracy, and Jennifer Lyn Simpson. *Leading Organizations Through Transition: Communication and Cultural Change.* Thousand Oaks, CA: Sage Publications, 2000.

Dixon, Tom. *Communication, Organization and Performance.* Norwood, NJ: Ablex Publishing, 1996.

Dowling, Michael J. "Adapting to Change: Creating a Learning Organization," *Public Relations Strategist* 10 (spring 2004): 10–14.

Downs, Cal W., and Allyson D. Adrian. *Assessing Organizational Communication: Strategic Communication Audits.* New York: Guilford Publications, 2004.

Eisenberg, Eric M., H. L. Goodall, and Angela Trethewey. *Organizational Communication: Balancing Creativity and Constraint*, 5th ed. New York: Bedford/St. Martin's, 2006.

Ewing, Michelle E. "An Engaged Work Force—Selling the Value and Incorporating Best Practices of Employee Communications," *Public Relations Tactics* 12 (March 2005): 10–12.

Frey, Thomas. "Employee Relations: The Facade of Communication," *Public Relations Strategist* 10 (fall 2004): 22–24.

Gargiulo, Terrence L. *The Strategic Use of Stories in Organizational Communication and Learning.* Armonk, NY: M.E. Sharpe, 2005.

Grates, Gary F. " 'Why Don't I Know?' The Strategic Role of Today's Internal Communications," *Public Relations Strategist* 10 (fall 2004): 14–18.

Harris, John. "Employee Engagement: An Easy Investment with Large Returns," *Public Relations Tactics* 11 (January 2004): 13.

Harris, Thomas E. *Applied Organizational Communication: Principles and Pragmatics for Future Practice*, 2d ed. Mahwah, NJ: Erlbaum, 2002.

Hickman, Gill Robinson, ed. *Leading Organizations: Perspectives for a New Era.* Thousand Oaks, CA: Sage Publications, 1998.

Holtz, Shel. *Corporate Conversations—A Guide to Crafting Effective and Appropriate Internal Communications.* New York: AMACOM, 2003.

Keyton, Joann. *Communication and Organizational Culture.* Thousand Oaks, CA: Sage Publications, 2004.

Khan, Julie. "Internal Communications: Ensuring Strategy and Measurement Coexist," *Public Relations Tactics* 7 (February 2000): 20.

Klein, Karen E. "A Company Blog Keeps People Connected," *Business Week Online* (21 August 2006): 5.

Klubnik, Joan P. *Rewarding and Recognizing Employees.* Burr Ridge, IL: Irwin Professional Publishing, 1994.

Madlock, Paul E. "The Link Between Leadership Style, Communicator Competence, and Employee Satisfaction," *Journal of Business Communication* 45 (January 2008): 61–78.

Manchester, Alex. *How to Use Social Media to Engage Employees.* London: Melcrum Publishing, Ltd., 2006.

Milite, George. "Getting Staffers to Read Company Manuals," *Supervisory Management* 39 (April 1994).

Miller, Katherine. *Organizational Communication: Approaches and Processes*. Belmont, CA: Wadsworth, 2008.

Papa, Michael J., Tom D. Daniels, and Barry K. Spiker. *Organizational Communication: Perspectives and Trends*. Thousand Oaks, CA: Sage Publications, 2007.

Parker, Glenn. *Team Players and Teamwork*, 2d ed. San Francisco: Jossey-Bass, 2008.

Perkins, Lisa. "Inspiring Change and Driving Results: What Can your Employee Publication Do for You?" *Public Relations Tactics* 12 (May 2005): 10.

Peterson, Gary L. *Communicating in Organizations: A Casebook*, 2d ed. Needham Heights, MA: Allyn & Bacon, 2000.

Profolio: Internal Communications. New York: Public Relations Society of America, 1998.

Rayburn, Jay. "A Matter of Trust (And More)," *Public Relations Tactics* 14 (March 2007): 21.

Sanchez, Paul. "Defining Corporate Culture," *Communication World* 21 (November–December 2004): 18–21.

Selame, Elinor. "Public Relations' Role and Responsibility in Reflecting Changes in Companies' Culture, Structure, Products and Services," *Public Relations Quarterly* 42 (summer 1997): 12–17.

Thilmany, Jean. "Showing Up Happy," *Mechanical Engineering* 126 (November 2004): 3–5.

"Using social media for internal innovation networks," *Knowledge Management Review* 9 (January/February 2007): 7.

Voeller, Greg, and Kelly Groehler. "Employees—Always the Primary Audience," *Public Relations Strategist* 10 (fall 2004): 27–30.

Wright, Marc. "Moving into the Mainstream," *Communication World* (January/February 2008): 22–25.

Member Relations Cases

Case 4-4

The Fraternal Order of Eagles (FOE) resembles many nonprofit social and community service organizations that continually evolve with new programs designed for emerging interests of its members and needs of the local communities where its members live and work. Changing demographics and memberships present special communication challenges for these organizations. Exhibit 4-4a is an introductory letter for the FOE "toolkit," and Exhibit 4-4b provides brochure pages describing the Memorial Foundation from a brochure and the Jimmy Durante Children's Fund.

Fraternal Order of Eagles Increases Understanding and Awareness

Fraternal Order of Eagles with Fahlgren Mortine Public Relations

OVERVIEW

The FOE is an international nonprofit organization, united fraternally in the spirit of liberty, truth, justice, and equality. Since its founding in 1898, the organization has worked consistently to advance the causes of workman's compensation laws, Social Security benefits, protection from age discrimination, and national recognition of Mother's Day. The FOE has also helped to fund research in the areas of heart disease, kidney disease, diabetes, and cancer. It comprises both male and female members; the males serve the aerie and the females serve the auxiliary.

As the organization has matured, its growth has slowed due to a lack of brand recognition and an aging membership. In recent years, membership growth has been largely the result of member loyalty rather than market-driven programs. The FOE first came to Fahlgren Mortine for public relations and community relations support. As the organization progressed in those areas, work began on the internal audiences to fully extend awareness and the programs.

RESEARCH

Qualitative research included twelve 60-minute focus groups conducted between February and April 2006, with representatives of the FOE at six different locations around the country. The intent of the qualitative research was to identify and explore issues of importance to local members and officers, to understand what led them to join and remain members of the FOE, and to gain a perspective of the relationship between these local members and Grand Aerie national leadership. The focus-group participants represented members and officers from 42 different states, and 4 of 7 Canadian provinces.

Quantitative research also included a questionnaire administered during a 10- to 15-minute telephone interview with volunteer members. The interviews were conducted by a third-party organization. Sample population comprised 431 members. The questionnaire included 16 closed-end and 3 open-ended questions.

Respondents to the telephone survey were recruited using a variety of methods:

- Solicitation postcards were sent to the 50 largest Aeries and Auxiliaries in North America.

- Solicitation postcards were also distributed at the six meetings and conferences where focus groups were conducted.

- A notice was posted on the Eagles Web site inviting members to register for telephone survey consideration.

The research findings were varied from continuing focus on charitable work, solidifying the brand image of "People Helping People," further understanding how members want to be communicated to and to develop a leadership program for members. These findings assisted in goal setting through providing a benchmark of current status and desires of members, as well as areas worthy of growth.

PLANNING

Goal

Communicate the Eagle brand by arming members with tools and consistent messaging for more awareness in Eagle communities.

Objectives

- Enhance awareness of local aerie via local community outreach through media relations programs.

- Identify the programs, events, and communication tools to best engage with members and potential members.

- Increase membership by 15 percent and increase attendance of nonmembers at aerie/auxiliary functions by 20 percent.

Target Audience

- FOE membership
- FOE leadership
- Grand Aerie national office support team
- Potential members and general public

Strategies

- With one voice, communicate image-enhancement efforts to membership and the general public.
- Provide easy-to-use guidelines and assistance for media relations outreach.
- Reduce number of FOE member communication vehicles to streamline messages and increase readership.
- Reduce and clarify the number of national charitable properties to create greater awareness.

EXECUTION

The following tactics were developed and executed based on research findings.

Local Aerie Toolkit

Research findings revealed that local members wanted a resource to further extend member recruitment opportunities and assist with connecting their club to the community and media. A Local Aerie Toolkit was developed. It is a multiuse binder designed to assist local aeries and auxiliaries nationwide to host more community events, bolster member recruitment parties, connect with the local media, and much more. The binder is developed so that each year additional programs can be added.

PR 101 Programs

In addition to introducing the Toolkit, it was necessary to provide a seminar on using the Toolkit and understanding the media and Fahlgren Mortine's role in the organization. To achieve this, the agency developed PR 101 programs that were presented at conferences throughout the country. These one-hour workshops were hosted by agency representatives and served as an introduction to the Local Aerie Toolkit. The presentations focused on the basics of public relations, marketing, and community relations.

Charity Brochure

Through further understanding of the importance of sending a clear message and developing the brand, leadership requested a new brochure that would encompass all the Grand Aerie charities, Fahlgren Mortine developed a full color brochure detailing the different charitable funds supported by the FOE.

Local Aerie Media Relations Program

Research also showed that local aerie leadership needed assistance announcing and publicizing current events and international leadership visits; as a result, we developed the Local Aerie Media Relations Program. When local leadership submits information to the Grand Aerie for local events, a follow-up form requesting information for local media is sent back to the local contact. This form is completed and returned to the Fahlgren Mortine team. The forms include event details that are pitched to local media.

Eagle Magazine

Eagle Magazine is a long-standing communication vehicle for members, which has recently been the topic of a debate over its value to members. Focus-group findings revealed that members like the publication, but wanted more quality information delivered in a timely manner. As a result, editorial content and member submission process are being evaluated.

Fraternal Order of Eagles Web Site

Opinions leading to changes for *Eagle Magazine* also provided insight on updating and enhancing the Eagles' Web site. A program and budget were developed and approved by the Board of Trustees, and Fahlgren Mortine is currently developing a site map and wireframes. The Web site update is scheduled to launch at the Eagles' 2007 International Convention in July.

EVALUATION

Enhance local aerie to local community outreach through media relations programs:

- The Local Aerie Media Relations Program, to date, has provided the Eagles with approximately 40 newsworthy media outreach opportunities with 98 percent receiving coverage by local media.

- The PR 101 programs have been presented at 10 regional conferences and 1 international convention, influencing approximately 20,000 leading members of the organization. Requests have been made for an updated version of PR 101 to be presented at five upcoming regional conferences and the 2007 International Convention.

- Identify the programs, events, and communication tools to best communicate with members and potential members. Development of the Local Aerie Toolkit allowed for consistent FOE branded programs to be distributed across North America. The identified programs and events combined with messaging elements in the Toolkit were first introduced at the 2006 International Convention, where books were available for $25 and 80 percent of books available at the convention were sold. By January 2007, the inventory of 900 books was depleted.

- The charity brochure was an extension of streamlining communications and identifying the best means of communicating with members and potential members. This brochure is unique for the Eagles, with all charitable entities identified in one document. Brochure distribution has increased understanding and awareness of the various funds.

- *Eagle Magazine* was trimmed to meet member needs. The monthly publication is now published five times a year without time-sensitive information. Value was added to the magazine by beefing up content to include more "how-to" articles on leadership, business, and communication skills. Additionally, an "In the News" section was added to *Eagle Magazine* to support and announce the local media relations outreach for events.

- The Eagle Web site is the last to see the necessary improvements to communicate with members and potential members. Recommendations from research include moving time-sensitive information and shorter, more "fun" stories to the Web.

Increase membership and attendance of nonmembers at functions:

- In 2006, through these initiatives and others, membership increased by 172,286 members, a 21 percent boost. As other fraternal groups announce declining membership and are closing clubs, the Eagles is experiencing steady growth.

- Feedback from membership tells us that attendance of nonmembers at functions has increased on average by 50 percent. Aerie/Auxiliary visitation logs, reviewed on a monthly basis, detail the number of people across the country visiting the clubs as nonmembers.

E X H I B I T 4-4a Introductory Letter

Dear Brothers and Sisters,

In many communities across the United States, the Eagles are working to "reintroduce" themselves as an organization as well as attract new members by involving local residents through hosting events and activities at the aeries. Successful events have driven the Eagles to raise awareness of their important contributions to the communities and increased membership on the local level.

During the first quarter of 2006, many members participated in focus groups or a telephone survey to identify needs on a local, state and national level. One need, highlighted in every conversation was the ability and tools to successfully host events, connect with the media and promote the local FOE club. In response to that need, we are providing you with this toolkit full of valuable information to move forward with a more successful aerie and/or auxiliary.

This Fraternal Order of Eagles toolkit was designed in hopes of allowing and assisting local aeries and auxiliaries nationwide host community events, member recruitment parties, connect with the media in their area and much more. The toolkit begins with a section on communication and media support to aid you in getting your message to the media. We have also included a crisis communication toolkit and quick reference guide. These items will help you in tough or sensitive media situations. The crisis plan was developed in response to the recent law suits and other needs and should aid your aerie if ever in this sort of situation.

You now have the tools to implement many member recruitment events, member appreciation events, talk to the media and so much more. The toolkit will be updated quarterly with new plans, tips and other needs you express through the FOE Web site media assistance request page (coming Fall 2006). In addition, the toolkit provides a CD that includes the templates and plans electronically.

Congratulations and good luck as you begin the journey of building a better club!

Courtesy Fraternal Order of Eagles

E X H I B I T 4-4b   Memorial Foundation Description

Memorial Foundation

The **Memorial Foundation** supports children (including those legally adopted) of members who die while serving their country or at work. All Eagle members and their families are automatically protected by this unprecedented safety net.

Memorial Foundation Benefits

With the Memorial Foundation children of deceased members who die while serving their country or at work are able to attend college or vocational school with grants up to $30,000. They can also receive medical assistance including payments to physicians, dentists, orthodontists, and hospitals. The cost of eyeglasses, prescriptions, as well as medical and dental devices is also included.

Aside from member support, the Memorial Foundation also provides educational benefits to graduates of Home on the Range in Sentinel Butte, North Dakota; High Sky Girls Ranch in Midland, Texas; and Bob Hope High School in Port Arthur, Texas.

H.O.M.E.

The **H.O.M.E. Charity Fund** is an acronym for Hands of Many Eagles. This fund is administered by the Memorial Foundation and allows donors from Eagle Communities to designate and support various charitable organizations. Organizations benefiting from H.O.M.E. are those not included in any other Eagle charity fund.

Courtesy Fraternal Order of Eagles

EXHIBIT 4-5c   (Continued)

Jimmy Durante
Children's Fund

Jimmy Durante Children's Fund

Money raised through the **Jimmy Durante Children's Fund** and **Child Abuse Fund** are one of the Eagle's greatest achievements.

The fund was named in honor of Jimmy Durante. One of the Eagle's most beloved human beings and an active life-member of the Fraternal Order of Eagles. Jimmy entertained without charge at fourteen consecutive Grand Aerie International Conventions and at many other Eagle gatherings until his death in 1980. Because of Jimmy's gentle and kind manner, the children's fund was named after him in 1966.

All money raised for the Jimmy Durante Children's Fund or Child Abuse Fund is returned to that state or province in the form of grants to children-helping organizations of the state's choosing. The selection of the recipients is up to the State Aerie President, with the approval of the State Executive Board utilizing the money available in the state's account.

Children's AIDS Awareness and Medical Research

The Fraternal Order of Eagles will pursue a mission to increase the amount of available information for at risk families and educate young people as to the dangers of the AIDS virus. Donations will also be set aside for medical research for this terrible disease.

Nearly 10,000 children under age 13 are currently living with HIV in North America.

| Jimmy Durante Children's Fund | Spinal Cord Injury Fund | Golden Eagle, Alzheimer and Parkinson Funds | Memorial Foundation and H.O.M.E. |

Case 4-5

Professional associations provide support for member organizations and also represent the best interests of its members in public policy discussions and in the media. The Minnesota Hospital Association (MHA) implemented a campaign to support its members during the implementation of a new law concerning patient safety. Exhibit 4-5a is a preannouncement draft of newsletter article and Exhibit 4-5b is an e-mail to key leaders.

First Do No Harm

Minnesota Hospital Association with Weber Shandwick Worldwide

SUMMARY

The MHA and member hospitals faced the intimidating challenge of being the first state in the nation to pass a law that mandated a public, hospital-specific report of 27 kinds of medical errors. There were concerns that releasing this sensitive data could cripple the intent of the reporting law, which was to increase the reporting of errors in order to learn from them. Along with broad efforts to partner with policy makers and other stakeholders, MHA used research, careful planning, and a thoughtful media strategy that resulted in the successful positioning of Minnesota as a leader in patient safety, secured public trust, and ultimately protected the integrity of the error reporting system.

SITUATION ANALYSIS

In 2000, the Institute of Medicine, a division of the government's National Academy of Sciences, released its groundbreaking report, "To Err is Human," that estimated up to 98,000 hospital patients die each year due to medical errors. The statistic alarmed the public and initially met with denial and scrutiny within the health care community.

In 2003, the MHA led the effort toward transparency and accountability by championing a medical error reporting law. Minnesota was going to be the first state in the nation to publicly report 27 measurable and preventable medical errors.

The goal of the Adverse Health Events (AHE) reporting system is to report medical errors, to learn what went wrong, and to develop safety measures to

Courtesy Minnesota Hospital Association

prevent the errors from happening again. The first public report would be released in January 2005 and would list medical errors by hospital including those resulting in serious harm or death.

The central communications question focused directly on the reputation of hospitals: "Will Minnesota hospitals be congratulated as leaders in improving patient safety or will they be perceived as dangerous places to receive care?"

RESEARCH

MHA conducted a literature review (secondary research) to analyze other public reporting efforts and to identify best practices. No directly relevant information existed and few insights were gained. MHA and Weber Shandwick conducted a public opinion survey (primary research: $N = 402$, ± 4.9 percent at 95 percent confidence level) to guide the release of the report, establish baselines, and evaluate effectiveness.

Pivotal findings

- Reporting system's focus is a selling point. In an unaided question, the public said the two items they most want to hear when they learn about an error are how did the error occur and what is being done to prevent it from reoccurring.

- Ninety-three percent support mandatory reporting of errors.

- Sixty-one percent stated they would be worried if their local hospital reported errors.

- Forty-four percent said they would be less likely to use a hospital that reported errors or it would depend on the error.

- Message testing revealed that the most effective messages centered on improving patient care and preventing errors.

- Message testing also identified that those who were least likely to use hospitals that reported errors strongly agreed with all key messages; however, they believed those involved with errors needed to be punished. The finding resulted in shifting key messages to include how individuals are held accountable.

PLANNING

Communications planning for the Adverse Event Report released in January 19, 2005, began in May 2004 and included everything from assuring data accuracy to how the report would be released.

- Convened communications officers from hospitals to participate in planning and key message development that would be tested.
- Engaged the active support of stakeholders from health plans, medical liability insurers, quality improvement organizations, business consortiums, and health agencies in an effort to build a large base of credible third-party spokespeople.
- Required hospital CEOs to sign a form verifying their data to eliminate the potential for public disputes over accuracy.
- Conducted weekly calls with hospitals that would be listed in the report to coordinate efforts.

Audiences

Previous research and association experience guided prioritization of audiences and the level of communication:

- Hospitals' internal audiences: employees, physicians, board members, volunteers
- Opinion leaders from labor, purchasers, payers, providers, and academia
- State and federal policy makers
- Consumers/hospital patients and their families
- Local, regional, state, and national news media

Objectives

- Instill confidence in the AHE reporting system, and in turn, temper any negative public opinion and media coverage (evaluation: hold steady or decrease public worry and those less likely to seek care at hospital that reported errors).
- Position Minnesota hospitals as national leaders in the area of standards for reporting medical errors (evaluation: use of key messages, national media placement, and securing national interest in system).
- Reinforce the need for all Minnesota hospitals to actively participate in the new system for reporting adverse health events (evaluation: hold steady public support for reporting, gain support of opinion leaders).

Strategies

- Assure data are accurate, report format is appropriate, and member hospitals are prepared.
- Provide hospitals with templates to educate and prepare internal audiences.
- Redirect the focus on individual errors to the broader policy issue of patient safety.

- Publicize and sustain interest in Minnesota's leadership in tackling the medical errors.

- Assure consistency in messages from hospitals and opinion leaders.

- Seek a top-tier publication that would focus on the policy of patient safety, not the local death count, thereby providing national recognition for pursuing a difficult but important effort.

EXECUTION

- Achieved sign off on data by 100 percent of hospital CEOs.

- Coordinated with the Minnesota Department of Health on report content and public release.

- Developed effective key messages and proof points based on research.

- Developed communications guidelines for hospital spokespeople and conducted media training.

- Developed comprehensive package of internal communications materials for hospitals.

- Recruited national, regional, and local patient safety commentators to discuss Minnesota's leadership.

- Provided all stakeholders (insurers to labor) with information on the system and gained their support in talking to the media.

- Educated media in advance of the report's release on the broader patient safety story so they would understand the context before the numbers were released.

- Briefed *The Wall Street Journal* for a feature story on the first results of the AHE reporting system.

- Held background briefings with the two major daily newspapers in Minneapolis and St. Paul.

- Conducted an advance desk-side media tour and editorial board meetings in nine Minnesota cities (those with hospitals that had events in the report).

EVALUATION

Instill confidence in the AHE reporting system, and in turn, temper any negative public opinion and media coverage.

- Eighty-nine news articles generated, 48 percent were positive, 51 percent were neutral, and 1 percent was negative.

- Survey showed the public's level of worry about their hospital reporting a medical error did not increase (11/04: 61 percent worried; 2/05: 62 percent worried).

- More importantly, the survey showed that the number of people who were less likely to go to their local hospital if it reported an error decreased, which reduced individual hospital vulnerability (11/04: 44 percent less likely to go/ depends; 2/05: 31 percent less likely to go/depends).

Position Minnesota hospitals as national leaders in the area of standards for reporting medical errors.

- Every article included at least one of MHA's four key messages and most used multiple messages. The top two messages used are:
  1. Reporting allows hospitals to share and learn, and
  2. Minnesota is a pioneer/leader in the area of patient safety. Message one ties directly to the objective of the reporting system and was identified as the strongest key message by our research.
- *The Wall Street Journal* feature article "Minnesota Issues a Hospital Report Card" positioned Minnesota as a leader in a top-tier national publication. An additional article in March referenced Minnesota's leadership.
- Secured letter from nationally recognized expert, National Quality Forum's President and CEO, that was included with the report, "…this document demonstrates that Minnesota is in the vanguard of public reporting of medical errors."
- Six states have passed similar legislation. Illinois even dubbed their law the "Minnesota Law."
- Editorials in support of Minnesota's system were published in Iowa and North Dakota.

Reinforce the need for all Minnesota hospitals to actively participate in the new system for reporting adverse health events.

- Public opinion supporting medical error reporting remained strong (11/04: 93 percent; 2/05: 92 percent).
- Twelve different third-party influencers were quoted, all but one were supportive of the effort.
- Received Safety Leadership Award from a business consortium, the Buyer's Health Care Action Group, a key audience for Minnesota hospitals.
- Supportive editorials published in the two largest Minnesota daily newspapers reinforced the public value of the reporting system.
- Received personal notes from opinion leaders and influencers voicing their support.

E X H I B I T 4-5a   **Preannouncement Newsletter Article**

Adverse Health Events Report on Minnesota Hospitals Due Out This Month

In late January, the Minnesota Department of Health (MDH) will release the first-ever Adverse Health Events (AHE) public report, which will disclose the number of 27 serious reportable events, or medical errors, that have occurred in Minnesota hospitals from July 1, 2003 to October 6, 2004. The list of 27 events includes wrong-site surgery, retention of a foreign object in a patient after surgery, and death or serious disability associated with medication error, a fall or use of restraint.

Minnesota is in the forefront of states implementing such an adverse health events reporting system. Legislation creating its Adverse Health Event Reporting Law was passed in 2003 and Minnesota hospitals, including (NAME OF HOSPITAL), have been electronically reporting their adverse events through the Minnesota Hospital Associations' Web-based Patient Safety Registry since July of that year.

In addition to reporting each event, hospitals also must complete a root cause analysis to help them determine exactly what happened and why it happened, and they must develop and implement a corrective action plan to prevent the error from reoccurring again.

"The AHE system represents a pioneering new approach to reduce medical errors and improve patient safety," said (HOSPITAL SPOKESPERSON). "It's designed to create a culture that promotes reporting, encourages shared learning across hospitals and focuses on fixing problems."

The AHE report will include an overall statewide report with the total number of reported events during the reporting period; a statewide report by event category (surgical, product or device, patient protection, care management, environmental, and criminal); and hospital-specific events reported at each hospital (the reported number for each of the 27 event types organized under each category).

The AHE reporting system was developed in response to a 1999 report by the Institute of Medicine, which stated that medical errors in U.S. hospitals kill between 44,000 and 98,000 people each year, making medical errors the eighth leading cause of death in the country.

# # #

Courtesy Minnesota Hospital Association

EXHIBIT 4-5b   Suggested E-mail to Leaders/Managers

Subject Line: Adverse Health Events Report To Be Released on January XX

On January XX, the Minnesota Department of Health and the Minnesota Hospital Association will be releasing the first-ever Adverse Health Events (AHE) public report, disclosing the number of 27 serious reportable events, or medical errors, that have occurred in Minnesota hospitals from July 1, 2003 to October 6, 2004. (NAME OF HOSPITAL) will be included in this report. (The list of 27 events includes wrong-site surgery, retention of a foreign object in a patient after surgery, and death or serious disability associated with medication error, a fall, or use of restraint.)

Reporting medical errors is not easy, but it's the right thing to do. The reason the AHE reporting system was passed by the Minnesota legislature in 2003 was because a coalition of Minnesota hospitals, doctors, nurses, and patient advocates all believed that one serious medical error is too many. Our state is leading the way in this effort and we have much to be proud of.

The most important thing to keep in mind about the AHE report is that it is designed to improve patient safety and to learn what went wrong. Every hospital that reports an event must complete a root cause analysis of what happened and why it happened, and develop and implement a corrective action plan to prevent errors from reoccurring. The goal is truly to create a culture of shared learning across hospitals and fixing problems, and I'm encouraged that this is already happening, as you will hear when the report is released.

In the days ahead, we will be sending you additional communications to help you prepare to talk to your employees about this report.

As always, if you receive a call from the news media regarding this report, we ask you to refer them to (NAME OF MEDIA RELATIONS PERSON) at (PHONE NUMBER OR EMAIL ADDRESS).

(NAME OF EXECUTIVE)

# # #

Courtesy Minnesota Hospital Association

5

Community Relations

One of the most important audiences an organization has is its community, the home of its offices and operations. Maintaining good relations with the community usually entails management and employees becoming involved in and contributing to local organizations and activities. In addition, the organization may communicate with the community in other ways, such as distributing house publications or meeting with community leaders. Often community relations activities involve face-to-face interaction between an organization and a public, one of the most powerful forms of influencing attitudes.

Solving community relations problems may follow the usual sequence of research, objectives, programming, and evaluation.

RESEARCH

Research for community relations includes investigation to understand the client, the reason for the program, and the community audiences to be targeted for communication.

Client Research

Client research for community relations concentrates on the organization's role and reputation in the community. What is its level of credibility? Have there been significant community complaints in the past? What are the organization's present and past community relations practices? What changes in the community and political landscape are affecting relations with the organization? What are its major strengths and weaknesses in the community? What opportunities exist to enhance community relations? These questions provide a helpful framework for a community relations program.

Opportunity or Problem Research

Why have a community relations program in the first place? Considering the cost and benefits involved, this is a question worthy of detailed justification. The public relations practitioner should assess problems the organization may have had with community groups and make a searching analysis of community relations opportunities. Many organizations conduct ongoing proactive community relations as a form of insurance against any sudden problem requiring a reactive public relations solution. It is often easier to communicate with an organization's current community network than to build a new communication program from scratch.

Audience Research

The final aspect of community relations research consists of carefully identifying audiences to be targeted for communication and learning as much about each audience as possible. Community publics can be subdivided into three major groups: community media, community leaders, and community organizations. These categories can then be further subdivided as shown in Exhibit 5-a.

E X H I B I T 5-A   Community Publics

Community media
  Mass
  Specialized
Community leaders
  Public officials
  Educators
  Religious leaders
  Professionals
  Executives
  Bankers
  Union leaders
  Ethnic leaders
  Neighborhood leaders
Community organizations
  Civic
  Business
  Service
  Social
  Cultural
  Religious
  Youth
  Political
  Special interest groups
  Other

In conducting community relations programs, it is important for the practitioner to develop contact lists of journalists, community leaders, and organizations.

The media contact lists will be similar to those discussed in Chapter 3, on media relations. These lists should include the type and size of audience reached by each media outlet in the community, the type of material used by each outlet, the name and title of appropriate editors who handle organizational news, and deadlines.

The list of community and organization leaders should be equally thorough. It should include the name, title, affiliation, address, and telephone number of all important community leaders. These data should be categorized according to occupational fields, such as public officials, educators, or religious leaders. In addition to a listing of leaders alone, there should be a list of organizations that includes frequently updated names of officers, their addresses, and telephone numbers. It is often a real challenge to identify the influentials or opinion leaders who have exceptional credibility with others in the community through reputation, expertise, economic clout, or political power. It is not always those individuals in "official positions of leadership." For example, the president of the local Parent Teacher Association (PTA) may be important, but the real power behind decisions about education may be a former school board member or a highly respected principal. When these people talk, others are careful to listen.

Research for community relations, then, consists of investigation of the client, the reason for the program, and the target audiences in the community.

OBJECTIVES

Impact and output objectives for community relations, like those for other forms of public relations, should be specific and quantitative.

Impact Objectives

Impact objectives for community relations involve informing the community audiences or modifying their attitudes or behaviors. Some examples are:

1. To increase (by 30 percent this year) community knowledge of the operations of the organization, including its products, services, employees, and support of community projects

2. To promote (20 percent) more favorable community opinion toward the organization (during a specified time period)

3. To gain (15 percent) greater organizational support from community leaders (during a particular campaign)

4. To encourage (20 percent) more feedback from community leaders (during the current year)

5. To increase the number of employees participating as leaders in local youth sport programs by 20 percent

Output Objectives

Output objectives consist of the efforts made by the practitioner to enhance the organization's community relations. Some illustrations are:

1. To prepare and distribute (15 percent) more community publications (than last year)
2. To be (10 percent) more responsive to community needs (during this year)
3. To create (five) new community projects involving organizational personnel and resources (during this calendar year)
4. To schedule (five) meetings with community leaders (this year)

Thus, both impact and output objectives are helpful in preparing community relations programs. They serve as useful and necessary precursors to programming.

PROGRAMMING

Programming for community relations includes planning the theme and messages, action or special event(s), uncontrolled and controlled media, and using effective communication principles.

Theme and Messages

The theme and messages for community relations are situational and grow out of research findings related to the organization, the reason for conducting the program, and the existing and past relationships with the targeted community audiences.

Action(s) or Special Event(s)

Actions and special events most often associated with community relations are:

1. An organizational open house and tour of facilities
2. Sponsorship of special community events or projects
3. Participation of management and other personnel in volunteer community activities
4. Purchase of advertising in local media
5. Contribution of funds to community organizations or causes
6. Meetings with community leaders
7. Membership of management and personnel in a variety of community organizations—civic, professional, religious
8. Participation of management and workers in the political affairs of the community—service in political office and on councils and boards

Involvement of the organization, its management, and its other personnel in the affairs of the community is the most significant aspect of a community relations program. With this kind of link to the community, there should be relatively smooth community relations, with few or no surprises.

Uncontrolled and Controlled Media

In the communications part of a community relations program, the practitioner should think first of servicing community media outlets with appropriate uncontrolled media, such as news releases, photographs or photo opportunities, and interviews of organizational officers with local reporters.

The use of controlled media, on the other hand, should include sending copies of house publications to a select list of community leaders. The practitioner should also help the organization develop a speakers bureau, and publicize the availability of organizational management and expert personnel to address meetings of local clubs and organizations. It is also appropriate to target community leaders on a timely basis for selected direct mailings, such as important announcements or notices of organizational involvement in community affairs.

Above all, the organization must develop an informative and appropriate Web site. This can be used for both uncontrolled and controlled communication. Journalists should be able to obtain background information and up-to-date news about the organization on the Web site. This should include recent photographs of organizational leaders and facilities as well as other important and relevant data.

Both uncontrolled and controlled media in the community relations program should be focused on the eight types of community involvement listed earlier. These are the heart of the program.

Effective Communication

Three principles of effective communication deserve special attention in community relations programs.

First, the targeting of opinion leaders or community leaders for communication is crucial to the success of such a program. The leadership provides the structure and substance of the community itself.

Second, group influence plays a substantial role in effective community relations. Organizations exercise varying degrees of cohesiveness and member conformity. The community relations program must cultivate community groups, their leaders, and their memberships. The effective speakers bureau is a primary means for accomplishing this.

Finally, audience participation is highly significant. Targeted community media, leaders, and groups can be encouraged to participate in the client's organizational events. Most important, the client should reach out to the community by sponsoring attractive activities.

EVALUATION

If the objectives of the community relations program have been phrased specifically and quantitatively, their evaluation should be relatively easy. For example, it is simple to measure the number of presentations by the organization's speakers bureau or to measure the number of people attending special events sponsored by the organization. The success of a program should be directly linked to its attainment of the objectives stated at the program's outset.

SUMMARY

Research for community relations assesses the organization's reputation and its existing and potential problems with the community. Targeting audiences usually includes a detailed analysis of community media, leaders, and organizations.

Impact objectives for community relations are such desired outcomes as informing or influencing the attitudes and behaviors of the community. Output objectives consist of a listing of public relations efforts to enhance the organization's relations with the community.

Programming concentrates on organizational involvement with the community through sponsorship of events, employee participation in community activities, contributions to community causes, meetings, and the like. The uncontrolled media used in community relations are aimed at servicing local journalists with appropriate news releases, photographs, and interviews with organizational officers. Controlled media usually include house publications, speakers bureaus, and appropriate direct mailings to community leaders.

It is also important for the organization to develop an attractive and informative community-oriented Web site.

Evaluation of stated objectives uses methods appropriate to the type of objective. Impact objectives are usually measured by a survey or other appropriate quantitative methods, while output objectives may call for simple observation of whether the desired output was achieved.

READINGS ON COMMUNITY RELATIONS

Aldrich, Leigh S. *Covering the Community: A Diversity Handbook for the Media.* Thousand Oaks, CA: Sage Publications, 1999.

Bete, Tim. "Eight Great Community Relations Ideas," *School Planning and Management* 37 (May 1998): 49ff.

Bruning, Stephen D. "Examining the Role That Personal, Professional, and Community Relationship Play in Respondent Relationship Recognition and Intended Behavior," *Communication Quarterly* 48 (fall 2000): 437–448.

Bruning, Stephen D., and Meghan Ralston. "Using a Relational Approach to Retaining Students and Building Mutually Beneficial Student-University Relationships," *The Southern Communication Journal* 66 (summer 2001): 337ff.

Burke, Edmund M. *Corporate Community Relations: The Principle of the Neighbor of Choice.* Westport, CT: Quorum Books, 1999.

Few, Roger. "Containment and Counter-Containment: Planner/Community Relations in Conservation Planning," *The Geographical Journal* 167 (2) (June 2001): 111–124.

Flocks, Joan, Leslie Clarke, Stan Albrecht, Carol Bryant, Paul Monaghan, and Holly Baker. "Implementing a Community-Based Social Marketing Project to Improve Agricultural Worker Health," *Environmental Health Perspectives* 109 (June 2001): 461–468.

Forrest, Carol J., and Renee H. Mays. "The Practical Guide to Environmental Community Relations," *Journal of Environmental Health* 67 (January–February 2005): 30ff.

Gaschen, Dennis J. "Play Ball: Community Relations and Professional Sports," *Public Relations Tactics* 7 (August 2000): 10.

Heath, Robert L., and Michael Palenchar. "Community Relations and Risk Communication: A Longitudinal Study of the Impact of Emergency Response Messages," *Journal of Public Relations Research* 12 (2) (2000): 131–161.

Holtzhausen, Derina R. "Public Relations Practice and Political Change in South Africa," *Public Relations Review* 31 (September 2005): 407–416.

Keswick, Renée, and LaDon McNeil. "Reaching out to the Arabic Community," *Behavioral Healthcare* 26 (11) (November 2006): 32.

Ledingham, John A., and Stephen D. Bruning. "Building Loyalty Through Community Relations," *Public Relations Strategist* 3 (summer 1997): 27–29.

Lucy-Allen, Dale, Dennis Brunton, Jenny McDade, Jennifer Seydel, and Dennis Vogel. "Springfield College Collaboration with the Springfield Public Schools and Neighboring Community," *Peabody Journal of Education* 75 (3) (2000): 99–114.

Lukaszewski, James E. *Building Quality Community Relationships: A Planning Model to Gain and Maintain Public Consent.* White Plains, NY: Lukaszewski Group, 1995.

———. "Getting to 51 Percent: Building Community Relationships That Gain and Maintain Public Consent," *Public Relations Tactics* 12 (May 2005): 11.

Matson, Judy. "Creating the Intersection Between Corporate Values and Community Service," *Public Relations Strategist* 10 (Summer 2004): 30–31.

McDermott, David. "The 10 Commandments of Community Relations," *World Wastes* 36 (September 1993): 48ff.

Milstein, Eric, and David S. Coles. "Don't Hate San Francisco! Engage, Don't Estrange," *U.S. Naval Institute Proceedings* 134 (1) (January 2008): 88.

Parker, Rani. "Community Impacts of Corporate Social Responsibility in the Mining Sector: Examples from Peru, Canada and Mali," *Conference Papers—International Studies Association* (2007): 1.

Poston, Patty. "Grassroots Communications Reconsidered," *Public Relations Tactics* 9 (September 2002): 12–13.

Profolio: Community Relations. New York: Public Relations Society of America, 1998.

Reish, Marc S. "Chemical Industry Tries to Improve Its Community Relations," *Chemical & Engineering News* (February 1994): 8ff.

Sandman, Peter M. "Responding to Community Outrage: Strategies for Effective Risk Communication," *Journal of Environmental Health* 67 (January–February 2005): 30ff.

Schultz, David L. "Strategic Survival in the Face of Community Activism," *Public Relations Strategist* 7 (spring 2001): 36–38.

St. John, Burton. "Public Relations as Community-Building: Then and Now," *Public Relations Quarterly* 43 (spring 1998): 34ff.

Wiser, Nancy. "After the storm: PR efforts help quell public frustration in Kentucky," *Public Relations Tactics* 11 (January 2004): 11–12.

Community Relations Cases

Case 5-1

Aligning a corporate mission and products with a national community issue makes good community relations. This case highlights hunger in America. Exhibit 5-1a is a news release announcing a "New National Hunger Relief Partnership" in 2006, Exhibit 5-1b is the "talking points" used by Tyson Foods Chairman of the Board John Tyson at the national launch event in Washington, and Exhibit 5-1c is a news release for a new partnership in 2007.

Tyson Foods Powers the Fight Against Hunger

Tyson Foods, Inc. with Mitchell Communications Group, Inc.

SUMMARY

Protein is one of the most essential nutrients for a healthy body, yet it is the least donated and most sought-after item at food banks. With its "Powering the Fight Against Hunger" campaign, Tyson Foods significantly stepped up its hunger relief work in 2006 with a fresh new approach to food donations and community engagement. Through partnerships with America's Second Harvest (A2H), Share Our Strength, NBA and NFL teams, and dozens of non-profit and advocacy groups, Tyson donated 7.5 million pounds of protein and staged 68 food donation events nationwide.

The public relations team executed a broad range of tactics to tell Tyson's empowering story, resulting in widespread media coverage, sales-impacting activities, team member involvement, and participation from community influencers from the local to the national level.

SITUATION ANALYSIS

Tyson Foods, Inc., the world's largest protein provider and processor of chicken, beef, and pork, is committed to the fight against hunger. Since 2000, the company has donated approximately $3 million and 25 million pounds of protein to hunger relief through a major partnership with Share Our Strength. But Tyson wanted to develop a more strategic overall approach to hunger relief that would engage stakeholders on a more meaningful level, including its team members; community leaders and elected officials; retail and food service customers; and a larger number of organizations and individuals involved in hunger relief nationwide.

On a broader front, the company was also facing significant business and reputation challenges: widespread concerns about avian influenza, unprecedented bans on beef imports in foreign markets, ongoing debates with groups on animal welfare, and environmental issues, and during 2006, Tyson also experienced major plant closings and layoffs.

RESEARCH

Tyson and Mitchell Communications Group (MCG) researched hunger in America, various national nonprofit hunger relief organizations, peers' and competitors' accomplishments in this area, and issues or causes that meant the most to key stakeholders. A pilot food donation event was also tested and evaluated.

- Archival research revealed a growing hunger problem in America. In October 2005, the U.S. Department of Agriculture reported in its annual study that 38 million people were "food insecure" and 13.9 million of those were children. More than 42 percent of those served by the A2H National Network reported in 2005 having to choose between paying for food or utilities. Other data showed hunger was a timeless issue Americans cared about.

- Competitive research of other major food producers showed widespread support for hunger relief, but no one protein producer had managed to stand out as a major player.

- Qualitative research conducted through phone and in-person interviews at nonprofits, food banks, and agencies around the country determined the need for protein products. A key finding is that protein is the least donated item and the most sought-after food product at food banks and pantries.

- Quantitative research of consumers through a monthly telephone study conducted by Tyson showed a significant increase in support when asked "Is Tyson a good corporate citizen?" after the company tested a new food donation event concept in two pilot markets during 2004 and 2005.

PLANNING

Based on our research, Tyson and MCG developed a new approach to the company's hunger relief efforts.

Goals

In the fall of 2005, Tyson and MCG set out to accomplish three goals:

- Develop a more strategic approach to hunger relief that would achieve meaningful results around its hunger relief commitment and events.

- Create and implement greater opportunities for the company to communicate much-needed positive news to both internal and external stakeholders.

- Most importantly, give Tyson an opportunity to involve and engage these critical groups in a significant, sustainable way.

Strategies

- Broaden Tyson's partnerships to include national relationships with not just Share Our Strength but also A2H, Lift Up America, and Feed the Children.

- Align more closely the company's national branding campaign "Powered by Tyson" and consumer appeal with its corporate giving strategy.

- Create visual events in major markets that would gamer involvement from target audiences and capture the attention of media.

- Reach special targeted audiences by partnering with African American and Latino groups or causes.

Target audiences

- Business customers (grocery retailers)
- General consumers of Tyson products
- Key business and civic community influencers and elected officials
- Tyson team members in markets throughout the country
- Hunger relief and other direct service agencies

Objectives

- Expand food donation events to at least 20 major media markets and 15 additional markets with Tyson plants or operations.

- Involve key community influencers and newsworthy individuals such as sports celebrities at food donation events.

- Engage Tyson team members in the cause.

- Generate at least 100 placements that mention Tyson or pick up at least one key message.

- Place stories in targeted online, specialty, and diversity publications in at least half of the markets.

- Involve grocery customers in food donation activities in at least five major markets and increase sales of Tyson products by 5 percent in selected donation markets.

- Earn positive feedback from community influencers.

EXECUTION

Using new partnerships, engaging donation events, and the "powering" branding theme, Tyson donated 7.5 million pounds of protein and staged 68 major food donation events from fall 2005–end to 2006.

America's Second Harvest

- In May 2006, Tyson announced its three-year national partnership with A2H during a Capitol Hill event featuring U.S. Senator Blanche Lincoln, chair of the Senate Hunger Caucus. Along with Senator Lincoln, Tyson announced a three-year commitment to include donation of more than 6 million pounds of protein to the A2H food bank network nationwide. The donation was the largest commitment of protein ever given in the fight against hunger in America.

- In June, Tyson and A2H unveiled the first "Almanac of Hunger and Poverty in America," underwritten by Tyson, at a National Hunger Symposium in Washington, D.C. The symposium was attended by leaders from the federal government, antihunger community, conservation groups, and faith community nationwide. The almanac is the first all-inclusive resource that includes data on federal and state food insecurity. In a short time, it has become a highly respected information resource used by media and elected officials across the country.

- From June to November 2006, Tyson and A2H undertook an ambitious food donation program, staging highly visual, engaging donation events in major media markets around the country. For the first time ever, Tyson's food donation events consistently attracted and involved key community influencers such as elected officials and business and civic leaders.

Celebrity Events, Prime-Time Television
Donation, and Diversity Initiatives

- To support its "Powered by Tyson" national brand campaign, Tyson created 10 celebrity-focused food donation events during 2006, highlighting partnerships with U.S. Olympic gymnasts, celebrity chef G. Garvin, and the Miami Heat's Alonzo Mourning.

- Tyson also donated a semitruck load of chicken products during prime-time television on the top-rated TV show "Extreme Home Makeover." Five special donations were held in conjunction with the NBA's Hispanic community relations initiative "Es Tu Cancha."

- Finally, Tyson staged food donation announcements throughout the fall at major football games with Historically Black Colleges and Universities and at a movie studio premier of a new Latino movie in Houston.

Share Our Strength

- Tyson revamped its partnership with Share Our Strength to develop and launch a major team member fund-raising initiative tied to the company's branding campaign. "Powering the Spirit" asked team members to hold grilling or other cooking events in Tyson plant communities.

- Through these events and the production and sale of a new cookbook featuring recipes from Tyson team members, thousands of team members could volunteer their time to support local hunger relief efforts.

Lift Up America

- Tyson worked with Lift Up America in both 2005 and 2006 to donate 1.25 million pounds of protein at 40 donation events with professional and college athletes appearing in major markets.

- Partnerships included New York Giants, Washington Redskins, Atlanta Falcons, Miami Dolphins, Chicago Bulls, Houston Texans, Memphis Grizzlies, Orlando Magic, Denver Nuggets, Kansas City Chiefs, Phoenix Suns, Los Angeles Lakers, San Diego Chargers, San Jose Sharks, and Dallas Stars.

- In 2005, Tyson was able to secure valuable in-store display space through grocery partnerships with Publix, Albertson's, Minyard's, Kroger, and HEB.

EVALUATION

Tyson and MCG achieved the following results based on our measurable objectives:

- We significantly exceeded our objectives by planning and implementing 68 visual and engaging food donation events. Of those, 25 events were held in Tyson plant communities, exceeding our objective of 15.

- Tyson established highly recognizable and widely covered partnerships with 25 professional or NCAA sports teams and U.S. Olympic gymnasts. Also attending donation events were a wide variety of community influencers such as U.S. Senator Blanche Lincoln; U.S. Senator Mark Pryor; Texas State Senator Juan "Chuy" Hinojosa; numerous state, county, and community officials; United Way presidents; Salvation Army leaders; and food bank board members.

■ In its first year, thousands of Tyson team members volunteered through "Powering the Spirit" and held more than 30 fund-raising events, raising more than $150,000 to support local hunger relief efforts.

■ Quantitative media results: Media coverage included more than 40 million impressions through 260 stories in print, broadcast, and online placements. The story was very effective with TV, and examples of major publication coverage included *Chicago Sun-Times, Arizona Republic, Kansas City Star, New York Daily News, Richmond Times-Dispatch,* and *Memphis Commercial Appeal.*

■ Qualitative results: 98 percent of stories had a positive tone and charitable-giving message; 85 percent mentioned Tyson in the top third of the story; 41 percent included key messaging regarding Tyson's commitment to hunger.

■ There was broad coverage in diversity and special audience media: Web sites for the Denver Nuggets, Miami Dolphins, Dallas Stars, Minnesota Vikings, and Memphis Grizzlies; NBA's en Espanol Web site; www.terra.com; Hispanic portal/Web site; and also Telemundo, Univision, Dos Mundos, and several food bank Web sites and newsletters.

■ Grocery partners were secured in 6 markets and Tyson sales increased 14.9 percent, much more than the 5 percent anticipated. (NOTE: Non-donation markets achieved only a 4.8 percent increase during the same period.)

■ Eighty percent of food bank directors surveyed responded that their perception of Tyson had increased, and they considered it to be an excellent corporate citizen. "This donation from Tyson will help us put this important source of nutrition on the plates of thousands of Oklahomans that may have otherwise had to go without," said Rodney Bivens, executive director, Regional Food Bank of Oklahoma.

E X H I B I T 5-1a   **News Release New Program**

America's
Second Harvest
The Nation's
Food Bank Network
Ending Hunger.

FOR IMMEDIATE RELEASE

FOR MORE INFORMATION CONTACT:

Ross Fraser, America's Second Harvest, rfraser@secondharvest.org, 312-263-2303
   ext. 6611

Katie Laning, Office of Senator Blanche Lincoln,
   Katie_Laning@lincoln.senate.gov, 202-224-4843

Gary Mickelson, Tyson Foods, Inc. 479-290-6111

Michael Clark, general information, 479-443-4673, 479-879-1571 (cell) or
   michael@mitchcommgroup.com

New National Hunger Relief Partnership Launches In Nation's Capital

Tyson and America's Second Harvest announce three-year national partnership; U.S. Senator Blanche Lincoln helps to raise awareness in the fight against hunger

WASHINGTON D.C., May 10, 2006–Millions of people at risk of hunger across the United States will add high-quality protein to their plate, thanks to a six-million pound donation of chicken by Tyson Foods, Inc., to America's Second Harvest–The Nation's Food Bank Network. The donation is the largest commitment of protein ever given in the fight against hunger in America.

Tyson Foods and America's Second Harvest also announced today a three-year partnership, with Tyson Foods pledging at least 10 million pounds of protein to the nationwide food bank network and charitable domestic hunger-relief organization. The network consists of more than 200 food banks that provide food and grocery products to agencies that serve people at the greatest risk of hunger.

EXHIBIT 5-1a   (Continued)

"We face significant challenges in the fight against hunger," said U.S. Senator Blanche Lincoln, co-founder of the U.S. Senate Hunger Caucus. "I'd like to commend Tyson Foods and America's Second Harvest, who have come together to form this important partnership to fight hunger in America's communities. This collaborative partnership is a great example of how charitable organizations and corporations can come together to gain significant ground towards our shared goal of ending hunger in America."

The six-million pound donation will make a significant impact on the fight against hunger, according to Vicki B. Escarra, president and CEO of America's Second Harvest. "We have thus far been able to distribute 4.4 million pounds of the donation to dozens of food banks from New York to Honolulu, helping us serve working families, children at our Kids Cafe programs, senior citizens, the disabled, the homeless and victims of domestic violence."

The Second Harvest Network of food banks and food-rescue organizations provides emergency hunger-relief services to an estimated 25.3 million people each year, or roughly nine percent of all Americans, according to the recently released report *Hunger in America 2006*. This represents an 8% increase since *Hunger in America 2001*, and an 18% increase since *Hunger in America 1997*.

"It's very important to our team members to assure a ready supply of much needed protein to people in critical need of nourishment," said John Tyson, CEO of Tyson Foods. "Through this donation and our partnership with America's Second Harvest, we want to continue making an impact where we can," he added.

Protein is one of the most efficient and long-lasting sources of energy. The chicken donated today is one of the most concentrated sources of protein—an essential nutrient of life. The average person — man, woman or child — needs to eat about 0.4 grams of protein for every pound of body weight, every day. This is approximately equivalent to 50–65 grams (6–8 ounces) of chicken, beef, or pork. In addition to being good sources of protein, meat and poultry supply other essential nutrients (e.g., B6, B12, iron and zinc) that are important to good health.

Tyson's Ongoing Commitment to Hunger Relief

Since Tyson's partnership with hunger relief agencies began in 2000, the company has provided more than 35 million pounds of chicken, beef and pork–supplying more than 201 million meals with essential protein–to benefit more than 400 hunger-relief organizations across the U.S. Tyson has made a significant impact leading the fight against hunger through its relationships with nationwide organizations. For example, Share Our Strength (SOS) is a national nonprofit that inspires and organizes individuals and businesses to share their strengths in innovative ways to help end childhood hunger in America and abroad. Tyson helps to sponsor the SOS Operation Frontline, a nutrition education program that fights childhood hunger by teaching families how to make healthy and budget-wise food choices. USDA information indicates that 12% of Americans are food insecure; meaning their access to enough food is limited by a lack of money and other resources, according to its 2004 report by the Economic Research Service. Tyson supports programs to include in-kind contributions, team volunteer programs, advertising and marketing support, and national sponsorships. It's through collaboration and partnerships of government, charitable organizations and corporations that will help organizations accomplish their missions.

# # #

E X H I B I T 5-1b   CEO Talking Points

Event Messages
Announcement in Washington, DC
John Tyson

- We're honored to be here today to be a part of this event to remind people of Hunger Awareness Day on June 6, and to celebrate the partnership we've formed with America's Second Harvest.

- Senator Lincoln, and other members of the Senate Hunger Caucus, we're grateful to you for using your positions to help create awareness for the problem of hunger in our country, and for creating initiatives that move us toward sustainable solutions. Senator Lincoln, thanks so much for the hard work you and your staff did to pull this event together. It really does emphasize the fact that, if we're going to find sustainable solutions to hunger in America, it's going to take a significant collaboration among the government, the non-profit sector, and the private sector. We're particularly proud of Senator Lincoln for her leadership role in the Hunger Caucus, since she's from our home state of Arkansas.

- Six years ago this week Tyson Foods made a commitment to be actively engaged in the fight against hunger with the announcement of a partnership with Share Our Strength.

- Since that time, we've met some incredibly inspiring people, who are doing great work to end this problem that affects so many lives in so many ways.

- That partnership with Share Our Strength is ongoing, and we want to thank our partners there for helping us understand the challenges of hunger, and helping us become involved in a meaningful way in the fight against hunger. We couldn't have asked for a better partner than Share Our Strength has been in the past six years. Billy Shore is, without a doubt a visionary in this area, and he's assembled a marvelous team of incredibly dedicated people. Chuck Scofield from Share Our Strength is here. Chuck, thanks, and we look forward to continuing the work we've been doing with you as your group focuses on ending childhood hunger in America.

- We're very excited about announcing this new partnership today, with America's Second Harvest. We're, of course, very familiar with America's Second Harvest, since a great deal of the 35 million pounds of food we've donated over the past six years has gone to Second Harvest Food Banks across the country. When it comes emergency food relief, nobody does it better than Second Harvest. You all have been directly involved in creating some innovative initiatives such as the Kids Café, and the backpack program that sends children at risk of hunger home from school at the end of the week with needed food. We look forward to exploring ways we can participate in these programs.

Courtesy Tyson Foods, Inc.

E X H I B I T 5-1b   (Continued)

- We're accenting this partnership announcement today by committing six million pounds of Tyson products to Second Harvest Food Banks across the country. We're told it's the largest single private commitment of protein that's ever been made toward hunger relief. We began to make these products available about a month ago, and as we've discovered over the years, the demand for protein is great among food banks. Already, almost four and a half million pounds of this donation have either been delivered or are on their way to Second Harvest Food Banks. We anticipate the remainder being delivered in the next 30 to 60 days.

- It's very important to our team members to assure a ready supply of much needed protein to people in critical need of nourishment. Through this donation and our partnership with America's Second Harvest, we want to continue making an impact where we can.

EXHIBIT 5-1c   News Release on New Partnership

Powered by Tyson

FOR MORE INFORMATION CONTACT:
Gary Mickelson, Tyson Foods, Inc., 479-290-6111
Cydnee Cochran, Mitchell Communications Group, 479-254-8618 or 479-366-8618
cydnee@mitchcommgroup.com

America's Second Harvest, LULAC and Tyson Foods Team Up to Fight Hunger

Tyson Foods announces donation of one million pounds of protein over the next three years and an initial donation of 35,000 pounds to the Chicago Food Depository

CHICAGO, July 10, 2007—Three leaders in very different fields are uniting to address the issue of hunger among Latino communities in the U.S. today. The League of United Latin American Citizens (LULAC), America's Second Harvest–The Nation's Food Bank Network (A2H), and Tyson Foods, Inc. (NYSE: TSN) announced that the three organizations have formed a coalition that will produce an in-depth study of the extent and root causes of hunger among Latinos. The announcement was made at Chicago's Navy Pier in conjunction with LULAC's annual convention, which is currently underway in Chicago. Tyson Foods also pledged to donate one million pounds of food over a period of three years to America's Second Harvest foodbanks serving Latino and Hispanic populations. To announce the collaboration and to kick-off the pledge, representatives from Tyson Foods made an initial donation of a truckload of more than 35,000 pounds of protein products to the Chicago Food Depository, whose member agencies serve Latino communities in the Chicago area.

"These three organizations are uniquely qualified to address the issue of hunger in Latino communities," said Vicki Escarra, president and CEO of America's Second Harvest. "We have worked with Tyson Foods for years to help alleviate hunger across the country, and by working with LULAC, we can specifically target hunger among the Latino population." According to the 2007 Hunger Almanac, the nation's most comprehensive guide to understanding the facts about domestic hunger and poverty,

Courtesy Tyson Foods, Inc.

E X H I B I T 5-1c   (Continued)

---

approximately 17 percent of individuals who are served by foodbanks in America's Second Harvest's network are Latino or Hispanic.

"Food security is a human right and LULAC believes everyone should have access to nutritional and culturally relevant food" said Rosa Rosales, National LULAC President. "We are excited about partnering with American's Second Harvest and Tyson Foods to meet the moral obligation that we have as leaders to participate in meaningful efforts to insure no one goes to bed hungry."

The ongoing partnership will draw on the strengths of all of the partners to explore the issue of hunger in Latino populations, and where possible to initiate solutions. Some potential questions that could be addressed in ongoing research include: How does the percentage of the Latino population utilizing foodbank-served resources compare with other populations? If Latinos in need are not accessing social services provided by hunger relief agencies, then why not? What is the role of faith-based organizations in serving this population? Are there cultural differences relevant to this issue from Latinos of different countries of origin? How do social support systems in other countries differ from those in the U.S.?

Protein is one of the most efficient and long lasting sources of energy. The protein products donated by Tyson Foods is one of the most concentrated sources of protein—an essential nutrient of life. The average person—man, woman or child—needs to eat about 0.4 grams of protein for every pound of bodyweight, every day. This is approximately equivalent to five ounces of chicken, beef or pork.

About Hunger Relief Nationwide

Tyson has made significant impact in their fight against hunger nationwide through a partnership with Share Our Strength, and America's Second Harvest-The Nation's Food Bank Network. Share Our Strength is a nonprofit that inspires and organizes individuals and businesses to share their strengths in innovative ways to help end childhood hunger in the United States. America's Second Harvest is the largest charitable domestic hunger-relief organization in the country with more than 200 food banks in its network.

Since Tyson's partnership with hunger relief organizations began in 2000, the company has provided more than 39 million pounds of chicken, beef and pork–supplying more than 156 million meals with essential protein–to benefit more than 400 hunger relief organizations across the U.S. Tyson has made a significant impact in leading the fight against hunger through its ongoing partnerships with America's Second Harvest, Share Our Strength, Lift Up America and others.

According to the Census Bureau's Current Population Survey released in August 2005 which studied conditions in 2004, the poverty rate in America rose by 4 percent to 35.9 million people, one-third of which are children.

For more information on how to get involved in the fight against hunger, go to www.tyson.com, http://www.secondharvest.org/ or www.strength.org

America's Second Harvest® — **The Nation's Food Bank Network** is the largest charitable domestic hunger-relief organization in the country with a Network of more than 200 Member food banks and food - rescue programs serving all 50 states, the District of Columbia and Puerto Rico. The America's Second Harvest Network secures and distributes more than 2 billion pounds of donated food and grocery products annually; and supports approximately 50,000 local charitable agencies operating more than 94,000 programs including food pantries, soup kitchens, emergency shelters, after-school programs, and Kids Cafes. Last year, the America's Second

---

EXHIBIT 5-1c (Continued)

Harvest Network provided food assistance to more than 23 million low-income hungry people in the United States, including more than 9 million children and nearly 3 million seniors. For more on America's Second Harvest, please visit www.second-harvest.org.

League of United Latino American Communities (LULAC) has approximately 115,000 members throughout the United States and Puerto Rico. It is the largest and oldest Hispanic organization in the United States. LULAC advances the economic condition, educational attainment, political influence, health and civil rights of Hispanic Americans through community-based programs operating at more than 700 LULAC councils nationwide. The organization involves and serves all Hispanic nationality groups. For more information, go to www.lulac.org.

Tyson Foods, Inc., www.tyson.com, [NYSE: TSN], founded in 1935 with headquarters in Springdale, Arkansas, is the world's largest processor and marketer of chicken, beef, and pork, the second-largest food company in the Fortune 500 and a member of the S&P 500. The company produces a wide variety of protein-based and prepared food products, which are marketed under the "Powered by Tyson™" strategy. Tyson is the recognized market leader in the retail and foodservice markets it serves, providing products and service to customers throughout the United States and more than 80 countries. The company has approximately 110,000 Team Members employed at more than 300 facilities and offices in the United States and around the world. Through its Core Values, Code of Conduct and Team Member Bill of Rights, Tyson strives to operate with integrity and trust and is committed to creating value for its shareholders, customers and Team Members. The company also strives to be faith-friendly, provide a safe work environment and serve as stewards of the animals, land and environment entrusted to it.

#

Case 5-2

Keeping blood donation programs alive and vibrant requires extensive community relations efforts. Whether through special events or personal contacts, communication campaigns encourage people to join the community of donors. Exhibit 5-2a is a news release, and Exhibit 5-2b is a poster promoting the blood drive.

"Descubre el Regalo que llevamos dentro": Discover the Gift Inside Tour

American Red Cross, Puerto Rico Region, with GCI Group Puerto Rico

SUMMARY

GCI Group, Puerto Rico, organized the "Discover the gift inside" tour for the American Red Cross. The objective was to educate the public, through an interactive mobile museum, on what is blood donation, how to do it, and where to do it; debunk the myths associated with it; and, as a result, increase blood donations.

Blood donations increased by 20 percent from February to June 2005 versus the same period the year before, surpassing objectives by 10 percent. This program was the winner of the 2005 Excel Award for outstanding public relations campaign by the Association of Public Relations Practitioners of Puerto Rico.

SITUATION ANALYSIS

In Puerto Rico, we need 87,000 units of blood annually to comply with the needs of patients. The Red Cross could only supply 74,000 units of blood during 2004. Hospitals in Puerto Rico to which the Red Cross supplies blood use approximately 350 units every day. The blood provisions are regularly spent during vacation seasons—summer months and the Christmas holidays.

Only 3 percent of the medically eligible population donates blood in Puerto Rico. The average transfusion requires 3.4 units of blood. New donors are needed to counteract the decrease of donors due to the aging of the donating population, fatigue of the traditional recruiting channels, and hectic work and life routines. Among the reasons for not donating blood are:

- The fear of getting some infectious disease
- The mistaken belief that there is already a blood substitute
- Ignorance about the process and of how to do it

These facts emerge from formal and informal research since it was obtained from the perceptual survey: SALT Survey of 1,600 adults, carried out in the summer of 2003, and market information submitted by the American Red Cross Puerto Rico office.

PLANNING

Use a trailer vehicle as an interactive Museum on Wheels and take it to various places on the island, including towns, schools, universities, and parks. The program goal was to educate the public, through this museum, about what is blood donation, how to do it, and where to do it; debunk the myths associated with it; and, as a result, increase blood donations.

Objectives

- Increase blood donations by 10 percent from February to June 2005, versus the same period the previous year.
- Increase by 5 percent blood donations for the fiscal year 2005 (July 2004– June 2005), versus the previous fiscal year.
- Get an average of 360 persons to visit the museum daily and surpass the number of visits in the United States (average of 275 persons daily).
- Educate the public about the importance of donating blood with special attention on youths.
- Establish a positive relationship with the health secretary, the government, and the municipalities of Puerto Rico.
- Get ample media coverage about the Museum on Wheels with a value equivalent of $90,000.

Target Audiences

- Students from 16 years of age and higher
- General public medically eligible to donate blood
- Officials from the Government of Puerto Rico and of the public health sector
- Civic groups and community organizations
- The news media of the island

Strategies

- Use the Interactive Museum on Wheels to educate the public about blood donation.

- Make a strategic alliance with Univision TV station of Puerto Rico and its news staff to follow the Museum on Wheels throughout the month and to guarantee ample news coverage.

EXECUTION

A 37,280 pounds custom made trailer was used for this program. It measured 10 feet wide, 74 feet long, and 16 feet high. All the exterior and interior signage was done in Spanish. An interactive technology system that attracts youths was integrated into the vehicle, and it included 3 cameras, 6 DVDs, 11 computers, 7 TV screens, 1 plasma screen, 10 touch-sensitive computer screens, and a system to record personal anecdotes plus mailing of photos taken in the museum through the Internet.

The tour would begin on February 1 with an inauguration activity at the Plaza Las Americas shopping center and would end on March 3 with a closing activity in the same place. A total of 23 stops of six hours each would be made. Visits would be made to 17 towns in the island, 12 universities, 4 shopping centers, and 4 parks or community centers. We would be visited by over 35 high schools.

As part of our recommendation, each school would get an educational lecture called teach-ins prior to visiting the museum. The objective of these lectures was to increase the learning experience and receptivity of the message. The visits were coordinated with health educators so that they would take the Teach-in curriculum to high school students the week before the museum arrived to their area. We would have the teach-ins available to schools even when they would not be able to participate in the museum tour.

There would be 8–10 promoters for each activity, depending on the amount of public expected in each locality. A press conference for the inauguration of the Museum on Wheels was held on February 1 at Plaza Las Americas, with the participation of government officials, mayors, and health representatives, including the health secretary of the Government of Puerto Rico. Supplementary visits of schools, community organizations, or neighbor clubs would be coordinated to guarantee assistance. One hour of each visit would be dedicated to a welcome ceremony and a VIP tour by the regional press, government officials, hospital directors, and university administrators.

The communications tactics with the media would have two roles:

- Educate the public about the importance of blood donation. For this purpose, news reports were generated about the museum and the Red Cross.

- Disseminate the visitation calendar. (For this purpose, news were generated in the calendar of events sections of the news media.)

We also implemented paid publicity. El Nuevo Dia newspaper was used to place press ads to announce the calendar of visits. The ad placing was made through a sponsorship exchange with the newspaper. A poster was designed and placed in universities a week prior to each museum visit.

EVALUATION

- We increased blood donations by 20 percent from February to June 2005, versus the same period the year before, surpassing objectives by 10 percent.

- The donations for fiscal year June 2004–2005 increased by 14 percent, surpassing the proposed 5 percent objective.

- The total number of visitors to the museum from February 1 to March 2, 2005, was 8,247.

- An average of 390 persons visited the museum each day.

- The average visits per day objective for Puerto Rico were surpassed by 9 percent and that of the United States by 42 percent.

- A total of 38 private and public schools visited the museum. The following groups and organizations visited the museum: Bayamon Lions Club, Home Schooling Girl Scouts, The Police Loss Prevention Program, Youth Home, Office of Youth Affairs, the Santa Rosa II, and the Guaynabo Elderly Centers.

- A total of 17 cities were visited: San Juan, Guaynabo, Bayamon, Arecibo, Utuado, Mayaguez, Hatillo, San German, Yauco, Ponce, Guayama, Cayey, Gurabo, San Lorenzo, Humacao, Fajardo, and Carolina.

- The following universities were visited: Universidad de Puerto Rico and its campuses in Rio Piedras, Arecibo, Utuado, Mayaguez, and Cayey; Umversidad Interamericana and its campuses in San German, Guayama, and Fajardo; Pontificia Universidad Catolica de Puerto Rico and its campuses in Ponce and Mayaguez; Universidad del Turabo; and Universidad del Este.

- The Museum on Wheels also visited the following shopping centers: Plaza Rio Hondo, Bayamon; Plaza Norte, Hatillo; Plaza del Caribe, Ponce; Plaza Palma Real, Humacao, and Plaza Las Americas.

Teach-ins

Six hundred and twenty-seven students of public and private schools between 10th and 12th grades received educational lectures from the Red Cross health educators.

- Colegio de Lourdes, Rio Piedras
- Madame Luchetti, Carolina

- Colegio La Inmaculada, Santurce
- UHS, Rio Piedras
- Colegio Sagrados Corazones, Guaynabo
- Colegio San Felipe, Arecibo
- Colegio Capitan Correa, Arecibo
- Colegio San Jose, Caguas
- Colegio La Milagrosa, Mayaguez
- Colegio San Miguel, Utuado
- Escuela Luis Munoz Mann, Yauco
- Escuela Loaisa Cordero, Yauco
- Escuela Lola Rodriguez de Tio, San German
- Colegio Ponceno
- Escuela Betzaida Velasquez, Ponce
- Colegio San Antonio, Guayama
- Colegio Corazon de Maria, Juncos
- Escuela Superior Vocacional de Fajardo

One hundred and thirty VIPs visited the Museum on Wheels; among them were government officials, hospital directors of each city, and university directors.

Media

- Over 30 media from local and regional newspapers, magazines, television, and radio visited and published information about the museum.
- Twenty-seven newscasts and televised mentions were generated during the month of February.
- Approximately 40 articles and mentions in newspapers were generated during the month of February.
- Three radio interviews were generated plus three radio mentions about the press conference.
- The news value equivalent was $119,465; this represents a 32.7 percent increase versus the objective.

E X H I B I T 5-2a   **News Release**

Servicios de Sangre

Comunicado de Prensa

Contacto   Ivana Cruz Román   Teléfono: 787.999.6709

Fecha   1 de febrero de 2005

            E-mail: icruz@gcipuertorico.com

La Cruz Roja Americana lanza el Museo Rodante Interactivo *"Descubre el Regalo que llevamos dentro"*

1 de Febrero de 2005- La Cruz Roja Americana, Región de Puerto Rico, junto al Departamento de Salud, presentaron la iniciativa educativa más grande en la historia de la Cruz Roja Americana: el Museo Rodante Interactivo *"Descubre el regalo que llevamos dentro"*. El mismo visitará 18 pueblos alrededor de la Isla por primera y única vez durante el mes de febrero y llevará información sobre la necesidad e importancia de la donación de sangre a sobre 15,000 personas. Toda la información pertinente a las 23 paradas que realizará la el Museo Rodante Interactivo se presentó hoy en conferencia de prensa celebrada en Plaza las Américas junto a la Secretaria de Salud, Honorable Rosa Pérez Perdomo y el CEO de los Servicios de Sangre de la Cruz Roja Americana Región de Puerto Rico, el Sr. Antonio de Vera.

El museo rodante interactivo de la Cruz Roja utiliza la tecnología más reciente para ofrecer una experiencia educativa única que incluye exhibiciones, juegos y actividades atractivas utilizando computadoras, DVD, monitores de pantalla táctil, pantallas plasma, cámaras de vídeo e Internet. Los visitantes al museo rodante interactivo

EXHIBIT 5-2a (Continued)

disfrutarán de actividades que le darán vida a la donación de sangre a través de datos y hechos curiosos, escuchando historias de la vida real que los inspirarán y aprendiendo lo que realmente significa dar un regalo de vida.

"El mensaje de prevención es uno muy relevante en nuestros días ya que una población educada es una población saludable" dijo la Secretaria del Departamento de Salud, la Dra. Rosa Pérez Perdomo.

El Museo Rodante Interactivo de 10 pies de ancho por 74 pies de largo y 16 pies de alto será visitado por aproximadamente 15,000 personas a través de sus 23 visitas alrededor de la Isla. El mismo visitará 14 universidades, 5 centros comerciales y cuatro parques o centros comunales. Además se han invitado sobre 35 escuelas superiores públicas y privadas para que visiten alguna de las paradas que hará el Museo Rodante Interactivo.

"El Museo Rodante Interactivo es parte de nuestra campaña para cambiar las motivaciones del donante de sangre tradicional; de hacerlo cuando un familiar está en necesidad, a hacerlo de manera totalmente altruista y voluntaria sin conocer quien pueda ser beneficiado por ese regalo de vida" aseguró Antonio de Vera, CEO Servicios de Sangre de la Cruz Roja Americana Región de Puerto Rico. "El Museo le provee la oportunidad al pueblo de sumergirse en lo que realmente significa dar un regalo de vida, esta experiencia educativa hará que los visitantes tomen un momento para pensar sobre el valor que tiene el regalo que todos llevamos dentro".

El Museo Rodante Interactivo *Descubre el regalo que llevamos dentro"* de la Cruz Roja

Americana estará abierto al público durante las siguientes fechas:

- Martes, 1 de febrero: Plaza las Américas, San Juan, de 12:00 p.m. a 4:00 p.m.
- Miércoles, 2 de febrero: Universidad de Puerto Rico Recinto de Río Piedras de 12:00 p.m. a 4:00 p.m.
- Jueves, 3 de febrero: Universidad de Sagrado Corazón, Santurce de 12:00 p.m. a 4:00 p.m.
- Viernes, 4 de febrero: Paseo Tablado Guaynabo de 12:00 p.m. a 4:00 p.m.
- Sábado, 5 de febrero: Plaza Río Hondo en Bayamón de 11:00 a.m. a 5:00 p.m.
- Martes, 8 de febrero: Universidad de Puerto Rico Recinto de Arecibo de 12:00 p.m. a 4:00 p.m.
- Miércoles, 9 de febrero: Universidad de Puerto Rico Recinto de Utuado de 12:00 p.m. a 4:00 p.m.
- Jueves, 10 de febrero: Universidad de Puerto Rico Recinto de Mayagüez de 12:00 p.m. a 4:00 p.m.
- Viernes, 11 de febrero: Universidad Católica de Mayagüez de 12:00 p.m. a 4:00 p.m.
- Sábado, 12 de febrero: *Pueblo* en Plaza del Norte en Hatillo de 11:00 a.m. a 5:00 p.m.
- Martes, 15 de febrero: Universidad Interamericana Recinto de San Germán de 12:00 p.m. a 4:00 p.m.
- Miércoles, 16 de febrero: Coliseo Raúl *Pipote* Olivera de Yauco de 12:00 p.m. a 4:00 p.m.
- Jueves, 17 de febrero: Pontificia Universidad Católica de Puerto Rico, Ponce de 12:00 p.m. a 4:00 p.m.

EXHIBIT 5-2a   (Continued)

- Viernes, 18 de febrero: Albergue Olímpico, Salinas de 12:00 p.m. a 4:00 p.m.
- Sábado, 19 de febrero: *Pueblo* en Plaza del Caribe en Ponce de 11:00 a.m. a 5:00 p.m.
- Martes, 22 de febrero: Universidad Interamericana Recinto de Guayama de 12:00 p.m. a 4:00 p.m.
- Miércoles, 23 de febrero: Universidad de Puerto Rico Recinto de Cayey de 12:00 p.m. a 4:00 p.m.
- Jueves, 24 de febrero: Universidad del Turabo, Gurabo de 12:00 p.m. a 4:00 p.m.
- Viernes, 25 de febrero: Parque Cristóbal Colón, San Lorenzo de 12:00 p.m. a 4:00 p.m.
- Sábado, 26 de febrero: *Pueblo* en Centro Comercial Palma Real en Humacao de 11:00 a.m. a 5:00 p.m.
- Martes, 1 de marzo: Universidad Interamericana de Fajardo de 12:00 p.m. a 4:00 p.m.
- Miércoles, 2 de marzo: Universidad del Este, Carolina de 12:00 p.m. a 4:00 p.m.
- Jueves, 3 de marzo: Plaza las Américas, San Juan de 9:00 a.m. a 3:00 p.m.

Para más información sobre el calendario del museo rodante interactivo puede comunicarse con la Cruz Roja Americana, Región de Puerto Rico al 787-759-8100 ext. 300.

-FIN-

E X H I B I T 5-2b Blood Donation Schedule Poster

DESCUBRE EL REGALO QUE LLEVAMOS DENTRO

Ven al Museo Rodante Interactivo

Disfruta de la experiencia del Museo Rodante Interactivo de la Cruz Roja Americana. Todo un fascinante recorrido educativo relativo al tema de la sangre, el regalo que llevamos dentro. A través de exhibiciones, juegos interactivos e interesantes presentaciones tendrás la oportunidad de aprender de manera divertida e innovadora sobre la necesidad e importancia de la donación de sangre. Durante tu visita, descubrirás extraordinarios datos, escucharás poderosas historias y aprenderás lo que puedes hacer para salvar una vida.

VEN DE 12:00 M. A 4:00 P.M. Y VIVE LA EXPERIENCIA DEL MUSEO RODANTE INTERACTIVO:

+ MARTES 1 DE FEBRERO: Plaza Las Américas, San Juan
+ MIÉRCOLES 2 DE FEBRERO: Universidad de Puerto Rico, Recinto de Río Piedras
+ JUEVES 3 DE FEBRERO: Universidad del Sagrado Corazón, Santurce
+ VIERNES 4 DE FEBRERO: Paseo Tablado, Guaynabo
+ SÁBADO 5 DE FEBRERO: Pueblo Plaza Río Hondo, Bayamón

PARA MÁS INFORMACIÓN, LLAMA AL 787-759-8100 EXT. 300.

Cruz Roja Americana

Servicios de Sangre

UNIVISION PUERTO RICO   univision

Courtesy American Red Cross, Puerto Rico Region

Case 5-3

Dedicated volunteers give many nonprofit organizations a special advantage in supporting local community programs, yet encouraging volunteers to join an organization is a perpetual challenge for most organizations. One partnership used insightful research to focus on increasing youth volunteerism. Exhibit 5-3a is a "current news" posting about a volunteer project, Exhibit 5-3b is the Web site "About RockCorps," and Exhibit 5-3c is the concert schedule.

Boost Mobile RockCorps
Boost Mobile with Miles Ahead Entertainment

SUMMARY

Combining the power of music, community, and volunteerism, Boost Mobile RockCorps (BMRC) offered entrance to exclusive concerts featuring today's chart-topping hip-hop and rock artists. However, the only way to get into the show was to earn a ticket by contributing four hours of volunteer service. BMRC volunteers work on a range of service projects in partnership with local nonprofit organizations, including school and playground renovations, environmental initiatives, food distribution, and more. By the end of the 2006 tour, BMRC volunteers contributed approximately 40,000 hours of community service and transformed close to 125 project sites in 8 cities across the country.

RESEARCH

In a time when youth are perceived to be apathetic and uninvolved in their communities, Boost Mobile and RockCorps developed a program—100 percent dependent on youth volunteerism—designed to drive young people to support their local community and dispel the widely perceived myth.

In 2005 Boost Mobile conducted research through Marketing Research Services, Inc. (MRSI) and Wagner Research & Consulting to determine if today's youth are willing to give four hours of community service to earn a free concert ticket. Almost three-fourths of those surveyed were in favor of and also preferred the idea of giving back to the community in exchange for a concert ticket (regardless of ethnicity, age, or gender). After evaluating the results from MRSI, BMRC was created with the program premise "you got to give to get," producing exclusive events for youth volunteers who donate four hours of their time to their local community.

To further substantiate the trend, in spring 2006, Boost referred to secondary research conducted by Teenage Research Unlimited, Inc. (TRU), which stated that more than half (56 percent of youth aged 12–19) of all youth surveyed think that volunteering is an "in," compared to 54 percent in spring 2005.

The BMRC movement was launched in June 2005 and, throughout the summer, traveled to six cities across the United States where local youth were given the opportunity to give back in their community. An additional 78 projects touching neighborhoods across the five boroughs of New York City were successfully completed in BMRC's inaugural year. The signature concert event at Radio City Music Hall brought together 5,000 volunteers and chart-topping hip-hop artists to celebrate the efforts and accomplishments of this unprecedented nationwide initiative.

PLANNING

In its second year, BMRC remains the only community program of its kind, but it has also expanded its reach across the nation and added an additional reward concert in Atlanta. Boost Mobile collaborated with the Miles Ahead Entertainment public relations agency to develop a twofold public relations strategy.

Objectives

- To continue to drive awareness of and participation in the program within targeted communities through tactical media relations highlighting the uniqueness and goals of the program
- To drive specific coverage of the exclusive Atlanta and New York concerts

Target Audiences

Target audiences for BMRC included Boost Mobile customers and potential customers (street-savvy, active, irreverent youth aged 14–24 who live large yet aspire to the next level in their lives), strategic partners, and BMRC's targeted media list.

Participation goals were set at 4,000 youth volunteers and 50 million media impressions. The 2005 goal was 25 million impressions.

EXECUTION/TACTICS

In April 2006, the BMRC movement kicked off its second year in Atlanta, followed by a signature reward concert in June. Volunteers worked on a range of service projects, including building playgrounds, renovating schools, distributing food, and preserving the environment. The BMRC program continued its momentum throughout the summer with stops in Houston, Chicago, Minneapolis/St. Paul, Detroit, Los Angeles, and Washington, D.C. By the end of the 2006 tour, which wrapped up with another signature reward concert in NYC in September, BMRC volunteers transformed close to 125 project sites in 8 cities across the nation.

Pre-Event

- Boost Mobile created hard and soft media materials to assist in BMRC media outreach. Media materials such as news releases, fact sheets, media alerts, and electronic press kits (EPKs) and resources such as B-roll production and a photowire service were coordinated.

- Boost Mobile reached out to multiple genres of media, including entertainment, marketing/advertising trades, philanthropic trades, lifestyle, urban, alternative, fashion, music, business, and major dailies, in addition to national and local TV and radio stations.

- BMRC also hosted a media launch event in NYC to drive additional awareness and increase participation in the movement.

- Local and national media targets were invited to learn more about the program and interview the Atlanta and New York concert host, Nick Cannon; one of the concert artists, Young Jeezy; RockCorps cofounder Chris Robinson; and Boost Mobile executive Daryl Butler.

Post-Event

- At both the Atlanta and New York BMRC concerts, Boost Mobile created high-tech working media rooms that exceeded media expectations. The media rooms served as the location for photo ops against a BMRC-branded step and repeat, live audio interviews with performing artists, live streaming BMRC concert video, and Internet feeds (through a localized media station).

- Immediately following each concert, Boost Mobile serviced media with a post-event news release, copy of B-roll, and concert photos with BMRC branding.

EVALUATION

The BMRC public relations campaign was a huge success and executed on schedule and within budget. All program objectives and goals were met and exceeded.

Through Boost Mobile's strategic media approach, BMRC awareness more than doubled the initial volunteer goal with 10,000 youth volunteers.

One hundred percent of BMRC youth development key messages were utilized and incorporated into Boost Mobile's multiple communications materials for its target audience.

The BMRC program and concert received more than 250 million impressions on 11 network TV segments, including coverage on MTV, CNN, BET, WNYW FOX, WXYZ ABC, WJBK FOX, WDIV NBC, and WXTA NBC.

National and local print media coverage garnered more than 23 million impressions, including coverage in:

- *Washington Sun*
- *Vibe Magazine*
- *Chicago Tribune-City*
- *Detroit News*
- *Houston Style Magazine*
- *Fairfax Times*

The BMRC program and concert was also heavily promoted on a number of local radio stations, including

WVEE V-103, BET Radio, American Urban Radio, Premiere Radio, KKDA 104.5 Dallas, DC 101, and WPGC.

Overall, the BMRC program and concert total media impressions surpassed the set goal with 376 million impressions.

EXHIBIT 5-3a   Rockcorps Volunteer News

June 7, 2008

Treating L.A. Students To Greener Spaces

Volunteers nurture the soil, plant trees and flowers, and promote fruit growth in underserved Middle School.

The Backstory

The Mission of Community Services Unlimited, Inc. is to foster the creation of communities actively working to address the inequalities and barriers that make sustainable communities and self-reliant life-styles unattainable. They have partnered with John Muir Middle School to implement a dynamic after-school program called Growing Healthy. Participants learn first hand how to grow and cultivate there own fruits and vegetables. With the help of BMRC volunteers, CSU will be care for and beautify the green spaces at this underserved middle school.

The Synopsis

BMRC volunteers laid down compost and mulch around the apple trees and shade trees on campus. In the courtyard we planted trees and flowers, built fencing around

Courtesy Boost Mobile

E X H I B I T 5-3a   (Continued)

the new trees, chipped off the tagged paint on several flower boxes, and repainted them. We also repotted the banana trees in the vegetable garden to increase their productivity.

The Rewind
This project tied in beautifully with the progressive and important work that Community Services Unlimited is accomplishing throughout Los Angeles. In schools like John Muir Middle School, youth have little access to green spaces or information about sustainability. Knowledge such as how to grow one's own food is no longer being passed on between generations of city-dwellers. Through CSU, students are learning to reconnect to and better appreciate nature. BMRC volunteers partnered with this mission by nurturing the green spaces at this school to make them more beautiful. The volunteers laid down 6 tons of mulch & 6 tons of compost, planted 160 flowers & 2 trees, prepped and repainted 8 flower boxes, and separated & repotted a banana tree so that it will bear much more fruit. Because of this project students will be able to enjoy peaches and apples grown from nurtured soil, bananas from the vegetable garden, and a beautiful courtyard full of two new black walnut trees, loads of marigolds, and a fresh coat of paint.

Outtakes
BMRC volunteers rise to even the most daunting challenges with gusto. While attempting to dig a deep hole in which to place the sapling walnut tree, volunteers encountered a daunting dilemma. After digging a foot into the soil they discovered a large stump, right where the tree was to be planted. The previous tree was so large that the root ran far too deep for volunteers to pull out. Equipped only with shovels, the volunteers hacked away at the stump to break it apart. Finally we were able to procure a pick axe and volunteers took turns chopping away the dead trunk and pulling apart the wood. After an hour and a half of work and a stubborn task ahead, not one complaint was heard. Instead these volunteers rose to the challenge with excitement and with a purpose. Finally the tree was planted with compost and mulch, and fencing was built to protect it. Now that the tree has been planted, the evidence of the volunteer's labor is hidden. Perhaps they alone will know the effort that was required to plant that single tree. Even so the result was well worth the trouble—and BMRC volunteers can be proud of completing a job well done even when the going got tough.

About Boost Mobile
Based in Irvine, CA, Boost Mobile is a lifestyle-based telecommunications brand focused on offering premium wireless phones and services to the youth market with exclusive Boost™ Walkie-Talkie service and Re-Boost® Cards available nationwide at locations where youth prefer to shop, including national retailers and convenience stores, and merchants that focus on fashion, music, and action sports-related activities. Boost Mobile is dedicated to boosting the lives of today's youth by contributing to development programs. Boost's community relations efforts are vast and aim at helping young people enhance their lifestyle and status, and build stronger connection and greater independence. Get more at www.boostmobile.com.

E X H I B I T 5-3b   Web Site "About Rockcorps"

About the Boost Mobile RockCorps Movement

Boost Mobile and RockCorps have partnered to spread a national youth movement: Boost Mobile RockCorps. The movement encourages volunteerism in young people. It was created to effect social change and act as a bridge between communities in need and the young people who want to make them better. Every volunteer who gives 4 hours of service, receives a ticket to a concert featuring the hottest artists today. Boost Mobile RockCorps introduces youth to service opportunities in their own neighborhood starting them on a lifelong commitment to civic engagement and service.

Established in 2002, RockCorps evolved from a concept executed by the Greenbucks Foundation that began in 1995. Boost Mobile RockCorps (BMRC) launched in the summer of 2005. Since then our "Around the Way Revolution" has motivated 16,000+ young people throughout the U.S. to get involved, connect with their community and become a part of a youth movement for social change. In 2007 we are even bigger. Los Angeles, Oakland, Miami, Atlanta, Houston, Chicago, Minneapolis, Detroit, Portland, Baltimore, Philadelphia,Washington DC and New York. 175+ volunteer projects. Concerts at the Kodak Theatre, the Fox Theatre, Radio City Music Hall and points in between. **Are you in?**

Results

"In 2006, the RockCorps volunteers worked over *250,000 hours* proudly rebuilding our homes & neighborhoods."

BMRC is a movement. And it's growing.

BMRC volunteers are significantly more likely than others to volunteer again in the future.

1. 69% of RockCorps volunteers say they can make time to volunteer versus 44% of non-participants
2. Close to 80% of BMRC volunteers are likely to volunteer again in future - without a concert ticket
3. 38% have reported volunteering again in the 6–12 months after their RockCorps concert experience. Participating in BMRC provides increased likelihood to volunteer again and improves view towards volunteering and their community
4. More than 90% enjoyed volunteering with RockCorps and attending the RockCorps concert
5. 73% said that attending the RockCorps concert gave them a sense of how powerful volunteer work can be

EXHIBIT 5-3b   (Continued)

	Stats		
	2005	**2006**	**2007**
Volunteer hours generated	24,000	40,000	60,000 (est)
Volunteers	6,000	10,000	15,000
Non Profit Partners	29	49	120 (est)
Volunteer Projects	88	119	180 (est)

EXHIBIT 5-3c   Concert Schedule

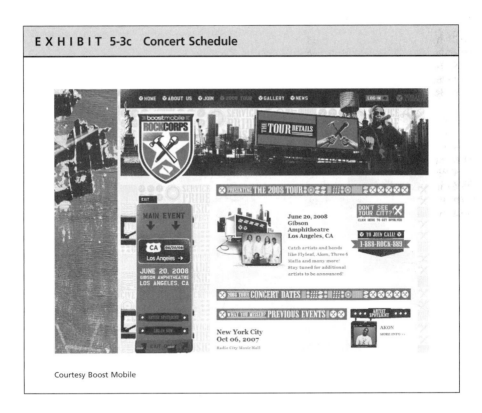

Courtesy Boost Mobile

6

Public Affairs and Government Relations

In the last decades, many U.S. corporations have subsumed what was formerly known as government relations within the broader enterprise now called public affairs. To add further semantic confusion, the U.S. government in the early 1980s decreed that the term public affairs would replace public information in all its departments and agencies.

Our principal concern here will be with how the enactment of legislation is influenced. This process includes the creation of political coalitions, direct and indirect lobbying, political action and political education activities, communication on political issues, and political support activities.

RESEARCH

The research process of public affairs includes investigation of the practitioner's client or organization, the opportunity or problem that accounts for the need for communication—including the important area of issues management—and the audiences to be targeted for public affairs programs.

Client Research

Client research for public affairs is similar to that for other forms of public relations. Background information about the client or organization should be obtained, including its personnel, financial status, and reputation, especially with government and community audiences. The practitioner should pay particular attention to past and present relations with the government and the community, along with any particular client strengths or weaknesses in these areas. Finally, the practitioner should catalog all opportunities for profitable communication with government or community audiences.

Opportunity or Problem Research

In public affairs programs, the process of issues management can make assessment of the client's opportunity or problem much easier. *Issues management* consists of listing and giving priority to all issues of interest to the client and then determining options and strategies for dealing with them. This process includes assessing political risks and monitoring social and political developments of concern to the client at the local, state, national, and international levels. An examination of each of these areas on a priority basis is a useful means of targeting the client's public affairs program.

Audience Research

The final aspect of research for public affairs consists of identifying target audiences, the necessary data regarding each one, and the methods of research necessary to obtain this information.

Public affairs programs target three audiences: community publics, government, and ancillary publics—this last group consisting of client allies, constituents of legislators, and media that reach both of them. Community publics were examined in the preceding chapter (see Exhibit 5-a). Government publics can be considered at the federal, state, county, or city level; they and the ancillary publics are listed in Exhibit 6-a.

Data necessary for understanding members of the legislative branches of government include officials' voting records on issues of concern to the client; their general attitudes or past and present reactions to the client; the size, location, and general demographics of their voting constituencies; their committee assignments; and their general interests and areas of expertise. Government officials in the executive branch may or may not hold elective office; this is their single most important characteristic. Beyond that, the nature and authority of the offices they hold, along with as much background about them as possible, should prove helpful. For officials in both legislative and executive positions, of course, the highest priority information about them is their degree of involvement with each issue or piece of legislation affecting the client, along with their stand, and how they are expected to vote. Officials often rely on key staff and advice from leaders in organizations specializing in public policy issues. It is valuable to determine who has the ear of a representative or government official, and to analyze what values underlie their advice.

Methods of gathering information about government officials are usually nonquantitative. Voting records or accomplishments are public knowledge and easily accessible. Beyond that, conducting surveys among officials is usually not feasible. Thus, the practitioner must rely on other sources of information, such as conversations with staff people, the officials' past behavior, and their public statements regarding issues of concern to the client.

EXHIBIT 6-A   **Government and Ancillary Publics**

Government Publics

Federal

    Legislative branch

        Representatives, staff, committee personnel

        Senators, staff, committee personnel

    Executive branch

        President

        White House staff, advisers, committees

        Cabinet officers, departments, agencies, commissions

State

    Legislative branch

        Representatives, delegates, staff, committee personnel

        Senators, staff, committee personnel

    Executive branch

        Governor

        Governor's staff, advisers, committees

        Cabinet officers, departments, agencies, commissions

County

    County executive

    Other county officials, commissioners, departments

City

    Mayor or city manager

    City council

    Other city officials, commissions, departments

Ancillary Publics

Allies

Think tanks

National/local public policy activist groups

Constituents of legislators

Media

    Mass media

    Specialized media

        Trade

        Allied organizations' publications

    Constituent media

Research on the ancillary publics listed in Exhibit 6-a is also of considerable value. Allies of the client must be identified and cultivated with the goal of building a coalition. The home districts, communities, and constituents of legislators must also be identified and studied. Old friends, business or professional partners, and local civic leaders are trusted sources of grassroots information for a legislator. Government leaders maintain close connections with their constituents to capture a sense of local concerns. They monitor local media in their district to gain a pulse on the body politic. Try to monitor these same sources. Finally, mass and specialized media for reaching constituents and client allies should be identified, and media contacts lists should be prepared, as discussed in Chapter 3.

OBJECTIVES

As in other forms of public relations, objectives for public affairs programs should be specific and quantitative.

Impact Objectives

A sampling of impact objectives for public affairs includes such statements as:

1. To increase knowledge of the client's current activities and field of operations among legislators (by 50 percent during the current year)
2. To create or enhance favorable attitudes toward the client's new initiative among officials (by 30 percent before the February vote)
3. To influence a favorable vote on a bill (by 30 members of the House of Representatives during the current session)

Output Objectives

Output objectives represent the effort of the practitioner without reference to potential audience impact. Such objectives might use such statements as:

1. To make oral presentations to 30 lawmakers
2. To distribute printed information to 45 lawmakers

PROGRAMMING

Public affairs programming includes the same four planning and execution elements used in other forms of public relations: (1) theme and messages, (2) action or special event(s), (3) uncontrolled and controlled media, and (4) principles of effective communication.

Theme and Messages

Always be aware that government audiences may be the most knowledgeable and sophisticated of all audiences for public relations communication. For this reason, the use of catchy themes or slogans may not be helpful; at times, they can even be counterproductive. When addressing public affairs programming to ancillary audiences, however, more traditional use of themes or slogans may be appropriate. Messages, of course, should be carefully coordinated with the program objectives and actions or special events.

Action(s) or Special Event(s)

Public affairs programming, like other forms of public relations, is structured around actions and special events. The practitioner should review the types found in Exhibit 2-c.

The actions unique to public affairs programming are:

1. Fact-finding
2. Coalition building
3. Direct lobbying
4. Grassroots activities (indirect lobbying)
5. Political action committees
6. Political education activities
7. Communications on political issues
8. Political support activities

Fact-finding.   Information gathering is an important aspect of public affairs. It includes attendance at openly conducted hearings, generally scheduled by both the legislative and the executive branches of government when considering legislation or regulations. This monitoring function is indispensable for all public affairs programs.

In addition to monitoring hearings, fact-finding often includes exchanging information with government officials, representatives of trade associations or interest groups, and other sources of reliable data. Fact-finding may also include entertainment, since the relaxed atmosphere of most social gatherings can be conducive to exchanging information.

A final aspect of fact-finding is the reporting of data and findings to the client, along with recommendations for appropriate responses.

Coalition Building.   It is useful to organize groups or individuals with a common interest in the passage or defeat of legislation or regulations. Such coalitions can be much more effective in attaining goals than groups or individuals working alone. The power of a coalition is often based on the "perceived" cohesiveness and political clout of the group. Some coalitions will claim a large number of members to enhance the credibility of the organization, even though many members may actually be relatively small local activist organizations. Coalitions can pool such resources as staff time, legal help, and printing and mailing costs. Working together, they can set priorities and devise operational strategies more effectively. In brief, the building of coalitions is one of the most important and effective tactics in public affairs.

Direct Lobbying.   The two "core" activities of public affairs are direct and indirect lobbying. In direct lobbying, the practitioner contacts legislators or officials who can influence the passage or defeat of a bill or proposed regulation. It is an overt advocacy process, although it takes the sometimes subtle forms of information exchange and hospitality.

Information exchange includes providing the lawmaker or official with data about the client's field of interest and the effect the proposed legislation or regulation would have on this field. The practitioner, or lobbyist, usually makes an authoritative oral presentation, including the publicity potential for the legislator or official and the potential interest or impact of the proposals on constituents. These two aspects—*publicity value* and *constituent interest*—strike the most responsive chords in the ears of legislators or officials. They should always be central to a public affairs presentation. In addition to presentations, the practitioner usually offers the official a sample draft of the proposed legislation or regulation that incorporates the views of the client. Position and background papers are a staple of information exchange.

Finally, information exchange may include providing authoritative testimony or offering witnesses for the hearings that are usually held in conjunction with proposed legislation or regulations. The practitioner often writes the testimony that is usually given by the client or the chief executive officer of the client's organization.

The second form of direct lobbying is still more subtle than information exchange. It involves offering *hospitality* to the legislator or the agency official. The days of extravagant gifts, yachting trips, weekends in hunting lodges, and the like have passed. Legislators and agency officials are now very sensitive to the ubiquitous investigative journalist, constantly in search of untoward political influence by moneyed interests or wrongdoing in high places. Nonetheless, hospitality still plays an important role in public affairs or, more particularly, in lobbying. Lawmakers and agency officials often accept invitations to social functions sponsored by influential associations or corporations. Personal relationships are still the realm of many political decisions and face-to-face exchanges work well in convincing an official of the merits of your initiative.

These social gatherings provide a relaxed and conducive atmosphere for the subtle conduct of the business of public affairs.

A more recent and widespread variety of hospitality has turned the tables. Now, more often than not, the legislator provides the hospitality in the form of thousand-dollar-a-plate breakfasts, lunches, dinners, or other special events at which the corporation, association, or union representatives pay or make large contributions to attend, and thus gain access to the lawmaker.

Access is a major goal of all lobbying, and to an increasing degree, hospitality events—usually linked to fund-raising for the legislator—have become the most used avenue for reaching this goal.

Grassroots Activities (Indirect Lobbying).   Indirect lobbying, or grassroots activities, is the second of the two core aspects of public affairs. This form of indirect lobbying involves mobilizing support for or opposition to proposed legislation or regulations at the state or local level, especially in the home districts of elected legislators. In the case of government departments or agencies, this grassroots level may be the location where a large agency is considering constructing or closing an installation that will profoundly affect the local economy.

Grassroots activities include working with national, state, or local mass media; the use of interpersonal communication; and the orchestration of campaigns to bring constituent pressure on legislators or officials.

The grassroots use of the mass media includes publicizing the client's position in national, state, or local media, demonstrating that this position will be beneficial to the media audience. This action is usually performed in cases where an elected official is in opposition to the client's position or is uncommitted. The practitioner, on behalf of the client, will use all feasible forms of media, including paid advertising, to generate news coverage about the situation. If the legislator has taken a stand contrary to that of the client's, the media messages will call attention to that, to voting records, and to the harm such a position will bring to the constituency. Care must be taken not to engage in overkill in this endeavor. In some cases, besieged legislators have also used the media, successfully portraying themselves as the victims of "fat-cat lobbyists." A second effective type of grassroots activity is the use of various forms of interpersonal communication at the national, state, or local level. This includes targeting key groups of opinion leaders in the home districts of legislators and getting expert and highly credible representatives of the client's viewpoint invited to their meetings, conferences, or conventions as guest speakers.

In addition to addressing important grassroots audiences, the client can meet with key executives at breakfast, with editorial staffs of newspapers, or with small groups of community leaders. Dyadic interactions may include interviews and meetings with key public officials, executives, and/or union leaders.

Interpersonal communication, then, in the form of speeches, small group meetings, or dyadic interactions can be a highly useful form of grassroots activity. When organizations host annual conventions in Washington, they arrange short meetings between legislators and association members who are constituents. The constituents arrive with specific talking points related to the organization's public policy agenda.

Finally, grassroots activities culminate in the orchestration of campaigns at the national, state, or local level designed to bring pressure from constituents directly on legislators or officials. These campaigns can be orchestrated by small or large membership groups, associations, or other affected groups. They may take the traditional form of organized letter writing to a legislator from home district constituents; or they may use more contemporary forms, such as e-mail, faxing, or the formation of "telephone trees." The "telephone tree" consists of groups of constituents who each may call 5 to 10 friends, who in turn each call 5 to 10 more friends, and so on, all of whom then call or otherwise communicate with the office of the lawmaker with a common request or purpose.

The National Rifle Association (NRA) is a membership group that uses all of these forms of constituent communication effectively to influence the course of national legislation. The NRA boasts the ability to mobilize its membership within 24 hours to flood Congress with enough constituent communication to shape the course of gun legislation.

Of the two public affairs core methods, grassroots activities usually prove more effective. These actions—working with mass media, interpersonal communication, and constituent communication campaigns—can provide legislators and other officials with unmistakable evidence regarding the will of the electorate.

Political Action Committees.   Political action committees (PACs) are an outgrowth of the reform in federal election campaign practices that followed the Watergate scandal. A PAC is a group established for the purpose of contributing an organization's money toward the election of political candidates. The Federal Election Commission (FEC) permits PACs to contribute a maximum of $5,000 per candidate per election. Thus, PACs may contribute a total of $10,000 to a candidate who is in both a primary contest and the general election. FEC limits are indexed for inflation and adjusted for every election cycle. Individuals may only contribute $2,300 per candidate per election and $5,000 per year to a PAC.

Since their inception in the mid-1970s, PACs have enjoyed phenomenal growth. Each year PACs provide funds to several thousand candidates for federal office. Such money may be solicited (but not coerced) from an organization's employees. Large groups, such as the banking and finance industry, labor unions, and the insurance industry, have the resources of hundreds of PACs at their disposal. Of course, PAC money can be used collectively for candidates who support legislation favorable to an entire industry.

The use of such funds to support the campaigns of elected officials guarantees access to those officials. Thus, PACs have become a significant force in public affairs.

Political Education Activities.   During the past 30 years, corporations have increasingly attempted to politicize their employees. They issue newsletters on the major political issues confronting given industries along with the company's positions on these issues. Employees are instructed in the methods of grassroots lobbying: writing letters to legislators, taking action through membership groups, or visiting legislators in their home district offices. Moreover, some large organizations provide their employees with political education seminars. Elected officials and candidates are invited to corporate facilities, where they make presentations and meet groups of employees. In return, the officials are often given honoraria, usually in accordance with legally allowable limitations. Political education activities, then, play an increasingly important role in the conduct of public affairs programs.

Communications on Political Issues.   Corporations communicate on political issues chiefly through advocacy advertising and targeted communications, such as direct mail to community leaders or special audiences.

Advocacy advertising has become increasingly popular since the early 1970s, when Herbert Schmertz, vice president for public affairs of Mobil, decided that major media outlets seemed interested only in condemning large oil companies for their alleged role in the creation of the gasoline shortages of the day. Schmertz abandoned the use of news releases and other uncontrolled media to give the oil companies' side of the controversy. Instead, he began to buy advocacy advertising space in the nation's most prestigious newspapers and later bought time on cooperative broadcast networks. Schmertz's success in calling attention to his corporation's political views gave rise to a boom in the corporate use of advocacy advertising. Expect to see advocacy ads not only in national newspapers such as the *Washington Post* with its political emphasis in the Capital, but in the local newspaper of a legislator who is the target of a campaign.

Their proliferation has probably diminished their effectiveness, but they remain a major vehicle for corporate communication on political issues.

Political communications can also be aimed at community leaders or occupational groups. Professors of communication, for example, are frequently the recipients of slick reprints of speeches by the chief executive officers of television networks and other corporations. These reprints are only one of many forms of mailings to community leaders and members of various professions.

Political Support Activities.   A final public affairs action is the support a corporation, association, or other organization offers an incumbent legislator or a candidate. Some organizations offer free media training, with expert consultants hired for the occasion. Guidance in effective public speaking, group communication management techniques, and other interpersonal communication skills are also offered. Some organizations provide volunteers to work on political campaigns. Additionally, political support can be offered in the form of expertise and other services needed for orchestrating election campaign events such as fund-raisers and testimonial dinners. Donations of facilities, recruiting celebrities to appear at the events, and any number of other services can be offered.

Like other forms of public affairs activities, political support can ensure access to the officeholder at a later time.

Another form of political support called "soft money" became the hottest—and most controversial—form of lobbying in the 1990s. Corporations and individuals were allowed to give unlimited amounts of money to national political parties for voter registration, television advertising, get-out-the-vote campaigns, and other party activities. This unlimited "soft money" could be contributed to support the party, but not specific candidates. Federal legislation passed in 2002, however, now prohibits corporations, unions, and individuals from giving unlimited contributions to national political parties. But this ban on "soft money" does not apply to independent groups or PACs. They are free to raise as much money as corporations, unions, or individuals will give them. They can spend unlimited sums of money to influence federal elections as long as they operate independently of election campaigns, stop short of calling for a specific candidate's election or defeat, and stop airing advertising within 30 days of a primary election and 60 days of a general election.

To counter the flow of this "soft money," the 2002 Bipartisan Campaign Reform Act limited the flow of large contributions to the political parties, but groups soon exploited Section 527 of the Internal Revenue Code, which had been added in 1974 to allow tax-exempt contributions for political activities, including voter mobilization efforts and issue advocacy. The 527 groups claimed to rely on grassroots efforts by small donors to encourage civic engagement, yet one study found the biggest 527s got 44 percent of their contributions from just 25 deep-pocket donors. During the 2004 political campaigns, MoveOn.org and the Swift Boat Veterans for Truth were some of the most visible and passionate in activating political engagement; however, neither was in the top 5 among all 527 groups that raised an estimated $550 million to influence the political process. For the 2006 election cycle, the top four organizations in terms of financial contributions were the Service Employees International Union, American Federation of State, County and Municipal Employees, America Votes and Emily's List. During the 2008 campaign, Senators Obama and McCain expressed concern about the role of these independent groups in presidential campaigns and urged their donors to not support these groups. "Hard money" contributions to candidates for federal office continue to be strictly limited by the Federal Election Committee. However, with increasingly close relationships between candidates, especially incumbents, and PACs, it is likely that multimillion-dollar contributions of "soft money" to PACs will become the most certain of all paths to officeholder access.

Uncontrolled and Controlled Media

The practitioner's communication with public officials must largely be direct and interpersonal. The lobbyist or practitioner of public affairs uses uncontrolled media at the grassroots level. However, all forms of controlled media can be used both in direct contact with lawmakers and in grassroots communication with constituents. In general, then, the uniqueness of public affairs communication lies in the interaction that occurs directly with lawmakers and officials. To be effective, it should emphasize interpersonal, preferably one-on-one, communication.

Effective Communication

The communication flow in public affairs is best described as triangular (see Exhibit 6-b). The flow is targeted ultimately at lawmakers, in the legislative branch, or at regulation-makers, in the executive branch. Thus, communication is generally initiated from the private sector and flows appropriately toward those two targets. In many cases, however, communication is initiated in the executive branch. Presidents, governors, and mayors may lobby their respective legislative branches for the passage or defeat of a law. Sometimes officials in the executive branch lobby a particular audience in the private sector to bring pressure on the legislative branch. Legislators often refer to this as "going over their heads to the people." Some U.S. presidents have been particularly fond of this form of lobbying.

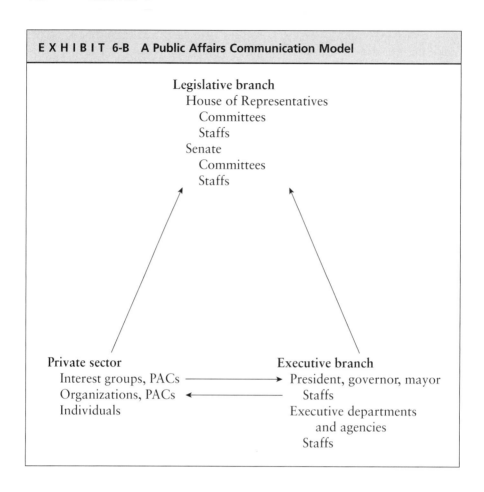

EXHIBIT 6-B   A Public Affairs Communication Model

Legislative branch
　House of Representatives
　　Committees
　　Staffs
　Senate
　　Committees
　　Staffs

Private sector
　Interest groups, PACs ⟶
　Organizations, PACs ⟵
　Individuals

Executive branch
　President, governor, mayor
　Staffs
　Executive departments
　　and agencies
　Staffs

The nine principles of effective communication discussed in Chapter 2 all apply in public affairs. Of special concern, however, is *selective exposure*. Public affairs, more than other forms of public relations, deals with legislation and regulations that are controversial. Therefore, it is important that the practitioner categorize the targeted receivers based on their agreement or disagreement with the public affairs messages. As suggested in Chapter 2, the terms that coincide with the Likert scale can be useful in this process. Thus, targeted legislators or other officials should be rated as "positives," "somewhat positives," "undecideds," "somewhat negatives," or "negatives." The selective exposure principle is applicable in this situation. The practitioner should thus begin persuasive efforts with the positives. Next to be targeted are the somewhat positives, then the undecideds, and last, if at all, the somewhat negatives. The pure negatives have hardened attitudes against the practitioner's cause and should not be targeted for communication. To communicate with those strongly opposed to the message is usually counterproductive; it simply makes them more determined and sometimes more active in their opposition.

Thus, the selective exposure principle of effective communication bears reiteration because of its special significance in public affairs. It is not necessary to convince everyone, just a few key votes that will swing the outcome. During the 2008 presidential election, selective exposure largely explained how some areas of the country seldom saw a political advertisement while other "swing states" were bombarded with thousands of ads and a flood of direct mail appeals.

All other principles of effective communication should also be observed. Each one can contribute to the success of public affairs programs.

EVALUATION

In public affairs, the measurement of impact and output objectives is somewhat different from the general methods of assessment presented in Chapter 2.

Evaluating Impact Objectives

There are two differences in the measurement of impact objectives for public affairs. First, message exposure, message comprehension, and message retention are not measured in the same way. The primary target audiences for public affairs are legislators and officials. The media, however, are used essentially to reach the *constituents* of these public officials. And though the officials themselves are usually media sensitive, message exposure in public affairs usually refers to *constituent* exposure.

The second difference in the measurement of impact objectives is that surveys or other quantitative methods of research cannot be used with the primary target audiences because legislators and officials will not usually take the time to respond to such PR surveys. Thus, nonquantitative measurements of message exposure and message retention are used in assessing the results of informational objectives.

Message comprehension, of course, can be measured, as usual, by the application of readability formulas. This will give the practitioner an indication of the *potential* for comprehension, not actual audience comprehension, which can be measured using nonquantitative research methods.

These same generalizations are applicable to attitude and behavioral objectives. Surveys among the primary audience are generally impossible, so the practitioner must rely on the nonquantitative research methods discussed earlier in this chapter—voting records or accomplishments, conversations, use of the practitioner's materials, and public statements by the targeted legislators or officials. At the grassroots level, of course, surveys are useful and should be employed to evaluate the impact objectives.

Evaluating Output Objectives

The practitioner needs to evaluate both forms of public affairs objectives. Output objectives can be measured through counting presentations and materials and through making qualitative value judgments. This is especially important in public affairs since surveys are impractical with the primary audiences. Evaluation of public affairs, then, ultimately focuses on observing the voting behavior or actions of legislators and other public officials. The practitioners in this chapter's cases accomplished all of their stated objectives remarkably well. In addition to informing their various targeted audiences, they also met their legislative or regulatory goals.

SUMMARY

Research for public affairs concentrates on problem assessment through issues management and on identifying and understanding target audiences. Audiences are usually in the legislative or executive branch of government, at various levels. Information about these officials consists of voting records, accomplishments, and public stands on issues.

Impact and output objectives are both useful in public affairs. Impact objectives consist of providing the target audience with information or influencing its attitudes or behavior, in this case, voting behavior. Output objectives catalog the practitioner's communication efforts without reference to the desired impact.

The most essential activities in public affairs programming are fact-finding, coalition building, direct lobbying, grassroots (indirect) lobbying, the use of PACs, political education, communications on political issues, and political support activities. Of special significance in lobbying is the principle of selective exposure. Lawmakers to be lobbied should be categorized as "positives," "somewhat positives," "undecideds," "somewhat negatives," or "negatives." The positives through the undecideds should be targeted for lobbying; the somewhat negatives should be targeted with caution, and the negatives, not at all.

Evaluation is not the same for public affairs as for other forms of public relations. Media exposure or placement does not ensure contact with legislators, and legislators and officials are often unresponsive to PR surveys. Nonquantitative measurements of impact objectives are thus more useful. Output objectives, of course, are measured by the same means as usual—observation and quantification. The ultimate means of evaluation in public affairs, however, is the voting behavior of the target audience.

READINGS ON PUBLIC AFFAIRS

"The Advocacy Book: Directory of Public Affairs & Grassroots Lobbying Firms," *Campaigns & Elections* 26 (2005): 84–95.

Alexander, Robert M. *Rolling the Dice with State Initiatives: Interest Group Involvement in Ballot Campaigns.* Westport, CT: Praeger, 2002.

Beder, Sharon. "Public Relations' Role in Manufacturing Artificial Grass Roots Coalitions," *Public Relations Quarterly* 43 (summer 1998): 20–23.

Brown, Clyde, and Herbert Waltzer. "Organized Interest Advertorials," *Harvard International Journal of Press/Politics* 9 (fall 2004): 25–48.

Cigler, Allan J., and Burdett A. Loomis. *Interest Group Politics*, 7th ed. Washington, DC: Congressional Quarterly, 2007.

Cook-Anderson, Gretchen. "Effectively Winning over Young Voters," *Public Relations Tactics* 11 (July 2004): 12.

Dennis, Lloyd B. *Practical Public Affairs in an Era of Change*. Lanham, MD: University Press of America, 1995.

Gabriel, Edward M. "The Changing Face of Public Affairs in Washington," *Public Relations Quarterly* 37 (winter 1992): 24ff.

Goldstein, Kenneth M. *Interest Groups, Lobbying and Participation in America*. Port Chester, NY: Cambridge University Press, 1999.

Graziano, Luigi. *Lobbying, Pluralism, and Democracy*. New York: Palgrave, 2001.

Grefe, Edward A., and Martin Linsky. *The New Corporate Activism: Harnessing the Power of Grassroots Tactics for Your Organization*. New York: McGraw-Hill, 1996.

Grossman, Gene M., and Elhanan Helpman. *Special Interest Politics*. Cambridge, MA: MIT, 2001.

Guyer, Robert L. *Guide to State Legislative Lobbying*. Gainesville, FL: Engineering THE LAW, 2003.

Hallahn, Kirk. "Inactive Publics: The Forgotten Publics in Public Relations," *Public Relations Review* 26 (winter 2000): 499.

Harris, Phil, and Craig S Fleisher, eds. *Handbook of Public Affairs*. London: Sage Publications, 2005.

Heath, Robert L. *Strategic Issue Management: Organizations and Public Policy Challenges*. Thousand Oaks, CA: Sage Publications, 1997.

Jeffries, Leo W. *Urban Communication Systems: Neighborhoods and the Search for Community*. Cresskill, NJ: Hampton Press, 2001.

Johnson, Haynes, and David Broder. *The System: The American Way of Politics at the Breaking Point*. Boston: Little, Brown, 1997.

Kaid, Lynda Lee, ed. *Handbook of Political Communication Research*. Mahwah, NJ: Erlbaum, 2004.

Kramer, Tony, and Wes Pedersen, eds. *Winning at the Grassroots: A Comprehensive Manual for Corporations and Associations*. Washington, DC: Public Affairs Council, 2000.

Ledingham, John A. "Government-Community Relationships: Extending the Relational Theory of Public Relations," *Public Relations Review* 27 (fall 2001): 285.

Lerbinger, Otto. *Corporate Public Affairs: Interacting With Interest Groups, Media, and Government*. Mahwah, NJ: Erlbaum, 2005.

Levin, David. "Framing Peace Policies: The Competition for Resonant Themes," *Political Communication* 22 (January–March 2005): 83–108.

Lipsitz, Keena, Christine Trost, Matthew Grossmann, and John Sides. "What Voters Want From Political Campaign Communication," *Political Communication* 22 (July–September 2005): 337–354.

Long, Rich. "PR and GR: So Happy Together?" *Public Relations Strategist* 8 (summer 2002): 14–18.

Lordan, Edward J. "Trivial Pursuit in the '04 Campaign: Simple, Issue-free and Happy to Stay That Way," *Public Relations Quarterly* 49 (fall 2004): 27–29.

Mack, Charles S. *Business, Politics, and the Practice of Government Relations*. Westport, CT: Quorum Books, 1997.

Murray, Bobbi. "Money for Nothing," *The Nation* 277 (September 8, 2003): 25.

Ortega, Felix. "Politics in the New Public Space," *International Review of Sociology* 14 (July 2004): 205–207.

Park, Hyun Soon, and Sejung Marina Choi. "Focus Group Interviews: The Internet as a Political Campaign Medium," *Public Relations Quarterly* 47 (winter 2002): 36.

Pinkham, Doug. "What it Takes to Work in Public Affairs and Public Relations," *Public Relations Quarterly* 49 (spring 2004): 15ff.

Poston, Patty. "Grassroots Communications Reconsidered," *Public Relations Tactics* 9 (September 2002): 12–13.

Richards, Barry. "The Emotional Deficit in Political Communication," *Political Communication* 21 (July–September 2004): 339–352.

Smith, Hedrick. *The Power Game: How Washington Works*. New York: Random House, 1988.

Solomon, Dan. "Getting Involved: Health Care Reform in a Web 2.0 World," *Public Relations Tactics* 15 (March 2008): 14.

Terry, Valerie. "Lobbying: Fantasy, Reality or Both? A Health Care Public Policy Case Study," *Journal of Public Affairs* 1 (August 2001): 266ff.

Thomson, Stuart, Steve John, and George J. Mitchell. *Public Affairs in Practice: A Practical Guide to Lobbying*. London: Kogan Page. 2007.

Trento, Susan. *Power House: Robert Keith Gray and the Selling of Access and Influence in Washington*. New York: St. Martins Press, 1992.

Ward, Hugh. "Pressure Politics: A Game-Theoretical Investigation of Lobbying and the Measurement of Power," *Journal of Theoretical Politics* 16 (January 2004): 31–52.

Public Affairs and Government Relations Cases

Case 6-1

Funding for medical care remains a top concern of the public and most years there are new Congressional initiatives affecting the funding of specific programs. In this case, the American Medical Association (AMA) felt compelled to weigh in on major changes to funding for the Medicare program. Exhibit 6-1a is news release about the impending Medicare program cuts, and Exhibit 6-1b is a news release outlining the campaign.

Keep Medicare's Promise: Stop Medicare Cuts to Doctors

American Medical Association

SUMMARY

Steep Medicare physician payment cuts would begin January 1, 2007, unless Congress intervened, and getting Congress to act during an election year posed a challenge. The AMA launched a national public affairs campaign to engage physicians and seniors to focus congressional attention on the issue. Using existing and AMA-created news-hooks, including the release of primary research, the AMA gained 741 news reports, including 12 supportive editorials. The media attention resulted in nearly one million contacts to Congress, and ultimately congressional action to stop the 2007 payment cut in December 2006.

RESEARCH

Concerned that seniors' access to physician care would be harmed if Medicare cuts occurred as planned, the AMA needed data to back up the claim. It was also important to show the depth of the cuts and that the AMA was not alone in calling for congressional action. Using both primary (two AMA surveys) and secondary research (MedPAC and Medicare Trustees reports), the AMA was able to state with confidence that:

- Nearly half, 45 percent, of the physicians surveyed say the 2007 Medicare cut will force them to either decrease or stop seeing new Medicare patients.

- Seven out of 10 Americans are not aware of impending Medicare physician payment cuts.

When told about the cuts:

- Eighty-six percent are concerned that access to care for Medicare patients will be hurt.

- Eighty-two percent of current Medicare patients (age 65+) are concerned that access to care will be hurt.

- A staggering 93 percent of baby boomers age 45–54 are concerned that access to care will be hurt.

- About 25 percent of Medicare patients seeking a new primary care physician already have problems finding one.

Congress should update 2007 Medicare physician payments 2.8 percent in line with practice cost increases, per the recommendation of MedPAC, the commission that advises Congress on Medicare. Without action, Medicare would cut physician payments nearly 40 percent over the next nine years, while practice costs increased about 20 percent. The 2007 cut alone was estimated at 5 percent.

PLANNING

Through the public affairs campaign, the AMA needed to motivate physicians and Medicare patients to contact members of Congress and demand action to stop the Medicare cuts. Key objectives included:

- Field physician survey in the first quarter of 2006.

- Focus media outreach in 14 states based on congressional targets, with an emphasis on television outreach and op-eds.

- Keep pressure on lawmakers to act with consistent coverage on the issue in Washington health policy trade press.

- Identify a partner outside of medicine who could help highlight the cuts impact on patients. (Because Medicare rates also apply to Tricare, we looked for a partner who could highlight the cuts impact on military families.)

- Increase number of contacts to Congress through the AMA grassroots network by 20 percent over the previous year.

Because of the congressional calendar, the bulk of the campaign was implemented in the second half of 2006, and a proactive media plan was created specifically for June to October 2006.

EXECUTION

With an emphasis on the message that Medicare cuts would harm seniors' access to physician care, the AMA media relations team focused on proactive outreach to gain media coverage on the issue.

Tactics included

- Released primary research on physician reaction to the Medicare cuts. Timed to coincide with the AMA's National Advocacy Conference in March, a press release and a video news release featuring the AMA immediate-past president, a Medicare patient and a concerned citizen highlighted the key finding that 45 percent of doctors would limit the number of new Medicare patients they treat if the cuts occurred. The VNR reached over two-million viewers and ran on NBC News in NYC and FOX News. Associated Press, UPI, and health policy papers like Congressional Quarterly and Inside CMS all covered the survey.

- Wrote and customized an op-ed by the AMA president that included a call to action, which was placed in nine target state newspapers during the critical months of August to October. Placements included the *Cincinnati Inquirer* and the *Rochester Democrat and Chronicle*.

- Wrote and placed six letters to the editor by AMA Board members in high-profile publications, including *The Wall Street Journal, Washington Post, Chicago Tribune* online version, and *Modern Healthcare*.

- Conducted eight local media tours in key states between May and August featuring an AMA Board member and local physicians. Tours included press conferences and editorial board meetings, and the Florida media tour included a spokesman from the Military Officers Association of America (MOAA) to highlight the cuts impact on military families.

- Released primary research on public reaction to the cuts with a satellite media tour and telephone press briefing for print reporters, which gained 30 broadcast interviews, all in key congressional markets, and articles in *Los Angeles Times, Fort Worth Star-Telegram,* and *CharlotteObserver*. New York City's ABC affiliate created its own segment on the issue featuring the AMA and local, sympathetic patients, and doctors provided by the AMA—and a positive statement from Senator Clinton.

- Held the "Clock is Ticking" press conference at the National Press Club in Washington, D.C., in early September with MOAA and doctors from across the nation to lobby Congress on the urgent need for action. The press conference was covered by *CQ HealthBeat, The Hill, InsideHealthPolicy, UPI, All Headline News,* BNA's *Health Care Daily Report,* and *CongressDaily*.

- Wrote and posted four blogs by the AMA Board chair to The Hill "Congress Blog" Web site, an inside-the-beltway print and online publication aimed at members of Congress and their staff. The blogs were posted in November and December as the window for congressional action narrowed.

- Wrote a mat release on the theme of "Helping Seniors Stay Active and Healthy: A Doctor's Care Makes a Difference" that included healthy living tips and a direct call for seniors to call Congress if they wanted their doctor to be there for them. The article was published in 100 papers, including the *FresnoBee, The Star-Ledger,* and *JournalStar*.

- Pitched target states on straight news articles, resulting in articles on the Medicare cuts impact on local seniors in key newspapers, including *The Star-Ledger, Kansas City Star,* and *St. Louis Post-Dispatch.*

EVALUATION

On December 9, 2006, Congress voted to stop the 2007 Medicare physician payment cut and continue to pay physicians at the current payment rate.

More than 741 news reports on Medicare physician payment cuts that included an AMA mention, resulting in 237 million media impressions. Of the 475 articles tracked through Vocus, 86 percent were positive and 14 percent were neutral.

Nearly one million contacts to Congress were made through the AMA grassroots network Web site and phone number, an 87 percent increase over the previous year.

Engaged the MOAA as a partner to bring home the impact of Medicare cuts on military families' access to care.

E X H I B I T 6-1a News Release on Medicare Cuts

For Immediate Release:
September 7, 2006
As "Grandparents' Day" Approaches

Most Americans Alarmed by Impending Medicare Cuts That Will Harm Seniors' Access to Care

Congressional Action Needed Now to Avert Medicare Physician Payment Cuts

WASHINGTON—A new national poll released today shows that the vast majority of Americans, 86 percent, are concerned that seniors' access to health care will be hurt if impending cuts in Medicare physician payment go through beginning January 1, according to the American Medical Association (AMA). Without congressional action, Medicare will cut physician payments nearly 40 percent over the next nine years, while practice costs increase at least 20 percent. As Congress returns to Washington this week, there's less than one month left on the congressional calendar to stop Medicare physician payment cuts.

"Seven out of 10 Americans are not aware of impending Medicare physician payment cuts, but when told about the cuts, 86 percent are concerned that access to care for Medicare patients will be hurt," said AMA Board Member Dr. William A. Hazel, Jr., M.D.

"Seniors are concerned about their own access to health care services as physicians are forced to make difficult practice decisions because of Medicare cuts," said Dr. Hazel. "Eighty-two percent of current Medicare patients are concerned about the cuts impact on their access to health care. What's really startling is the huge number of baby boomers concerned about the cuts impact on Medicare patients' access to care."

"A staggering 93 percent of baby boomers age 45-54 are concerned about the cuts impact on access to care," said Dr. Hazel. "No doubt this grave concern reflects

EXHIBIT 6-1a (Continued)

worry for parents who currently rely on Medicare, and for their own future as Medicare patients."

In just five years, the first wave of baby boomers will reach age 65, and will turn to Medicare for health care. The government plans to cut almost 200 billion dollars over the next nine years from physician care for seniors—just as baby boomers are aging into the Medicare program by the millions.

"Congress needs to stop the Medicare cuts and instead tie physician payments to the cost of caring for America's seniors," said Dr. Hazel. "Physicians are committed to caring for their senior patients, but year after year of payment cuts that fall far below practice cost increases make it difficult to continue doing so."

The AMA is asking Congress to set Medicare on the right course for the future by stopping the cuts and tying physician payments to increases in practice costs. Next week, physicians from across the country representing many state and medical specialty societies will unite to pay a "House Call" on their lawmakers in Washington and urge them to act before time runs out.

American's concerns about the cuts impact on seniors' access to health care are legitimate. A national survey of physicians conducted earlier this year by the AMA found that nearly half, 45 percent, will be forced to decrease or stop taking new Medicare patients if the planned cuts go through.

"The government made a promise to provide America's seniors with health care, now this Congress must fulfill that promise," said Dr. Hazel. "Congress must preserve seniors' access to health care by stopping Medicare physician payment cuts now, before its too late."

EDITORS NOTE: A telephone survey of 1,031 adults 18 years of age and older living in the continental United States was conducted by Opinion Research Corporation for the AMA from July 14–17, 2006. The margin of error for the survey is +/–3 percent.

EDITORS NOTE: Data on the number of Medicare patients per state and the amount of federal dollars each state will lose that should go toward caring for seniors is available at www.ama-assn.org.

BROADCAST NOTE: Audio soundbite of AMA Board Member William A Hazel, Jr., M.D. is available at www.ama-assn.org for your use.

EXHIBIT 6-1b   News Release Outlines Campaign

For Immediate Release
September 13, 2006

AMA Outlines End-of-Congress Campaign to Protect Seniors' Access to Health Care

Physicians Pay a "House Call" on Congress to Demand Action on Medicare Cuts

WASHINGTON, DC—This week, physicians are converging on Washington to push for Congress to stop Medicare cuts and tie physician payments to practice cost increases before recessing in just a few weeks.

Hundreds of physicians from across the country, representing the AMA, state and specialty societies, are visiting Capitol Hill over the next two weeks to pay a "House Call" on Congress to urge immediate action on Medicare physician payment cuts.

The government plans to cut Medicare physician reimbursement by about 40 percent over the next nine years, forcing physicians to make tough practice choices. The physician visits are just one piece of the AMA campaign to stop the cuts, unveiled today at a press conference in Washington, D.C.

"The clock is ticking," said AMA Board Chair Cecil B. Wilson, M.D. "With less than one month until Congress recesses and goes home for the November election—the time for action is now."

"An AMA poll released last week shows that, when told about the cuts, 86 percent of Americans are concerned that access to care for Medicare patients will be hurt," said Dr. Wilson. "Patients concerns are justified. If Congress lets the cuts go through, physicians will be forced to make difficult practice decisions. Nearly half, 45 percent, of physicians tell the AMA they will be forced to reduce or stop taking new Medicare patients if the cuts take place January 1. These cuts follow five years during which Medicare payments have not kept up with practice cost increases. In fact, 2006 payment rates are about the same as they were in 2001."

E X H I B I T 6-1b   (Continued)

The AMA campaign includes a $1.5 million advertising campaign. Print advertisements are currently running in inside-the-Beltway and national media outlets, including *US News & World Report, Newsweek, Prevention, Parents,* and *Ladies Home Journal.* The national ads portray seniors' "hands" and relay the message that seniors shouldn't have to fight for the health care Medicare promised them. Washington issue ads include a stop watch with the message "time is running out."

The AMA is educating and activating patients across the country through its 1.2-million member "Patients' Action Network," that lets patients contact their legislators and make their voices heard. This year the network has generated more than 560,000 patient contacts to Congress urging immediate action to stop Medicare physician payment cuts.

Throughout the summer and into the fall, AMA leaders and local physicians have barnstormed states across the country through the AMA "House Call" program to raise awareness among seniors and lawmakers of the impending cuts and the impact they will have on seniors' access to care.

Congress knows it needs to stop the cuts. Eighty Senators sent a letter to the U.S. Senate leadership urging immediate action before the congressional recess at the end of the month. This week, a similar sign-on letter is expected to be delivered to the U.S. House of Representatives leadership with more than 240 signatures.

"Patients need action," said Dr. Wilson. "Nothing less than access to health care for America's seniors hangs in the balance."

Case 6-2

Changes in behavior often involve public education efforts coupled with public policy initiatives. California decided to eliminate unhealthy food and beverages from all public schools in an effort to reduce childhood obesity. Exhibit 6-2a is news release about a study of overweight children, Exhibit 6-2b is a program fact sheet, and Exhibit 6-2c is a policy brief on "The Growing Epidemic."

Giving Legislators a Role in Correcting California's Childhood Obesity Crisis

California Center for Public Health with Brown-Miller Communications, Inc.

SUMMARY

In the face of a growing childhood obesity crisis, California's legislators had repeatedly taken a back seat role, dismissing obesity as a personal choice issue. A new opportunity to address this crisis arose in 2005 when landmark legislation was introduced that would make California the nation's leader in mandating healthy school environments. Similar legislation had been roundly defeated in heated partisan battles, but the California Center for Public Advocacy (CCPHA), working with Brown-Miller Communications, created a campaign to win passage of the legislation using media advocacy to make legislators accountable for the rising obesity numbers in their own district.

SITUATION ANALYSIS

The childhood obesity crisis in California is unparalleled and increasing at an uncontrolled rate. One out of four children in California is overweight, at risk for diabetes and other chronic diseases, and likely to be an obese adult who suffers from expensive and preventable illnesses. Despite this reality, little political action has been taken to address the problem, with politicians regularly dismissing obesity as a personal choice issue.

A new opportunity to address this crisis arose in 2005 when landmark legislation (SB 12, eliminating junk food in all public schools K–12; and SB 965, banning sodas in high schools) was introduced that would make California the nation's leader in mandating healthy school environments. Similar legislation had

Courtesy California Center for Public Health

been roundly defeated in heated partisan battles, but the CCPHA, working with Brown-Miller Communications, created a campaign to win passage of the legislation using an innovative combination of research, education, media advocacy, and community relations.

RESEARCH

Research focused in three separate areas:

- To best understand and present the local impact of the childhood obesity crisis, data from the California FitnessGram, administered to every fifth, seventh, and ninth grade public school student in California, was analyzed by California legislative district.

- The voting records of all 80 California State Assembly members were researched to determine who traditionally supported healthy standards, who opposed similar legislation and, finally, which legislators were sitting on the fence and susceptible to media pressure.

- Media content research was conducted to determine which news outlets were likely to play a supporting role based on former editorial positions.

Collectively, the research informed the entire advocacy campaign and allowed for precise targeting that would maximize the very limited resources available. The analyzed data also served as a powerful tool to educate policy makers and community advocates on the severity of the issue and the need for action.

PLANNING

Based on the research, the following plan was developed:

Goal

- Revolutionize the nutrition environment for California children by passing legislation that removes unhealthy food and beverages from all public schools.

Target Audiences

- Primary—State legislators, with an emphasis on undecided legislators
- Secondary—Influential media in markets where research showed undecided legislators live and local community advocates

Objectives

- Surround 15 targeted "undecided" legislators with media attention on the rising obesity rates in their districts to influence a "yes" vote for passage of the bills

- Enlist papers throughout the state to take a supportive editorial position and call on their legislators to vote for passage of SB 12 and SB 965

- Build a historic coalition, including former adversaries, to lobby for bill passage

- Provide Governor Schwarzenegger a leadership platform to support the health of California's children by appealing to him to push for legislative passage, break partisan blocks, and sign the landmark legislation

Strategies

- Launch a coordinated media advocacy campaign strategically timed to coincide with key voting dates and to negate the chance for the opposition to release a counter campaign.

- Create and release localized research studies for every legislative district that translate statewide information to community-level data and stimulate a rising tide of concern that the problem is worsening and demands immediate action.

- Foster an expectation among the media that legislators have the responsibility and authority to address the local obesity crisis and encourage reporters to quote legislators in their articles.

- Treat small daily, weekly, and ethnic papers in targeted legislative districts like major papers by offering embargoed stories and scheduling local, state, and national expert interviews.

EXECUTION

Following are some of the specific actions taken:

- A policy brief, The Growing Epidemic: Child Overweight Rates on the Rise, was developed showing the rise in childhood obesity rates by legislative districts over a three-year period and supplemented by fact sheets tailored for each legislative district. Complete press materials were created to assist in the release of this information.

- Local and statewide spokespersons were identified and message trainings held. Each spokesperson was given specific children's health information for their legislative district as well as background on their legislator's voting record and a battery of media advocacy tools, including op-eds and template letters to the editor.

- The study was released on an embargoed basis to local media in targeted legislative districts. Each reporter was personally contacted and given specific fact sheets for their geographic jurisdiction as well as a list of local spokespersons and legislators.

- All of the research study information and press materials were simultaneously released to California legislators and their Sacramento and district staffs so that they could make wise voting decisions and respond to media inquiries.

- A positive media environment was created through editorial board meetings, letters to the editor, and locally generated opinion editorials.

- Regular meetings were held with the Governor's office to gain his support and show him how to use the study and bills to maximize his political clout and safely break with his party.

- Media alerts and press releases were issued for the release of the study and after the vote on each bill.

- Additional press outreach was conducted during the Governor's obesity conference in support of all partners and the supportive legislators.

EVALUATION

The success of the campaign was realized with the decisive passage of both SB 12 and SB 965. The following are some additional measures of success:

- The targeted media outreach campaign to media in all 15 targeted legislative districts swayed 12 of the 15 Assembly members to vote for SB 12 and 11 of the 15 to support SB 965.

- The strategy to capture legislators on the record was also successful. Nearly half of the 80 Assembly members were quoted or mentioned in articles. For example, the headline of the Fremont Argus said, "Oh Torrico: Your area's kids put on pounds."

- Large- and small-circulation newspapers throughout California, including the *Los Angeles Times, The Sacramento Bee, San Francisco Chronicle, San Diego Union-Tribune, La Opinión, San Bernardino Sun, The Modesto Bee,* and *Ventura County Star,* all used their editorial power to urge local lawmakers to vote for passage of the bills. "We favor the legislation. Schools should be part of the solution not part of the problem," said an editorial in the *Inland Valley Bulletin.* In addition, editorial space was given to letters to the editor, opinion editorials, and open forum submissions.

- The media and promotional campaign helped build and solidify a coalition of influential businesses, education and associations, including a former adversary, the California School Food Service Association, to mobilize their constituents and work together for passage of the bills.

- Governor Schwarzenegger culminated his September Obesity Summit by signing both the bills. He highlighted in his 2006 State of the State speech that one of California's biggest accomplishments was making "our schools healthier by becoming the only state in the union to ban sodas and junk food from our schools." He closed his speech with a story about the success of working in a bipartisan manner. "One day I ran into Senator Martha Escutia, and she told me about her bill to get sodas and junk foods out of schools. And I said, 'I love that idea. It's great to fight obesity. Let's do it together.' And we did. And we got it passed."

EXHIBIT 6-2a   News Release

CONTACT: **Dr. Harold Goldstein**   -or-   **Paula Hamilton**
            CA Center for Public Health Advocacy   Brown≡Miller Communications
            (530) 297-6000   (800) 710-9333

Embargoed Until August 25, 2005

New Study Shows 6 Percent Jump in the
Number of Overweight Children in California

Sacramento, CA, August 25, 2005... While Californians may be better informed about the obesity crisis than ever before, a study released today shows the number of overweight children in California continues to rise. Based on their analysis of children's fitness statistics, the California Center for Public Health Advocacy (CCPHA) reports that the state's prevalence of overweight children has increased 6.2 percent in three years.

"Though we may all know there's a problem, far too little has been done to address the childhood obesity epidemic. The crisis is getting worse," says Dr. Harold Goldstein, CCPHA executive director. "In nearly 90 percent of all state Assembly Districts, we saw the number of overweight children increase. Correcting this crisis must become a top priority for California lawmakers."

Using data from the 2004 California Physical Fitness Test, which is administered in California public schools to fifth, seventh and ninth graders, the study shows that childhood overweight rates have climbed to 28.1 per 100 students, up from 26.5 per 100 students in 2001. The study also reports that the prevalence of overweight increased for every ethnicity, age and gender group studied. More than a third of the state's Assembly Districts saw double-digit rates of growth.

To understand the extent of the crisis from a local perspective, *The Growing Epidemic: Child Overweight Rates on the Rise in California Assembly Districts* reports the information by

Courtesy California Center for Public Health

E X H I B I T 6-2a   (Continued)

state Assembly District. The Los Angeles region reported some of the most disturbing data, where eight out of the state's ten Assembly Districts with the highest percentage of overweight children were recorded.

"This study highlights the childhood obesity epidemic growing across California. More than one out of every four children in our state is overweight. This crisis poses serious health risks for our children and will negatively impact the future of California," said Governor Schwarzenegger. "All of us must respond boldly and decisively to address this problem and as Governor I am committed to educating and motivating our children to live an active, healthy lifestyle. I urge all Californians - government leaders, parents, teachers, coaches, business owners and citizens - to join me as we work together to address this serious problem."

The growing epidemic of overweight children is already taking its toll. Pediatricians today regularly treat children afflicted with type 2 diabetes, a disease once referred to as adult-onset diabetes and virtually unheard of among children a decade ago. Additionally, overweight children are more likely to be obese adults and suffer from expensive and preventable illnesses, and they may die prematurely. If policymakers ignore this trend, experts warn that state and local governments face a future marred by runaway healthcare costs, a jeopardized work force and an increasing burden on government finances.

Given the increasing prevalence of overweight children, the report suggests that it is not enough to tell children to eat better and get more exercise. "State and local leaders must enact polices to change conditions in schools and communities that undermine parents' efforts to protect their children," Goldstein said.

CCPHA is an independent, nonpartisan, nonprofit organization founded by the California Public Health Association-North and the Southern California Public Health Association. Support for the 2004 study was provided by a grant from the California Vitamin Cases Consumer Settlement Fund. The 2001 analysis was funded by a grant from The Robert Wood Johnson Foundation. Copies of the study, policy brief and Assembly District fact sheets are available at the CCPHA Web site at: http://www.publichealthadvocacy.org.

-0-

NOTE TO EDITORS: copy of the policy brief and press materials are available at: http://www.publichealthadvocacy.org/policy_brief/overweight2004.html

E X H I B I T   6-2b   Fact Sheet

CALIFORNIA CENTER FOR
PUBLIC HEALTH ADVOCACY

Overweight Children in California, 2004

1st Senate District

THE PROBLEM

The California Center for Public Health Advocacy analyzed results of the 2004 California Physical Fitness Test for 5th, 7th and 9th graders. The analysis shows that among all students in the 1st Senate District:

- **21.0% of children were overweight in 2004, up from 18.3% in 2001.**

THE EFFECT

- **Overweight children face a greater risk of developing many health problems during childhood,** including type 2 diabetes, high blood pressure, asthma, orthopedic problems and gallstones, as well as low self-esteem, poor body image, and depression.

- **Overweight children are more likely to be obese as adults,** putting them at a much higher risk for heart disease, cancer, stroke, and diabetes later in life.

- **Overweight, obesity and physical inactivity are estimated to cost California $28 billion during 2005** for medical care, worker's compensation, and lost productivity.

WHAT CAN BE DONE

To address the epidemic of overweight chidren, state and local leaders must address the conditions in schools and communities that contribute to this crisis and that undermine parents' efforts to protect their children's health. The California Center for Public Health Advocacy recommends the following actions:

- Institute healthy food and beverage standards in places where children spend time.
- Ensure quality physical education for all children.
- Eliminate advertising of unhealthy foods and beverages to children.
- Require health insurance to cover nutrition counseling and physical activity.
- Make school recreation facilities available for after-hours use.
- Provide safe roadway access for walking and biking.
- Provide financial incentives that bring grocery stores and recreation facilities to low-income communities.

NOTE: The term overweight as used in CCPHA's analysis of the California Physical Fitness Test data is based on the assessment standards therein. For additional information and references, see CCPHA's full report on this study, available at www.publichealthadvocacy.org.

Support for this project was provided by a grant from The California Vitamin Cases Consumer Settlement Fund. © August 2005 CCPHA

The California Center for Public Health Advocacy is a nonpartisan, nonprofit organization established by the Northern and Southern California Public Health Associations.

Post Office Box 2309, Davis CA 95617   (530) 297-6000   http://www.publichealthadvocacy.org

Courtesy California Center for Public Health

E X H I B I T 6-2b   (Continued)

Overweight Children in California, 2004

1st SENATE DISTRICT
http://republican.sen.ca.gov/web/1/
State Capitol - (916) 445-5788; District Office - (916) 969-8232

The 1st S.D. consists of all of Alpine, Amador, Calaveras, El Dorado, Lassen, Modoc, Mono, Plumas and Sierra Counties, as well as parts of Nevada, Placer and Sacramento Counties, including the cities of Folsom, Roseville, and parts of Arden-Arcade, Carmichael and Elk Grove.

Dave Cox (R) represents the 1st District; he was elected for a four-year term in November 2004. Term limit: 2012.

Overweight Students: 1st S.D. and California - 2004
By Gender, Grade and Ethnicity

	1st SENATE DISTRICT	CALIFORNIA
All Students Tested	21.0%	28.1%
GENDER		
Girls	15.9%	22.0%
Boys	25.8%	33.9%
GRADE		
5th Graders	21.3%	29.3%
7th Graders	22.3%	29.1%
9th Graders	19.4%	25.4%
ETHNICITY		
African-American	27.3%	28.7%
American Indian / Alaskan Native	27.3%	31.7%
Asian	19.3%	17.9%
Filipino	21.0%	24.7%
Latino	30.2%	35.4%
Pacific Islander	29.3%	35.9%
White	18.7%	20.6%
Other	17.7%	24.4%

NOTE: The terms overweight and unfit as used in the California Center for Public Health Advocacy analysis of the California Physical Fitness Test are based on the assessment standards therein. For additional information see the Center's full report on the analysis, available at http://www.publichealthadvocacy.org/.

Demographics of Students Tested: 1st S.D. and California - 2004

	1st Senate District	California
Total of All Students Tested	37,830	1,375,214
Percentage of Students Tested		
African-American	5%	8%
American Indian / Alaskan Native	2%	1%
Asian	5%	8%
Filipino	2%	3%
Latino	14%	45%
Pacific Islander	1%	1%
White	68%	33%
Other	3%	1%

Data source: from the California Center for Public Health Advocacy (CCPHA) analysis of the 2001 and 2004 California Physical Fitness Test. For additional information contact CCPHA at Post Office Box 2309, Davis CA 95617; (530) 297-6000; http://www.publichealthadvocacy.org. Support for this project was provided by a grant from The California Vitamin Cases Consumer Settlement Fund. © August 2005 CCPHA

EXHIBIT 6-2c   Policy Brief

CALIFORNIA CENTER FOR
PUBLIC HEALTH ADVOCACY

THE GROWING EPIDEMIC

POLICY BRIEF NO. 4   AUGUST 2005

CHILD OVERWEIGHT RATES ON THE RISE IN CALIFORNIA ASSEMBLY DISTRICTS

SUMMARY

In 2002, the California Center for Public Health Advocacy (CCPHA) released a study reporting that 26.5 out of every 100 children enrolled in grades 5, 7, and 9 in California in 2001 were overweight. In this updated study, CCPHA reports that in 2004 childhood overweight rates had increased by 6%, to 28.1 out of every 100 children. Between 2001 and 2004, the percentage of overweight children increased among all demographic groups: boys and girls, students in all grades studied, and children of all racial/ethnic backgrounds.

The growing levels of childhood overweight point to two of the most serious public health crises facing California today: unhealthy diets and low levels of physical activity among our children. Poor eating and inadequate physical activity put California children at risk for diabetes and other chronic diseases in their youth, can lead to expensive and preventable adult illnesses, and may reduce their life expectancy.

These crises reflect not only factors under the control of children and their parents, but also conditions in schools and communities that encourage children to eat and drink unhealthy foods and beverages and that limit their physical activity. Unfortunately, not enough has been done to address these problems. To address this growing epidemic, the California Center for Public Health Advocacy calls on policy makers to establish comprehensive policies that support parents in providing opportunities for their children to make healthy choices about eating and physical activity.

BACKGROUND

During the past three decades, the prevalence of overweight among young people in the United States more than tripled among children 6 to 11 years and more than doubled among adolescents aged 12 to 19 years.[1] These figures are particularly alarming because of the health problems associated with children being overweight. Children and adolescents who are overweight are at increased risk for type 2 diabetes mellitus, asthma, and orthopedic problems; they are more likely to have risk factors for cardiovascular disease (such as increased blood pressure and cholesterol); and they are more likely to have behavioral problems and depression.[2,3] In addition, children and adolescents who are overweight are more likely to remain so as adults,[4,5] with an estimated 75% of overweight adolescents being obese as young adults.[5]

Obese adults are at increased risk for heart disease, stroke, osteoarthritis, and several forms of cancer.[6-8] These health risks result in increased human suffering, reduced quality of life, and premature death.[9-11] In addition, costs for health care attributable to excess body weight account for up to 7% of annual U.S. health-care expenditures among adults, at a cost of more than $90 billion per year.[12,13] In 2005, medical care, workers' compensation, and lost productivity attributable to overweight, obesity, and physical inactivity among adults will cost California an estimated $28 billion.[14]

Courtesy California Center for Public Health

EXHIBIT 6-2c (Continued)

The increasing prevalence of overweight is a reflection of critical and fundamental health problems that plague our children: poor diet and a lack of regular physical activity. These problems are the result of a variety of individual, social, and environmental factors. These factors include increased availability and consumption of soft drinks and high-fat, high-calorie foods; increasing amounts of time spent in sedentary activities, including television viewing; and limited access in many neighborhoods to healthy foods and safe places to be physically active. Since CCPHA released its 2002 report on overweight children in California, far too few significant statewide policies have been enacted to promote healthy eating and physical activity in California.

The Study

The California Center for Public Health Advocacy (CCPHA) analyzed data collected in the 2004 California Department of Education Physical Fitness Test from almost 1.4 million children to determine the number of children enrolled in grades 5, 7, and 9 who were overweight.[15] The California Physical Fitness Test evaluates children using the *FITNESS*GRAM assessment tool, which consists of six measures of physical fitness.[16] The Healthy Fitness Zone is the *FITNESS*GRAM term used to describe the minimum level of fitness (that is, the level thought to provide some protection from health risks imposed by a lack of fitness) in each component of the test. Each Healthy Fitness Zone is based on criterion-referenced standards that have been tested and shown to be valid and reliable.

CCPHA analyzed one of these measures, body composition, as an indicator of whether or not children were overweight. Each student's body composition was assessed based on either body mass index (BMI) calculated from measured height and weight, triceps skin fold thickness, or bioelectrical impedance.[17] Children who exceeded the Healthy

Fitness Zone were considered to be overweight. In this study, overweight is generally equivalent to the 90th percentile of BMI-for-age, and is slightly lower than the commonly used Centers for Disease Control and Prevention (CDC) definition of overweight as a BMI-for-age at or above the 95th percentile.[18]

CCPHA used data from the California Senate Office of Demographics to assign children to the 80 Assembly districts in California based on their school zip codes.[19] The percentage of overweight children was determined for each Assembly district by gender, grade, and race/ethnicity. The percentage of children who were overweight in 2004 was compared to the percentage of children who were overweight in 2001 as determined by CCPHA's prior analysis.[20]

Results

TABLE 1. Overweight Children in Grades 5, 7, and 9—California, 2004

Category	Overweight (%)
ALL CHILDREN	28.1
GENDER	
Boys	33.9
Girls	22.0
GRADE	
5th	29.3
7th	29.1
9th	25.4
RACE/ETHNICITY	
African American	28.7
American Indian/ Alaskan Native	31.7
Asian	17.9
Filipino	24.7
Latino	35.4
Pacific Islander	35.9
White	20.6
Other	24.4

EXHIBIT 6-2c (Continued)

STATEWIDE PERCENTAGES OF OVERWEIGHT CHILDREN

Overall, more than one in four (28.1%) children enrolled in grades 5, 7, and 9 in California were overweight in 2004 (TABLE 1). Boys (33.9%) were more likely to be overweight than girls (22.0%). The percentage of children who were overweight decreased with increasing grade level, from almost one out of three in grades 5 and 7 to one out of four in grade 9.

The percentage of children who were overweight was highest among Pacific Islanders (35.9%), followed by Latino (35.4%), American Indian/Alaskan Native (31.7%), and African-American (28.7%) children. Lower percentages of overweight were found among non-Latino white children (20.6%) and Asian children (17.9%).

CHANGE IN PERCENTAGE OF OVERWEIGHT CHILDREN FROM 2001 TO 2004

Statewide, the percentage of children enrolled in grades 5, 7, and 9 who were overweight increased from 26.5% in 2001 to 28.1% in 2004 (FIGURE 1). The percentage of overweight children increased among both boys and girls, among children in all three grade levels, and among children of all racial/ethnic backgrounds.

The percentage of children who were overweight increased among all race/ethnicity categories from 2001 to 2004 (FIGURE 2). American Indian/Alaskan Native children experienced the largest increase in overweight, from 25.1% in 2001 to 31.7% in 2004.

FIGURE 1. PERCENTAGE OF CHILDREN IN GRADES 5, 7, AND 9 IN CALIFORNIA WHO WERE OVERWEIGHT IN 2001 COMPARED TO 2004, BY GENDER AND GRADE

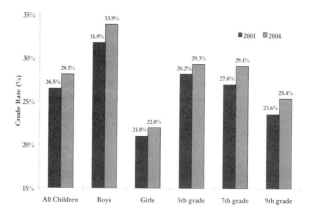

E X H I B I T 6-2c   (Continued)

FIGURE 2. PERCENTAGE OF CHILDREN IN GRADES 5, 7, AND 9 IN CALIFORNIA WHO WERE OVERWEIGHT IN 2001 COMPARED TO 2004, BY RACE/ETHNICITY

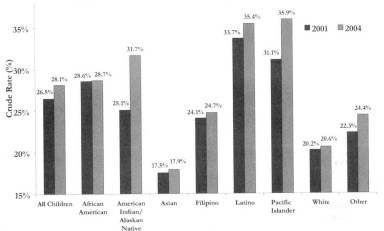

PERCENTAGE OF OVERWEIGHT CHILDREN BY ASSEMBLY DISTRICT

Across all 80 Assembly districts, the percentage of children enrolled in grades 5, 7, and 9 who were overweight in 2004 ranged from 18.2% to 39.1% (SEE MAP). In 55 out of 80 (69%) Assembly districts, at least one out of four (25%) children was overweight.

Assembly districts in the Los Angeles area had particularly high percentages of children who were overweight. Eight out of ten (80%) Assembly districts with the highest percentages of overweight children were located in the Los Angeles area.

CHANGE IN PERCENTAGE OF OVERWEIGHT CHILDREN BY ASSEMBLY DISTRICT FROM 2001 TO 2004

Between 2001 and 2004, the percentage of children enrolled in grades 5, 7, and 9 who were overweight increased in 71 out of 80 (89%) Assembly districts. Of the 80 districts, 50 experienced a 5% or greater increase in the percentage of children who were overweight (TABLE 2). Only nine out of the 80 districts (11%) experienced a decrease in the percentage of children who were overweight.

TABLE 2. CHANGE IN PERCENTAGE OF OVERWEIGHT CHILDREN FROM 2001 TO 2004 — CALIFORNIA ASSEMBLY DISTRICTS

CHANGE IN PERCENTAGE OF OVERWEIGHT CHILDREN FROM 2001 TO 2004	NUMBER OF ASSEMBLY DISTRICTS
Increase of > 10%	27
Increase of 5% - 10%	23
Increase of 0% -5%	21
No Change	0
Decrease of 0% - 5%	6
Decrease of > 5%	3

EXHIBIT 6-2c   (Continued)

CONCLUSION

Across California, the percentage of children in grades 5, 7, and 9 who were overweight increased 6% in three years to 28.1 per 100 children in 2004, from 26.5 per 100 children in 2001. The increase occurred among both boys and girls and among children of all racial/ethnic backgrounds. An increase in the percentage of children who were overweight occurred in 71 out of 80 Assembly districts – almost 90% of all districts. The increase in the percentage of overweight children in California is a reflection of two of the most critical public health problems facing California children today: unhealthy diets and low levels of physical activity. In order to address these problems, statewide policies must be implemented to support parents in helping their children make healthy choices about eating and physical activity.

POLICY RECOMMENDATIONS

The epidemic of childhood obesity will not be solved by calling for individual behavior change alone. To address this health crisis, state and local leaders must address the conditions in schools and communities that contribute to the epidemic and undermine parents' efforts to protect their children's health. The California Center for Public Health Advocacy (CCPHA) calls on policy makers throughout the state to take immediate action. The following recommendations are based on those made by a national Scientific Panel brought together by CCPHA and on recommendations recently developed by the Strategic Alliance for Healthy Food and Activity Environments.[21]

1. Institute healthy food and beverage standards for all items available in pre-school, school, and after-school programs. Standards should address levels of fat, sugar, and calories.

2. Ensure that all children receive physical education that meets minimum standards for quality, duration, and frequency. Students should be active, classes should be of appropriate size, and teachers should be credentialed and well-trained.

3. Establish grocery stores with produce and other fresh, healthy items in all underserved neighborhoods.

4. Eliminate advertising of unhealthy foods and beverages to children and youth.

5. Provide health plan benefits that cover age-appropriate nutrition counseling and education as well as physical activity programs.

6. Make school recreational facilities available for after-hours use by children and families, especially in neighborhoods that lack adequate, safe, and accessible park and recreational facilities.

7. Adopt and implement "complete streets" policies to provide safe and convenient roadway access for people who walk, bicycle, or use wheelchairs.

8. Provide financial incentives for establishing physical activity facilities, grocery stores, and farmers markets, and improving walkability, particularly in low-income communities.

Case 6-3

The ability to use symbols that have inherent emotional value gives a public policy debate a fighting chance. Here an environmental group used a powerful flipper friend to affect an animal protection act. Exhibit 6-3a is a news release, Exhibit 6-3b is a photo of a "protest event" on Capitol Hill, and Exhibit 6-3c is an open letter to Congress.

Save Flipper: Don't Kill the Dolphin Deadline

Oceana with The Wade Group, Inc.

SUMMARY

Dolphins, whales, and other ocean animals were under attack by some members of Congress who wanted to remove a key timeline—the "Dolphin Deadline"—from the Marine Mammal Protection Act. Without the deadline, tens of thousands of animals would continue to be harmed or killed each year. Dolphins can't speak and they can't vote, so Oceana launched a multiyear campaign, and with the assistance of their flippered friends, successfully stopped Congress from passing legislation that would have eliminated the deadline.

SITUATION

More than 30 years ago, Congress enacted the Marine Mammal Protection Act to protect dolphins, whales, and other ocean animals from harm by human activities, such as commercial fishing. Most important is a requirement that commercial fisheries reduce the killing and injury of marine mammals to insignificant levels. Congress set a reasonable time line for this to occur, but the deadline expired without reaching this goal. Instead of working harder to enforce it, some powerful members of Congress were trying to do away with the Dolphin Deadline altogether.

In the last three years, repeated attempts were made by Congress to eliminate the Dolphin Deadline, including proposals by House Resources Committee Chairman Richard Pombo (R–CA) and by Chairman of the House Subcommittee of Fisheries, Wildlife, and Oceans Representative Wayne Gilchrest (R–MD). In 2004 and 2005, Oceana was successful in preventing these bills from coming up for floor action, but 2006 promised to be the real battle to save the Dolphin Deadline. Prospects of achieving any environmental victory in a Republican-controlled Congress were daunting, but Oceana—unlike other environmental organizations—took on the challenge and was prepared with a sophisticated political strategy and a highly targeted PR and advocacy program to Save Flipper.

RESEARCH

Research was conducted initially to substantiate the need for the Dolphin Deadline and was employed strategically during the campaign to refine the program in its aim to change legislative and political environments. Research initiatives included:

Political Analysis

Review of voting records and lobbying history on similar issues to determine key targets; online research of targeted Congressional members; opposition research on Representatives Pombo and Gilchrest; campaign analysis to identify districts with tough Republican races to include in additional targeting; and review of Congressional activity to assess the issue "competition."

Constituent/Voter Targeting

Research by Yale University and Case Western Reserve University in conjunction with phone banks to test and refine advocacy messages.

Polling

Selected Ohio for special polling because of the following:

- It was the home state for key Republican leaders.

- Other key targets were in neighboring states and the poll results could be used in those states.

- Ohio represents "America"—a bellwether state for testing everything from toothpaste to elections.

- Commissioned a prominent Republican pollster to conduct a survey of Ohio Republican voters to quantitatively confirm what campaign activities and other research suggested: Republican voters support the Dolphin Deadline and do not want to kill Flipper.

SCIENCE

Primary research was conducted to assess the impacts on marine mammals of not enforcing the Dolphin Deadline, which provided important scientific information in support of Oceana's advocacy messages.

PLANNING

The campaign's ultimate goal was to prevent any legislation that eliminated the Dolphin Deadline from passing the U.S. House of Representatives. Initially, Representative Gilchrest was the primary target. When the bill became poised to move to the House floor, a two-part political strategy was initiated: (1) maintain solid Democratic support, and (2) generate broad Republican support by showing that "protecting Flipper" made good political and policy sense, particularly in a difficult election year (2006). Based on the research, the following PR strategies were implemented to support the legislative objectives:

- Increase the visibility of the Dolphin Deadline issue and differentiate it from the "clutter"
- Show strong voter/constituent support for protecting the Dolphin Deadline ("A vote for the bill is a vote to Kill Flipper")
- Demonstrate that protecting the Dolphin Deadline has important policy implications

EXECUTION

Oceana implemented a broad range of tactics and activities to gain and maintain support for protecting the Dolphin Deadline:

- Developed Dolphin Deadline brochure and outreach kit
- Placed billboards and newspaper ads in Representative Gilchrest's district, and displayed ads on the Washington, D.C., metro subway trains and in the Capitol Hill station to brand and "create" the issue
- Conducted media outreach to key outlets in Washington, D.C., and selected Congressional districts
- Brought the "Dolphin Brigade," a band of dolphin-costumed lobbyists, to Capitol Hill to ask Congress to Protect the Dolphin Deadline; the Dolphin Brigade commuted to Capitol Hill on the Metro, stopped for coffee at Starbucks, read the newspaper, and then got to work—holding a news conference and educating new Hill staff friends about the Dolphin Deadline

- Organized phone banks in Representative Gilchrest's and 13 other congressional districts to target and cultivate support from key voters

- Initiated outreach to opinion leaders in Representative Gilchrest's district to enlist their support

- Issued a report, "Pointless Peril: Deadlines and Death Counts," on the results of Oceana's scientific work, which found that nearly 10,000 marine mammals would have been saved in the last five years if the Dolphin Deadline had been enforced; the report was used to demonstrate the consequences of removing the Dolphin Deadline and to provide additional credibility to the key messages

EVALUATION

Despite widespread skepticism from many, including the environmental community, in July 2006, the U.S. House of Representatives passed legislation (H.R. 4075) amending the Marine Mammal Protection Act, but only after it took out language that would have eliminated the Dolphin Deadline. Ultimately, more than 20 environmental groups, which had not been previously engaged in this battle because they believed the legislation could not be beaten in the House and were content to "fix the bill" in the Senate, joined Oceana's efforts. Additional outcomes included:

- Media coverage in publications important to Capitol Hill and political leadership including *The Washington Times, Roll Call, Political Hotline, Washington Post Express*, and *Cleveland Plain Dealer*.

- Successful creation and branding of the Dolphin Deadline concept, which has become the regularly used term by Capitol Hill staff and media when referring to these provisions of the Marine Mammal Protection Act.

- Recruitment of more than 4,000 Republican voters in the target districts to call, e-mail, record a message, or post a yard sign telling their representative to Save Flipper.

- Recruitment of more than 20 local opinion leaders to sign on to a letter to Representative Gilchrest urging him to protect the Dolphin Deadline.

EXHIBIT 6-3a   News Release

OCEANA | Protecting The
         | World's Oceans.

PRESS RELEASE

2501 M Street NW, Suite 300   202.833.3900
Washington, DC 20037 USA   www.oceana.org

For Immediate Release

Oct. 20, 2005

Contact: Doralisa Pilarte

202.467.1909 (o)

202.486.6154 (c)

dpilarte@oceana.org

Dolphin Brigade Marches on Capitol Hill to Save Flipper

Congressman Gilchrest's Bill Would Kill Key Provision in Marine Mammal Protection Act

WASHINGTON – The Dolphin Brigade, a band of dolphin-costumed "lobbyists," marched on Capitol Hill today to demand that Congress reject a proposal by U.S. Rep. Wayne Gilchrest (R-Md.) that would undermine the Marine Mammal Protection Act, the best safeguard in American law that dolphins, whales, seals and other marine mammals swimming in U.S. waters have against death and injury from commercial fishing gear.

"This is just another attempt by this Congress to strip away key environmental protections," said Ted Morton, Oceana's federal policy director, who accompanied the Dolphin Brigade to Capitol Hill. "We welcome the Dolphin Brigade to Washington and urge Congress to maintain basic tools of survival for ocean wildlife."

H.R. 2130, sponsored by Congressman Gilchrest, would eliminate a key deadline requiring commercial fisheries to reduce the catch of marine mammals to insignificant levels. H.R. 2130 was passed by the House Resources Committee in May 2005, and is currently awaiting action by the floor of the House of Representatives. The bill currently has no co-sponsors. There have also been proposals by the House Resources Committee to include H.R. 2130 in other unrelated budget actions.

"Dolphins can't talk and they can't vote, but those of us who can need to speak up to keep the Marine Mammal Protection Act intact–particularly its deadlines for reducing marine mammal deaths and injuries in commercial fishing," said Morton.

Brigade members rode the Metro subway system, sipped latte grandes in Hill coffee shops and read newspapers on streets surrounding the Capitol. The objective was to raise the public's awareness of Gilchrest's H.R. 2130, which could mean life or

Courtesy Oceana

E X H I B I T 6-3a   (Continued)

death for Flipper and his marine mammal cousins. Joined by their human friends from Oceana, the Dolphin Brigadeers distributed copies of a new issue ad calling for Congress to not to kill "the dolphin deadline" and protect one of the compliance mechanisms in the Marine Mammal Protection Act.

"No deadlines means no action," Morton added. "We need to protect, not kill, the dolphin deadline."

Please see attached fact sheet for additional information about changes proposed to the Marine Mammal Protection Act under H.R. 2130. Information is also available at www.saveflipper.org.

Oceana campaigns to protect and restore the world's oceans. Our teams of marine scientists, economists, lawyers, and advocates win specific and concrete policy changes to reduce pollution and to prevent the irreversible collapse of fish populations, marine mammals, and other sea life. Global in scope and dedicated to conservation, Oceana has campaigners based in North America (Washington, DC; Juneau, AK; Los Angeles, CA), Europe (Madrid, Spain; Brussels, Belgium) and South America (Santiago, Chile). More than 300,000 members and e-activists in over 150 countries have already joined Oceana. For more information, please visit www.Oceana.org.

E X H I B I T 6-3b   Save Flipper Event

Courtesy Oceana

EXHIBIT 6-3c Open Letter to Congress

OPEN LETTER TO CONGRESSMAN GILCHREST

SUPPORT A DEADLINE FOR THE MARINE MAMMAL PROTECTION ACT

Dear Congressman Gilchrest:

Your historic support and concern for the environment have been a source of pride amongst your constituents. That is why we are writing to express our surprise and dismay that you have chosen to be the sole sponsor of **H.R. 2130, a bill that cripples the Marine Mammal Protection Act** by eliminating the deadline for commercial fishing operations to reduce the catch of marine mammals to insignificant levels.

What does this mean? *Passage of H.R. 2130 will continue the needless deaths of tens of thousands of dolphins, whales, sea otters, sea lions and other marine mammals.* **NO DEADLINE FOR COMPLIANCE MEANS NO ACTION!**

The Marine Mammal Protection Act, originally passed in 1972, is one of our country's foundational statements that the use of our ocean's resources should also preserve the dolphins, whales, sea otters, sea lions and other mammals that call the ocean home.

After years of debate, in 2004, the Bush Administration created the first, scientific definition of what it means to reduce the catch of marine mammals to insignificant levels.

Unfortunately, we may never reach the goal to save dolphins and whales if reasonable deadlines are not firmly in place for achieving it.

That is why we are urging you to fix H.R. 2130. Permanently eliminating the deadline for reducing the catch of marine mammals to insignificant levels takes away a key incentive to reach the goal defined by the Bush Administration to save the lives of thousands of dolphins and whales.

As a Congressional leader on resource issues, we know that you understand that mankind has a responsibility of good stewardship over our earth. Eliminating this key deadline in the Marine Mammal Protection Act through passage of HR. 2130 will set back our nation's commitment to that responsibility. **Please join us in insisting on a reasonable deadline for achieving the reduction of the killing of marine mammals to "insignificant levels".** We are counting on you!

Sincerely,

Joseph M. Okoh
Chairman, Biology Department
University of Maryland
Eastern Shore

John R. Schol
Bishop
Baltimore - Washington Conference
United Methodist Church
over 100,000 members

Courtesy Oceana

7

Investor and Financial Relations

Corporations that sell shares to the public must conduct a specialized form of public relations with the investment, or financial, community. Investor and other financial relations cannot be managed in the same aggressive manner that characterizes other forms of public relations. The U.S. Securities and Exchange Commission (SEC) prohibits the promotion of corporate stock under certain circumstances, and it has detailed regulations regarding the issuance of annual and quarterly reports and the timely disclosure of all information that will affect the value of publicly traded corporate shares. After a spate of scandals involving accounting irregularities by large corporations such as ENRON, Congress passed the Sarbanes-Oxley Act in 2002 to set standards for corporate responsibility and internal audit practices. It included measures requiring chief executive officers (CEOs) and chief financial officers (CFOs) to certify financial and other information in their companies' quarterly and annual reports and to force disclosure of non-GAAP (Generally Accepted Accounting Practices) financial measures. Coupled with SEC policy changes making company information more transparent for the general investor, investor relations is a challenging communications field.

How, then, does our four-stage process apply to this highly specialized form of public relations?

RESEARCH

Investor relations research includes investigation of the client, the reason for the program, and the audiences to be targeted for communication.

Client Research

The public relations practitioner needs to focus first on the company's past and present financial status, its past and present investor relations practices, and its strengths, weaknesses, and opportunities specifically related to the financial community. Both internal management practices and external factors such as new pressures from competitors, changes in the cost of goods, and unfounded rumors may all affect decisions by the investment community and will need to be explored.

Opportunity or Problem Research

The second area of research involves assessing the need for a program of financial public relations. Most corporations engage in ongoing investor relations programs that may involve routine communication with the financial media, the annual report to shareowners, the annual meeting, as well as miscellaneous meetings with and tours for shareowners. When problems develop with particular publics, special programs may be devised reactively. Thus, the need for the program should be clearly justified and explained in this phase of research.

Audience Research

Finally, research for investor relations involves identification of key audiences or groups that make up the financial community:

Shareowners and potential shareowners

Security analysts and investment counselors

The financial media

Major wire services: Dow Jones, Reuters Economic Service, AP, UPI, Bloomberg

Major business magazines: *BusinessWeek, Fortune*—mass circulation and specialized

Major New York City newspapers: *The New York Times, The Wall Street Journal*

Statistical services: Standard & Poor's, Moody's Investor Service

Private wire services: PR Newswire, Business Wire, and PRIMEZONE

Major broadcast networks: CNNfn, CNBC, Bloomberg TV

Securities and Exchange Commission.

OBJECTIVES

Investor relations objectives, both impact and output, should be as specific and as quantifiable as possible.

Impact Objectives

Impact objectives for investor relations include informing investor publics and affecting their attitudes and behaviors. Some examples are:

1. To increase the investor public's knowledge of significant corporate developments (by 40 percent during the current year)

2. To enhance favorable attitudes toward the corporation (by 30 percent this year)

3. To create (40 percent) more interest in the corporation among potential investors (during this year)

4. To raise (20 percent) more capital through the investor relations program (by our deadline of December 1)

5. To receive (45 percent) greater responses from shareowners and other targeted investor publics (during the next fiscal year)

Output Objectives

In investor relations, output objectives constitute the distribution and execution of program materials and forms of communication. Examples are:

1. To distribute corporate news releases to 12 major outlets among the financial media

2. To make 18 presentations to security analysts during the months of March and April

Public relations directors often prefer to use output objectives exclusively. These clarify public relations actions and are much simpler to evaluate than impact objectives.

PROGRAMMING

As in other forms of public relations, the element of programming for investor relations includes planning the theme and messages, the action or special event(s), the uncontrolled and controlled media, and the use of effective principles of communication in program execution.

Theme and Messages

The theme and messages for an investor relations program will be entirely situational. Such programs usually provide assurances of credibility and attempt to enhance relations between the company and the financial community.

Action(s) or Special Event(s)

Actions and special events unique to investor relations include:

1. An annual shareowners' meeting
2. An open house for shareowners or analysts
3. Meetings with members of the financial community
4. Teleconference or webcast with investors and analysts
5. Special seminars or other group meetings with analysts
6. Special visits to corporate headquarters or plant tours for analysts and shareowners
7. Presentations at meetings or conventions of analysts, in and outside of New York City
8. Promotional events designed to enhance the company's image in the financial community

Uncontrolled and Controlled Media

Uncontrolled media most frequently used in investor relations include:

1. News releases or feature stories targeted to the financial and mass media
2. CEO interviews with the financial and mass media
3. Media relations with key members of the financial press to stimulate positive news coverage of the company and its activities

Controlled media most often found in investor relations programs are:

1. Printed materials for shareowners, including the annual report, quarterly and other financial reports, newsletters, magazines, special letters, dividend stuffers, and announcements; much of this sent by e-mail and placed on the Web site
2. Company promotional films or videos
3. CEO and other corporate officers' speeches to key audiences in the financial community and professional blogs
4. Company financial fact books, biographies and photographs of corporate officers, special fact sheets, and news releases
5. Shareowner opinion surveys
6. Financial advertising
7. The company Web site, a repository for all of the above

Several examples of uncontrolled and controlled forms of communication are included with the cases in this chapter.

Effective Communication

The most relevant communication principles for investor and financial relations are source credibility and audience participation.

Much of the effort of the investor relations program is directed toward enhancing the credibility of the corporation inside the financial community. The financial media, security analysts, shareowners, and potential shareowners must have a favorable image of the corporation. To accomplish this, organizations have changed their stock offerings from regional exchanges to the NASDAQ, the American, or the New York Stock Exchange; have upgraded their printed materials, incorporating designs to convey a more "blue-chip" image; and have stepped up presentations to security analysts. Thus, corporate credibility must always be a paramount concern.

Audience participation is also a vital aspect of such programs. Prospective shareowners, financial media people, security analysts, and others targeted for communication are invited to as many corporate functions as possible. The ultimate form of "audience participation," of course, is the actual purchase of shares in the company.

EVALUATION

Evaluation of investor relations programs should be goal oriented, with each objective reexamined and measured in turn. Although there is a great temptation to cite analyst reports about the company and the company's performance, especially its stock price/earnings (P/E) ratio, these measures may not be related to investor relations programming, or there may be other intervening variables that overshadow the influence of such programming. Some firms use external measures of reputation to gauge success. These include such lists as the *Financial Times*' "World's Most Respected Companies," *Fortune*'s "100 Best places to work for," and *Washington Technology*'s "Fast 50" list of fastest growing technology firms.

SUMMARY

Research for investor relations aims at understanding the publicly owned company's status in the financial and investment community, the need for communicating with that community, and the makeup of that community as a target audience. The audience components are shareowners and potential shareowners, security analysts and investment counselors, the financial press, and the SEC.

Both impact and output objectives are used in investor relations. Impact objectives are oriented toward informing or influencing the attitudes and behaviors of the financial community, while output objectives cite distribution of materials and other forms of programming as desired outcomes.

Programming for investor relations usually consists of such actions and events as annual shareowners' meetings, an open house for shareowners, special meetings with analysts or other members of the financial community, and promotional events designed to enhance the company's image in the financial community. Uncontrolled and controlled media used in investor relations include news releases, interviews, printed literature, audiovisual materials, and/or speeches directed to targeted segments of the financial community.

Evaluation of investor relations should return to the program's specific, stated objectives and measure each one appropriately. Some practitioners attribute enhancement of the corporation's P/E ratio to the efforts of the investor relations program. However, the presence of intervening variables should always be suspected in such cases.

READINGS ON INVESTOR AND FINANCIAL RELATIONS

Adler, Rob. "Net Gain: An Effective Investor Relations Web Site Enhances Shareholder Communications," *Public Relations Tactics* 5 (November 1998): 19ff.

Bragg, Steven. *Investor Relations: The Comprehensive Guide.* Centennial, CO: Accounting Tools, 2008.

Burns, Stuart. "Minority Rights (Voting Rights) of Minority Shareholders," *Accountancy* 125 (February 2000): 44ff.

Casteel, Lynn. "Investing in an Effective Annual Report," *Public Relations Tactics* 9 (November 2002): 10.

Cole, Benjamin Mark. *The New Investor Relations—Expert Perspectives on the State of the Art.* Princeton, NJ: Bloomberg Press, 2003.

Corning, Beth. "Great Reputations: A PR Disaster Could Cost Your Corporation Dearly," *Accountancy* 123 (March 1999): 38ff.

Easley, Lisa. "Using Media Relations (Instead of Investor Relations)," *Public Relations Quarterly* 43 (summer 1998): 39ff.

Fernando, Angelo. "When Rumor Has It (or Not)," *Communication World* 22 (July–August 2005): 10–11.

Gaschen, Dennis John. "Restoring Public Confidence—The Challenges of Conducting Investor Relations in Today's Volatile Market," *Public Relations Tactics* 9 (November 2002): 8.

Hassink, Harold, Laury Bollen, and Michiel Steggink. "Symmetrical Versus Asymmetrical Company-Investor Communications Via the Internet," *Corporate Communications* 12 (spring 2007): 145–160.

Higgins, Richard B. *Best Practices in Global Investor Relations.* Westport, CT: Greenwood Publishing Group, 2000.

Hong, Youngshin, and Eyun-Jung Ki. "How Do Public Relations Practitioners Perceive Investor Relations? An Exploratory Study," *Corporate Communications* 12 (spring 2007): 199–213.

Jordan, Allan E. "Strategic Communication Plan Reassures Jittery Gold Investors," *Communication World* 20 (August/September 2003): 42ff.

Jones, Charles P. *Investments: Analysis and Management*, 10th ed. Somerset, NJ: Wiley, 2007.

Kanzler, Ford. "Poised for Public Offerings? Start Your Public Relations Efforts Now," *Public Relations Quarterly* 41 (summer 1996): 23ff.

Macintosh, William. "Getting Focused—The Communicator's Role When a CEO Fails," *Public Relations Strategist* 9 (winter 2003): 16ff.

Mahoney, William F. *Investor Relations: The Professional's Guide to Financial Marketing and Communications*. New York: New York Institute of Finance, a division of Simon & Schuster, 1991.

Marconi, Joe. "Taking Stock: Understanding Investor Relations," in *Public Relations: The Complete Guide*. Mason, OH: South-Western, 2004.

Marston, Claire. "Investor Relations Meetings: Evidence from the Top 500 UK Companies," *Accounting and Business Research* 38 (2008): 21–48.

Merchant, Hemant, and Dan Schendel. "How Do International Joint Ventures Create Shareholder Value?" *Strategic Management Journal* 21 (July 2000): 723ff.

Miles, Morgan P., and Jeffrey G. Covin. "Environmental Marketing: A Source of Reputational, Competitive, and Financial Advantage," *Journal of Business Ethics* 23 (February 1, 2001): 299ff.

Nekvsil, Charles. "Getting the Most Out of Your Investor Relations Conference Calls," *Public Relations Tactics* 6 (August 1999): 10ff.

Niedziolka, Dariusz A. "Investor Relations in Poland: An Evaluation of the State of Affairs from Empirical Studies," *Public Relations Review* 33 (November 2007): 433–436.

Parnell, Larry. "Making the Business Case for Corporate Social Responsibility: Why It Should Be Part of a Comprehensive Communications Strategy," *Public Relations Strategist* 11 (spring 2005): 49–51.

Radner, Greg. "The Promise of Web-based Disclosure," *Public Relations Tactics* 10 (November 2003): 13.

Savage, Michelle. "New Standards in Communicating to Financial Audiences—Why You Need to Understand XBRL," *Public Relations Strategist* 11 (winter 2005): 10–12.

Schneider, Carl W., Joseph M. Manko, and Robert S. Kant. *Going Public: Practice, Procedure and Consequences*. New York: Browne Publishing, 2002.

Silver, David. "Creating Transparency for Public Companies: The Convergence of PR and IR in the Post-Sarbanes-Oxley Marketplace," *Public Relations Strategist* 11 (winter 2005): 14–17.

Stapleton, Geof. *Institutional Shareholders and Corporate Governance*. New York: Oxford University Press, 1996.

Turner, Michael. "Surviving in the Era of Downsizing," *Public Relations Tactics* 4 (January 1997): 5ff.

Turnock, Madeline. "IR and PR: Come Together," *Public Relations Strategist* 8 (spring 2002): 13–15.

Vahouny, Karen. "Opportunities for Improvement," *Communication World* 21 (May/June 2004): 32–37.

Investor Relations Cases

Case 7-1

The market capitalization of a firm is tied to perceptions of senior leadership competencies and the distinctive identity of a company or brand. With so much attention on energy policy, the time was ripe for a communication initiative dealing with a producer of ethanol. Exhibit 7-1a is a news release announcing a presentation by the CEO, and Exhibit 7-1b is a news release about the firm acquiring interest in another production facility.

Pacific Ethanol: Creating an Industry Leader

Pacific Ethanol with Hill & Knowlton

SUMMARY

When Hill & Knowlton began work with Pacific Ethanol in September 2005, the stock was trading below $10 a share and at low volume. Its management was unknown to both the investment community and the business and financial media, and the company's market capitalization was under $200 million. During the eight months that ensued, Hill & Knowlton helped the company leverage market, media, and political opportunities to enhance its access to capital and position its CEO as a leading industry spokesperson. During that period, the company saw its stock price increase fivefold; it raised over $200 million in needed capital and CEO Neil Koehler became a regular source of information for media, industry, and the investment community, all achievements owing much to Hill & Knowlton's insights, research, and multidisciplined execution.

RESEARCH

In order to ensure a successful program for Pacific Ethanol, extensive research and planning was done in the months preceding the program launch.

Hill & Knowlton first examined the share of voice and sentiment for industry competitors such as ADM before crafting a plan. Media coverage, recent stock performance, and analyst sentiment of companies were analyzed.

Without the benefit of a big splash IPO or stock listing, Pacific Ethanol had foregone critical exposure to the financial media, coverage from analysts, and a place at sponsored investment conferences that give most companies recognition with the investment community.

There appeared to be great opportunity to share Pacific Ethanol's story in the media. Stories were being printed almost daily on the domestic oil industry, and it was clear from coverage that industry leaders were looking for alternative solutions in the marketplace.

Hill & Knowlton provided weekly media monitoring on Pacific Ethanol and industry competitors in order to accurately gauge current sentiments and awareness around the globe.

Hill & Knowlton's research helped determine which major investment banks would be hosting investment conferences appropriate to Pacific Ethanol's investment appeal—a challenging task given that there were few precedents for regular conferences featuring renewable or alternative fuels.

PLANNING

Hill & Knowlton assumed ongoing contact with institutional holders to determine evolving attitudes toward the market and Pacific Ethanol.

In order to prepare members of Pacific Ethanol management for media interviews, road shows, and other speaking opportunities, Hill & Knowlton team members in New York conducted an intense media training session for the company.

In order to be seen as a market leader, Pacific Ethanol would need to gain awareness with several stakeholders, including financial analysts, investors, and stockholders.

Goals/Objectives

- Communicate a compelling rationale for investment in company shares.
- Broaden appreciation of Pacific Ethanol's operations, financial structure, and business strategy.
- Build recognition of and long-term confidence in Pacific Ethanol's senior management team.

Strategies

With no internal staff dedicated to public relations or investor relations, the Hill & Knowlton team assumed a large amount of responsibility to execute on plans. Working directly with Pacific Ethanol's CEO, Neil Koehler, Hill & Knowlton crafted a strategy that focused on:

- Leveraging existing news to establish Neil Koehler as a leading expert and spokesman for the ethanol industry with national and business media

- Positioning Pacific Ethanol as a distinct corporate personality, directly emphasizing Pacific Ethanol's "destination" business model, making it distinct from that of Midwest producers like ADM

- Establishing rapport with top-tier sell- and buy-side analysts

Because gaining access to the capital markets to secure financing was a high priority for Pacific Ethanol, Hill & Knowlton crafted a plan that combined targeted media outreach and direct contact with buy-side institutions. This would provide the best and quickest payoff in terms of building awareness for the company and demand for its stock.

The awareness program was launched in October 2005, reaching out to all critical stakeholder groups.

EXECUTION

Hill & Knowlton began reaching out to targeted reporters covering the energy sector to pitch stories on the company, the progress of plant construction, and stock performance. The team also worked to position company executives as thought leaders for relevant day-two stories. For example, upon hearing that energy would be an important topic in the President's 2006 State of the Union address, Hill & Knowlton worked with Pacific Ethanol to issue a media alert the day before the address, offering the CEO for expert commentary. Other initiatives included:

- Meetings at two non-deal road shows: one in December 2005 and another in October 2006. Members of Pacific Ethanol's senior management team traveled to New York and Boston to meet with analysts and portfolio managers.

- A toll-free telephone hotline was set up for investors, and Hill & Knowlton team members handled all incoming inquiries.

- The team also developed an investor kit—both a physical and an online version—to send to current and potential investors.

- Hill & Knowlton also secured participation for Pacific Ethanol management at Goldman Sachs' first alternative fuels conference in May 2006, which drew over 400 attendees, and arranged a luncheon/conference call at Bear Stearns, which reached the majority of its institutional sales force and over 100 institutional clients.

EVALUATION

- Since October 2005, Pacific Ethanol has scored significant media coverage in several top-tier publications, including CNBC, *BusinessWeek*, *The Wall Street Journal*, Reuters, *San Francisco Chronicle*, *San Diego Union-Tribune*, MarketWatch "Commodities Corner," *Investor's Business Daily*, *Investment Dealers' Digest*, CBS Radio Network, and Bloomberg.

- Pacific Ethanol's stock rose from $8 in September 2005 to a high of $44.50 in May 2006, an increase of 456 percent over a period of eight months.

- The volume trading and liquidity for the stock increased equally as dramatically, from averaging 100,000 shares per day to a high of 11,015,100 on May 23—a 110-fold increase. The trailing three-month average trading volume has since settled to a respectable 2,269,570.

- The toll-free number set up was in high demand, especially during May and June 2006. The volume grew to over 50 calls a day from both individual and institutional investors.

Pacific Ethanol enjoyed great success with the capital markets; during 2006, the company raised over $200 million in debt and equity financing toward its plant expansion, including an $84 million investment by Cascade Investment, the investment vehicle of Microsoft Chairman Bill Gates.

CEO Neil Kohler has received a number of conference invitations from Jeffries, Bank of America, and Piper Jaffray. He was also invited to present at the prestigious Milken Institute's annual conference and will participate in several more investment conferences during the balance of 2006.

Today, Pacific Ethanol is among the best known alternative fuel in the U.S. investment community and among key media covering the space, despite the fact that the company only began production of ethanol in October 2006. Today, industry stories in the media regularly include a mention of Pacific Ethanol.

Pacific Ethanol is now in a position to accelerate its growth and expansion time frame, from 5 ethanol plants online by the end of 2008 to a new goal of 9 or 10 ethanol plants, all operational by 2010, which will put the company in the top 5 ethanol producers in the country.

E X H I B I T 7-1a   News Release on Presentation at Investment Conferences

Pacific Ethanol, Inc.

FOR IMMEDIATE RELEASE

CONTACTS
INVESTORS: MEDIA:
William G. Langley   Rory Mackin
Chief Financial Officer   Hill & Knowlton
PACIFIC ETHANOL, INC.   212-885-0455
(559) 435-1771   rmackin@hillandknowlton.com

PACIFIC ETHANOL TO PRESENT

AT TWO INVESTMENT CONFERENCES

CEO Neil Koehler to Present at Friedman, Billings, Ramsey 2006 Investor Conference and Bear Stearns Commodities and Capital Goods Conference

FRESNO, CA., Nov. 27, 2006 – Pacific Ethanol Inc. (NASDAQ GM: PEIX), today announced that Pacific Ethanol's CEO, Neil Koehler, will be presenting at two sponsored investment conferences in New York City this week.

Mr. Koehler will present at the Friedman, Billings, Ramsey Group, Inc. 2006 Investor Conference in New York City on November 28, 2006, at 2:45 PM EST. The conference will be held at the Grand Hyatt hotel located at Park Avenue at Grand Central Terminal.

Mr. Koehler will present at the Bear Stearns Commodities and Capital Goods Conference in New York City on November 29, 2006 at 11:30 AM EST. He will also serve on a panel discussing the current state of the biofuels industry at 2:20 PM EST. The conference will take place at Bear Stearns' headquarters, at 383 Madison Avenue in New York City.

559.435.1771
5711 N. WEST AVENUE
FRESNO, CALIFORNIA 93711
www.pacificethanol.net

Courtesy Pacific Ethanol

E X H I B I T 7-1a   (Continued)

Pacific Ethanol, Inc.

Details of webcasts of each conference will be available at the sponsors' respective websites and at www.pacificethanol.net.

About Pacific Ethanol, Inc.

Pacific Ethanol owns and operates an ethanol plant in Madera County, California, is constructing a second plant in Boardman, Oregon and owns a 42% interest in Front Range Energy, LLC which owns and operates an ethanol plant in Windsor, Colorado. Pacific Ethanol's goal is to become the leading marketer and producer of renewable fuels in the Western United States. In May 2006, Pacific Ethanol completed an equity funding of $138 million which provided the Company with sufficient cash to both accelerate its stated goal of completing five ethanol production facilities totaling 220 million gallons of capacity per year by the middle of 2008 and its plans to complete additional ethanol production facilities, increasing total capacity to 420 million gallons per year by the end of 2010. Pacific Ethanol, through its wholly-owned subsidiary, Kinergy Marketing, LLC, is the largest West Coast-based marketer of ethanol. In addition, Pacific Ethanol is working to identify and develop other renewable fuel technologies such as cellulose-based ethanol production and bio-diesel.

####

559.435.1771
5711 N. WEST AVENUE
FRESNO, CALIFORNIA 93711
www.pacificethanol.net

E X H I B I T 7-1b   News Release on Acquisition of Financial Interest in Front Range Energy

---

Pacific Ethanol, Inc.

FOR IMMEDIATE RELEASE

CONTACTS

INVESTORS:
William G. Langley
Chief Financial Officer
PACIFIC ETHANOL, INC.
(559) 435-1771

MEDIA:
Rory Mackin
Hill & Knowlton
212-885-0455
rmackin@hillandknowlton.com

PACIFIC ETHANOL ACQUIRES 42% OF FRONT RANGE ENERGY, LLC AND EXTENDS MARKETING CONTRACT

Transaction is Accretive to Earnings

October 17, 2006 Fresno, CA – Pacific Ethanol, Inc. (NASDAQ:PEIX) today announced the acquisition from Eagle Energy, LLC of a 42% minority interest in Front Range Energy, LLC ("Front Range"), the owner of a 40 million gallon nameplate ethanol plant located in Windsor, Colorado.

The ICM-designed Front Range facility is currently running at an annual production rate of 47 million gallons. The plant began full production in June, 2006.

Pacific Ethanol purchased 10,095 Class B Voting Units, representing a 42% interest in Front Range, in exchange for $30 million in cash, 2,081,888 shares of Pacific Ethanol common stock, and a warrant to purchase up to 693,963 shares of common stock at any time before October 17, 2007 at an exercise price of $14.41 per share. The number of shares issued to the seller was calculated to have a value of $30 million, based on the average of the closing prices of Pacific Ethanol's common stock for the 10 trading days preceding the closing, and has a value as of closing of $35,975,000 based on today's closing price of $17.28. The exercise price of the warrant was based on the average of the closing prices of Pacific Ethanol's common stock for the 10 trading days preceding the closing. The securities sold in this private placement have not been registered under the Securities Act of 1933 and may not be offered or sold in the United States in the absence of an effective registration statement or exemption from registration requirements. Pacific Ethanol has agreed to file a resale registration statement on Form S-3 within 10 days after the

EXHIBIT 7-1b   (Continued)

Pacific Ethanol, Inc.

closing of the transaction for the purpose of registering the resale of the shares of common stock issued at the closing and the shares of common stock underlying the warrant.

Pacific Ethanol and Front Range already have a significant relationship, announced upon the completion of Front Range's plant in June, 2006, pursuant to which Pacific Ethanol markets all of the output of the plant (fuel ethanol and wet distillers grain), procures the corn feedstock, and manages plant operations. As a part of Pacific Ethanol's purchase of an ownership stake in Front Range, the parties have extended the term of the ethanol marketing agreement until June 9, 2013.

Neil Koehler, President and CEO of Pacific Ethanol stated, "This transaction is immediately accretive to earnings and accelerates our goal to be the leading ethanol producer in the western US. Our acquisition of a stake in Front Range in effect adds approximately 20 million gallons to our annual operating production capacity. This represents a significant step in achieving our stated annual production capacity targets of 220 million gallons by the middle of 2008 and 420 million gallons by the end of 2010. This agreement further cements our close working relationship with Front Range Energy. And finally, as this plant supplies local markets for both fuel and feed, obviating the need to ship our product long distances, it is also a perfect fit with Pacific Ethanol's low cost destination business model."

Front Range Energy's majority owner, Dan Sanders, said, "We are delighted to have Pacific Ethanol as a partner in this operation, given our existing relationship and their proven expertise in the production and marketing of ethanol and feed products in the western US. Pacific Ethanol's ownership in our company also strengthens our position as we evaluate a potential expansion of the Windsor plant and other new production opportunities."

About Pacific Ethanol, Inc.

Pacific Ethanol has an ethanol plant in Madera County, California which has recently been completed and is undergoing startup, and a second plant under construction in Boardman, Oregon. Pacific Ethanol's goal is to become the leading producer and marketer of renewable fuels in the western US. Central to its growth strategy is its destination business model, whereby each respective ethanol plant achieves lower process and transportation costs by servicing local markets for both fuel and feed. In May 2006, Pacific Ethanol completed an

---

E X H I B I T 7-1b   (Continued)

Pacific Ethanol, Inc.

equity funding of $138 million which provided the Company with sufficient cash to both accelerate its stated goal of completing five ethanol production facilities totaling 220 million gallons of capacity per year by the middle of 2008 and its plans to complete additional ethanol production facilities, increasing total capacity to 420 million gallons per year by the end of 2010. Pacific Ethanol, through its wholly-owned subsidiary, Kinergy Marketing, LLC, is the largest West Coast-based marketer of ethanol. In addition, Pacific Ethanol is working to identify and develop other renewable fuel technologies such as cellulose-based ethanol production and bio-diesel.

About Front Range Energy

Front Range Energy owns an ethanol plant in Windsor CO with nameplate annual capacity of 40 million gallons . The majority owner of Front Range is Dan Sanders. The plant was designed by ICM, a leading technology company.

Safe Harbor Statement Under the Private Securities Litigation Reform Act of 1995

With the exception of historical information, the matters discussed in this press release are forward-looking statements that involve a number of risks and uncertainties. The actual future results of Pacific Ethanol could differ from those statements. Factors that could cause or contribute to such differences include, but are not limited to, the ability of Pacific Ethanol to successfully market all of Front Range Energy's ethanol and WDG produced at Front Range Energy's Windsor, CO ethanol production facility and to manage operations at this facility; the final determination by Front Range Energy to expand its Windsor, Colorado production facility; the ability of Pacific Ethanol to successfully capitalize on its internal growth initiatives; the price of ethanol relative to the price of gasoline; and those factors contained in the "Risk Factors" section of Pacific Ethanol's Form 10-Q filed with the Securities and Exchange Commission on August 18, 2006.

####

Case 7-2

The arrival of a new chief executive officer in a company offers prime opportunities to expand awareness of the tone and direction of the new leadership. Exhibit 7-2a is the ACS Fact Sheet, and Exhibit 7-2b is the CEO letter to stockholders.

Improved Connections to Investors: Only Clear Signs from Alaska Communications

Alaska Communications Systems Group with Lippert/ Heilshorn & Associates, Inc.

SUMMARY

Alaska Communications Systems Group (ACS) engaged Lippert/Heilshorn & Associates (LHA) to launch an investor relations (IR) program to eloquently communicate the new management team's strategy to change its capital market plan, grow revenue leveraging the strongest wireless offering in Alaska, reduce costs using process improvement teams, and conduct transactions to reduce interest expense and variable rate risk. LHA's plan educated the investment community and leading business press, priming Wall Street for capital market transactions in 2005. Efforts resulted in three articles in prominent, national financial publications, diversified institutional ownership, and increased analyst coverage, resulting in improved stock performance.

SITUATION ANALYSIS

Headquartered in Anchorage, Alaska Communications Systems Group (ACS; NASDAQ: ALSK) is a customer-focused, facilities-based integrated telecommunications provider. As the leading provider in Alaska, ACS offers local telephone, wireless, Internet, long distance, and TV services in partnership with DISH Network to business and residential customers throughout the state. On February 28, 2006, ACS' stock closed at $11.05, with a market cap approaching $460 million, a dramatic increase from a stock price of $5.08 and market cap approaching $150 million on September 30, 2004. In addition, the long-term debt on December 31, 2005, was $445 million, markedly lower than the long-term debt of $531 million on September 30, 2004.

In 2003, after ACS completed its strategy to acquire the best telecom assets in Alaska, the board of directors and Fox Paine, ACS' equity investment firm and major shareholder decided it was time to implement the next phase of the company's evolution: installing experienced telecom leadership, conducting savvy capital market transactions, and executing sound operational measures to drive growth. In October 2003, Liane Pelletier joined ACS as the new CEO, and in March 2004, David Wilson began as the new CFO. Although the new management team wanted to conduct investment community outreach, the company chose to enter a quiet period.

In April 2004, ACS filed an S-1 (used by public companies to register their securities) with the Securities Exchange and Commission to issue income deposit securities (IDS), a new type of hybrid security that would pay a dividend and interest, raise capital, and increase the float. However, during the summer of 2004, IDS offerings received less than favorable reactions from Wall Street. Therefore, management began to reformulate its strategy, which would most likely include withdrawing the IDS and introducing the next plan.

Management was faced with an investor communications dilemma. In September 2004, ACS engaged LHA to launch an IR program that would eloquently communicate a change in financial strategy as well as educate the investment community and leading business press about the "new ACS" with the goal of priming Wall Street for capital market transactions in 2005 and 2006.

RESEARCH/PLANNING/EXECUTION

LHA delivered an integrated IR and media program that supported the company as it withdrew its IDS, introduced its dividend policy, conducted public offerings of primary and secondary shares of common stock, implemented a dividend reinvestment plan (DRIP), and completed numerous debt transactions and repurchases that reduced the company's interest expense and interest rate volatility risk. The LHA team conceptualized a communications strategy that highlighted ACS as an attractive investment and facilities-based integrated telecommunications provider under the new leadership. LHA's goals were to:

- Increase investment community awareness of ACS to develop institutional investor support

- Diversify and broaden institutional ownership and increase sell-side coverage to drive average daily trading volume, improve stock valuation, and enable a private equity investor exit strategy

- Articulate key messages about the business, the new management team, and ACS as an equity investment to influential business columns

Research, beginning with an on-site due diligence meeting, included targeted studies of institutional investors and sell-side analysts based on ACS' peer group as well as business media.

The plan began with simultaneous IR and business media outreach. The IR team prepared management to conduct the third quarter 2004 results conference call. Due to the IDS quiet period, this would be the first opportunity for the new united management team to present its vision. To maintain the IR momentum, LHA proposed a non-deal road show immediately following the conference call. LHA arranged a nine-day nationwide tour during the first and second weeks of November, which reached 7 cities, 12 sell-side analysts, 64 investors, and 81 investment professionals.

LHA supported these events by preparing the company fact sheet; developing the IR presentation and IR kit; providing Web site recommendations; executing the press release strategy; and managing the company's investor conferences, among other activities. After events with the investment community, LHA surveyed participants, summarized feedback, and provided management with recommendations for the next IR effort. Throughout 2005, LHA continued the cycle, preparing management for quarterly earnings reporting and conducting additional road shows. Also, LHA delivered quarterly activity reports summarizing the program and strategy plans recommending actions to drive IR.

To complement the IR efforts, the LHA media team evaluated market-moving columns, corporate profiles, and management stories; established a time-line to reflect ACS' corporate and financial milestones; provided media training for management; and developed a New York media road show to introduce management to key columnists. As a result of LHA's research, the team was able to book meetings with *The Wall Street Journal, Barron's, BusinessWeek*, and *Forbes*, prior to the nine-day IR road show.

EVALUATION

The ACS–LHA integrated IR program has been a resounding success. LHA secured press interviews, leading to three significant media placements in renowned financial publications. The financial metrics improvements were also quite strong.

The stock price more than doubled, sell-side coverage doubled, the number of institutional holders almost tripled, and the three-month average of daily trading volume increased dramatically. Furthermore, Fox Paine was able to sell more than half of its position. Finally, between December 31, 2004, and 2005, the company reduced leverage from 4.9 times EBITDA (earnings before interest, taxes, depreciation, and amortization) to 3.9 times, deleveraged the balance sheet by $92 million, and cut interest expense by $16 million annually.

LHA's media component paired timely media placements with ACS' corporate milestones. ACS received excellent media coverage that articulated three of the most significant elements of the company: CEO Liane Pelletier and her new management team, the company's new customer service program, and ACS' investment thesis.

March 28, 2005

LHA secured a feature placement in *Barron's*, "Taking the Chill Off: A Revamped Alaska Communications Aims to be Friendlier to Customers and Shareholders." The story appeared shortly after ACS announced that it increased its dividend. LHA worked with reporter Neil Martin to emphasize the personality of ACS' new management. The article focused on ACS' customer service launch, financial overhaul, and dividend strategy.

June 27, 2005

LHA secured a profile in *BusinessWeek*, "Heading North to Alaska Communications." The story also ran shortly after the dividend increase. LHA worked with reporter Gene Marcial to highlight ACS' growth driven by its unique wireless service. The article touched on ACS' increasing EBITDA and the strong stock performance, noting a surge from $5.25 in October 2004 to $10.20 on May 30, 2005.

October 23, 2005

LHA secured a feature placement in the Boss column of *The New York Times*, "Adventure as a Team Sport." The story followed the news of a new ACS wireless plan and preceded third quarter results in which ACS increased guidance. LHA worked with reporter Elizabeth Olsen to highlight the unique, self-reliant personality of Liane Pelletier, as well as her ability to remake a company.

The following charts provide statistical data from the beginning of the program, September 30, 2004, through the last reported quarter, December 31, 2005.

Metric	September 30, 2004	December 31, 2005	Achievement
ALSK stock price	$5.08	$10.61	Doubled
Number of sell-side analysts	5	10	Doubled
Three-month average daily trading volume	31.303	286,908	Nine times greater
Number of shares outstanding	29.3 million	41.6 million	Lowered cost of capital
Number of shares held by institutions	23.7 million	29.4 million	Increased
% of shares institutionally held	80.8%	70.6%	Diversified
% of shares held by top 10 holders	78.6%	49.4%	Diversified
Number of institutional holders	34	91	Almost tripled

E X H I B I T 7-2a   Alaska Communication Systems Fact Sheet

Alaska Communications Systems Group, Inc.
Corporate Fact Sheet

Alaska's Premier Telecommunications Provider

Headquartered in Anchorage, ACS is Alaska's leading provider of broadband and other wireline and wireless solutions to Enterprise and mass market customers. The ACS wireline operations include the state's most advanced data networks and, with the acquisition of Crest Communications and build of the AKORN fiber, will be the only company with a geographically diverse undersea fiber optic network connecting Alaska to the contiguous United States. The ACS wireless operations rely on the only statewide 3G network, reaching across Alaska from the North Slope to Ketchikan, with coverage extended via the best CDMA carriers in the Lower 49 and Canada. By investing in the fastest-growing market segments and attracting the highest-quality customers, ACS seeks to drive top and bottom-line growth, while continually improving customer experience and cost structure through process improvement.

ACS has a compelling strategy to drive growth

Targeted growth strategy: Increase market share in high-value segments

- Use Wireless and Broadband products to serve high-value customers
- Provide complete data networks with best-in-class components for Enterprise customers
- Provide bundle convenience for mass market customers

Within Alaska and beyond, ACS has an ideal asset mix

- Statewide wireline networks equipped with 10 Gig networking technology
- Statewide 3G CDMA wireless network with best quality voice and fastest mobile data
- Interstate submarine fiber to the Lower 48 via AKORN build and Northstar buy – complements the in-state networks and provides differentiation
- Two geographically diverse Network Operations Control Centers to manage traffic 7X24 and assure business continuity

Combined with a strong financial foundation and an attractive dividend policy, ACS provides a smart investment opportunity

Driven by three key operating principles

- Allocate resources toward strongest growth segments – Wireless and Enterprise
- Maximize cash return from segments undergoing structural decline
- Manage costs and improve customers' experience through process improvement

Stable revenues and cash flows

- Revenue growth of 27% 2004 to 2007
- EBITDA growth of 33% 2004 to 2007

Attractive dividend on common shares

- Long term payout ratio of 70-75%
- Current dividend of $0.86 per share annually, subject to quarterly Board approval
- Focused growth strategy positions ACS for future dividend growth

Strong balance sheet with liquidity

- Leverage at Dec. 31, 2007 was 2.9x EBITDA
- Interest rate risk significantly reduced by fixing 100% of term loan debt

Courtesy Alaska Communications Systems Group

EXHIBIT 7-2a   (Continued)

Alaska Communications Systems

Alaska Communications Systems Group, Inc.

Financial Highlights
(In thousands)

Corporate Fact Sheet

	Three Months Ended 3/31/08	Twelve Months Ended 12/31/07	Twelve Months Ended 12/31/06
Total operating revenue	$96,776	$385,785	$348,721
Total operating expense	79,868	325,346	305,100
Cash flow from operations*	24,866	104,935	91,824
Weighted average shares outstanding (basic)	42,939	42,701	42,045
EBITDA*	$34,890	138,127	$121,185

	As of 3/31/08	As of 12/31/07	As of 12/31/06
Cash & Short-Term Investments	$20,636	$38,587	$38,560
Total current assets	89,945	114,706	88,926
Property, plant & equipment, net	391,079	383,594	391,364
Total assets	655,071	663,203	556,216
Total current liabilities	69,583	74,901	77,182
Long-term liabilities, net	523,251	514,291	510,069
Tot liab. & stockholders' equity (deficit)	$655,071	$663,203	$556,216

Contacts

INVESTORS:
Investor Relations
Alaska Communications Systems
investors@acsalaska.com
907.564.7556

MEDIA:
Alaska Communications Systems
David C. Eisenberg
david.c.eisenberg@acsalaska.com
907.297.3000

Analyst Coverage

Banc of America Securities - *David W. Barden*
JP Morgan Equity - *Jonathan Chaplin*
Merrill Lynch (under review) - *Michael J. Funk*
Oppenheimer and Co. Inc. - *Tim Horan*
Raymond James - *Frank G. Louthan*
RBC Capital Markets - *David Coleman*
Standard and Poor's Equity Group - *Todd Rosenbluth*
Stifel Nicolaus & Company Inc. - *Christopher C. King*

Telecommunications Growth Opportunities supported by Alaskan demographics

► Alaska's population growth exceeds the national average.
► Federal spending is significant in Alaska.
► Median household income is 23% higher than the U.S. average.
► Alaskans spend roughly 33% more on communications services than other Americans.

Potential opportunity: Alaska could see significant population and economic growth in the next 5 to 10 years if proposed oil and gas development occurs.

Nasdaq symbol:	ALSK	Annual dividend policy (subject to quarterly Board approval):	$0.86 per share
Shares outstanding: 4/28/08	43.3 M	Dividend record date:	March 31, 2008

*A reconciliation of EBITDA to Cash flow from operations, its closest GAAP measure, is available on our investor web site at http://www.alsk.com.

Forward-Looking Statements: Statements about future results and other expectations constitute forward-looking statements within the meaning of the Private Securities Litigation Reform Act of 1995. These statements are based on current expectations and the current economic environment. The company cautions that these statements are not guarantees of future performance. Actual results may differ materially from those expressed or implied in the forward-looking statements. A number of factors in addition to those discussed herein could cause actual results to differ materially from expectations. The company's financial planning is affected by business and economic conditions and changes in customer order patterns. Any projections are inherently subject to significant economic and competitive uncertainties and contingencies, many of which are beyond the control of ACS. Important assumptions and other important factors, including risk factors, which could cause actual results to differ materially from those in the forward-looking statements, are specified in the company's Form 10-K, Form 10-Q, and other filings with the SEC, including under headings such as "Risk factors" and "Management's discussion and analysis of financial condition and results of operations." The company undertakes no obligation to update forward-looking statements, whether as a result of new information, future events, or otherwise.

E X H I B I T   7-2b   Letter to Stockholders

Alaska Communications Systems

2005

Letter to Stockholders

ACS
Alaska Communications Systems

WIRELESS   INTERNET   LOCAL   LONG DISTANCE   TELEVISION

introduced, after much research into customer needs, a Pocket PC, which offers users the consistency, simplicity and security of their office desktop Microsoft-based computer in a device that fits in the palm of their hands. Life outside the office is as stress-free as it can be with a quality device, full office functionality, and a fast and reliable network, both in and outside of Alaska.

Results in 2005 included a 15% growth in wireless subscribers, growth faster than the market, so ACS gained share with its premier wireless capabilities.

Grow Within Our Cost Structure

ACS exceeded our financial goals in 2005. We funded top line growth by trimming costs everywhere, and in a sustainable manner, by driving efficiencies through Process Improvement. The Process Improvement teams are central to how we work and the results we deliver.

Throughout the year, ACS also exercised smart capital market moves by lowering and fixing interest rates on the majority of our debt and at the same time reducing total debt levels.

On the back of substantial operating progress and strategic refinancing in 2005, ACS again increased its annual dividend early in 2006 to what is now $0.86 per share.

We are pleased that the performance of ACS created the conditions appropriate for our largest investor, Fox Paine & Company, to sell its holdings in a two-step process concluded in the first quarter of 2006. The sale diversified our stockholder base and increased the liquidity of the stock. We welcome our new investors and appreciate the confidence they demonstrate in the team at ACS.

We entered 2006 with strong cash flow, a strong balance sheet, an increased dividend, strong operating metrics and a team increasingly confident in its ability to deliver. Our work for the rest of this year, and always, centers on the understanding that loyal customers drive our results

Total Shareholder Return (TSR)			
	Stock	Dividend	TSR*
Q1 2005	$10.05	$0.200	19%
Q2 2005	$9.91	$0.200	20%
Q3 2005	$11.44	$0.200	40%
Q4 2005	$10.16	$0.200	27%
Q1 2006	$12.13	$0.215	52%

*assuming initial purchase of ACS stock on 12/31/04, quarter-end pricing and no reinvestment of dividends

and that with our distinctive assets, we have the ability to deliver quality services at home, at work, on the road, and virtually anyplace in between.

Thank you for your support and I look forward to reporting to you on the progress realized in 2006.

Sincerely,

Liane Pelletier

Liane Pelletier
President, CEO and Board Chair

Corporate Headquarters
Alaska Communications Systems
600 Telephone Avenue, Anchorage, AK 99503

Telephone: 907.297.3000

NASDAQ: ALSK
Investors' Web Address: www.alsk.com
Corporate Web Address: www.acsalaska.com

Courtesy Alaska Communications Systems Group

EXHIBIT 7-2b   (Continued)

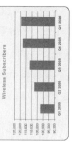

ACS understands that a company easy to do business with is the one that wins loyal customers.

Liane Pelletier
President, CEO and Board Chair

ACS   Building the Business through Customer Focus

Dear Fellow Stockholders:

It gives me great pleasure to share with you the achievements of 2005 at Alaska Communications Systems, specifically against the three goals laid out last year – to enhance the overall customer experience, to be known as Alaska's premier wireless provider, and to grow within our cost structure.

Enhance the Overall Customer Experience

At ACS, it is all about growing the number of loyal ACS customers – those who choose ACS, buy more from ACS, and refer ACS to others. Loyal customers are profitable. We win loyal customers through competitive differentiation, quality customer experience and effective marketing, sales, and service.

Competitive differentiation. ACS is the only statewide telecom provider in Alaska that owns the assets of local, long distance, wireless and Internet and therefore is the only company able to profitably combine and package products into valuable services for customers, who increasingly demand answers to their communications needs in an easy-to-use format. One expression of such packaging is ON ACS, launched mid-year 2005. ON ACS is a strategic program that encourages our customers to use more ACS services, and for that, ACS shares in the value created. It performs well in both acquiring and retaining our customers. The *first expression* of ON ACS offers free mobile-to-home and home-to-mobile calls (or any and all members of a household who buy ACS residential service and ACS wireless service. It is a program so innovative that it earned a mention in the Wall Street Journal near its launch in 2005.

Quality customer experience. ACS understands that a company easy to do business with is the one that wins loyal customers. The company is transforming itself through a strategy of tightly focused Process Improvement, with the aim of delivering streamlined, simpler, error-free and efficient operations. We organized the Process Improvement initiative into ten process teams - most of them concentrated on our many interfaces with customers, all of them focused on quality. Even those teams tackling internal processes derive important benefits that

accrue to our customers. The transformation is entirely employee-driven; all resources deployed are internal, so that the knowledge developed and solutions deployed are completely retained and embraced by the organization.

Effective marketing, sales and service. The creativity and professionalism of our marketing distinguishes ACS in Alaska. The organization of our sales and service teams and their participation in Process Improvement, is a direct translation of our customer centric strategy, as front line employees are asked to *specialize* in a customer segment and are *cross trained* on all products. The Process Improvement initiatives are eliminating seams conventionally found between the service delivered by a call center representative and the service delivered by a field technician. The targeted experience for our customers is one-stop-shopping and one-and-done servicing.

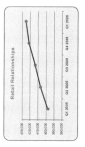

Retail Relationships

Our daily measure of success is growth in retail relationships. From the first quarter of 2005 through the first quarter of 2006, we grew ACS retail relationships by over 7%, to 425,000.

Be Known as Alaska's Premier Wireless Provider

At ACS, we understand that what matters to wireless users is network ubiquity, service reliability, voice clarity, data speeds and a range of high performing devices. ACS invested $12 million in our CDMA network and more in our wireless customer functions during 2005, driven by these customer requirements.

Wireless Subscribers

ACS is the *only* statewide wireless provider that offers third-generation (3G) services. For ACS, which deploys CDMA technology, that means we offer the *fastest mobile data speeds possible,* and the *clearest voice quality possible.* 2005 was a major build year for ACS as we expanded our CDMA footprint to 75% of the population at year end, and extended reach for our customers into the Lower 49 through roaming agreements for *both voice and data.* As the Alaska footprint expanded we implemented a quality measurement program via drive testing to assure we deliver the most reliable service. Drive test results prove ACS has the fewest dropped calls when measured against competitors in the state: high end users value such differentiation. To bring alive the richness of the data capabilities embedded in the ACS network, we

Case 7-3

Moving into a new product line to meet an emerging need, especially a critical need for military operations, offers rare opportunities for increased visibility for a company. An active investor relations program can take advantage of the new products through normal investor communications and even special events to highlight the product. Exhibit 7-3a is a news release about a New York City investor event, Exhibit 7-3b is a news release announcing a presentation to investors and analysts by the CEO/president, and Exhibit 7-3c is a release about a digital road show.

Spartan Motors 2006 Investor Relations Program
Spartan Motors, Inc. with Lambert, Edwards & Associates, Inc.

SITUATION ANALYSIS

Spartan Motors (NASDAQ: SPAR), a manufacturer of custom chassis and vehicles for specialty vehicle markets, ended 2005 with an increase in sales for the year. Moving into 2006, Spartan was focused on growing market share for its existing recreational vehicle (RV) and emergency-rescue products, while also moving into a new market for mine-blast resistant ambush-protected (MRAP) military vehicles—armored vehicles the U.S. military desperately needed to protect troops from improvised explosive devices (IEDs) in the Middle East.

Spartan needed to effectively tell its evolving story to its existing shareholder base, potential new shareholders, and decision makers via targeted communications and the media. Lambert, Edwards & Associates (LE&A), Spartan's investor relations (IR) firm for the past seven years, was tasked with crafting a broad IR program for what ultimately became the best performing year in Spartan's history.

RESEARCH

LE&A's first step was to analyze Spartan's IR activity for 2005 and develop an expanded strategy that built on the company's existing IR initiatives. This included research with investors that concluded Spartan Motors, thought "only" a supplier, should be positioned alongside its OEM partners as a key manufacturer. During 2006, LE&A also conducted two perception studies with Spartan's current institutional investors and sell-side analysts. In the course of these perception studies, LE&A discovered new investor interest and excitement generated by Spartan's new military business. At the same time, LE&A uncovered the investment community's increasing demand for time with Spartan's management.

Further, LE&A learned investors who followed the RV and emergency-rescue markets were unfamiliar with the military business, and those following the military business were unfamiliar with Spartan's other existing markets. Lastly, LE&A researched what was driving the military's demand for MRAP armored vehicles, including the deadly threat of IEDs (roadside bombs), which cause 62 percent of all fatalities in Iraq. LE&A also learned the biggest obstacle to the military's deployment of MRAP vehicles (which were preventing IED-related fatalities at a 100 percent rate in 2006 despite thousands of explosions) was a lack of awareness about the threat and solution by the general public, the Pentagon, and Congress. Ultimately, the research into IEDs helped sell the MRAP story to investors and the media, and, in the process, helped to elevate awareness of the issue among these broader audiences.

PLANNING

The fee budget for the IR plan included standard IR best practices such as quarterly conference calls, letters from the CEO, and financial press releases, as well as unique elements such as conferences and a video road show. As a build on the previous year's IR plan, the 2006 program was aggressively focused on getting management on the road and to investor conferences to tell Spartan's story. It also deliberately focused the bulk of the activity for the second half of 2006, to allow management to focus on executing the business and driving results.

Included in the plan were two LE&A-hosted investor conferences to help elevate Spartan's visibility: the first-ever Lambert-Edwards Recreational Vehicle Investor Conference, held in New York City in June, and the Lambert-Edwards SMID-West Stock Conference, held in Chicago in December (SMID is the industry shorthand for small-mid capitalization). As a supplement to the IR plan, LE&A also launched an interactive, online presentation for shareholders. This "virtual management presentation" allowed investors to experience management's investor presentation similar to what they would see in person. The initial plan also included a large-scale, high-profile event to simultaneously reach a large audience of investors and media, generating excitement among Spartan's existing and potential shareholder base.

LE&A presented the initial plan in December 2005. Beginning in the first quarter of 2006, Spartan began receiving substantial orders for its new military products, although the orders were constrained because of a lack of funding for the project from Congress. From its research and perception studies with shareholders, LE&A determined the need to present Spartan's military growth story to investors while simultaneously educating the general public, media, and politicians about the need for increased MRAP vehicle funding to save lives in Iraq. With this in mind, LE&A began focusing its plan for a high-profile IR event to highlight Spartan's work with MRAP vehicles.

EXECUTION

Following management's focus in the first half of 2006 on business execution and results, LE&A began planning Spartan's investor events to commence in the summer. In June 2006, LE&A executed the first-ever Lambert-Edwards Recreational Vehicle Investor Conference at the Four Seasons Hotel in Manhattan, providing a platform for Spartan to communicate about its established RV business line to the financial community. The event drew 30 fund managers and analysts for live presentations, and another 130 investors and analysts listened to LE&A's webcast.

Moving into the second half of 2006, LE&A's task was to get a message to the Wall Street investment community and government officials that highlighted the new MRAP vehicles' operational record; namely, no soldier using an MRAP vehicle had sustained fatal injuries from an IED despite enduring 1,000 mine blasts. To build a platform for this message, LE&A partnered with Spartan and the latter's primary military customer, Force Protection (NASDAQ: FRPT), to create a high-profile investor and media event in New York City in late June 2006. The aim of the event was to showcase the capabilities of the vehicles, with the ultimate goal of driving new orders and increased investor awareness.

The first challenge was bringing the "Cougar," a 22-ton armored transport, and the "Buffalo," a 26-ton mine-sweep (which is four times the size of a Hummer) MRAP military vehicles into Midtown Manhattan, in the city's post 9/11 security environment. The second challenge was that LE&A had less than six weeks to pull the event together because the vehicles themselves were in production and testing for immediate deployment to Iraq. Both of the vehicles were, at the time, located at the West Point Military Academy for cadet training.

LE&A developed a target list of all possible venues that would offer reasonable access to the investment community and the media in Midtown, eventually deciding on the St. Regis Hotel on 55th Street, a location that puts us in the heart of Manhattan; maintained the stringent security demanded by the military; and allowed us to host an invitation-only investor conference—all at one venue. LE&A began coordinating with the New York City Port Authority, the New York City Police Department, the West Point Military Academy, and even a high-ranking U.S. Army general to obtain all necessary transit and parking permissions and related security to deliver these 22-ton vehicles into the heart of Manhattan under the cover of night.

LE&A also instituted a tiered approach to pitching the business, financial, and general media, starting with buzz-building through press releases, fact sheets, and phone pitches, while keeping the handful of available public photos under wraps to build curiosity. LE&A followed with targeted pitches to local, regional, and national outlets, as well as key photo outlets such as AP, Reuters, and AFP. The massive vehicles on a Manhattan city street would make a great photo opportunity: One vehicle is equipped with a 20-foot robotic arm that allows troops to remove roadside bombs without being put in harms way.

On hand with the vehicles was a uniformed officer from West Point to speak with investors and media, give tours of the vehicles, and provide demonstrations. LE&A also invited a soldier who had survived an IED detonation to attend the event for media interviews. With the assistance of the New York City police, LE&A shut down 55th Street between Madison and 5th Avenues in the middle of the day to give the media exclusive shots of the two vehicles in action.

The investor portion of the event drew more than 60 members of the investment community to attend, representing some of the top financial institutions in the city (J.P. Morgan, Citibank, Robert W. Baird, Thomas Weisel, etc.), an impressive feat for any company, let alone a small-cap company. LE&A also secured stories on CNN and four NYC TV network affiliates and in *USA Today, The New York Times, The New York Sun, The New York Post, The New York Daily News*, AFP, Getty Images, Reuters, and AP. These stories were syndicated to 50 publications nationwide, including the *San Francisco Chronicle, L.A. Times, Cleveland Plain Dealer, Miami Herald, Seattle Post Intelligencer, Houston Chronicle, Washington Times*, and *Forbes.com*.

In December 2006, as an end point to Spartan's 2006 program, LE&A hosted the SMID-West Investor Conference in Chicago. By hosting the event in Chicago and branding it region-wide, LE&A was able to draw investors from across four states. In all, the event drew 30 analysts and portfolio managers, and 130 investors and analysts listened to Spartan's webcast. Much of the investor interest focused on Spartan and its military business, a result of the previous New York event, as well as targeted outreach to investors following other military suppliers.

EVALUATION

LE&A's execution of Spartan's IR plan in 2006, and especially its execution of the three consecutive investor events, helped drive tangible results in terms of market capitalization, share trading volume, and increased institutional ownership.

Spartan's return to shareholders included the following:

- Spartan's market capitalization doubled to around $300 million; average daily trading volume grew 500 percent.

- The stock increased 142 percent in 2006 and moved up an additional 51.5 percent once the company reported its year-end.

- Spartan's 2006 results included significant sales and profits from the military.

- On December 27, Spartan's stock hit $15.79, its highest level since the early 1990s.

- Spartan increased dividends and executed a three-for-two stock split in October 2006.

Additionally, Spartan received $79 million in new military revenue in 2006, a 876 percent increase, and had military orders in its backlog valued at $49 million at the end of 2006. It continued to receive new military orders in the first quarter of 2007. After Spartan's record 2006 results were reported in February 2007, investors pushed the stock up 25 percent on the day of the announcement. The Pentagon is currently in the process of awarding new MRAP contracts worth $1 billion. The awareness built by LE&A through its 2006 IR plan helped drive enormous shareholder value and led to the tangible business result of creating future revenue for Spartan Motors.

EXHIBIT 7-3a   New York City Investor Event

SPARTAN MOTORS, INC.

1165 REYNOLDS RD. • CHARLOTTE, MI 48813 • U.S.A.
TELEPHONE 517-543-6400 • FACSIMILE 517-543-7727
WEB - WWW.SPARTANMOTORS.COM

FOR IMMEDIATE RELEASE

Spartan Motors and Force Protection to Host Investor Event with Cougar and Buffalo Military Vehicles in New York City

Event to Mark Three Years of Combat Operations without a Reported Fatality

CHARLOTTE, Michigan, June 27, 2006–Spartan Motors, Inc. (NASDAQ: SPAR) and Force Protection, Inc. (OTC-BB: FRPT) will display a Cougar and a Buffalo military vehicle in front of the St. Regis Hotel in New York City on June 28 from 10 a.m. ET to 3 p.m. Both companies' management teams will also present the same day to a group of professional investors at a special analyst lunch event.

"Both of these vehicles are deployed today in places such as Iraq and Afghanistan and are saving the lives of our military men and women," said John Sztykiel, president and CEO of Spartan Motors. "Our aim in bringing these vehicles to New York City is to make the people aware of the new technology our military is using to defeat the deadly threat of IEDs (Improvised Explosive Devices).

"At the same time, it's an opportunity for Spartan Motors and Force Protection to inform the investment community of our technical expertise in manufacturing these unique specialty vehicles and the impact of recent significant orders on our business."

Courtesy Spartan Motors

E X H I B I T 7-3a   (Continued)

The Cougar is a medium-sized, blast-protected vehicle produced in both four- and six-wheel configurations which can be customized for multiple tasks including urban patrol, route clearance support, troop transport, mine and explosive ordnance disposal, command and control, reconnaissance and as a lead convoy vehicle.

The Buffalo is an anti-mine/IED vehicle that uses a 30-foot robotic arm and iron claw with a specialized camera and sensing equipment to allow soldiers to examine and disarm potential threats without leaving the safety of the armored hull. Both vehicles utilize a unique V-shaped hull designed to deflect the force of explosions away from passengers inside the armored hull. To date, not a single fatality has been reported in either a Cougar or Buffalo despite over 1,000 mine detonations.

About Spartan Motors

Spartan Motors, Inc. (www.spartanmotors.com) designs, engineers and manufactures custom chassis and vehicles for the recreational vehicle, fire truck, ambulance, emergency-rescue and specialty vehicle markets. The Company's brand names– **Spartan™**, **Crimson Fire™**, **Crimson Fire Aerials™**, and **Road Rescue™**–are known in their market niches for quality, value, service and being the first to market with innovative products. The Company employs approximately 900 at facilities in Michigan, Alabama, Pennsylvania, South Carolina, and South Dakota. Spartan reported sales of $343.0 million in 2005 and is focused on becoming the premier manufacturer of specialty vehicles and chassis in North America.

About Force Protection

Headquartered near Charleston, South Carolina, Force Protection, Inc. (OTC Bulletin Board: FRPT) manufactures ballistic and mine protected vehicles through its subsidiary. These specialty vehicles are designed to offer significant protection against landmines, hostile fire and IEDs. For more information about Force Protection, visit http://www.forceprotectioninc.com.

The statements contained in this news release include certain predictions and projections that may be considered "forward-looking statements" under the securities laws. These forward-looking statements are identifiable by words or phrases indicating that the Company or management "expects," "believes" or is "confident" that a particular result "may" or "should" occur, that a particular item "bodes well," that the Company "looks forward" to a particular result, or similar statements. These

---

E X H I B I T 7-3a   (Continued)

statements involve many risks and uncertainties that could cause actual results to differ materially, including but not limited to economic, competitive, governmental and technological factors affecting the Company's operations, markets, products, services and prices. Accounting estimates are inherently forward-looking. Additional information about these and other factors that may adversely affect these forward-looking statements are contained in the Company's reports and filings with the Securities and Exchange Commission. The Company undertakes no obligation to update or revise any forward-looking statements to reflect developments or information obtained after the date of this news release.

CONTACT:

John Sztykiel, CEO, or Jim Knapp, CFO   Ryan McGrath or Jeff Lambert

Spartan Motors, Inc.   Lambert, Edwards & Associates, Inc.

(616) 233-0500/

(517) 543-6400

rmcgrath@lambert-edwards.com

###

E X H I B I T 7-3b **CEO Presentation to Investors and Analysts**

 SPARTAN MOTORS, INC.

1165 REYNOLDS RD. • CHARLOTTE, MI 48813 • U.S.A.
TELEPHONE 517-543-6400 • FACSIMILE 517-543-7727
WEB - WWW.SPARTANMOTORS.COM

FOR IMMEDIATE RELEASE

Spartan Motors to Present at Lambert-Edwards SMID-West Stock Conference on Dec. 5

CHARLOTTE, Michigan, Dec. 1, 2006–John E. Sztykiel, president and CEO of Spartan Motors, Inc. (Nasdaq: SPAR), will present to investors and analysts at the Lambert-Edwards SMID-West Stock Conference at 10:15 a.m. ET (9:15 a.m. CT) on Dec. 5 at the Drake Hotel in Chicago.

A live webcast of the presentation will be available to investors, analysts and media at http://www.lambert-edwards.com/smid. An archive of the webcast will be available for 30 days.

SMID-West 2006 is an invitation-only event to introduce Midwest-based buyside and sellside analysts to the management teams of top-performing small- and mid-cap (SMID) companies. Lambert, Edwards and Associates, Inc., one of the Midwest's top investor relations firms, in partnership with NASDAQ, BetterInvesting.org, PR Newswire and Roadcast™, will host SMID-West 2006.

About Spartan Motors

Spartan Motors, Inc. (www.spartanmotors.com) designs, engineers and manufactures custom chassis and vehicles for the recreational vehicle, fire truck, ambulance, emergency-rescue and specialty vehicle markets. The Company's brand names– **Spartan™**, **Crimson Fire™**, **Crimson Fire Aerials™**, and **Road Rescue™**–are known for quality, value, service and being the first to market with innovative products. The Company employs approximately 900 at facilities in Michigan, Pennsylvania, South Carolina, and South Dakota. Spartan reported sales of $343.0 million in 2005 and is focused on becoming the premier manufacturer of specialty vehicles and chassis in North America.

CONTACT:

John Sztykiel, CEO, or Jim Knapp, CFO	Ryan McGrath or Jeff Lambert
Spartan Motors, Inc.	Lambert, Edwards & Associates, Inc.
(517) 543-6400	
(616) 233-0500/rmcgrath@lambert-edwards.com	

Courtesy Spartan Motors

E X H I B I T 7-3c   News Release on "Digital Roadshow"

 SPARTAN MOTORS, INC.

1165 REYNOLDS RD. • CHARLOTTE, MI 48813 • U.S.A.
TELEPHONE 517-543-6400 • FACSIMILE 517-543-7727
WEB - WWW.SPARTANMOTORS.COM

FOR IMMEDIATE RELEASE

Spartan Motors Updates "Digital Roadshow" For Investors

CHARLOTTE, Michigan, July 27, 2006–Spartan Motors, Inc. (NASDAQ: SPAR) launched a new version of its "Digital Roadshow" this week, updating and adding content to give investors the most up-to-date information about the company's growth story.

Spartan teamed with PDB Connect (www.pdbconnect.com) to update its life-like computerized video investor presentation, which is similar to the one the Company uses when meeting analysts and portfolio managers in person.

To launch the Digital Roadshow, please visit www.spartanmotors.com on the web and look for the "Click here to view Spartan Motors Virtual Road Show" link near the top of the page. Spartan's Digital Roadshow is also featured on BetterInvesting's website at: http://www.betterinvesting.org/stocks/resources

"With a click of a mouse, our Digital Roadshow allows the individual investor to see the same content we present to institutional investors and analysts," said John Sztykiel, president and CEO of Spartan Motors. "We encourage all of Spartan's stakeholders to take a look at the Digital Roadshow and learn more about our growth story."

The Digital Roadshow utilizes video of CEO John Sztykiel and CFO Jim Knapp to tell the Spartan story while allowing users to interact and "click through" to different sections of the presentation. The Digital Roadshow is approximately 40 minutes and covers all content of the Company's standard analyst presentation, including company background, products, markets and financial information.

About Spartan Motors

Spartan Motors, Inc. (http://www.spartanmotors.com) designs, engineers and manufactures custom chassis and vehicles for the recreational vehicle, fire truck, ambulance, emergency-rescue and specialty vehicle markets. The Company's brand names– **Spartan™**, **Crimson Fire™**, **Crimson Fire Aerials™**, and **Road Rescue™**–are known for quality, value, service and being the first to market with innovative products. The Company employs approximately 900 at facilities in Michigan, Pennsylvania, South Carolina, and South Dakota. Spartan reported sales of $343.0 million in 2005 and is focused on becoming the premier manufacturer of specialty vehicles and chassis in North America.

Courtesy Spartan Motors

E X H I B I T 7-3c (Continued)

CONTACT:

John Sztykiel, CEO, or Jim Knapp, CFO

Spartan Motors, Inc.

(517) 543-6400

(616) 233-0500/rmcgrath@lambert-edwards.com

Ryan McGrath or Jeff Lambert

Lambert, Edwards & Associates, Inc.

8

Consumer Relations

A development almost as significant to business as the Industrial Revolution has been the "Age of the Consumer." This emphasis on consumerism began with the establishment of the National Consumers League in 1899. It received added impetus with the establishment of the Consumers Union and the publication of Consumer Reports in 1936. The creation of government regulatory agencies such as the Food and Drug Administration (FDA) and the Federal Trade Commission (FTC) added to the movement's impact, and consumerism finally came of age with the installation of a consumer affairs adviser in the White House during the presidency of John F. Kennedy.

Today, no corporation can ignore the need for a fully functioning program in consumer relations or, as it is often known, consumer affairs. The ROPE process model is a useful means of preparing and executing a consumer relations program.

RESEARCH

Research for consumer relations includes investigation of the client, the reason for the program, and the consumer audiences to be targeted for communication.

Client Research

In the case of consumer relations, client research will be centered on the organization's reputation in its dealings with consumers. How credible is the organization with activist consumer groups? Has it been a frequent target of their attacks? What are its past and present consumer relations practices? Does it have a viable program in place? What are its major strengths and weaknesses in this area? What opportunities exist to enhance the organization's reputation and credibility in consumer affairs? The answers to these questions will provide a reasonably complete background for further development of a consumer relations program.

Opportunity or Problem Research

Explanation and justification of the need for a consumer relations program is part of the research process. The need grows out of the client research phase in determining past and present dealings with consumers. If problems already exist, a reactive program will be necessary. If there are no problems with consumers at the moment, the practitioner should consider preparing a proactive program. The organization's "wellness" in its relations with consumers should be made a matter of priority concern to management. Also, opportunities and challenges are often connected to the competition faced by the organization. For example, other companies are vying for the same audience by capturing market share or consumer loyalty.

Audience Research

The final aspect of research consists of identifying and examining audiences to be targeted in a consumer relations program. These audiences usually include:

Company employees

Customers

    Professionals

    Middle class

    Working class

    Minorities

Other

    Activist consumer groups

    Consumer publications

    Community media—mass and specialized

    Community leaders and organizations

Information about the customer groups and activist consumer groups should be of particular interest. Their attitudes and behaviors toward the company and their media habits are especially important.

OBJECTIVES

Consumer relations programs may use both impact and output objectives.

Impact Objectives

Some likely examples of impact objectives are:

1. To increase consumers' knowledge about the company's products, services, and policies (by 30 percent during the current year)

2. To promote (30 percent) more favorable consumer opinion toward the company (before December 1)

3. To increase sales (15 percent) for a company's specific product or service (this year)

4. To encourage more positive feedback (20 percent) from consumer groups to the company's programs (in the coming year)

Output Objectives

Output objectives for consumer relations involve the practitioner's measurable communication efforts with targeted audiences:

1. To distribute (10 percent) more consumer publications during the period June 1 to August 31

2. To develop three employee consumer seminars for this fiscal year

3. To meet with five important consumer groups during the next six months

4. To prepare and distribute recipes for using the product to 12 major food editors in the state during the campaign

PROGRAMMING

Programming for consumer relations includes planning the theme and messages, action(s) or special event(s), uncontrolled and controlled media, and effective communication principles to execute the program.

Theme and Messages

The theme and messages will grow out of the consumer relations situation and will reflect research findings and objectives for the program.

Action(s) or Special Event(s)

Organizational actions and special events in a consumer relations program generally include:

1. Advising management and all employees about consumer issues

2. Developing an efficient consumer response system

3. Handling specific consumer complaints through a customer relations office

4. Creating a company ombudsman, whose role is the investigation and resolution of complaints

5. Maintaining liaison with external activist consumer groups

6. Monitoring federal and state regulatory agencies and consumer legislation that might affect the company

7. Developing emergency plans for a product recall
8. Establishing a consumer education program, including meetings, information racks with printed materials on product uses, training video on product uses, celebrity endorsements and tours, online interactive quiz, and paid advertising on consumer topics
9. Holding employee consumerism conferences, seminars, and/or field training
10. Establishing a presence on a social media or virtual world Web site

These actions and events form the basis of a thorough consumer relations program.

Uncontrolled and Controlled Media

Community, and sometimes state or national, media should be targeted for appropriate news releases, photo opportunities or photographs, interviews, and other forms of uncontrolled materials reporting the company's actions or events in consumer affairs.

Controlled media for a consumer relations program usually include printed materials on the effective use of the company's products or on health, safety, or other consumer-oriented topics. In addition, specific printed materials are developed for meetings, conferences, and other special events. Audiovisual materials such as training videos and DVDs are often used as vehicles for consumer education. One of the most important mechanisms for effective consumer communication is the company Web site. This can contain virtually unlimited amounts of information useful to consumers. The cases included in this chapter illustrate a variety of forms of both uncontrolled and controlled media.

Finally, interpersonal communication should play a significant role in any consumer relations program. Ideally, the company can employ a consumer affairs spokesperson whose tasks may include conferring with consumer groups, addressing community organizations, or even representing the company in mass media appearances, including paid consumer advertising. Interpersonal communications should also be used generously in the company's consumer response system, its customer relations office, and other meetings and conferences in the consumer relations program.

Effective Communication

The principles of special interest for effective communication in consumer relations are source credibility, two-way communication, and audience participation.

A major purpose of consumer relations programs is credibility enhancement. For example, Giant grocery chain employs a consumer adviser who produces a "weekly column" for radio stations and listens to customers. One woman held the position for more than 25 years and captured considerable name recognition and credibility for her nutritional and shopping information.

Consumers are increasingly quality conscious in their purchases of goods and services. To cite another prominent example, U.S. automobile manufacturers have suffered a loss of public confidence and credibility in comparison with the high-quality standards of their Japanese competitors. Because of this stiff overseas competition, the U.S. companies have been forced to improve their quality controls, their warranties, and their treatment of consumers in general. Once lost, corporate credibility is difficult to rebuild, but effective programs in consumer relations can be a decisive factor in that rebuilding process.

Two-way communication and audience participation go hand in hand in consumer relations. There can be no substitute for direct, interpersonal communication in some situations. The proper treatment of consumers demands that their grievances be heard and, in most cases, personally resolved. The most effective consumer education programs are those that go beyond mere distribution of literature on store information racks. The best programs involve the consumer personally in meetings, interviews, conferences, and/or other interpersonal presentations that allow audience feedback and participation.

EVALUATION

There are no surprises and nothing out of the ordinary in the evaluation of consumer relations programs. The practitioner uses the previously discussed methods to evaluate the program's stated objectives. Measures of reputation and sales are frequent mainstays of evaluating successful programs.

SUMMARY

Research for consumer relations concentrates on an organization's reputation with its consumers and on the reason for conducting a program of this kind. In some instances, the consumer publics are segmented, with different messages and media designed for communication with each group.

Consumer relations uses both impact and output objectives. Impact objectives propose outcomes that increase consumers' knowledge or influence their attitudes and behaviors. Output objectives propose outcomes in terms of measurable practitioner efforts without regard to impact.

Programming involves organizational actions such as advising management about consumer affairs, developing consumer-oriented programs, and/or holding meetings or conferences about consumerism. Communication for consumer relations includes uncontrolled, controlled, and interpersonal formats, although the use of controlled printed materials is often emphasized. But interpersonal communication is increasingly being used.

Evaluation, as in other forms of public relations, consists of discovering appropriate measurements for the program's stated objectives.

READINGS ON CONSUMER RELATIONS

Abboud, Leila. "Stung by Public Distrust, Drug Makers Seek to Heal Image," *Wall Street Journal* 40 (August 26, 2005): sec. B.

Beaupre, Andre. "Getting Your Customers to Help with Public Relations," *Public Relations Tactics* 10 (October 2003): 9.

Bell, Chip R. *Customers as Partners: Building Relationships That Last.* San Francisco: Berrett-Koehler, 1994.

Benett, Andrew. "Consumers Are Watching You," *Advertising Age* 79 (April 7, 2008): 19.

Bush, Lee. "Focusing on Strategy: Moving Beyond Media Relations and Getting to the New Brand Marketing Table," *Public Relations Strategist* 13 (Spring 2007): 30–32.

Choi, Chong Ju, Tarek Ibrahim Eldomiaty, and Sae Won Kim. "Consumer Trust, Social Marketing and Ethics of Welfare Exchange," *Journal of Business Ethics* 74 (August 2007): 17–23.

Colgate, Mark R., and Peter J. Danaher. "Implementing a Customer Relationship Strategy: The Asymmetric Impact of Poor Versus Excellent Execution," *Journal of the Academy of Marketing Science* 28 (Summer 2000): 375ff.

Crawford, Alan Pell. "Why We Need to Begin Our Work With a Customer-First Approach," *Public Relations Tactics* 7 (April 2000): 12.

DeVries, Dave. "Oprah's Car Giveaway: Marketing or Public Relations? A PR Pro Decides," *Public Relations Tactics* 11 (December 2004): 9.

"Eat Me, I'm Safe," *Onearth: Environmental Politics People* 27 (fall 2005): 9.

Falbo, Bridget. "Wow Customers with Service to Build Positive PR," *Hotel and Motel Management* 213 (May 4, 1998): 45.

Fornell, Claes. "A Method for Improving Customer Satisfaction and Measuring Its Impact on Profitability," *International Public Relations Review* 15 (1992): 6ff.

Greene, Richard. "Two Steps to New Product Success," *Public Relations Tactics* 11 (December 2004): 17.

Guiniven, John. "The Less-is-More Approach: Extending Campaigns' Lives," *Public Relations Tactics* 14 (April 2007): 6.

Holtz, Shel. "Establishing Connections," *Communication World* 22 (May–June 2005): 9ff.

Krauss, Michael. "Create Customer Promoters, Avoid Detractors," *Marketing News* 40 (April 1, 2006): 8–9.

Miller, Steve. "Toyota CGM Exec Monitors the Good, the Blog, the Ugly," *Brandweek* 48 (September 3, 2007): 8.

Nail, Jim. "A Distorted Image?: How Public Relations Can Cure Blu-Ray's Blues," *Public Relations Tactics* 14 (March 2007): 10.

Quick, John, and Anna Dé. "Update to the Direct-to-Consumer Debate: The Risks and Benefits of Pharmaceutical Promotion Across the Atlantic," *Public Relations Strategist* 10 (spring 2004): 29–31.

Rappleye, Willard C., Jr. "Customer Relationship Management," *Across the Board* 37 (July 2000): 47ff.

Rhea, Darrel. "Understanding Why People Buy," *Business Week Online* (August 15, 2005), http://www.businessweek.com/innovate/content/aug2005/id20050809_077337.htm.

Schneider, Joan. "Countdown To Launch: 10 Lessons Learned About Publicizing New Products," *Public Relations Tactics* 8 (May 2001): 24.

Scott, David Meerman. "The New News Cycle," *EContent* 28 (July–August 2005): 48.

_____. *The New Rules of Marketing and PR: How to Use News Releases, Blogs, Podcasting, Viral Marketing and Online Media to Reach Buyers Directly.* Hoboken, NJ: Wiley, 2007.

Sernovitz, Andy. *Word of Mouth Marketing: How Smart Companies Get People Talking.* Chicago: Kaplan, 2006.

Stern, Barbara B. "Advertising Intimacy: Relationship Marketing and the Services Consumer," *Journal of Advertising* 26 (winter 1997): 7–19.

"Target Practice," *Economist* (April 2, 2005): 13ff.

Thompson, Gary W. "Consumer PR Techniques in the High Tech Arena," *Public Relations Quarterly* 37 (winter 1992): 21–22.

Trudel, Mary R. "Consumer Marketing Synergy: PR Comes of Age," *Public Relations Quarterly* 36 (spring 1991): 26ff.

Ventura, Michael. "No Such Thing as a Free Lunch," *Advertising Week* 49 (May 12, 2008): 18.

Weber, Larry. *Marketing to the Social Web: How Digital Customer Communities Build Your Business.* Hoboken, NJ: Wiley, 2007.

Willing, Paul. "Be a Partner with Your Community" *Nursing Homes* 54 (August 2005): 14–16.

Zoda, Suzanne M. "Rebuilding Credibility with a Hostile Public," *Communication World* 10 (October 1993): 17ff.

Consumer Relations Cases

Case 8-1

Effective campaigns often focus on the "influentials" within a broader target audience. A large product association used a health-based theme and generated large returns on its communication campaign investment. Exhibit 8-1a is brochure to nurses, Exhibit 8-1b is a news release, and Exhibit 8-1c is a survey on consumer attitudes.

Improving Patient Care with Cranberries' Round-the-Clock Bacteria Protection
Cranberry Marketing Committee with Publicis Consultants PR

SUMMARY

The Cranberry Marketing Committee (CMC), representing U.S. cranberry growers, retained Publicis Consultants PR with the goal of increasing domestic consumption of fresh cranberries and cranberry products. The campaign leveraged the greatest motivator for dietary change—advice from a health professional. Through research, we identified critical subgroups to reach (dietitians, nurse practitioners, and physician assistants) and learned what communications tools would be most appreciated. By performing direct outreach, as well as placing health and nutrition stories in the publications their patients read, we delivered on all tactical measurements and contributed to clear economic value for U.S. cranberry growers.

RESEARCH

The CMC, representing U.S. cranberry growers, retained Publicis Consultants PR with the goal of increasing U.S. consumption of fresh cranberries and cranberry products by improving awareness of the health, flavor, and convenience benefits

Courtesy Cranberry Marketing Committee

that cranberries offer. Not only is CMC's budget smaller than major pharmaceuticals communicating their medicinal products' health benefits, but its promotions budget is even significantly smaller compared to much of its competition within its own world of healthy agricultural products. Therefore, we recognized the need to target influencers with the strongest impact on consumer behavior.

According to original research conducted on behalf of CMC by an independent research firm, we learned that U.S. consumers feel that information from a medical professional about the health benefits of cranberries is most likely to increase their consumption. This is the single greatest motivator, at 64 percent for both men and women.

Once we determined that health professionals (HPs) would comprise our primary influencer target, we examined which specific types of HPs would be most beneficial. Often, clients assume HPs equals doctors. However, our target analysis (conducted through secondary research, both online and print, as well as anecdotal evidence from conversations with leading HPs) showed that doctors tend not to prescribe preventative dietary interventions.

In contrast:

- Fifty percent of nurse practitioners prescribe dietary agents, and they reach significant numbers of patients: 74 percent treat three or more patients per hour, 68 percent provide the patient's primary care in a high-volume setting, and 65 percent spend over 80 percent of their time in clinical practice.

- Dietitians determine menu choices at hospitals and long-term care facilities, often single-handedly; 70 percent counsel patients and 80 percent have a role in product purchasing.

- Finally, physician assistants also make hundreds of thousands of nonprescription recommendations annually and treat precisely the conditions cranberries may help prevent, with 10 million cases of urinary tract infections (UTIs), 8 million cases of heart failure, and 14 million health maintenance consultations to patients annually.

- We also included health media in order to assist HP advocacy: patients are doubly motivated to act on a message when they hear it from their HP and read it in a respected news source.

PLANNING

We tapped into original research to determine strategies and tactics to move HPs from passive interest to active advocacy.

- According to an HP survey also conducted on behalf of CMC by an independent research firm, they generally viewed cranberries favorably, particularly for prevention of UTIs.

- However, less than half understood why cranberries may prevent UTIs, and that the same reason might play a role in preventing many other medical problems (some stomach ulcers, gum disease and other oral health problems, and possibly even respiratory conditions) by blocking bacteria.

- This was important to counteract, because this incorrect belief was important to counteract because it caused the HPs to lack urgency in recommending cranberries for overall wellness to non-UTI patients. Only 36 percent recommended cranberry consumption on a daily or weekly basis.

The research also demonstrated where we would need to communicate our messages: 9 in 10 HPs said they are most receptive to cranberry information at health care conferences/trade shows, where they have taken time out of their busy schedules to focus on information gathering. Therefore, we employed trade shows, along with several other high-scoring communications vehicles (information to give directly to patients, technical information for the health care professional and recipes) in our plan.

Objectives

- Demonstrate increased interest in cranberries' health benefits, with the goal of tripling voluntary opt-ins to the HP database (for further information, such as a quarterly e-newsletter), presenting information to at least 2,500 trade show attendees and securing a speaking opportunity

- Improve likelihood of patients hearing about cranberry health benefits, as measured by at least a 10:1 return on investment (ROI) on media relations

- Deliver value to the cranberry growers, as evaluated by U.S. market representing at least 50 percent of global sales and reaching at least $200 million in agricultural crop value

Strategy

Promote cranberries' unique bacteria blocking mechanism as a tool for HPs to help prevent a variety of health problems and, therefore, make patient care easier.

EXECUTION

Tactics

- Stage exhibitions at the following trade shows: American Dietetic Association's Food & Nutrition Conference & Expo (ADA, St. Louis, October 22–25, 2005); American Association of Nurse Practitioners (AANP, June 20–25, 2006, Grapevine, Texas); and American Academy of Physician Assistants (AAPA, May 27–June 1, 2006, San Francisco). Please note that we exhibit under the name of the Cranberry Institute, CMC's partner in funding and promoting credible scientific research.

- Secure speaking opportunities for our technical expert, Dr. Marty Starr, during the trade shows as well as positioning him in the trade show booth to answer questions.

- Promote our trade show exhibition in advance by direct e-mails and follow-up with a special issue of our Cranberry Health News e-newsletter dedicated to that trade show's specific audience.

- Develop requested literature at the trade show booth (technical brochures and fact sheets for HPs, and simpler brochures with health information in laymen's terms and recipes for HPs to share with patients). Distribute at trade shows, promote in e-newsletters as free tools, and mail bulk copies to individual HPs upon request.

- Communicate to the health media via a radio news release and radio media tour on oral health, health press kit on cancer, run-of-press on daily wellness, healthy recipes, and desk-side briefings and editor luncheons with spokesperson dietitians from CMC's Speakers Bureau.

- Editor luncheons—Reinforce health messages of cranberries to at least 50 editors by conducting luncheons in Birmingham and New York City.

Challenges and Materials

We successfully addressed the challenges set forth in the planning stage as described below. Please see the appendix for samples of our high-quality materials, designed and produced with consistent branding and high standards for communicating credible health information.

EVALUATION

Trade Show Measurements

- HPs grew the e-newsletter database fivefold, through voluntary opt-ins from inception to end of this program year. This exceeded our goal of tripling the database.

- Additionally, 4,500 influential trade show attendees visited our booths at ADA, AANP, and AAPA (combined), nearly twice our goal.

- One-hundred powerful dietitians attended Dr. Starr's two presentations at Nutrition Educators for Health Professionals and Nutrition Education of the Public dietary practice groups, twice our goal.

Health Media Relations Measurements

- Total number of stories: 184
- Total impressions: 382,003,635
- Total publicity value: $17,748,059
- Return on investment: 91:1 (far exceeding a goal of 10:1 ROI)

Editor Luncheons

- Fourteen Birmingham editors and 41 New York City editors attended the luncheons, for a total of 55 editors (surpassing the goal of 50 attendees).

Final Evaluation of Success—Value to U.S. Cranberry Growers

- An independent evaluation by an agricultural economist with the University of California at Davis found that the U.S. market still represents 77 percent of sales despite a variety of successful export markets, exceeding a goal of 50 percent. To quote: "Does the emphasis on health benefits make economic sense? Yes."
- We helped U.S. cranberry growers earn their highest crop value in the last four years, rising from $182 to $211 million. This more than doubled the value of the crop just five years ago ($96 million in 2000) and significantly exceeded the $200 million goal.

EXHIBIT 8-1a   Brochure—Power of Cranberries

THE POWER OF
CRANBERRIES

MAKING PATIENT CARE
EASIER FOR NURSES

CRANBERRY
INSTITUTE

Cranberry Institute
3203-B Cranberry Highway
East Wareham, MA 02538

www.cranberryinstitute.org

CRANBERRY: BENEFITS COME IN A VARIETY OF FORMS

Research indicates that consuming 8–10 ounces of cranberry juice cocktail daily achieves bacterial antiadhesion benefits. In addition to juice, other forms of cranberry products contain similar amounts of the active flavonoids responsible for this effect.

BACTERIA BLOCKING EQUIVALENCIES:

POPULAR CRANBERRY PRODUCTS

8–10 oz. of 27% juice = 1 1/2 cups fresh berries = 1/2 cup sauce = 1 oz. sweetened dried cranberries

Source Amy Howell, PhD

To receive cranberry research updates, sign up for a FREE e-subscription to the Cranberry Health News through the Cranberry Institute Web site at www.cranberryinstitute.org.

Courtesy Cranberry Marketing Committee

EXHIBIT 8-1a (Continued)

IMPROVING QUALITY OF CARE

An ever-increasing amount of patient-care responsibility falls on the shoulders of registered nurses and nurse practitioners. With limited time and resources, finding efficient, cost-effective forms of disease prevention and treatment remains a primary goal.

While pharmaceutical interventions certainly have their place, an expanding body of scientific evidence suggests bioactive compounds in certain fruits and vegetables have disease-fighting properties that may stave off the need for prescription medications for certain conditions.

A diet high in antioxidant-rich fruits and vegetables is associated with decreased risk of cancer, heart disease and type 2 diabetes. Among common fruits, cranberry has one of the highest concentrations of antioxidant polyphenols and exhibits potent antiproliferative activity.

FRUIT / SERVING SIZE (g)	TOTAL PHENOLS PER SERVING (mg)
CRANBERRIES 1/2 cup (55)	373
PEAR 1 medium (166)	317
RED GRAPES 1/2 cup (80)	296
APPLE 1 medium (138)	256
CHERRIES 1/2 cup (73)	231
STRAWBERRIES 8 medium (147)	199
WATERMELON 1 large wedge, 2 cups diced (286)	183
CULTIVATED BLUEBERRIES 1/2 cup (79)	181
BANANA 1 medium (128)	174
GREEN GRAPES 1/2 cup (80)	155

Amount of total phenols in fruits on the basis of serving size.

UTIs COME IN ALL SHAPES & SIZES

Cranberry has received most of its attention for maintaining urinary tract health, due to the antiadhesion properties of proanthocyanadins (PACs). These condensed tannins found in cranberries have a unique chemical structure that inhibits key E. coli bacteria from adhering to the uroepithelium and proliferating.

UTI IMPLICATIONS FOR NUMEROUS PATIENT POPULATIONS:

Women's Wellness

- An estimated 11 million U.S. women suffer from UTIs and 25% have recurring infections.
- Regular cranberry consumption reduced recurrent infections by as much as 40%.
- Cranberry can help reduce the need for antibiotics and decrease antibiotic resistance.

Elderly Care

- A randomized, placebo-controlled, double-blind trial involving elderly patients in a hospital setting demonstrated a 50% reduced risk of developing additional urinary bacteria in the group that consumed cranberries.

Pediatrics

- Among infants who have a UTI during their first year, 18% of boys and 26% of girls will have additional infections.
- Reduction of antibiotic use prevents depletion of beneficial bacteria in the gut and helps reduce antibiotic resistance.

This same mechanism may also play a role in reducing oral health problems, ulcers and even respiratory infections.

BENEFITS BEYOND THE BLADDER

Additionally, cranberries appear to possess several other protective properties that could have far-reaching public health benefits.

HEART HEALTH

Cardiovascular disease (CVD) is the leading cause of death in the United States and claims more lives than the next five diseases combined. The annual CVD death rate exceeds one million and associated annual costs are estimated at over $350 billion.

Cornell University researchers examined the potential role of cranberries in the prevention of CVD, using cranberry extracts on various CVD markers in vitro, and found:

- Reduction in LDL oxidation
- Induction of hepatic LDL receptors
- Increased uptake of cholesterol by hepatocytes

COGNITIVE FUNCTION

Researchers have hypothesized that cranberries may protect brain cells from free radical damage and subsequent motor and cognitive function losses. Preliminary results in both animal and human models are encouraging and additional research is being explored.

Potential public health benefits are far-reaching.

EXHIBIT 8-1b   News Release

CRANBERRY'S

PUNCH

FOR IMMEDIATE RELEASE
November 27, 2006

Contact:
Diana Steeble
Cranberry Institute
c/o Publicis Dialog
(206) 270-4637
Diana.steeble@publicis-usa.com

CRANBERRIES OFFER BIG BANG FOR THE BITE!
One of a kind, the delicious berry provides a double-dose of disease prevention

EAST WAREHAM, MA — As trends go, being a health-conscious consumer tops the list. From beauty products to gym memberships, we aspire to a healthy lifestyle. The most integral, and perhaps challenging, part of that lifestyle is nurturing a healthy diet. It's not just about counting calories, but finding foods that optimize health and prevent disease. With so many foods claiming healthy attributes, the choices can overwhelm us. That's why it may be surprising to learn that one of the smallest, simplest foods truly delivers the biggest bang for the bite — cranberries.

In addition to conventional vitamins and nutrients, **cranberries pack a one-two punch** of both **antioxidant** and **antiadhesion** properties. Known for being a rich source of antioxidants — those substances that protect cells from damage and disease — cranberries may help prevent cancer and heart disease. And because cranberries contain the **most antioxidants per calorie** among popular fruits, they're the perfect choice.

In addition to antioxidants, cranberries possess unique bacterial **antiadhesion** — or **bacteria blocking** — **benefits** essential to maintaining good health. Martin Starr, PhD, Science Advisor to the Cranberry Institute explains, "The distinctive structure of specific compounds found in cranberries create these antiadhesion properties. And, the accumulating research shows that the bacteria that cause urinary tract infections, gum disease, some stomach ulcers and other infections are inhibited by cranberry consumption." In layman's terms, cranberries prevent bad bacteria from sticking to our bodies. If they can't stick, they can't multiply and cause an infection.

Cranberries aren't just exceptionally nutritious, they're delicious, versatile and easy to incorporate into your daily diet. Whether you prefer fresh or dried berries, refreshing juice, potent powders or a tangy sauce, there are endless ways to bring cranberries to the table.

The Cranberry Marketing Committee offers these easy, great-tasting recipes. In just 10 minutes, you can prepare the delicious **Cranberry Bean Salad**. A hint of curry spikes this tangy mix of cranberries, apples and chickpeas to make a flavorful no-cook side dish. If you're looking for a light entrée, you'll savor the **Cranberry Tuna Salad**. Featuring tuna and dried cranberries mixed with edamame in a wasabi-ginger dressing, it's loaded with nutrition and takes just minutes to prepare. Finally, try the delicious **Cranberry Earl Grey Granita**. Its cool, crisp flavor makes the perfect afternoon refresher or elegant dessert. Any way you prepare them, cranberries make eating right effortless.

The Cranberry Institute is dedicated to supporting research and increasing awareness about the health benefits of cranberries. For more information, visit www.cranberryinstitute.org or www.uscranberries.com.

###

Editors Note: For interviews, photographs or additional recipes, contact Diana Steeble via e-mail at Diana.steeble@publicis-usa.com.

Courtesy Cranberry Marketing Committee

EXHIBIT 8-1b (Continued)

CRANBERRY TUNA SALAD

CRANBERRY'S
one-**two**

CRANBERRY TUNA SALAD
Prep time: 15 minutes | Makes: 4 servings

1 cup Edamame, cooked, drained
1 cup Cherry tomatoes, halved
1 cup Carrots, peeled, diced
1 can (6 oz) Tuna, packed in water, drained
1/2 cup Dried Cranberries
1/2 cup Radishes, halved, thinly sliced
1/4 cup Green onions, thinly sliced
2 tablespoons Olive oil
4 teaspoons Lime juice
1 to 2 teaspoons Wasabi paste
1 teaspoon Fresh ginger, grated
1 teaspoon Sugar

Mix edamame, tomatoes, carrots, tuna, cranberries, radishes, and green onions in large bowl.

Blend olive oil, lime juice, wasabi paste, ginger, and sugar in small bowl. Pour over tuna mixture; toss until blended.

Nutritional Analysis per Serving: Calories 240 (34% Calories from Fat), 16g Protein, 24g Carbohydrate, 5g Fiber, 9g Fat, 1g Sat. Fat, 0g Trans Fat, 15mg Cholesterol, 190mg Sodium

CRANBERRY
INSTITUTE

E X H I B I T 8-1c   Survey on Consumer Attitudes

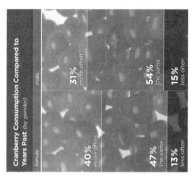

Cranberry consumption is on the rise. More people are actively increasing cranberry consumption than decreasing it (38 percent vs. 13 percent, respectively), and women are more likely than men to have increased their consumption of cranberries.

Cranberry Consumption Compared to Years Past (by gender)

female | male
more often | more often
40% | **31%**

the same | the same
47% | **54%**

less often | less often
13% | **15%**

The likelihood of purchasing cranberries is influenced by gender, age and region of the country. Women are much more likely to have purchased a cranberry product in the last six months then men (76 vs. 24 percent), consistent with women being more likely to do the grocery shopping for their household overall. Consumers aged 55 and older are more likely to purchase cranberry products, as are those who live in New England or the West Coast. Income level, parental status and ethnicity do not play strong roles in determining usage.

Frequency of Cranberry Purchases in the Last Six Months

TOTAL

27% weekly
24% monthly
22% every few months
13% once
6% never
8% daily

PURCHASED JUICE

35% weekly
29% monthly
19% every few months
4% once
2% never
11% daily

CONSUMER ATTITUDES ABOUT CRANBERRIES

Introduction

Bold, healthy and versatile, cranberries make a persuasive case for belonging in American shopping carts. But how do U.S. consumers perceive the cranberry? How often do they purchase cranberry products, and why? How much of a role do the health benefits play?

This report answers those questions, based on responses from a nationwide survey on consumer attitudes about cranberries. Sponsored by the Cranberry Marketing Committee (CMC), and financially supported in part by the USDA Federal State Marketing Improvement Program and the Wisconsin Cranberry Board, the study occurred in April 2005.

Conducted by an independent research firm, the study includes 1,000 random telephone interviews, providing a sample that is consistent with the total American population. All respondents purchase at least half of their household groceries, and 83 percent purchase three-quarters or more of the household groceries. The study's margin of error is +/- 3.0 percent and its confidence interval is 95 percent.

For information on the health benefits of cranberries and recipes, please visit www.uscranberries.com.

Cranberry Consumption

Americans know their cranberries. Approximately 79 percent of all U.S. consumers have purchased cranberry products at the grocery store in the last six months, and 90 percent have purchased cranberry products at some point in their lives. Among the total population, 59 percent purchase cranberry products once a month or more. And, people who specifically consume cranberry in juice form have a higher frequency rate, with 75 percent purchasing juice monthly or more.

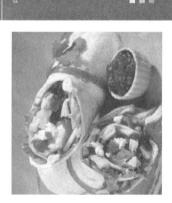

EXHIBIT 8-1c   (Continued)

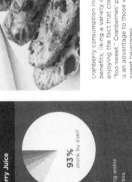

Usage of Cranberry Product Forms

Cranberry juice is the most common form purchased at the grocery store (61 percent of cranberry product purchases). Cranberry juice drinkers are also the most frequent cranberry consumers overall. Most do not mix the juice with other beverage products, preferring to drink the juice by itself.

Popular Uses for Cranberry Juice

TOTAL
note: multiple responses result in statistics exceeding 100%

93% drink by itself

9% added to alcohol/cocktails
3% added to punch
3% added to sparkling water
2% added to smoothies
3% other

Turning to other cranberry products such as sweetened dried cranberries, cranberry sauce and fresh or frozen whole cranberries, consumers report a variety of recipe-oriented uses. They use non-juice products primarily for snacks, salads, adding to breads or muffins, and turning into relishes or spreads. Fewer consumers use cranberries for adding to cereals, baking in pies or tarts or adding to granola. Reasons for

cranberry consumption include taste, health benefits, liking a variety of beverages, and enjoying the fact that cranberries are not "too sweet." Cranberries' pleasantly tart taste is an advantage to those who dislike very sweet beverages.

Younger adults seek cranberry products that are very easy to prepare, rather than using cranberry ingredients in complicated recipes. They also are less likely to choose traditional uses, such as making a cranberry relish, in favor of more contemporary approaches like snacking on dried cranberries out of hand. Consumers in the 35 to 54 age range with children who eat cranberries are also more likely to have cranberries by themselves as a snack.

Consumers are most likely to name cranberry juice as the type of cranberry product they will purchase over the next six months (67 percent). Results are higher (72 percent) when examining just the 18 to 34 year old population. Seniors (aged 55+) drive sales of cranberry sauces and relishes into second place at 46 percent. Other frequent answers include products with whole cranberries such as muffins, dried cranberries, fresh or frozen cranberries, light cranberry juice and specialty products like cereals, barbecue sauces and mustards.

How Consumers Use the Cranberry Products They Purchase (by age)	Total%	18-34%	35-54%	55+%
Eat by themselves as a snack	30	29	37	24
Turn into relish/spread	27	16	25	34
Add to breads or muffins	23	23	22	25
Add to salads	23	23	25	21
Add to drinks	10	10	14	6
Add to cereal	8	4	7	12
Add to pies or tarts	8	14	5	8
Add to granola or other mixes	5	9	5	2

Future Cranberry Consumption: Likely Purchases in the Next Six Months (by age)	Total%	18-34%	35-54%	55+%
Cranberry juice	67	72	66	66
Cranberry sauce/relish	46	34	43	56
Products with whole cranberries such as muffins	31	26	33	32
Dried cranberries	26	21	29	25
Fresh or frozen cranberries	26	17	26	31
Light cranberry juice with reduced calories, carbs and sugars	25	21	26	27
Specialty cranberry products such as cereals, BBQ sauces, mustards or others	21	18	26	17

EXHIBIT 8-1c (Continued)

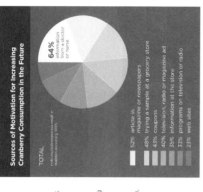

Sources of Motivation for Increasing Cranberry Consumption in the Future

TOTAL *(with multiple responses result in statistics exceeding 100%)*

64% information from a doctor or nurse

52% article in magazine or newspapers
48% trying a sample at a grocery store
45% coupons
40% television, radio or magazine ad
35% information at the store
33% programs on television or radio
23% web sites

Health's Role in Cranberry Consumption

Health benefits are a major factor driving increased consumption. Among the total population, 63 percent have consumed cranberries for their health benefits. Among those increasing their frequency, 74 percent do so for health benefits.

Those using cranberries more often are also more likely to be aware of the health benefits, suggesting an advantage in increasing the awareness of health benefits. Nearly half of all consumers are aware of the UTI prevention benefit (49 percent), and women are even more likely to be aware of it (53 percent).

All women surveyed and men over 35 are likely to have recently increased cranberry consumption, likely due to the health benefits. Consumers aged 55-64 are even more likely to have increased cranberry consumption, and are very interested in staying healthy as they age. Households with children also tend to be very interested in the health benefits of cranberries.

Those who recall seeing information about the health benefits of cranberries are most likely to name magazine articles (38 percent) and

television ads (33 percent) as the sources of that information. Weekly consumers are more likely than infrequent consumers to report seeing cranberry health information in print or on the Web.

Power of the Health Professional's Advice

Consumers feel that information from a medical professional about the health benefits of cranberries is most likely to increase their consumption. This is the single greatest motivator, at 64 percent for both men and women. A health professional's opinion is slightly more influential to consumers with children than those without children (69 vs. 61 percent).

Other significant motivating factors for consuming cranberries include learning about cranberries through the media and trying samples at the grocery store. Consumers say they are most interested in heart health (60 percent), cancer prevention (59 percent), anti-aging (57 percent), fighting bacteria (56 percent) and oral health (51 percent).

Cranberries for the Holidays

While cranberries offer year-round health benefits and most consumers eat them throughout the year, cranberries will always have a special place on the holiday table. In fact, 88 percent of Americans include cranberries in their Thanksgiving celebrations every year.

Consumer Awareness of Health Benefits *(by gender)*

	Total	Male	Female
Help prevent urinary tract infections	49	37	53
Contain more antioxidants than most commonly eaten fruits	11	9	12
Vitamin C/vitamins	5	3	5
Reduce ulcers & other intestinal problems	5	4	5
Good for kidneys	4	2	5
Contribute to heart health	4	5	3
Fight bacteria	3	3	3
Reduce risk of certain types of cancers	2	2	1
None/don't know	32	44	27

Cranberries Pack a Punch with Health Benefits

Cranberries possess powerful bacteria blocking properties that may help prevent urinary tract infections (UTIs), some stomach ulcers and even gum disease. Additionally, as a rich source of antioxidants, they may help protect against heart disease and cancer. Consumers have many good reasons to incorporate cranberries into their daily diet:

Case 8-2

Special events provide a method to accent a new product or service. In this case, competition between the fastest talker and the fastest "texter" for text messages provided a backdrop for national publicity. Exhibit 8-2a is the news release announcing text ordering and Exhibit 8-2b is the news release promoting "Big Game" points.

Papa, What's Next? Text! Papa John's Pizza First with Text Ordering Option

Papa John's with Fleishman-Hillard, Inc.

SITUATION ANALYSIS

In the late 1960s, consumers reveled at the idea of picking up the phone and having a pizza delivered to their door. Decades later, in 2001, Papa John's made ordering pizza even more convenient with the introduction of online ordering at www.papajohns.com. And in November of 2007, Papa John's led the entire quick-service restaurant industry across yet another technology threshold as the first national pizza chain to offer text message ordering.

But is text message ordering truly faster and easier than ordering via phone? And how does it work?

Fleishman-Hillard easily answered both questions with a three-part strategy to first tell the business story of this technological breakthrough to business partners, shareholders, and even competitors; then appeal to consumers and media with an attention-grabbing event pitting the World's Fastest Talker (speaking 10 words/second) against the World's Fastest Texter (typing 3.6 characters/second) in a pizza ordering challenge at the Mall of America in Minneapolis; and ultimately educate tech-savvy customers via blog outreach and an engaging online flash demonstration that illustrated the step-by-step text ordering process.

RESEARCH AND AUDIENCE ANALYSIS

Research revealed a number of trends in mobile communications. Text messaging is quickly becoming the communications vehicle of choice, with more than 48 percent of mobile phone owners sending daily text messages to friends and

Courtesy Papa John's International, Inc.

family. Texting is even more popular among the younger demographic, with 74 percent of Americans aged 18–24 using their mobile phones for more than chatting.

- Twenty-nine percent of cell phone users say they could not live without their cell phone.

- Forty-eight percent of cell phone users consider text messaging a "must have" option.

- Thirty-five percent of cell phone users say they send text messages to friends/family/business colleagues, including 65 percent of those ages 18–29 and 37 percent of those ages 30–49.

- Fifty-two percent of people keep their cell phone turned on at all times.

- Fifty percent of people say they have encountered people talking too loudly on their cell phone.

- Eight percent of cell phone users have texted in a vote to hit television programs such as "American Idol" and/or "Dancing with the Stars."

PLANNING AND STRATEGY

Objectives

- Drive media and consumer awareness of Papa John's text message ordering option

- Increase opt-in registrations for the www.papajohns.com e-mail and mobile phone customer database

- Drive consumers online to www.papajohns.com to view the text message ordering flash demonstration

Though Papa John's is the third-largest pizza chain in the United States, the company has continuously been regarded as the technology leader among the pizza industry's Big Three, thanks in large part to its seamless online ordering platform that allows customers to order from any Papa John's restaurant in the country via www.papajohns.com. And while competitors were busy streamlining their own online ordering process, Papa John's was one step ahead of everyone in the quick-service restaurant industry as the first pizza company to introduce text message ordering via a simple four-step process:

1. Customers first register online at www.papajohns.com and save their favorite orders, delivery, and payment preferences with the Papa John's "Favorites Wizard."

2. Once registered online, the Papa John's consumer can simply text FAV1, FAV2, etc., to 4PAPA (47272).

3. Papa John's then sends a text message detailing the order and requesting confirmation from the consumer.

4. The consumer presses Y1 to confirm the order for FAV1 or N1 to change the order. Once confirmed, the closest Papa John's restaurant processes the order.

Working closely with Papa John's, FH secured an exclusive story in *The Wall Street Journal* to debut this breakthrough technology to business partners and shareholders. The following morning, an Associated Press story (also secured by FH) was picked up by numerous print publications around the country—leading directly into a late-morning event at the high-traffic Mall of America, in which the World's Fastest Talker faced off against the 14-year-old World's Fastest Texter in a pizza ordering challenge to determine what was faster—ordering pizza the old-fashioned way via phone or ordering via text message. The event, in turn, provided vivid visuals to broadcast media, successfully making the business/technology story relevant to a broader consumer audience.

At the same time, FH conducted extensive online editorial outreach to the country's most popular and influential bloggers—identified as savvy "early adopters" of such technology. To further complement the Mall of America event and online outreach, FH created a flash demonstration to be featured on www.papa-johns.com, giving Web site visitors a step-by-step tutorial on how text message ordering works.

EXECUTION

- Research, contact, and negotiate participation of the World's Fastest Talker, Fran Capo (Capo is featured in the Guinness Book of World Records, having been clocked at 603.32 words a minute, or 10 words a second).

- Research, contact, and negotiate participation of the World's Fastest Texter, LG National Texting Champion 14-year-old Morgan Pozgar (Pozgar beat out more than 300 competitors by texting the winning phrase "Supercalifragilisticexpialidocious! Even though the sound of it is something quite atrocious. If you say it loud enough you'll always sound precocious" in just 42 seconds, or 3.6 characters per second).

- Partner with LG Mobile Phones to obtain high-resolution branded images of the LG enV—designed specifically for multimedia messaging with a QWERTY keyboard and large internal screen—to be used in the online flash demonstration and event signage.

- Obtain 10 free enV mobile phones (valued at more than $200 each) from LG for the event giveaway.

- Coordinate with local Papa John's franchisee to conduct pizza delivery and sampling at mall.

- Work directly with Mall of America staff on event location, staging, food permits, insurance, "victory" balloon drop, and other logistics.

- Set up wireless laptop stations at the Mall of America, allowing event attendees to learn more about text message ordering and register at www.papajohns.com.

- Create a flash demonstration to be hosted online at www.papajohns.com, giving customers a step-by-step illustration of how text message ordering works.

- Conduct selective media outreach to national outlets announcing Papa John's text message ordering system and previewing the Mall of America event.

- Conduct local media outreach in Minneapolis, driving crews to the Mall of America event for footage and interviews with the World's Fastest Talker and Texter.

- Conduct blog outreach to food and technology writers, providing access to the online flash demonstration.

Work with a local Minneapolis video crew to film the event and create a B-roll package that would be sent directly to news stations across the country.

EVALUATION

Drive media and consumer awareness of Papa John's text message ordering option:

- Developed 629 media placements that totaled more than 53 million impressions, with an ad value of nearly $350,000.

  Print—128 articles, including exclusive, pre-event business story in *The Wall Street Journal* (followed by AP story and later, *USA Today*)

  Television—462 segments and utilized B-roll and merchandised national feeds to garner coast-to-coast coverage about the event

  Radio—35 segments

Online

- Eighty-four blogs/Web forums that focused on influencer tech and food bloggers; provided flash demo for them to place on their own blog for easy consumer use.

- Post-event, FH posted a highlight reel of the Mall of America online at YouTube, garnering more than 12,000 views.

- Online buzz initiated by FH was not only heard by customers, but by media, with *USA Today* reporter Bruce Horowitz reading about text message ordering on a blog and subsequently writing his own story to spur a second wave of media coverage weeks after the initial launch.

Increase opt-in registrations for the www.papajohns.com e-mail and mobile phone customer database:

- Following the launch of text message ordering, more than 114,000 people registered their mobile phone number with Papa John's, opting to receive special offers via text.

Drive consumers online to www.papajohns.com to view the text message ordering flash demonstration:

- In just the first week following the text message ordering launch, more than 6,100 people viewed the flash demonstration at www.papajohns.com—a more than 2,000 percent increase from the mere 300 customers that had viewed a written tutorial posted online two weeks earlier.

EXHIBIT 8-2a   News Release on Text Ordering

Better Ingredients.
Better Pizza.

Papa, What's Next? Text! Papa John's Pizza First with Text Ordering Option

Ordering Pizza is Now Easier Than Ever with a Text Message to 4PAPA (47272)

LOUISVILLE, Ky.–(Nov. 15, 2007)–In the late 1960s, consumers reveled at the idea of picking up the phone and having a pizza delivered to their door. Decades later, in 2001, Papa John's made ordering pizza even more convenient with the introduction of online ordering at www.papajohns.com. Today, Papa John's is leading the entire quick-service restaurant industry across yet another technology threshold as the first national pizza chain to offer text message ordering.

Sound too good to be true? This is nothing to LOL about.

"Just a few years ago, e-mail was a revolutionary way to keep in touch with friends and family, and Papa John's responded in-kind with online ordering," said Jim Ensign, vice president, marketing communications for Papa John's International, Inc. "Now, more than 48 percent of mobile phone owners use text messaging to communicate with their friends and family every day. And just as we did with online ordering, Papa John's is proud to take the ease of text message communication one step further with our convenient text message ordering option."

The introduction of Papa John's text ordering comes just before one of the three busiest pizza delivery days of the year, the night before Thanksgiving. And with 74% of Americans age 18–24, using their mobile phones for more than chatting, busy college students cramming for finals can now discreetly order a late-night snack without violating their library's "no talking" policy.

BTW, text message ordering with Papa John's will put a :) on anyone's face with this simple four-step process:

1. Customers first register online at www.papajohns.com and save their favorite orders, delivery and payment preferences with the Papa John's "Favorites Wizard."

2. Once registered online, the Papa John's consumer can simply text FAV1, FAV2, etc. to 4PAPA (47272).

3. Papa John's then sends a text message detailing the order and requesting confirmation from the consumer.

Courtesy Papa John's International, Inc.

EXHIBIT 8-2a (Continued)

4. The consumer presses Y1 to confirm the order for FAV1 or N1 to change the order. Once confirmed, the closest Papa John's restaurant processes the order.

Earlier today, hundreds of busy holiday shoppers at the Mall of America in Minneapolis watched as Papa John's pitted the World's Fastest Talker, Fran Capo, against LG National Texting Champion Morgan Pozgar, to determine what was faster - ordering a Papa John's pizza the old-fashioned way via phone or ordering via text message.

Amid much suspense, 13-year-old Pozgar was all thumbs, emerging victorious and leaving the fast-talking Capo in her text message dust. Mall of America shoppers then learned firsthand how to text message their order to Papa John's and ten lucky people were randomly selected to win a enV by LG - designed specifically for multi-media messaging with a QWERTY keyboard and large internal screen - from LG Mobile Phones.

"Text ordering a Papa John's pizza was really easy," said Pozgar. "I think even my mom could handle it."

Capo, meanwhile, accepted her defeat in stride.

"For the first time ever, I am speechless," said Capo. "Who would have ever thought that ordering a pizza could be done with just a few keystrokes? I may be the World's Fastest Talker, but when it comes to technology, Papa John's is obviously winning the race."

Headquartered in Louisville, Kentucky, Papa John's International, Inc. (NASDAQ: PZZA) is the world's third largest pizza company. For eight years running, consumers have rated Papa John's No. 1 in customer satisfaction among all national pizza chains in the highly regarded American Customer Satisfaction Index (ACSI). For more information about the company or to order pizza online, visit Papa John's at www. papajohns.com.

For more information on LG Mobile Phones, please visit: www.LGusa.com.

CONTACT: Papa John's International, Inc.

Tish Muldoon, 502-671-9488	Fleishman-Hillard
Papa John's Director, Media Relations	Doug Terfehr, 314-550-0934
tish_muldoon@papajohns.com	doug.terfehr@fleishman.com

E X H I B I T   8-2b   **News Release on Big Game Points**

TEXTra, TEXTra Read All about It: Papa John's Text-Ordering is Go-to Play for Football Fans

Compete in the Papa John's "TEXTra Points 4 Pizza" Promotion: Big Games, Big Points, Big Savings

LOUISVILLE, Ky.–Jan. 4, 2008–When professional football playoffs begin this weekend, fans across the country will gather around televisions and tailgates with the hope that their favorite team will advance to the Big Game in Phoenix ... and score big points in the process. And this playoff season, high-scoring games mean big wins for pizza lovers - thanks to the Papa John's "TEXTra Points 4 Pizza" promotion.

As the first pizza company in America to offer text message ordering on a national basis, Papa John's wants football fans everywhere to get off the bench and begin experiencing the benefits of being a Papa John's mobile customer.

With Papa John's "TEXTra Points 4 Pizza" promotion, by texting "POINTS" to 47272 (4PAPA) or registering to receive text messages from Papa John's at www.papajohns.com ahead of the games, fans will be signed up for the chance to receive super deals on pizza at participating restaurants throughout the playoffs, based upon the number of points scored on the field. The promotion kicks off wild card weekend on Saturday, January 5, and extends throughout the playoffs and the Big Game, February 3. Here's how it works:

- For the wild card and divisional rounds, if the score of any playoff game totals 25 points or more, fans registered in the promotion will receive a text message from Papa John's with an exclusive promo code worth 25 percent off the average national regular menu price of a large, three-topping pizza ordered online the following week. This means scoring a large pizza with a national average regular menu price of $15.99, for only $11.99!

- Stakes will be raised for conference championship day - Sunday, January 20 - when Papa John's challenges the teams in contention for the Big Game to score a cumulative 50 points in either game, so that registered fans will receive 50 percent off the average national regular menu price of a large three-topping pizza ordered online the following week. It happened in both divisional

Courtesy Papa John's International, Inc.

EXHIBIT 8-2b (Continued)

championship games last season. A $15.99 pizza for $7.99 - can it get any better? Yes!

- When the Big Game takes place in Phoenix on Sunday, February 3, if the cumulative score is 75 points or more, fans registered for the promotion will receive 75 percent off the average national regular menu price of a large three-topping pizza ordered online the following week, or a $15.99 pizza for only $3.99!

Complete promotion rules at www.papajohns.com.

"This playoff season, Papa John's wants to make the excitement of a high scoring game even more exciting by giving all fans - no matter their team allegiance - a reason to cheer for extra points," said Jim Ensign, Papa John's vice president of marketing communications. "And as the only national pizza company to offer text message ordering throughout the country, Papa John's is eager to introduce customers to the newest and most convenient way to order their game day essentials."

Fast Stats About the Promotion:

- The lowest weekly average combined score during the 2007 regular season was 36.1 (week eight), so cashing in on the promotion during the first two playoff weekends is virtually a lock.
- The highest cumulative score in the history of the Big Game is 75 points - when San Francisco beat San Diego 49-26 in 1995.
- During the 2007 season, 75 points or more was scored in an incredible six regular season games!
- Papa John's expects football playoffs to be especially busy, with predictions to sell nearly three quarters of a million pizzas on Sunday, February 3, making it one of the busiest days of the year.

This year, advance online ordering from Papa John's makes life even easier for football party planners. Fans can log on to www.papajohns.com and follow the online ordering menu to place their order well in advance of the Big Game. Place an order up to 21 days in advance - including all the pizzas, wings, breadsticks, sodas and other sides the party needs - and indicate a time of delivery. It's that simple.

Headquartered in Louisville, Kentucky, Papa John's International, Inc. (NASDAQ: PZZA) is the world's third largest pizza company. For eight years running, consumers have rated Papa John's No. 1 in customer satisfaction among all national pizza chains in the highly regarded American Customer Satisfaction Index (ACSI). For more information about the company or to order pizza online, visit Papa John's at www.papajohns.com.

CONTACT: Papa John's International, Inc.

Tish Muldoon, 502-261-4987

Director, Community & Public Relations

Case 8-3

Companies often find new ways to engage customers and to customize their products, but seldom do they find one that resonates with personalized music. Exhibit 8-3a is a news release announcing the new "sound cards," and Exhibit 8-3b is a news release about the signing of a new recording artist.

Hallmark Sound Card Product Launch:
Sweet Music!

Hallmark Cards with Fleishman-Hillard, Inc.

SITUATION ANALYSIS

With the overwhelming growth of cell phones, Blackberries, and iMs, it has never been easier to communicate. And with more options than ever to say "Happy Birthday" or "Congrats" rather than using a traditional greeting card, many card companies realized they needed to work to remain relevant. Industry-wide, card sales have been flat for years. So how does a company whose brand is built on greeting cards grow sales?

In 2005, Hallmark Cards created the answer. The company set out to invent a new type of card—something that tapped into deep human emotion—and more specifically tied into our culture's music obsession. From iPods to ring tones, Hallmark knew personalized music was hot and there had to be a way to merge it with the emotion of greeting cards. The "sound card" was born.

Although a card that plays music was not new, Hallmark's approach with original songs by original artists—partnered with relevant editorial—was like nothing the industry had ever seen.

After an initial "test run" during Valentine's Day 2006, the 24 new sound cards were a hit ... leading Hallmark to embark on a mission to create 200 new cards in five months. With the ink still wet on the music licensing agreements, the expanded card line launched in summer 2006. Featuring recognizable songs selected for multigenerational appeal, it was the only sound card line to use original recordings by the original artists. And because of that, a key to success would be alerting music fans—potential new consumers—to the product.

One key strategy implemented by the Hallmark Cards and Fleishman-Hillard teams was to leverage extensive research about the consumer need/desire for the cards to raise awareness. The team showcased the cards via media sampling and unique direct-to-consumer tactics.

In the end, the Hallmark Gold Crown-exclusive sound cards created *buzz*, drove traffic, and generated purchases from both Hallmark Gold Crown Card (HGCC) members and nonmembers.

Specifically, the sound cards:

- Helped card sales jump 9 percent over previous year's sales

- Formed the foundation of Hallmark's new "innovations" platform, demonstrating Hallmark cards' relevancy

- Reminded consumers of the power of a card

RESEARCH

Four research studies led to the expanded sound card line launch and were key to the communications strategies.

Product Research (2005)

Prior to the card line development, Hallmark researched the use of music as a marketing vehicle, finding trends in two areas:

- "Social expression" (personal playlists, favorite songs as gifts)

- "Brand relevance" (using music for branding)

Research showed we identify ourselves by our favorite music, which crosses generations. Song cards are a way for adults to show kids they're hip. For kids, there's play value in the card.

Consumer Focus Groups (December 2005)

This research showed consumers believe the "wow" impact of a sound card is a motivator to purchase.

Sales Data Research (Valentine's Day 2006)

Preliminary results show broad appeal from both current HGCC consumers and new consumers.

- Equivalent appeal between HGCC consumers (49 percent) and non-HGCC (51 percent) consumers.

- Attracted "new" consumers, as HGCC members who bought song cards during Valentines 2006 but did not shop at HGC in Valentines 2005 were more likely to be newer to the HGCC program and younger.

Consumer Online Idea Exchange Research (April 2006)

Through an online study, Hallmark polled 1,000 consumers on what they liked/didn't like about the cards, showing:

- Song cards rated highest with 91 percent finding them appealing.
- Eighty-two percent indicated they were likely to purchase song cards.
- The appeal is in the surprise or "wow" factor for many.

Research Findings

Through this research, Hallmark found consumers want to use music to communicate a unique message. The element of sound adds a whole new contemporary way of connecting—and it will surprise and delight both the giver and the receiver. With this finding, the team knew they had to showcase that "surprise and delight" element in the publicity tactics. In addition, the research showed these cards were a hit with a new, non-HGCC consumer, giving the team the ability to reach out to new consumers in new ways.

PLANNING

Objectives

- Raise consumer awareness of the new sound cards.
- Increase sales by driving traffic to Hallmark Gold Crown stores to try the new "shopping experience."

Strategies

- Create a sense of surprise and excitement to generate media attention, drive traffic, and attract consumers.
- Leverage product's ability to reach beyond the core target and speak to a "nontraditional" secondary audience.
- Use Hallmark's inherent creative experts to tell the story.
- Leverage cards themselves (demonstrate key attributes of product and sound technology) to garner media attention.

The target audience for the campaign was consumers who wanted a fun and unique way to enhance the experience of giving a greeting card. It included both current Hallmark consumers and new ones (music and pop culture fans).

The campaign was conducted over a five-month timetable. Planning sessions took place in April/May 2006, and rollout occurred in July/August 2006.

EXECUTION

The team wanted to build excitement and awareness of the "wow" factor, and the cards were our best ambassadors. You didn't "get it" until you were able to experience it for yourself. Therefore, card samples were included with media materials and opened up to demonstrate during interviews. By providing samples and venues where key opinion leaders could "experience" the product, the team was able to combat the "song card" stereotype. (Prior to Hallmark's song card launch, most other products were of poor sound quality and featured studio bands doing covers of songs.)

The team employed several nontraditional tactics to showcase the cards throughout the campaign. The key was to demonstrate the card—which worked best either direct-to-key-influencer or in a broadcast outlet—as the star.

These buzz-generating tactics reached new audiences for Hallmark:

- MTV Video Music Awards—To start building buzz among the music industry—and to attract new music artists to the concept—Hallmark provided sample products at the "AOL Style Suite" at the MTV Video Music Awards. The sound cards were an unequivocal hit drawing comments such as "I have to have one of these," and "How can we get our band in a card?" More than 200 celebrities came through including Snoop Dogg, Fall Out Boy, The All American Rejects, and Panic! At the Disco. In addition, several music executives expressed interest in having their label's artists included in future sound cards. To expand the buzz, celebrities ordered 100 holiday sound cards custom printed with a personal message to send to their friends and families.

- Fan club sites—The team targeted new consumers by reaching out to the fan sites of artists featured on the cards, leading to buzz-generating copy on sites for artists including Louis Armstrong, Blondie, Earth Wind & Fire, KISS, and The Village People.

- Radio trade-for-mentions—To generate more buzz among music fans, the team reached out to radio stations to offer "trade-for-mention" giveaways. The top five callers were given a "box set" of cards that matched the genre of that station. For example, R&B station listeners won "box sets" of cards featuring Earth Wind & Fire. The team also provided trivia questions that the DJ could use on air.

- Radio media tour—Key messages were delivered by Hallmark creative spokespersons. DJs received the cards prior to the interviews so they could play them on the air.

- Customized pitching—The team targeted media outlets with card samples and story ideas to fit their niche. As the campaign progressed, the team also pitched the top selling cards, posting them similar to Billboard's weekly music list.

- Satellite media tour—The success of the product line led to being featured in a "Best Products of 2006" SMT.

EVALUATION

Sales Results:

Ultimately, the success of the product launch was proven by sales results. In Hallmark Gold Crown stores, sound cards fueled a 9 percent increase in sales of everyday cards compared with 2005.

The growth continued past the launch in July 2006 and into the holidays, the busiest season for Hallmark:

- Total season greeting cards were up 9 percent.

- Christmas counter card sales increased 10 percent; sound cards contributed 6 percent of counter sales.

- Sound cards contributed more than half of the counter card dollar increase.

More importantly, the success of sound card sales helped overall sales for Hallmark Gold Crown stores. In 2006, total store sales were up 3.1 percent.

Media Results

The campaign successfully raised consumer awareness via national and local television, radio, newspapers, magazines, and Internet. As demonstrated by the enclosed clips, the media clearly communicated the message that Hallmark sound cards were a new way for consumers to communicate. PR strategies and tactics generated nearly 122 million trackable impressions.

- Radio/TV outreach resulted in more than 59 million impressions, including national hits on "The View," "The CBS Early Show," ABC News "Nightline," "CNN Headline News," Sirius Satellite Radio, and XM Satellite Radio; local interviews were secured in cities ranging from New York to Seattle. As part of the radio trade-for-mention program, the team secured more than 50 giveaways of 270 "box sets" including WLTW, the No. 1 station in NYC, resulting in 45 million impressions.

- The print media outreach resulted in nearly 50 million impressions, including articles in key music industry publications such as *Billboard, Country Weekly*, and *RollingStone* (online). And, in addition to homerun hits in *The Wall Street Journal* and a positive Associated Press article, news about sound cards appeared in hundreds of newspapers across the country.

E X H I B I T 8-3a   **News Release on the Launch**

FOR IMMEDIATE RELEASE
Contact: Deidre Parkes
(816) 274-5768 or dparke1@hallmark.com

Hallmark Has a Hit with Sound Card Collection

Expanded offering, includes new musical gift bags and gift-card boxes

(Kansas City, Mo., July 7, 2006)–Saying 'I love you' the first time can be nerve-wracking–but what if you had Willie Nelson or the Rolling Stones helping you out? Or what if you could cheer someone up by sending them the sounds of James Brown inside a card? Now, with a little help from Hallmark, you can.

This month, Hallmark Gold Crown® stores will offer an expanded collection of 223 sound cards featuring more than 100 original music artists as well as dialogue and theme songs from popular movies and TV shows. The collection also includes musical gift bags and gift-card boxes, as well as gift bags designed with pockets to hold a sound card.

Unlike any other cards in the market today, Hallmark sound cards feature CD-quality recordings of original music and sound clips. Each clip plays up to 30 seconds when the card is opened, and stops when the card is closed.

Tap into the Emotional Power of Sound
The addition of sound evokes more passion than a traditional card, according to Tim Bodendistel, art director for the line. "Music and favorite movie and TV shows evoke incredibly strong emotions," Tim says. "They recall memories, moments, times and feelings—so many tangible connections that the sender and recipient share. They allow you to share secret jokes from movies, relate to someone over an old TV show or evoke an emotion with a song.

Adding sound to a greeting card is a perfect way to help the card's sender express more meaning and to prompt that extra 'wow' from the recipient."

Hallmark sound cards are printed on high-quality card stock and feature a mix of special processes to make them sparkle, shimmer or stand out. The extraordinary sound quality from the cards' internal speaker is designed to be played again and again. The cards, priced at $4.99 each, are available exclusively in about 4,000 Hallmark Gold Crown® stores nationwide.

Courtesy Hallmark Cards, Inc.

E X H I B I T 8-3a   (Continued)

Appeal Across the Generations

The cards cover a range of sending situations including birthday, thinking of you, friendship, love, anniversary, encouragement, support, new baby, congratulations and cope. Clips featured in the cards have multigenerational appeal. The cards include classics songs such as "Unchained Melody" by The Righteous Brothers and "What a Wonderful World" by Louis Armstrong, as well as trendy tunes such as "All Star" by Smash Mouth, and "Wild Thing" by The Troggs.

Hollywood-themed cards feature sound clips and photos from popular movies, such as "Star Wars" and "Napoleon Dynamite." TV greetings showcase clips from shows such as "I Love Lucy" and "Law & Order." The clips include theme songs and well-known quotes from the TV show or movie.

The Hits Keep Coming

"When we introduced our original 24 sound cards last October, we approached two record labels and received licensing agreements for stock songs," says Tom Esselman, Hallmark greetings innovation director. "As word got out about the quality of our cards and their popularity with consumers, more record labels became interested in working with us. Today, we have much greater collaboration with everyone from major record labels to small publishing houses, and we're thrilled to introduce more than 180 new cards."

With this next generation of sound cards, "Hallmark has just taken the time and cared enough to make them meaningful—to get licensing rights to the original songs from the original artists and to put it together into a quality card that consumers love," Esselman says.

About Hallmark Cards, Inc.

Kansas City-based Hallmark is known throughout the world for its greeting cards, related personal expression products, and television's most honored and enduring dramatic series, the Hallmark Hall of Fame. The company's Binney & Smith subsidiary, maker of Crayola® crayons and markers, is the leading producer of art materials for children and students. Through licensing leadership and joint ventures, Hallmark continues to expand its product formats and distribution avenues. The company publishes products in more than 30 languages and distributes them in more than 100 countries through a multi-national strategy. In 2005, Hallmark reported consolidated net revenues of $4.2 billion.

EXHIBIT 8-3b   News Release on New Recording Artist

New Faith Hill Hallmark Cards With Sound to Exclusively Benefit (RED)™

Share Faith Hill's music with a loved one and do some global good

KANSAS CITY, Mo. (June 16, 2008) — Hallmark Cards, Inc. today announced one of country music's top recording artists, Faith Hill, as the latest performer to be exclusively featured in Hallmark's (PRODUCT) RED™ Cards With Sound. The cards will feature five of Hill's originally recorded songs, and like other items in Hallmark's (PRODUCT) RED collection, the cards will raise money for the Global Fund to help eliminate AIDS in Africa.

"It's always great to find new ways for people to share music in a positive way," said Jill Rosen, Hallmark director of licensing. "To know that fans of Ms. Hill will save lives in Africa simply by purchasing a Hallmark card with one of her songs inside, that's a powerful thing."

Cards With Sound featuring Faith Hill's popular songs including "This Kiss," "If My Heart Had Wings," and "Breathe," are now available for $4.99 at Hallmark Gold Crown stores nationwide.

With eight percent of net wholesale sales from all Hallmark (PRODUCT) RED products going to the Global Fund, the purchase of one Faith Hill Card With Sound results in a contribution equivalent to a single-dose treatment used to reduce the risk of transmission of HIV from mother to child during childbirth. Find out more about Hallmark's partnership with (RED) at Hallmark.com/RED and JOINRED.COM.

About Hallmark Cards, Inc.
Kansas City-based Hallmark has been helping people communicate, celebrate, and connect for nearly 100 years. Hallmark greeting cards and other products can be found in more than 43,000 places in the U.S. alone, with the network of Hallmark Gold Crown stores providing the very best selection. The Hallmark brand also reaches consumers online at Hallmark.com, on newsstands through *Hallmark Magazine,* and on television through Hallmark Hall of Fame original movies and the top-rated Hallmark Channel. In addition, Hallmark publishes products in more than 30 languages and distributes them in 100 countries across the globe. The company's Crayola subsidiary provides fun and imaginative ways for children to colorfully express themselves. In 2007, privately held Hallmark reported consolidated net revenues of $4.4 billion. Charitable giving of $16 million a year focuses on the well-being of children and families, vibrant arts and cultural experiences, and basic services for people in need in the communities where Hallmark operates. For more information about the company, visit http://corporate.hallmark.com.

###

Courtesy Hallmark Cards, Inc.

Case 8-4

People may wish to quit smoking but face a daunting challenge in overcoming the addiction to nicotine. A new flavor of nicotine replacement therapy presented an opportunity for a communication campaign that offered alternatives to the unpleasant taste of other products. Exhibit 8-4a is a news release, and Exhibit 8-4b is the "Million Challenge Fact Sheet."

Nicorette Fruit Chill's Smoking Cessation Challenge

GlaxoSmithKline Consumer Healthcare with CKPR

SITUATION ANALYSIS

While nicotine replacement therapies (NRTs), such as Nicorette gum, are clinically proven to double a smoker's chances of quitting, their unpleasant taste often prevents quitters from completing the course of treatment, increasing the chances of a relapse. To increase compliance and success rates, GlaxoSmithKline (GSK) Consumer Healthcare developed Nicorette Fruit Chill, a coated, fruit-flavored nicotine gum similar in taste to confectionery gums. To launch the new product, GSK engaged CKPR to develop and lead an integrated marketing campaign to support the product's national rollout. Rising to the challenge, CKPR brought a 360-degree idea to the table: "The Nicorette Fruit Chill Million Challenge," a nationwide movement to encourage and help one million smokers kick the habit. CKPR's multifaceted campaign included advertising, mobile marketing, a sweepstakes, and a Web site—which were executed by other GSK marketing partners—but the campaign was clearly conceived, launched, led, and sustained by PR. It changed smokers' perceptions about the NRT category and built widespread awareness of Nicorette Fruit Chill as a new, effective, and palatable form of NRT, setting the brand on fire and torching every weekly sales projection during the course of the campaign. Who says quitters can't be winners?

RESEARCH

CKPR used primary and secondary research to fully understand smokers and their habits, barriers to compliance with NRTs, the role of influences, the media environment and the competitive landscape, and to develop tools and messages that would resonate with smokers.

Courtesy GlaxoSmithKline Consumer Healthcare

Established a Smokers Panel

- CKPR recruited a diverse panel of current and former smokers from across the country for a day of learning. They provided vital input on program elements.

Interviewed Leading Smoking Cessation Experts

- Guided the development of program tools, messages, and materials.

Fielded a National Consumer Survey

- Showed that smokers feel pressured by family or friends to quit smoking (72 percent) and that nearly half have felt judged for failing to quit.

Pinpointed Relevant Health Statistics

- Smoking kills 440,000 Americans each year. The leading cause of preventable death, it lessens normal life expectancies by 13 to 15 years and costs the U.S. $75 billion in annual health care costs.

Evaluated 10 Years of Behavioral Research

- Proprietary brand data provided audience psychographics.

Probed the Media Environment

- A media audit validated the news value of program elements and identified inconsistencies in smokers' understanding of what it takes to quit successfully.

Analyzed the Competitive Environment

- Revealed opportunities to differentiate Fruit Chill within its category.

Evaluated Geographic Data

- Nielsen Scanner Data and research on local antismoking legislation and geographic prevalence of smoking helped establish markets and timing for local events.

Key research findings dictated a multifaceted campaign designed "for smokers by smokers," that would give them ready access to the most clinically proven approach to quitting—counseling combined with NRT—and establish Nicorette Fruit Chill as an effective aid in their attempts to quit smoking successfully.

PLANNING

Objectives

- Drive trial and repeat purchase of new Nicorette Fruit Chill through an integrated launch platform and a strong call to action that encourages trial.
- Generate 65.5–102.5 million unweighted media impressions (goal set by GSK Corporate Communications).
- Ensure 90 percent of coverage is "branded" and delivers at least one key message:
  - new Nicorette Fruit Chill is a coated, fruit-flavored nicotine gum that could finally be the ticket to helping smokers quit
  - the Nicorette Fruit Chill Million Challenge is a multifaceted education and outreach campaign to encourage smokers to commit to quitting
  - at www.fruitchillminion.com, smokers can access tools to help them quit and sign up for a chance to win $1 million

Target Audience

- Primary: Smokers 25–44 who are thinking about quitting
- Secondary: Concerned loved ones of smokers; key influencers, such as government officials and health organizations

Strategies

- Engage consumers and immerse them in the brand.
- Create a supportive environment in which smokers feel comfortable seeking out the help they need to quit.
- Build awareness of Nicorette Fruit Chill as a new, effective, and palatable form of NRT.
- Educate smokers on the barriers to complying with NRTs and communicate the brand differentiators intended to help smokers overcome those barriers.
- Recruit panel of physicians, psychologists, and other smoking cessation experts (the Nicorette Quit Team) to provide input on campaign tools, materials, and messaging; serve as credible, third-party spokespersons; and counsel smokers one-on-one.
- Set an aspirational goal (encourage 1 million smokers to quit smoking) on a scale that would drive media interest.

- Tap the knowledge and insights of current and exsmokers to arrive at a proper campaign tone and tenor.

- Obtain the support and buy-in of key influencers.

EXECUTION

Nicorette Stop Shops

At the heart of the campaign were first-of-their kind, "pop-up" smoking cessation centers that CKPR designed, managed, and publicized. They appeared for one week's time in New York, Atlanta, Houston, Phoenix, and Chicago, offering smokers free professional counseling valued at hundreds of thousands of dollars; quit tools such as podcasts and educational videos; and health assessment tools.

Quit Tools

CKPR developed guides to empower smokers and help them quit successfully, which were posted on the campaign's Web site and used in collateral materials distributed at local-market events. CKPR also wrote and produced podcasts hosted by Nicorette Quit Team experts, which were available online and on-site at the Stop Shops.

Collateral Materials

CKPR wrote and produced FCM, *Fruit Chill Magazine*, which presented the Quit Tools in an easy-to-read magazine format; wallet card that offered tips for getting back on track after a relapse; postcards that offered Stop Shop visitors a guide to all the tools available; and localized postcards inviting smokers to visit the Stop Shop and "Take the Challenge," which were distributed by street teams and mailed to area businesses and influencers in Stop Shop markets.

Press Kit/Creative Mailer

CKPR targeted national, major-market, and long-lead media by delivering a creative mailer inviting them to "Take the Challenge"; the mailer highlighted the various "tools" available to smokers through the campaign. Also included press materials, Fruit Chill placebos, a product demo DVD, and a branded tool belt.

Launch Event

CKPR kicked off the campaign with a media event at the inaugural Stop Shop in the heart of New York's Times Square, which was attended by more than 50 journalists as well as various influencer groups.

National Media Blitz

The national media launch included: a remote SMT (aired live on 27 stations, including New York, LA, and Dallas); a B-roll newsfeed that resulted in 60+ airings; an ANR that produced 680 hits; targeted pitching to national and major-market outlets; and a mat release that extended the story to media in second- and third-tier markets.

Influencer Outreach

CKPR enlisted the support of more than a dozen influential national organizations, including the American Cancer Society, American Lung Association, and National Cancer Institute, as well as local smoking control and prevention programs and government and health officials in each Stop Shop market. It resulted in local proclamations declaring "Quit Smoking Week" in Atlanta and Houston while the Stop Shop was open in those markets.

EVALUATION

Objective

- Drive trial and repeat purchase of new Nicorette Fruit Chill

Result

- PR drove significant and immediate Nicorette Fruit Chill sales increases, as shown by client-supplied Nielsen Scanner Data collected over four-week periods ending immediately before and after key campaign milestones.
- National sales increased 221 percent following the campaign media launch, before TV ads were on air.
- New York sales increased 1,029 percent post Stop Shop.
- Atlanta sales increased 74 percent post Stop Shop.
- Houston sales increased 55 percent post Stop Shop.
- Chicago sales increased 25 percent post Stop Shop.
- Nicorette Fruit Chill sales surpassed weekly sales forecasts by 28 percent during a period of the campaign when all marketing activities, except PR, were dormant.
- Exceeded every weekly Nicorette sales forecast during the course of the campaign.

Objective

- Generate 65.5 to 102.5 million unweighted media impressions

Result

- More than 2,100 print, broadcast, and online stories were generated, resulting in excess of 204.6 million unweighted media impressions, exceeding the low-end goal by 212 percent and the high-end goal by 100 percent.

Objective

- 90 percent of coverage is "branded."

Result

- 99.8 percent of coverage was "branded."

Objective

- 90 percent of coverage conveys at least one key message.

Result

- 99.2 percent of coverage conveyed at least one key message.

E X H I B I T 8-4a   News Release

Media Contacts:

Jen Dobrzelecki or Audrey Laricchia

CKPR

212 251 1204 / 212 251 1209

jdobrzelecki@ckpr.biz/alaricchia@ckpr.biz

Jennifer May

GlaxoSmithKline Consumer Healthcare

412 200 3729

jennifer.l.may@gsk.com

Nicorette Challenges One Million Smokers to Commit to Quitting as Part of Its Introduction of a New Fruit Chill Flavor

"Fruit Chill Million" Education and Outreach Campaign Puts Up $1 Million Prize in Effort to Help Smokers Quit

PITTSBURGH (April 2006) — For the nearly 50 million smokers who need a reason to quit, Nicorette® is offering one million of them.

As part of its introduction of new Nicorette Fruit Chill™, the only fruit-flavored coated nicotine gum, the brand is launching the "Nicorette Fruit Chill Million Challenge," a multi-faceted consumer education and outreach campaign designed to encourage one million smokers to finally make a commitment to quitting. Among the resources it offers smokers are free counseling and first-of-their-kind smoking cessation centers, which offer quit tools like podcasts, educational videos and a learning center where smokers can assess the impact smoking could have on their health.

And what is in it for the participants, aside from the obvious health benefits of giving up their smoking habit, is the chance to win $1 million. The winner will also receive free counseling with a smoking cessation expert and free Nicotine Replacement Therapy product.

The Nicorette Fruit Chill Million, Nicorette's largest quit smoking challenge ever, is unique in that its key elements were designed for smokers by smokers to increase the chance of a successful quit attempt. The brand leveraged years of research, and recruited and worked with a diverse panel of current and former smokers to develop tools and messages that would resonate with other smokers.

The brand also established a Nicorette Quit Team of smoking cessation experts, including: Matthew H. Carpenter, Ph.D., research psychologist at the Medical University of South Carolina (MUSC); Robin J. Mermelstein, Ph.D., clinical psychologist, smoking cessation researcher and director of the Center for Health Behavior Research at the University of Illinois at Chicago; Arden G. Christen, D.D.S, M.S.D., M.A., co-director of the Nicotine Dependence Program at Indiana University and at

Fairbanks Addiction Hospital in Indianapolis and private smoking cessation counselor; and Kimberly Jeffries Leonard, Ph.D., smoking cessation and public health expert with specific expertise on substance abuse prevention and treatment in special populations. They will provide ongoing input on tools and materials for the Fruit Chill Million Challenge and will be present at consumer events throughout the year, along with certified GlaxoSmithKline (GSK) Consumer Healthcare smoking cessation counselors, who will provide professional counseling and support to smokers face-to-face.

"Our research shows that four out of five (81 percent) smokers would be willing to try to quit smoking for a chance to win a million dollars," says Bill Slivka, vice president, smoking control, for GSK Consumer Healthcare. "But more important than the money, we are giving them access to educational materials, quit tools and counseling–all free of charge–to help make their quit attempts more successful."

Among the campaign's key elements are Nicorette Stop Shops, first-of-their-kind "pop-up" smoking cessation centers that will open this summer, offering tools, support and FDA-approved nicotine replacement therapy in one place. The Stop Shops will appear for limited periods of time in Atlanta, Chicago, Houston, New York and Phoenix, with the first opening in New York in April.

Inside the Stop Shops, smokers will find a comfortable waiting area where they can relax and interact with one another; a private counseling area for free one-on-one consultation with certified GSK Consumer Healthcare smoking cessation counselors; a retail area; and a learning center where they can assess the impact smoking has had on their own health, view educational videos, download useful podcasts and access online resources.

Another key campaign element is a nationwide Fruit Chill Million Tour. Two specially equipped Nicorette sport utility vehicles will roll into high-profile events and high-traffic areas across the country between July and December, where certified GSK Consumer Healthcare smoking cessation counselors will provide one-on-one counseling and education to smokers. Smokers will also have a chance to learn how the great new taste of Nicorette Fruit Chill can provide a new option to help in quit attempts.

Smokers who don't have access to the Nicorette Stop Shops or the Fruit Chill Million Tour can take advantage of the exciting tools and resources designed to help them quit at www.FruitChillMillion.com, the official campaign website. Fruit Chill Million Challenge participants can also enter for a chance to win the $1 million prize by visiting the site. Participants can earn up to 74 additional entries–and stay fully engaged in their quit attempt–by enrolling in programs, completing surveys and downloading and viewing the quit tools available on the site, such as the "10 Step Quit Plan," relapse "Trigger Tamers" and "If You Slip" wallet card.

"The Nicorette Fruit Chill Million Challenge provides smoking cessation tools and personalized support that smokers will find helpful to get started and help them with their quit attempts," says Slivka. "Plus, with the potential to win a million dollars, and a great new fruit flavor for their nicotine replacement therapy, smokers have never had a better motivation than right now to stop smoking."

Gum Flavor Can be a Barrier to Compliance

Nicotine replacement therapies, such as nicotine gums, are clinically proven to help smokers quit. For years, however, smokers have complained that the taste of the gum was a barrier to complying with the dosing regimen.

E X H I B I T 8-4a   (Continued)

A Harris Interactive® survey of more than 400 smokers showed that a better tasting nicotine gum could be just the ticket to finally kicking the habit, by helping to address the compliance issue by making the chewing experience more enjoyable. To help improve compliance, Nicorette launched Fresh Mint™ in 2005 and now is announcing the launch of another great-tasting flavor, Fruit Chill. Similar in texture to confectionary gums, Nicorette Fruit Chill has a crispy coating that releases a burst of fruit flavor with a cool mint finish, providing a surprisingly refreshing chewing experience. The sugar-free gum also contains the fast, flexible craving-fighting medicine that consumers have come to expect from Nicorette.

"There are two elements to smoking addiction—the craving for nicotine and the habit—and both must be addressed to increase the chances of successfully quitting," says Carpenter. "Nicotine Replacement Therapy, like Nicorette Fruit Chill, can help satisfy the body's physical need for nicotine, so smokers can focus on breaking their smoking habit using the tools, counseling and support available through the Fruit Chill Million."

For more information, including Nicorette Stop Shop locations and hours of operation, Fruit Chill Million Tour stops and dates and official sweepstakes rules, please visit www.FruitChillMillion.com.

About Nicorette

Nicorette is a stop-smoking aid in the form of sugar-free nicotine gum. It provides oral gratification and reduces nicotine withdrawal symptoms, including cravings that make attempts to quit smoking so difficult. Convenient to carry and use, Nicorette allows smokers to control how much nicotine they use, and gives them the added flexibility of chewing an additional piece during strong or frequent cravings. Plus, exciting new flavors, such as Fresh Mint and new Fruit Chill, may make the chewing experience more enjoyable for smokers who have complained about the taste of nicotine replacement gums.

About GlaxoSmithKline Consumer Healthcare

GlaxoSmithKline Consumer Healthcare is one of the world's largest over-the-counter consumer healthcare product companies. Its more than 30 well-known brands include the leading smoking cessation products, Nicorette®, NicoDerm® and Commit®, as well as a many medicine cabinet staples such as Abreva®, Aquafresh®, Sensodyne® and Tums®. GlaxoSmithKline Consumer Healthcare continues to develop innovative products to help all smokers find their best support system and achieve their goal of being cigarette-free.

About GlaxoSmithKline

GlaxoSmithKline is one of the world's leading research-based pharmaceutical and consumer healthcare companies. GlaxoSmithKline is committed to improving the quality of human life by enabling people to do more, feel better and live longer.

# # #

E X H I B I T 8-4b Fact Sheet

Nicorette® Fruit Chill™ Million Challenge Fact Sheet

The Nicorette Fruit Chill Million Challenge

As part of its introduction of new Nicorette® Fruit Chill™, the only fruit-flavored, coated nicotine gum, the brand is launching the "Nicorette Fruit Chill Million Challenge," a multifaceted consumer education and outreach campaign designed to encourage one million smokers to make a commitment to quitting. It is the largest quit smoking challenge ever developed by Nicorette.

Nicorette Quit Team

A team of smoking cessation experts, including physicians and psychologists, the Nicorette Quit Team will provide ongoing input on tools and materials for the Challenge and will be present at consumer events throughout the year.

Nicorette Stop Shops

Five "pop-up" smoking cessation centers, the first of their kind, will open in high-traffic locations in major cities, offering tools, support, and FDA-approved Nicotine Replacement Therapy (NRT) in one place. The Stop Shops will appear for limited periods of time in Atlanta, Chicago, Houston, New York, and Phoenix. Inside the Stop Shops, smokers will find:

- A comfortable waiting area where they can relax and interact with one another.
- A private counseling area for free one-on-one consultation with certified smoking cessation counselors.
- A Learning Center, which will include:
  - A risk suite with evaluative tools that can assess the impact smoking could have on a smoker's health.
  - Videos explaining how NRT works and how to get started on the path to a smoke-free life.
  - Podcasts that offer quit tools and tips from Nicorette Quit Team experts.
  - A computer kiosk where visitors can log on to the Nicorette Fruit Chill Million official Web site and register for the Challenge.
- A retail sales area, where smokers who want to start their quit attempt immediately can purchase Nicorette Fruit Chill.

Courtesy GlaxoSmithKline Consumer Healthcare

EXHIBIT 8-4b (Continued)

Fruit Chill Million Tour

Two specially equipped Nicorette sport utility vehicles will roll into high-profile events and high-traffic areas across the United States between July and December, where certified smoking cessation counselors will provide one-on-one counseling and education to smokers. Smokers will also have a chance to experience the great new taste of Nicorette Fruit Chill, though in special placebo samples that do not contain nicotine.

www.FruitChillMillion.com

The official campaign Web site is a virtual network that provides support for a community of smokers throughout their quit attempts. Smokers can go online and download "Quit Tools," including a quit plan that can be tailored to their individual lifestyles and tip sheets to help get started on a quit attempt, manage triggers, and deal with family and friends. Smokers can also view videos on how to get the most from Nicorette; identify Nicorette Stop Shop locations and hours of operation; obtain Fruit Chill Million Tour stops and dates; and enter the Fruit Chill Million $1 million sweepstakes.

$1 Million Sweepstakes

Participants in the Fruit Chill Million Challenge can enter to win $1 million by visiting the official campaign Web site and entering the Committed Quitters Personal Code from the User's Guide that is included in each box of Nicorette. Participants can earn up to 74 additional entries—and stay fully engaged in their quit attempt—by enrolling in programs, completing surveys, and downloading and viewing the Quit Tools available on the site.
The winner will also receive free smoking cessation counseling with a smoking cessation expert and free NRT product.

The sweepstakes is open from March 1, 2006, through December 31, 2006. For official rules, please visit www.FruitChillMillion.com.

Nicorette Manufacturer

GlaxoSmithKline Consumer Healthcare
1000 GSK Dr.
Moon Township, PA 15108
412 200 4000
www.gsk.com

About Nicorette

Nicorette is a stop-smoking aid in the form of sugar-free nicotine gum. It provides oral gratification and reduces nicotine withdrawal symptoms, including cravings, that make attempts to quit smoking so difficult.

E X H I B I T 8-4b (Continued)	
	Convenient to carry and use, Nicorette allows smokers to control how much nicotine they use, and chewing an additional piece during strong or frequent cravings is acceptable under normal usage. Plus, exciting new flavors such as Fresh Mint™ and new Fruit Chill, may make the chewing experience more enjoyable for smokers who have complained about the taste of nicotine gums.
About GlaxoSmithKline Consumer Healthcare	GlaxoSmithKline Consumer Healthcare is one of the world's largest over-the-counter consumer healthcare product companies. Its more than 30 well-known brands include the leading smoking cessation products, Nicorette®, NicoDerm®, and Commit®, as well as many medicine cabinet staples such as Abreva®, Aquafresh®, Sensodyne®, and TUMS®. GlaxoSmithKline Consumer Healthcare continues to develop innovative products to help all smokers find their best support system and achieve their goal of being cigarette-free.
About GlaxoSmithKline	GlaxoSmithKline—one of the world's leading research-based pharmaceutical and healthcare companies—is committed to improving the quality of human life by enabling people to do more, feel better, and live longer.

9

International Public Relations

During the past several decades, international public relations has become a major concern of practitioners. The two principal aspects of this field are counseling domestic clients in their programs to reach markets or audiences in other countries and counseling foreign clients, both corporate and governmental, in their efforts to communicate with American audiences.

International public relations problems should be approached using the ROPE process.

RESEARCH

The research process for international public relations includes understanding the client, the opportunity or problem involved, and the audiences to be reached.

Client Research

A thorough investigation of the client will begin with background information on their nationality or home country. The next need will be for knowledge of the client's reputation and status in the country of its target audiences, along with past and present public relations practices in that country. Finally, the client's public relations strengths and weaknesses in the host country should be assessed.

Opportunity or Problem Research

In this phase of research, the practitioner should determine why and to what extent the client needs an international public relations program. The program may be either reactive in response to a problem experienced in the host country, or proactive in the interest of establishing a presence and creating goodwill in the host country.

Audience Research

Whether domestic or foreign, the client—and, more important, the practitioner representing the client—must understand various aspects of the target audience, including the language and its centrality to the culture of the host country, its cultural values, patterns of thought, customs, communication styles—both verbal and nonverbal—and the target audience's cultural norms. In addition, the public relations practitioner must become acquainted with the host country's various systems: legal, educational, political, and economic. Moreover, knowledge of the host country's social structure, heritage, and, particularly, its business practices will greatly benefit communicating with target audiences. Finally, audience information levels regarding the client and its products or services, audience attitudes and behaviors relevant to the client, and specific audience demographics and media-use levels should be gathered as part of the research for an international public relations program.

As in audience research for community relations, international practitioners will need to investigate and understand the media, leaders, and major organizations of the host country. Collectively or singularly, they will often provide the key to success in communicating with a target international audience. Thus, audiences for international public relations will include those listed in Exhibit 9-a.

E X H I B I T 9-A   International Publics

Host Country Media

    Mass

    Specialized

Host Country Leaders

    Public officials

    Educators

    Social leaders

    Cultural leaders

    Religious leaders

    Political leaders

    Professionals

    Executives

Host Country Organizations

    Business

    Service

    Social

    Cultural

    Religious

    Political

    Special interests

OBJECTIVES

International public relations programs may employ both impact and output objectives. They should be both specific and quantitative.

Impact Objectives

Impact objectives for international public relations involve informing target audiences or modifying their attitudes or behaviors. Some possible examples are:

1. To increase (by 20 percent) the international audience's knowledge of the client, its operations, products, or services (during a specific time period)
2. To enhance the client's image (by 15 percent during the current year) with the target international audience
3. To encourage (20 percent) more audience participation in the client's international events (during a particular program)

Output Objectives

Output objectives for international public relations consist of the practitioner's measurable efforts on behalf of the client. They may include such operations as:

1. Preparing and distributing (20 percent) more international publications (than last season)
2. Creating (five) new international projects (during the current calendar year)
3. Scheduling (eight) meetings with international leaders (during a specified time period)
4. Developing (three) special events for the public

PROGRAMMING

Programming for international public relations includes planning theme and messages, action(s) or special event(s), uncontrolled and controlled media, and effective use of communication principles.

Theme and Messages

The nature of the opportunity or problem and the research findings in the situation will govern the messages and theme, if any, to be communicated in the international public relations program. Subtle differences in themes in countries may be required due to translation and cultural factors.

Action(s) or Special Event(s)

Client actions and special events for international programs often include:

1. Sponsorship of cultural exchange programs between the host and the client's countries

2. Establishment of institutes in the host country to teach the language and culture of the client's country

3. Meetings with leaders of the host country

4. Seminars or training programs held in schools, businesses, or institutions in the host country

5. Awards programs honoring leaders and other celebrities of the host country

6. Festivals in the host country celebrating the foods, dress, dance, art, or other aspects of the culture of the client's country. These may coincide with such holidays as creation of the client's country, its independence, victory in key battles or wars, birthdays of its founding fathers or heroes, and so on

7. Participation of the client organization, its management, and its personnel in the special holidays and events of the host country

A major key to successful international public relations is the client involvement and interaction that actions and special events in the host country can provide.

Uncontrolled and Controlled Media

In international public relations, the practitioner should service the media of the host country with such appropriate uncontrolled media as news releases, interviews with officers of the client organization, and photo opportunities, all centered around the actions or special events composing the program itself.

Controlled media may also use the client's actions and special events as a major focus, with related print materials mailed to a select list of leaders and a speakers bureau created to provide important organizations in the host country with oral presentations from officers of the client organization. Both uncontrolled and controlled media should be centered on the client's involvement with, participation in, and contributions to the interests of the host country.

The client's Web site may play a significant role in the program. It may provide a wealth of information available in the language of the host country and reflect the client's interest in the host country. The Web site may also establish a channel for interactive dialogue and exchange of information.

Effective Communication

The most important communication principles involved in the programming of international public relations are source credibility, nonverbal and verbal cues, two-way communication, the use of opinion leaders, group influence, and audience participation.

Nothing is of greater importance in international public relations than the perceived credibility of the client organization in the host country. Target audiences must believe that the practitioner's client has their best interests at heart and is not simply operating in the host country for purposes of exploitation of cheap labor, low production costs, lax environmental standards, and similar factors. In such situations, credibility enhancement requires tangible and visible contributions to the host country on the part of the client organization, its management, and its personnel. These organizational representatives simply cannot set themselves apart as an elitist enclave or separate community in the host country and expect to maintain their credibility. They must become active and constructive participants in the life and culture of the host country. This will be best reflected in constructive actions and special events as part of the organization's public relations programming.

Effective use of verbal and nonverbal cues in the programming will include an understanding not only of the official language of the host country, but of that country's special applications or dialectical usage of the language. Although French is the official language of France, Canada's province of Quebec, and Haiti, its usage varies as widely among these countries as does Spanish usage from Madrid to Santo Domingo. The astute practitioner will understand such verbal nuances, as well as the many nonverbal cultural differences in the uses of time, spatial relationships, and visual and vocal cues. Failure to take these verbal and nonverbal distinctions into account can spell doom for international public relations programming.

Two-way, or interpersonal, communication is especially important in an international context. This presupposes the use of native speakers and writers in the public relations programming. The deadly public relations sin of overreliance on the mass media or other forms of one-way communication (mainly print) can take a serious toll on the effectiveness of international public relations efforts.

The inclusion of opinion leaders and groups is another indispensable element in international public relations programming. While important in most American contexts, attention to and communication with important leaders and groups can become magnified in the international context. This requires a thorough understanding of the complexities of the social and political context in the host country. It may require the employment of authoritative consultants in the host country. Though the cost of getting this right may be high, the cost of getting it wrong will, in the long term, be unbearable if not disastrous.

Finally, there can be no substitute in any public relations program for audience participation. If interactive programming is the norm for American public relations, it should be an absolute requisite of international public relations. This principle again underlines the significance of participative actions and special events as the core of effective programs.

Effective use of these communication principles cannot be overemphasized. They serve to heighten the practitioner's sensitivity to and awareness of the interactive and participative nature of public relations, especially in the international context.

EVALUATION

The evaluation of an international public relations program should be driven by the monitoring and final assessment of its stated objectives. Both impact and output objectives can be evaluated using the same measurement tools as in other forms of public relations (see Chapter 2). A significant difference may lie in the necessity to use research firms with credible reputations in the host country. It could be a serious mistake to bring in firms and employees from the client's country to conduct surveys, focus groups, and the like in the host country.

SUMMARY

The ROPE process is a useful format for the conduct of international public relations. In all aspects of the process, unusual precautions must be taken to observe the social, political, and cultural norms of the host country of the program's target audience. Not only must successful practitioners understand effective public relations principles, they must also become working cultural anthropologists and sociologists versed in the host country's history and politics.

READINGS ON INTERNATIONAL PUBLIC RELATIONS

"An International Sensibility," *Public Relations Tactics* 6 (February 1999): 31.

Arfield, George. "As the World Changes, So Must Communicators," *Communication World* 10 (June–July 1993): 33–34.

Bates, Don. "Update on Japan: Tips on Dealing with the Press," *Public Relations Journal* 50 (October–November 1994): 14.

Braun, Sandra L. "The Effects of the Political Environment on Public Relations in Bulgaria," *Journal of Public Relations Research* 19 (May 2007): 199–228.

Busch, Per-Olof, and Jörgens Helge. "The International Sources of Policy Convergence: Explaining the Spread of Environmental Policy Innovations," *Journal of European Public Policy* 12 (October 2005): 860–884.

Chen, Ni, and Hugh M. Culbertson. "Two Contrasting Approaches of Government Public Relations in Mainland China," *Public Relations Quarterly* 37 (fall 1992): 36–41.

Clarke, Terence M. "An Inside Look at Russian Public Relations," *Public Relations Quarterly* 45 (spring 2000): 18ff.

Creedon, Pam, and Mai Al-Khaja. "Public Relations and Globalization: Building a Case for Cultural Competency in Public Relations Education," *Public Relations Review* 31 (September 2005): 344–354.

Culbertson, Hugh M., and Ni Chen, eds. *International Public Relations: A Comparative Analysis*. Mahwah, NJ: Erlbaum, 1996.

Curtin, Patricia A., and T. Kenn Gaither. "Contested Notions of Issue Identity in International Public Relations: A Case Study," *Journal of Public Relations Research* 18 (January 2006): 67–89.

_____. *International Public Relations: Negotiating Culture, Identity, and Power.* Thousand Oaks, CA: Sage, 2007.

_____. "Privileging Identity, Difference, and Power: The Circuit of Culture as a Basis for Public Relations Theory," *Journal of Public Relations Research* 17 (May 2005): 91–115.

de Souza, Cerena, et al. "Navigating New Seas: Advice on Communicating Internationally," *Communication World* 11 (June–July 1994): 33.

Drobis, David R. "The New Global Imperative for Public Relations: Building Confidence to Save Globalization," *Public Relations Strategist* 8 (spring 2002): 36–38.

Fawcett, Karen. "An Embassy Can Be a Communicator's Ally," *Communication World* 10 (May 1993): 24–27.

Fortner, Robert S. *International Communication: History, Conflict, and Control of the Global Metropolis.* Belmont, CA: Wadsworth, 1993.

Greenberg, Keith Elliot. "Indian PR Business Discovers Its Purpose," *Public Relations Tactics* 3 (April 1996): 15ff.

Guth, David. "The Emergence of Public Relations in the Russian Federation," *Public Relations Review* 26 (summer 2000): 191ff.

He, Mike H. "Working with High-Tech Media in China," *Public Relations Tactics* 10 (May 2003): 23.

Huang, Yi-hui. "The Personal Influence Model and Gao Guanxi in Taiwan Chinese Public Relations," *Public Relations Review* 26 (summer 2000): 219ff.

Katz, Michael E. "A PR Market Grows in Central America," *Public Relations Tactics* 5 (August 1998): 24.

Kiousis, Spiro, and Xu Wu. "International Agenda-Building and Agenda-Setting," *The International Communication Gazette* 70 (February 2008): 58–75.

Kobayashi, Sanae. "Characteristics of Japanese Communication," *Communication World* 14 (December 1996–January 1997): 14–16.

Kotcher, Raymond L. "The Changing Role of PR in Latin America," *Public Relations Tactics* 5 (March 1998): 26ff.

Kunczik, Michael. *Images of Nations and International Public Relations.* Mahwah, NJ: Erlbaum, 1996.

Leaper, Norm. "Ahh … the Pitfalls of International Communication," *Communication World* 13 (June–July 1996): 58ff.

Molleda, Juan-Carlos, and Candace Quinn. "Cross-National Conflict Shifting: A Global Public Relations Dynamic," *Public Relations Review* 30 (March 2004): 1–9.

Molleda, Juan-Carlos, and Deanna K.W. Pelfrey, "Intercultural communication: A key aspect of international media preparation," *Public Relations Tactics* 14 (December 2007): 18.

Morley, Michael. *How to Manage Your Global Reputation: A Guide to the Dynamics of International Public Relations.* New York: New York University Press, 1998.

Panol, Zenaida Sarabia. "Philippine Public Relations: An Industry and Practitioner Profile," *Public Relations Review* 26 (summer 2000): 237ff.

Parkinson, Michael, and Daradirek Ekachai. *International and Intercultural Public Relations: A Campaign Case Approach*. Upper Saddle River, NJ: Allyn & Bacon, 2005.

Reaves, Lynne. "One Country, Two Systems: PR in the New Hong Kong," *Public Relations Tactics* 4 (September 1997): 12ff.

Rieff, David. "Their Hearts and Minds?" *New York Times Magazine* 154 (April 9, 2005): 11–12.

Ritchey, David. "Mastering the Fundamentals: PR in China," *Public Relations Tactics* 4 (September 1997): 16ff.

Robles, Jennifer De, Carolyn Munckton, and Brian Everett. "Global Perspectives," *Communication World* 22 (September–October 2005): 138ff.

Rugh, William A. *Arab Mass Media: Newspapers, Radio, and Television in Arab Politics*. Westport, CT: Praeger, 2004.

Singh, Raveena, and Rosaleen Smyth. "Australian Public Relations: Status at the Turn of the 21st Century," *Public Relations Review* 26 (winter 2000): 387ff.

Sokuvitz, Sydel, and Amiso M George. "Teaching Culture: The Challenges and Opportunities of International Public Relations," *Business Communication Quarterly* 66 (June 2003): 97–113.

Sriramesh, Krishnamurthy, and Dejan Vercic, eds. *The Global Public Relations Handbook: Theory, Research, and Practice*. Mahwah, NJ: Earlbaum, 2003.

Stevens, Art. "Emergence of Global Public Relations Networks," *Public Relations Strategist* 4 (spring 1998): 18ff.

Sturaitis, Laura. "What's the Big Idea?" *Public Relations Tactics* 11 (December 2004): 11.

Taylor, Maureen. "Toward a Public Relations Approach to Nation Building," *Journal of Public Relations Research* 12, no. 2 (2000): 179ff.

Taylor, Maureen, and Michael L. Kent. "Challenging Assumptions of International Public Relations: When Government Is the Most Important Public," *Public Relations Review* 25 (summer 1999): 131ff.

Ting-Toomey, Stella. *Communicating Across Cultures*. New York: Guilford Publications, 1999.

van Ham, Peter. "The Rise of the Brand State: The Postmodern Politics of Image and Reputation," *Foreign Affairs* 80 (September–October 2001): 2ff.

Van Ruler, Betteke. "Communication Management in the Netherlands," *Public Relations Review* 26 (winter 2000): 403ff.

Wang, Jian. "Managing National Reputation and International Relations in the Global Era: Public Diplomacy Revisited," *Public Relations Review* 32 (June 2006): 91–96.

Wilcox, Dennis L., Philip H. Ault, and Warren K. Agee. "International Public Relations." In *Public Relations Strategies and Tactics*, 8th ed. New York: HarperCollins, 2006.

Wouters, Joyce. *International Public Relations*. New York: AMACOM, 1991.

Zaharna, R. S. "Intercultural Communication and International Public Relations: Exploring Parallels," *Communication Quarterly* 48 (winter 2000): 85–100.

———. "'In-awareness' Approach to International Public Relations," *Public Relations Review* 27 (summer 2001): 135–148.

International Public Relations Cases

Case 9-1

When a global company changes its name, it requires a global communication campaign to ensure the brand loyalty and reputation follows. Exhibit 9-1a is the news release announcing the new name, Exhibit 9-1b is the introductory brochure, and Exhibit 9-1c is a "frequently asked questions" about the change.

Holding Out for a Hero: NXP Revs Up the Semiconductor Industry
NXP with Text100

OVERVIEW

The story of NXP's launch is a classic underdog tale—with a twist. A year ago, things looked bleak for NXP. Its own parent company, Dutch electronics giant, Philips Group, had seemingly written it off when it announced that NXP (then Philips Semiconductors) was up for sale. Rather than give up, the company's young management team adopted a steely resolve, bringing in Text 100 Public Relations to beef up its global profile. The combined team's efforts were so successful that NXP attracted the eye of an elite consortium of private equity companies who shared CEO Frans van Houten's assessment of NXP's potential. Within months, Philips Semiconductors was reborn in a blaze of glory as an exciting new media technology company. The twist? En route to its relaunch, NXP became its industry's largest ever private equity buyout. How's that for a comeback!

CHALLENGE/OPPORTUNITY

At the start of 2006, Philips Semiconductors had a low profile and an uncertain future. The relative volatility of the semiconductor sector had caused its parent company, Philips Group, to deprioritize its technology division and focus on the health care and lifestyle "pillars" of the Group business strategy. Philips then announced its intention to spin-off or sell the semiconductors business by the end of the year. The business unit's reputation consequently became a lower priority in the overall communications program of Philips Group, drastically impacting its profile, lowering media awareness, and diminishing coverage favorability. In response, the PR team launched a global nine-month campaign to bolster media share around its "hero" products culminating in the high-profile launch of Philips Semiconductors as a new, independent vibrant company— NXP Semiconductors—whose business history and financial stability positioned it well for growth and success.

Objectives

Traditionally, Philips Semiconductors media efforts had focused on trade media for its product news, the media set it was permitted to engage by its parent company. Neither this focus nor the resulting coverage did justice to an energetic management team, nor to the success of its corporate business renewal program, which had delivered 11 consecutive quarters of profit. To address both issues head-on, Philips Semiconductors set out to create a clear identity, vision, and evidence of industry leadership to position it as a vibrant, successful entity and an appealing acquisition or investment target.

Target/Audience Analysis

The company creates semiconductors that deliver better sensory experiences in mobile phones, personal media players, TVs, set-top boxes, electronic passports, applications, cars, and other electronic devices. Its customers are product designers, engineers, and manufacturers who rely on semiconductor technologies to create ever-more powerful devices with richer features at lower cost and lower power consumption. This audience is served by the world's semiconductor and electronics media (e.g., *EE Times, Electronics News*), vertical sector media (automotive, mobile, consumer electronics), specialist analyst groups (Semico and iSuppli), and the world's business media. Markets addressed by the campaign included the United States, the UK, France, Germany, India, China, Taiwan, Japan, and Korea.

RESEARCH/PLANNING

To ascertain the state of Philips Semiconductors reputation among stakeholders, the PR team contracted research company Context Analytics to conduct a global media and analyst perception audit. Interviews took place with more than 100 leading media and analysts across the globe. The audit revealed three key issues: (1) Journalists and analysts had a lower level of familiarity with Philips Semiconductors industry vision than with that of competitors Texas Instruments, Freescale, and Infineon. (2) More than 10 percent of respondents said they had a "poor" understanding of Philips Semiconductors business strategy. (3) Respondents associated Philips Semiconductors with a wide range of technologies, but the company scored lower than competitors for technical innovation.

Strategy

To demonstrate the company's vision and business strategy, the PR team crafted a communications strategy demonstrating leadership in fast-growth "fashion" markets such as digital TV, contactless payment systems, and next-generation cell phones. By doing so, the team sought to highlight the value of the business unit's assets and pave the way for its emergence as an independent semiconductor powerhouse. The team selected a handful of "hero" technologies that typified the vision and specifically demonstrated technical innovation. These were TV-on-Mobile (Philips technology allows users to view live TV programs on a mobile phone), Next-Generation Digital TV (Philips chips are integral to lifelike images on digital TV products), and Near-Field Communication (Philips chips enable secure contactless transactions to be made using phones instead of credit or cash cards). These technologies were the focus for all global communications and activity.

EXECUTION

1. **TV-on-mobile—Making (air) waves in 2006.** The PR team began driving visibility with "intro-to-mobile-TV" press events in China and Europe. Featuring technical discussions and demonstrations of the handset technology, the events generated close to 100 pieces of print and online coverage. Next, the team focused on the three largest consumer technology events: CES, 3 GSM, and CTIA, where new smaller chips critical to reducing power consumption (essential to making TV-on-mobile devices feasible) were unveiled. PR efforts at these events culminated in a giant leap forward for Philips' perception as a leader in TV-on-mobile with over 70 pieces of coverage. Results for the Barcelona-based 3 GSM event alone included a 143 percent increase year-on-year in media interviews and a 211 percent increase in coverage; all generated by a more-focused 50 percent fewer press releases. The year's activities culminated with editors receiving a sneak-preview of TV-on-mobile at the 2006 FIFA World Cup in Germany. To capitalize on Philips sponsorship of the event, the PR team hosted 14 regional journalists at World Cup games where they could watch live coverage of several matches using mobile handsets supporting this promising new technology.

2. **IPTV and the home of the (not-too-distant) future.** To raise awareness of Philips Semiconductors leadership in IPTV (technologies combining TV images with Internet-like information features) the PR team had to engage Junko Yoshida, the Paris, France-based senior editor of the world's most influential electronics publication, *EE Times*. It did so by working with the marketing team at Philips Semiconductors' Silicon Valley campus to create a showcase where visitors could gain a realistic impression of what a home with an IPTV setup would look like and could view Philips IP-Set Top Box

technology (the Philips-powered device that melds internet and TV signals). The team convinced Junko to come see the demo first-hand. She loved the room, stating this was the first time a semiconductor vendor had combined technologies such as IPTV, VoIP (voice calls delivered by an Internet connection), and a wireless home network to demonstrate what a connected home could look like. Her visit resulted in a five-page feature in the global issue of *EE Times* touting Philips as the leader in the emerging IPTV market.

3. **Near-field communication—Demonstrating Philips Leadership in Contactless Payment Systems.** Philips Semiconductors is a pioneer of near-field communication (NFC), a short-range wireless communication technology used to enable contactless transactions. Philips sought to generate awareness for NFC and consumer demand by making global NFC trials central to its media strategy. First, journalists were invited to see how residents of the northern French city of Caen were boosting retail sales by 30 percent by conducting transactions of up to 1,500 Euros in retail stores, accessing car parking, and obtaining tourist information via NFC-enabled Samsung D500 mobile phones. The media were invited to see how NFC technology allowed residents to access and pay for use of the transportation system of Hanau, Germany—the world's first commercial rollout of NFC technology. These trials raised visibility worldwide through coverage in *La Tribune, EE Times, South China Morning Post, Financial Times, Economist, Handelsblatt,* and major TV networks including CNN, Fox News, BBC, and CBS. The promotion of the results of a subsequent usability study, commissioned jointly by Philips with finance partner VISA, further underscored the positive attitude of consumers, revealing convenience, ease-of-use, and "coolness" as reasons why NFC would catch on as a way to buy entertainment and services.

4. **The launch of NXP semiconductors—A truly global launch yields stunning results.** On September 1, 2006, after weeks of detailed behind-the-scenes planning, NXP Semiconductors was born out of Philips Semiconductors as an independent company. The global communications team planned customer and employee events worldwide, with high-profile media activity scheduled to take place in Europe, North America, and Asia to ensure the launch reverberated around the globe. In sum, more than 11.6 million viewers and listeners had witnessed CEO Frans van Houten announce the new brand and its core values on global broadcast television programs. Additionally, more than 335 journalists and analysts around the world had been briefed through a combination of nearly 100 one-to-one interviews and 7 regional press events.

RESULTS

Media results following the global company launch positioned NXP as more competitive than ever before, with high-profile publications acknowledging its newfound independence would allow NXP to grow and emerge as a stronger player. In addition, 90 percent of articles were positive and 75 percent of coverage was headline coverage (Source: CARMA).

One year after the first media and analyst audit, the PR team again contracted Context Analytics to conduct a global perception audit. Research showed a dramatic shift in perceptions with 25 percent of all editors and analysts reporting an improvement in their opinion of the company. More importantly, the audit revealed significant progress had been made against the three issues identified as impeding a positive reputation:

1. Ten percent improvement in familiarity with the company's vision

2. Eighty-nine percent of respondents said that their understanding of the company's business strategy was good or better, up more than 5 percent

3. Rating for technical innovation increased 12 percent

EXHIBIT 9-1a News Release

founded by Philips

Philips Semiconductors becomes NXP

Fifty years of innovation and a rich IP portfolio firmly establishes NXP as Europe's second largest semiconductor company

Berlin, Germany, 1ˢᵗ September 2006 – Philips Semiconductors CEO Frans van Houten today revealed the company will move forward as NXP, marking a milestone in its 53 year history as it becomes independent from Royal Philips. The name change announcement follows an agreement between Royal Philips and Kohlberg Kravis Roberts & Co. (KKR), Bain Capital, Silver Lake Partners, Apax and AlpInvest Partners NV that will see the consortium take an 80.1 percent stake in the semiconductor operation with Philips retaining a 19.9 percent interest. NXP is Europe's second largest semiconductor company and a global top 10 player.

Speaking at the Internationale Funkausstellung (IFA) consumer electronics show in Berlin, Mr. van Houten explained that the company's 'vibrant media' brand promise reflects its leadership in media technologies that enable better sensory experiences for consumers such as superior image and sound quality in digital televisions, mobile phones and other entertainment products.

"Today we take control of our own destiny and start to shape the future of the semiconductor industry. We enable our customers to build better products, based on our next generation vibrant media technologies," said Mr. van Houten. "NXP stands for Next Experience. Put simply, we're enabling the next generation of consumer entertainment products. In order to emphasize the rich heritage that NXP gained from 53 years as part of Royal Philips, the NXP name will be supported by the tagline *founded by Philips.*"

Derek Lidow, CEO of iSuppli said, "This largest technology leveraged buyout ever will create a real semiconductor powerhouse. Armed with its independence, and starting out as Europe's second largest semiconductor company, the management team has clearly just started re-writing the history books."

Commitment to Business Renewal Strategy Confirmed

Mr. van Houten confirmed that NXP will continue its current business renewal strategy, which has been underway for 18 months and has contributed to sustained profitability and cost savings, as a strong foundation for the future.

The new shareholders support the continuation of the strategy of NXP, which is driving for leadership in five markets on which the company focuses: Automotive, Identification, Home, Mobile and Personal, and Multimarket Semiconductors. This will be achieved through investment of one billion Euro in R&D, the asset light manufacturing strategy, a strong customer focus, the enormous talent base among its 37,000 employees, and the continued Business Renewal Program.

Explaining the financial structure of the equity funding, Mr. van Houten confirmed NXP will have over 1.2 billion Euro in cash and credit reserves. This financial buffer will also enable the company to explore options for acquisitions.

E X H I B I T 9-1a   (Continued)

founded by Philips

Mr. Johannes Huth from KKR, the leading partner in the private equity consortium, added: "We were attracted to a world class business with a global scale and presence. NXP is leading in markets with strong growth characteristics, for example Near Field Communication and digital TV. The business renewal strategy is a strong foundation for future growth, and we look forward to supporting the existing management team as it continues to add value to this business."

A center dedicated to emerging technologies has been established within NXP with close to 600 scientists joining from Philips Research and Applied Technologies, ensuring continued innovation. In total, NXP now has over 6,700 engineers in research & development. NXP will remain headquartered in Eindhoven, the Netherlands.

"We want to be a leader in everything we do," said Mr. van Houten. "NXP already has number one market share in areas such as TV chips, contactless identification for e-passports, RFID for electronic ticketing in public transport, car radio digital signal processors and key mobile phone system solutions."

About NXP:
NXP is a top 10 semiconductor company founded by Philips more than 50 years ago. Headquartered in Europe, the company has 37,000 employees working in 20 countries across the world. NXP creates semiconductors, system solutions and software that deliver better sensory experiences in mobile phones, personal media players, TVs, set-top boxes, identification applications, cars and a wide range of other electronic devices. News from NXP is located at www.NXP.com.

Chief Executive Frans van Houten will be hosting a press call at 11.00 CET on Friday 1 September to answer questions about the new company. To receive dial in details for this call please send an email to Press.office@text100.co.uk.

For further press information, please contact:

Europe:	Heather Drake	Greater China:	Terry Chiang
	Tel. +31 40 27 65949		Tel. +886 2 3789 2821
	heather.drake@nxp.com		terry.chiang@nxp.com
USA:	Paul Morrison	APAC:	Mark Chisholm
	Tel. +1 408 474 5065		Tel. +81 3 3740 4792
	paul.morrison@nxp.com		mark.chisholm@nxp.com

PLEASE DO NOT PRINT THESE CONTACT DETAILS IN YOUR PUBLICATION

Forward-looking Statements
This release may contain certain forward-looking statements with respect to the financial condition, results of operations and business of NXP and certain plans and objectives of NXP with respect to these items. By their nature, forward-looking statements involve risk and uncertainty because they relate to events and depend on circumstances that will occur in the future and there are many factors that could cause actual results and developments to differ materially from those expressed or implied by these forward-looking statements.

founded by
PHILIPS

Page 2 of 2

E X H I B I T 9-1b   NXP Brochure

Deliver a difference your customers can see, hear, and feel

It's not often that you find a partner that has the energy and enthusiasm of a newcomer but the wisdom and experience of a veteran. Yet that's exactly what we offer.

We're a new company driven by a single purpose – to deliver vibrant media technologies that create better sensory experiences – yet we begin life with more than 50 years of success to our credit.

We're proud of our Philips heritage and are keeping everything that's best about who we are. You'll find we still have the same remarkable consumer insight, and the same in-depth knowledge gained from billions of dollars invested in R&D. And, of course, we have the same confidence that comes from consistently delivering groundbreaking technology.

Take a closer look, and you'll see that we're the same exceptionally talented people you've come to know and trust. The only difference is that now we're lighter on our feet and have an even sharper focus on our customer relationships.

Our independence makes us better than ever, and we're ready to take on your most ambitious ideas. Together, we can deliver a difference your customers can see, hear, and feel.

Frans van Houten, President and CEO

NXP at a glance
- Founded in 2006 by Royal Philips Electronics
- 50+ years of experience in semiconductors
- Net sales of € 4.771 billion in 2005
- R&D investments of more than € 965 million in 2005
- 5,300+ patent families (25,000 patents)
- Roughly 37,000 employees in more than 20 countries
- Ten wafer fabs and 8 test and assembly sites worldwide
- Top rankings in mobile & portable, connected home, identification, automotive, and multimarket semiconductor sectors

"We're proud to become NXP. Our separation from Philips lets us invest in our future, accelerate our growth, and focus on our key customers – all with the same exceptional talent and ability for innovation we've always had."

Courtesy NXP Semiconductors/Text100

EXHIBIT 9-1b (Continued)

Put the world in the palm of your hand

Accomplishments in Mobile & Portable

- Number 1 in complete system solutions for GSM/GPRS/EDGE handsets, with more than 200 million Nexperia cellular system solutions shipped
- Number 1 in speaker systems for mobile phones
- Number 1 in FM radio ICs for portable applications
- Number 1 in USB
- Number 1 in digital cordless ICs
- Number 3 in ASSPs for all wireless communications
- Technology provider behind the world's first UMA-enabled mobile phone for voice calls and data sessions through cellular networks and Wi-Fi access points

The right handheld device adds spark to the daily routine and becomes a vital part of your personal adventure. Our industry-leading Nexperia cellular system solutions cover everything from ultra-low-cost (ULC) handsets to high-end smartphones, and our Nexperia-based technologies for personal media players raise the bar for multimedia performance. We excel in high-value options like TV-on-mobile and FM radio, and have cross-over technologies like WLAN for VoIP. We even let you extend the options with high-quality audio in the form of speakers, receivers and accessory sound panels. What's more, we build in flexibility at every point, so you can deliver products that are as individual as the people who use them.

"What if you could truly re-live the experience?"

Our Nexperia mobile multimedia processor PNX4103 delivers high-and still imaging and video functions, including real-time video recording and playback. It uses a standard parallel interface and is designed to work with any host processor.

Camcorder quality on your mobile phone, so you can really enjoy it all over again.

EXHIBIT 9-1b (Continued)

Create a personal oasis

Home is a place that should delight the senses and feed the soul. Our Nexperia-based solutions and audio/video components let you turn the digital home into a connected living experience, so it's easier than ever to enjoy and share media in every room. Time spent with friends and family has a new energy, down time is more relaxing, and you stay connected with the outside world in a whole new way. High-end audio and video surprise even the toughest critics, and wireless gives you the freedom to move. We also let you put your PC in the mix, so you can add your own creativity to media files of all kinds.

"What if you could make everything sharper, more life-like?"

Our Nexperia hybrid ATSC/DVB solution TV520 is a ready-to-manufacture design that combines best-in-class HD picture quality with ATSC/DVB operation. Copy-ready hardware and mature, field-proven software stacks dramatically reduce design time and even facilitate a cost-effective transition to digital TV.

A state-of-the-art LCD TV with HD quality, so you can enjoy greener grass and bluer skies.

Accomplishments in Digital Home
- Number 1 in silicon for TV, with 1 in 2 TVs worldwide using our IC
- Number 1 in silicon for PC TV, with 4 in 10 PC TVs using our silicon tuners
- Number 3 in ASSPs for all consumer applications
- 1 in 2 digital terrestrial set-top boxes uses our RF front-end module
- Best-in-class video quality for TV, STB, PC TV, with best digital natural motion, EDDI, active picture control, MPEG artifact reduction

EXHIBIT 9-1b   (Continued)

Add that something extra

As specialists in the sensory experience, we never underestimate the value of software – it is as essential to our work as breath is to life. To underline our commitment in this area, we've established a separate, fully independent company, NXP Software. They are the leading provider of software solutions that improve sound, voice, and video quality in mobile handsets. Their software adds brilliance and vitality, and is available on its own, whether you use our hardware or not. They're also members of our Nexperia partner program, so you get direct access to their industry-leading options for Nexperia-based technologies. The partner program is an extensive ecosystem of ISVs for mobile and home, so you can extend your options with state-of-the-art solutions developed by a variety of leading third-party companies.

"What if you could
put real life in a little box?"

LifeVibes™ software products, available from NXP Software, dramatically improve voice clarity, make music sound better, produce video that rivals that of a TV, and make things more fun with features like video shoot, edit, and share.

Truly incredible music, TV, video, and voice for mobile, so you can bring all your senses to life.

Accomplishments in Software
▶ Number 1 Independent Software Vendor for mobile multimedia software solutions
▶ More than 100 million devices use LifeVibes software

Software · Conquering Software   9

8 · Conquering Software

E X H I B I T 9-1c   Frequently Asked Questions

 founded by Philips

Frequently Asked Questions

Q.   Please explain the rationale behind the new name.
A.   The NXP name stands for Next Experience. The new name and value proposition reflect our company's expertise in technologies that deliver vibrant consumer experiences. To us, it is fitting that we should name our company after what we do. We create the next experience.

Q.   Please explain NXP's 'vibrant media' technologies positioning.
A: The semiconductor industry is driving the innovation that delivers the new and exciting consumer electronics, mobile communications and media devices that consumers demand. We believe that vibrancy is a core element of these types of applications.

We believe consumers want experiences, and not just gadgets, and vibrant media technologies are essential for:
- Creating, managing and sharing content
- Communications, both analog and digital
- Improving consumers' sensory experience, either directly or indirectly
- Creating superior sound quality
- Creating superior image quality
- Synchronizing audio and video

NXP has expertise in technologies that deliver these vibrant consumer experiences – such as crisp, high-quality audio or video content.

Q.   Please explain the rationale behind the new logo.
A.   Within the new logo, the *N* represents the next and the *P* represents Philips; they are linked by the *X* which represents the sensory experiences that our company aims to deliver.

Q.   What is the new company's business strategy?
A.   NXP Semiconductors will continue its current business renewal strategy, which has been underway for 18 months and has contributed to sustained profitability and cost savings, as a strong foundation for the future. This involves building leadership in the five markets on which the company focuses: Automotive, Identification, Home, Mobile & Personal, and Multimarket Semiconductors.

Q: What will happen to the management team?
A: The current management team that runs the Semiconductors activities will stay in place, led by CEO Frans van Houten. As part of the formal legal process, a board of management will also be established at NXP.

Courtesy NXP Semiconductors/Text100

Case 9-2

With a global economy come global communication challenges when setting new international standards for commerce. The radio frequency identification (RFID) system is quickly becoming a global standard for "scanning" products instead of the older bar code system, but it took considerable communication initiatives to make it happen. Exhibit 9-2a is a news release in Belgium, Exhibit 9-2b provides a video news release advisory, Exhibit 9-2c is an audio script, and Exhibit 9-2d is a "messaging" presentation.

The Electronic Product Code: From Concept to Commercialization in One Year

Creating the EPCglobal Brand—Real value. Right partner. Right now

SITUATION ANALYSIS

The bar code. Most of us only think of it in the supermarket checkout lane. But this technology—developed and commercialized by the Uniform Code Council (UCC)—is scanned 10 billion times every day. Now, the growing complexity of global commerce and the growing demand for more sophisticated and effective supply chain management has given the UCC the opportunity to bring to the marketplace the next-generation bar code—the Electronic Product Code (EPC). This exciting new technology harnesses radio frequency identification (RFID) to give companies the expanded ability to track products as they move from point to point, anywhere in the world. But in the fall of 2003, as the UCC began the commercialization efforts for EPC technology, it faced some real challenges. Some of the world's largest organizations, such as Wal-Mart, P&G, Gillette, Marks & Spencer, Tesco, and even the United States Dept. of Defense were clamoring to implement the technology. Their support created relentless demand for standardized products, which awaited guidance from the UCC and its soon-to-be-created affiliate, EPCglobal, Inc. Simultaneously, consumer privacy groups, fearful of the technology's capabilities, had organized an all-out misinformation campaign. Industry proponents were stunned into silence as state legislators and federal officials began considering regulation of the technology. The

Uniform Code Council, Inc., with Fleishman-Hillard, Inc.

media and analyst communities, woefully underinformed about EPC, played into the hands of its opponents. Within this environment, the UCC and Fleishman-Hillard, Inc. (FH) launched EPCglobal to focus and drive the commercialization of the technology forward. To date, the efforts are succeeding beyond expectations; with membership in EPCglobal soaring by more than 200 percent, and share of voice in the media reaching a height of 35 percent, up from 5 percent at the start of the program.

RESEARCH/PLANNING

To ascertain what brand recognition the UCC had in the marketplace, assess the key opinions of target audiences, and uncover obstacles, FH conducted primary and secondary research. The research can be clustered in three categories:

C-level and supply chain executives. FH conducted interviews with senior-level corporate executives across target industries. Findings uncovered high confidence in the UCC, high awareness of RFID, but low awareness of the EPC. Results also indicated business-driven messages were important and prioritized. As a result, the brand architecture, "Real value. Right partner. Right now" reflected the essence of each message.

Consumers. FH conducted a global audit of all existing information on consumer concerns around RFID. The firm was able to tap into additional research conducted by the client. It was discovered that consumers, when presented with the facts about EPC in the supply chain, overwhelmingly supported its use. As a result, EPCglobal's privacy platform is consumer benefits focused.

Member organizations (MO). Based on survey data from 103 MOs, FH created tools to help push the commercialization effort forward within their respective countries. Results included the creation of a global news summary and newsletter.

Strategy

Based on the research, FH and the client determined that efforts should focus on the following areas:

Gain momentum in the United States and then expand globally. With the majority of early adopter companies in the United States, the campaign first focused efforts domestically. Traction in the United States would then entice others to join in other regions.

Articulate the value of the organization to drive membership. The new standards body required membership fees to feed standards development efforts and push adoption quickly.

Simplify the technology to focus on real benefits for business. Key audiences simply wanted to hear the value proposition and how it could improve their business and the lives of their customers.

Seed the marketplace with factual information about the technology. Communicate developments through business, trade and vertical media, analyst reports, and the organization's Web site. Counteract negative coverage with aggressive response tactics to keep positive messages in front of key audiences.

OBJECTIVES

Establish credibility. Develop a brand that would effectively communicate the value and vision of the organization.

Gain subscribers. EPCglobal is supported by membership fees. To create a sustainable business model, EPCglobal needed subscribers fast.

Gain industry support. Although some of the world's largest organizations supported the technology, few had embraced its value proposition.

Audience

EPC technology is a global supply chain tool, but at launch, many early adopter companies were in the United States. To focus resources, tactics were first executed domestically, and additional elements were added to fuel adoption in the rest of the world.

Primary—U.S.-based C-suite executives, IT leaders and supply chain and logistics managers in the aerospace/aviation, automotive, consumer packaged goods, health care/pharmaceutical, and retail industries

Secondary—More than 100 MOs representing individual countries from around the world

EXECUTION

Phase I (September 2003 to present)

Brand identity. FH developed the core brand and brand positioning for the new organization. The selected name, EPCglobal, underwent a global name screen and was selected because of its connection to the technology and its emphasis on the global nature of the technology. The tagline emphasized "Real value. Right partner. Right now" to communicate the value of the technology, the viability of the organization, and the sense of urgency to begin implementing the EPC today. The brand mark was leveraged across multiple vehicles with the media launch conducted at a high-profile, industry trade show.

Steady drumbeat of information to key audiences through media relations. FH executed ongoing proactive and reactive media relations efforts throughout the year. To maximize exposure, FH planned significant events around the following:

Making the Technology Real, the Selection of VeriSign to Operate the EPCglobal Network—A key challenge was the natural tendency of companies to "put off" investing in the technology. By announcing a key contract with VeriSign, FH was able to reposition the conversation to begin tracking the buildup of the EPCglobal Network.

Hearing Consumer Concerns and Taking Steps to Address Them— To take a proactive stance on the issue of consumer privacy, EPCglobal formed a collaborative Public Policy Steering Committee (PPSC). Made up of experts from various industries, the PPSC published guidelines for the responsible deployment of EPC. At this time, EPCglobal also began proactively responding to media queries, balancing the conversation.

Wal-Mart Launches First Commercial Trials of EPC—To further highlight the rapid deployment of EPC in the marketplace, EPCglobal, in conjunction with Wal-Mart, opened the first commercial tests to the media. Though prepared for potential picketing from privacy advocates, the event coverage and customer feedback were positive.

Happy Birthday to the Bar Code—On June 26, the ubiquitous U.P.C. (Universal Product Code) turned 30 and offered an opportunity to reframe the conversation for the transition from the world of U.P.C. to EPC. Media coverage relentlessly connected the U.P.C. to the EPC, the next generation bar code.

EPCglobal US Fall Conference—Culminating a year's worth of effort, the conference provided a platform to update the industry on the incredible progress. Featuring high-level media secured by FH, including David Kirkpatrick of *FORTUNE*, Ron Insana of CNBC, and Mark Roberti of *RFID Journal*, attendance rocketed past projections and dwarfed a competitive show held weeks before.

Gen 2 Ratification—Built upon the excitement that occurred at the EPCglobal US Fall Conference, Generation 2 (Gen 2) Ratification marked the culmination of a year's worth of standards development efforts. Reported by major business publications, trade journals, and key verticals, the ratification was the landmark news event for the RFID industry in 2004.

Phase II (August 2004 to present)

Global Member Communications. As U.S. efforts took off, interest grew around the world. To capitalize on the growing interest, FH created an online newsletter that allowed each MO to brand the piece with their respective country. In addition, FH also distributes a weekly news roundup of international coverage to help keep interest high.

EVALUATION

Created a unified, global brand. Since the launch in September, 103 UCC Member Organizations have adopted the EPCglobal brand in their markets.

Created a sustainable organization and increased industry support. At the brand launch in September there were no members of EPCglobal. Today, after one year, there are nearly 400 subscribers worldwide with more than 200 headquartered domestically, including companies like Wal-Mart, Target, Johnson & Johnson, Abbott, Pfizer, Sun, HP, Boeing, and Michelin.

The EPCglobal US Fall Conference, the first one held, hosted nearly 2,000 attendees, with more than 70 media in attendance, successfully dwarfing a competing show held just weeks earlier.

Added EPC into the conversation. At the start of the campaign, the mentions of RFID significantly outweighed those of EPC. Through aggressive media relations, share of voice and inclusion of EPC in stories reached a high of 35 percent, climbing from less than 5 percent. The VeriSign partnership announcement achieved more than 20 million impressions. The bar code birthday celebration generated more than 17 million media impressions.

Aggressively addressed misinformation regarding privacy. Less than a year ago, consumer privacy groups owned the conversation and did not focus on consumer benefits. EPC is now consistently included in more than half of privacy coverage. Overall tone has shifted from predominantly negative to neutral, and in many cases positive with inclusion of key consumer benefits.

E X H I B I T 9-2a News Release

EPCglobal

FOR IMMEDIATE RELEASE

For More Information Contact:
Audrey Ni Cheallaigh, 011.32.2.227.10.25
audrey.nicheallaigh@gs1.org

EPCglobal Ratifies Royalty-Free UHF Generation 2 Standard

Announcement Marks Culmination of Collaborative Process; Opens Door for Proliferation of Standards-Based Hardware to Drive EPC Implementations Worldwide

BRUSSELS, Belgium – December 16, 2004 – EPCglobal Inc™, a subsidiary of GS1 a not-for-profit standards organization entrusted with driving global adoption of Electronic Product Code (EPC) technology, today announced the ratification of the royalty-free EPCglobal UHF Generation 2 candidate specification. Today's announcement marks the much anticipated completion of the UHF Generation 2 air interface protocol as an EPCglobal standard. With the Generation 2 standard now in place, technology providers will create products that will meet the requirements of suppliers, manufacturers, and end users; and industries as a whole can drive EPC implementation with standards-based equipment.

Today's announcement follows successful testing of prototypes from several technology providers, which illustrated that the ratified standard can meet the EPCglobal community end user requirements, as well as final determination that all intellectual property presented on a licensed basis during the standards development process was not necessary to the standard. Commercially available products are expected the first half of 2005.

"Today marks both an exciting culmination and a much anticipated beginning in the commercialization of RFID and EPC technology," said Chris Adcock, president, EPCglobal Inc. "Many of the world's leading technology companies collaborated to develop the UHF Generation 2 specification, and we celebrate and applaud their efforts as we launch the royalty-free UHF Generation 2 standard. With this standard in place, technology manufacturers and end users alike can begin exploring how to deploy the technology in such a way to make a significant impact in improving their own business."

- more -

EXHIBIT 9-2a (Continued)

EPCglobal Ratifies Royalty-Free UHF Generation 2 Standard
Page two

    The EPCglobal UHF Generation 2 protocol, a consensus standard built by more than 60 of the world's leading technology companies, describes the core capabilities required to meet the performance needs set by the end user community. The UHF Generation 2 standard will be used as a base platform upon which standards-based products and future improvements will be built. An EPCglobal standard ensures interoperability and sets minimum operational expectations for various components in the EPCglobal Network™, including hardware components. While EPCglobal oversees interoperability and conformance testing of standards-based products, the actual development of these products comes from leading solution providers around the globe.

    During 2004, EPCglobal has worked with the global community of end-users and solution providers to complete a number of activities aimed at building out the EPCglobal Network. The UHF Generation 2 standard is a foundational element in the continued build-out of the EPCglobal Network, a network that combines RFID technology, the Internet and the EPC to provide accurate, cost-efficient visibility of information throughout supply chains.

    Concurrent with the ratification of UHF Generation 2, EPCglobal has set up a special committee to consider whether additional numbering features are necessary to the EPCglobal standard. Following the outcome of this work group, EPCglobal plans to submit the Generation 2 standard to the International Organization for Standardization (ISO).

About EPCglobal Inc. EPCglobal Inc™, a subsidiary of GS1, is a not-for-profit organization entrusted by industry to establish and support the EPCglobal Network™ as the global standard for real-time, automatic identification of information in the supply chain of any company, anywhere in the world.

The EPCglobal Network combines radio frequency identification (RFID) technology, existing communications network infrastructure, and the Electronic Product Code™ (a number for uniquely identifying an item) to enable accurate, cost-efficient visibility of information in the supply chain. The end result helps organizations be more efficient, flexible, and responsive to customer needs. EPCglobal US is an affiliate of EPCglobal Inc, serving subscribers in the United States to help foster the adoption of the EPCglobal Network and related technology. For more information about EPCglobal visit: www.EPCglobalinc.org.

About GS1. GS1 is the global not-for-profit organisation that creates, develops and manages the EAN•UCC standards jointly with the Uniform Code Council, one of its Member Organisations. These are open, global, multisectoral information standards, based on best business practices. By driving their implementation, GS1 and its Member Organisations play a leading role in supply and demand chain management improvement worldwide. For more information on EAN International, please visit: www.GS1.org.

# # #

E X H I B I T 9-2b   VNR Advisory

---

* * * ATTN: NEWS / FEATURE / CONSUMER & FINANCIAL EDITORS * * *

U.P.C. BAR CODE CELEBRATES
30th BIRTHDAY ON JUNE 25TH

Uniform Code Council Returns to the Site of the History-Making First Product Scanned Was a Pack of Wrigley's Gum

VIDEO FEEDS FRIDAY, JUNE 25, 1:15 – 1:30 PM ET
PATHFIRE Story # NBN 23393

Lawrenceville, NJ/Troy, OH -- The Uniform Code Council (UCC) is celebrating the 30th anniversary of the Universal Product Code, or U.P.C., by returning to Marsh Supermarket in Troy, Ohio, the store that hosted the world's first live scan on June 26th, 1974. The original cashier, Sharon Buchanan, who scanned the first product – a pack of Wrigley's Gum – will join others in commemorating the occasion.

The U.P.C. was the outgrowth of meetings that took place in the late 1960's by leaders of the U.S. grocery industry, who were hoping to reduce food costs and congestion at the checkout line.

The U.P.C. is composed of a row of 59 black and white bars that vary in length and are read by a scanner. Beneath the bars is a series of 12 human-readable numbers, which together identify the manufacturer and the specific product.

Today, the U.P.C. is used by 23 major industry sectors, including retail, healthcare, government, foodservice, transportation and high-tech. **The UCC estimates that bar codes are scanned over 10 billion times a day in over 140 nations around the world**. The UCC is now standardizing its newest innovation, a "wireless bar code" called the Electronic Product Code.

The original pack of Wrigley's gum and the checkout scanning unit from the Marsh store are housed at the Smithsonian Institution's National Museum of American History in Washington, DC.

WHAT YOU'LL GET: B-roll and soundbites package
FOOTAGE of the first item scanned, a pack of Wrigley's chewing gum; Marsh Supermarket of Troy, OH, the first store to use the U.P.C. system; the U.P.C. on various products; new bar code technology
SOUNDBITES include Michael Di Yeso, President of the Uniform Code Council (UCC) and Sharon Buchanan, cashier who scanned first U.P.C

VIA SATELLITE, C-BAND FEED:
FRIDAY, JUNE 25   1:15 – 1:30 PM ET   IA 5, Tr. 14, DL 3980
                    ** IA 5 Formerly known as Telstar 5 **

Technical Info DURING FEED ONLY, NBN TOC, 212 – 684 - 8910 x 221

VIA PATHFIRE:
On the left panel of Pathfire, double click on News Broadcast Network, Story # NBN 23393.

FREE FROM NEWS BROADCAST NETWORK, 212 – 684 – 8910
Hard Copy Requests: Shannon Speck, 800 – 920 – 6397
shannon@newsbroadcastnetwork.com
Editorial Contact: Laura Ojile, 314 – 982 - 1740

w w w . n e w s b r o a d c a s t n e t w o r k . c o m

Courtesy GS1 US

EXHIBIT 9-2c Audio News Release

6.18.04

UNIFORM CODE COUNCIL
30TH BIRTHDAY ANR

ANNOUNCER:

MICHAEL DELL...BILL GATES. MANY OF US THINK OF THESE INDIVIDUALS AS BUSINESS ICONS. SATURDAY, JUNE 26TH ANOTHER BUSINESS ICON IS TURNING 30 – THE U.P.C. BARCODE.   THIS SATURDAY AT THE MARSH GROCERY STORE IN THE SMALL TOWN OF TROY, OHIO – WHERE THE WORLD'S FIRST SCAN OCCURRED – A CELEBRATION IS TAKING PLACE TO MARK THE OCCASION.   THE ORIGINAL CASHIER, SHARON BUCHANAN, WHO SCANNED THE FIRST BARCODED PRODUCT – A PACK OF WRIGLEY GUM – WILL JOIN OTHERS IN COMMEMORATING THE OCCASION. JACK GRASSO, FROM THE UNIFORM CODE COUNCIL, THE GROUP THAT BROUGHT THE BAR CODE TO LIFE WAS THERE.

SOUNDBITE:

"THE UNIFORM CODE COUNCIL IS THRILLED TO CELEBRATE THE 30TH YEAR OF THE REVOLUTIONARY UPC, WHICH PROVIDES TREMENDOUS COST-SAVINGS AND IMPROVED INVENTORY TRACKING FOR BUSINESSES AND CONSUMERS. THE UPC HAS PAVED THE WAY FOR TECHNOLOGIES IN DEVELOPMENT TODAY, LIKE THE ELECTRONIC PRODUCT CODE, OR EPC. EPC WILL HAVE AS REMARKABLE AN IMPACT ON THE FUTURE OF THE SUPPLY CHAIN AS THE UPC DID THREE DECADES AGO."

ANNOUNCER:

TODAY, THE UNIVERSAL PRODUCT CODE IS NOW USED BY 23 MAJOR INDUSTRY SECTORS, INCLUDING RETAIL, HEALTHCARE, GOVERNMENT, FOODSERVICE, TRANSPORTATION, AND HIGH-TECH. THE ORGANIZATION ESTIMATES THAT THESE BAR CODES ARE SCANNED MORE THAN 10 BILLION TIMES A DAY IN OVER 140 NATIONS AROUND THE WORLD.

#

EXHIBIT 9-2d Message Training Presentation

PRIVACY IS AS IMPORTANT AS ANYTHING ELSE WE ARE DOING.

COMMITMENT	BENEFITS	TECHNOLOGY
We are committed to understanding and addressing the complex questions that surround consumer privacy.	Consumers and businesses will reap benefits through the use of EPC technologies.	The technology creates data about products not people.

COMMITMENT

EPC subscribers adhere to published public policy guidelines relating to consumer privacy.

These guidelines provide that consumers should be given:
- **notice** when EPC technology is in use,
- **choice** over using or disposing of the tag after purchase,
- **education** about EPC technology and its uses and
- **control** of information retained through the use of EPC technologies.

• We established a multi-industry, global public policy steering committee (PPSC) to provide education and outreach to key stakeholders in the public and private sectors.

The PPSC has and will continue to:
• Reviewed all relevant, recent and future studies on consumer privacy to inform and guide our discussions.
• Study consumer perceptions and opinions regarding privacy and EPC.
• Provide various state and federal bodies information that includes, relevant facts on EPC and its benefits to consumers and business.

BENEFITS

• Consumers will have access to the right products at the right time.
• Consumers believe in the benefits of the technology.
• No longer will consumers receive expired or short-dated products.
• EPCs will help speed product recalls and aid in the recovery of stolen property, and reduce the opportunity for counterfeit items; especially in the pharmaceutical and electronics industry.
• Business can improve efficiency in their business processes through RFID in the supply chain.
• Retail theft costs retailers, and ultimately consumers, $50 billion per year. EPC will help retailers keep better track of items in the supply chain to reduce theft.
• Counterfeiting is a $500 billion problem. EPC technologies will help lessen counterfeiting.

TECHNOLOGY

• The EPC is merely a license plate for a product. It creates data about products not people
• Current applications help companies see how, when and where their products move within the supply chain helping them create new efficiencies in their business.
• The licensing arrangements for EPC specifically prohibit their use for tracking or identifying people.
• EPC tags are passive, they have no power of their own, transmitting data only when prompted by a signal emitted from a reader that is in close proximity.
• The technology currently has limitations:
  — EPC tags cannot be read at great distances. They have an average read range of less than five feet.
  — Radio waves cannot penetrate some materials; particularly dense materials such as frozen foods, foils and liquids.

Courtesy GS1 US

10

Relations with Special Publics

Special publics are defined as those unique or distinctive groups with which an organization needs to communicate. These groups may be minority publics, such as African Americans, Hispanics, or Asian Americans. Practitioners should be aware of the extensive national, geographic, and ethnic subsets that exist within each of these broadly defined minority groups in the United States. For instance, practitioners might mistakenly lump all Hispanics together under the Mexican umbrella. For a Hispanic special event, they could employ a mariachi band and serve Mexican dishes. However, such treatment would easily offend Spaniards, Argentines, or Dominicans, all of whose home cultures differ sharply from one another and from that of Mexico, although all share Spanish as a common language. A similar mistake would be to treat Asian Americans as a singular group or, worse, to refer to them as Orientals. These Asian groups share neither common languages nor common cultural heritages. Many of them, in fact, have been enemies for centuries.

When dealing with a minority group with national origins outside the United States, practitioners would be well advised to consult in advance the embassy or consulate of that group's homeland and certainly the group's local leaders as well.

In addition to ethnic or national minority publics, practitioners may target for special communications with such groups as women, students, educators, handicapped persons, environmentalists, school-age children, the business community, municipal officials, or community physicians. The list of potential special publics can actually be extended to include all the segments of society.

The fastest growing and most significant of these special groups in the United States is the "senior citizen" segment of the population, a segment expected to double in size by the mid-twenty-first century. Age groupings, such as 50–64 for the "active" seniors, 65–74 for the "less active," and 75-plus for the "elderly," are often used to describe subsegments of the senior citizen audience. These age groupings alone, though, are usually less useful in targeting senior audiences than are their organizational affiliations. Organizations such as AARP (formerly the American Association of Retired Persons), the National Council on the Aging (NCOA), the National Hispanic Council on Aging, the National Council of Senior Citizens, the National Senior Sports Association, and the Gray Panthers have chapter networks and affiliate organizations that can be used to reach their members. Thus, the key to reaching a senior audience lies in cosponsorship of an event or project with an organization such as AARP or the NCOA.

As with other forms of public relations, the four-part ROPE process model is a helpful format for preparing and executing programs that target special publics.

RESEARCH

Research for special programs includes investigation of the client, the reason for the program, and, most important, the distinctive audience to be targeted.

Client Research

Client research for an organization's relations with a special public should focus on the client's role and reputation with the particular audience. How credible is the organization with this public? Have there been significant complaints against it from this public in the past? What are its past and present communication practices toward this audience? What are its major strengths and weaknesses relative to this public? What opportunities exist to enhance its relations with this public?

Opportunity or Problem Research

Should a proactive public relations program be devised for this particular audience? Or has some problem arisen that must be addressed with a reactive program? Why should the organization communicate with this audience at all? Detailed answers to these questions will provide the necessary justification for the outlay of funds required for relations with a given special public.

Audience Research

Obviously, the practitioner should learn as much as possible about a special public. One way to do this is to regard such publics as differentiated communities. In community relations, practitioners address community media, community leaders, and community organizations. These same audience subsets may also be applicable in defining a special public:

Media utilized by this public

> Mass
>
> Specialized

Leaders of this public

> Public officials
>
> Professional leaders
>
> Ethnic leaders
>
> Neighborhood leaders
>
> Others

Organizations composing this public

> Civic
>
> Political
>
> Service
>
> Business
>
> Cultural
>
> Religious
>
> Age-based
>
> Recreational
>
> Other

As in community relations, practitioners should develop special contact lists for the appropriate media and for the special public's leaders and organizations. These materials are indispensable in relations with a special public. Remember, some audience segments are more actively engaged in an issue than others.

OBJECTIVES

Programs that target special publics can use both impact and output objectives; and, as in all other types of public relations, the objectives should be specific and quantitative.

Impact Objectives

Impact objectives represent the desired outcomes of informing or modifying the attitudes or behaviors of the special audience. Some examples include:

1. To increase the knowledge of the organization's minority-benefits program among members of this special public (by 50 percent before January 1)

2. To promote more favorable opinion (30 percent) toward the organization on the part of this special public (during the current year)

3. To stimulate greater participation (15 percent) in the organization's programs by this special public (during the summer months)

4. To reduce the incidence of sexually transmitted diseases among senior citizens by 20 percent.

Output Objectives

Output objectives comprise the specific efforts to enhance relations with special publics. For example:

1. To prepare and distribute materials to (30 percent of) the Hispanic community in Washington (during the coming year)

2. To schedule four meetings each year with leaders of the Chinese community in Houston

3. To develop five new projects for African American instructors' use in their classrooms (during the current school year)

PROGRAMMING

Programming for relations with special publics includes planning the theme and messages, action(s) or special event(s), uncontrolled and controlled media, and effective communication principles in the program's execution.

Theme and Messages

Both the theme and messages should reflect the desired relationship between the organization and the targeted special public. They will also be an indicator of past and present relationships that exist between the organization and this public. Cultural, ethnic, and gender values will likely affect the themes and messages used in a campaign so look for messages that will resonate with your public.

Action(s) or Special Event(s)

Actions and special events should concentrate on the major interests of the targeted audience. The most successful actions and special events address the interests, needs, and problems of the particular target group. The special events in the cases in this chapter clearly meet this criterion. For example, if the target audience is very attuned to "family and community," think in terms of family-oriented events.

Uncontrolled and Controlled Media

As mentioned earlier, representatives of both the mass and specialized media aimed at the special audience are an important segment of the audience itself. Uncontrolled media in the form of news releases, photo opportunities or photographs, feature stories, and/or interviews should be prepared in the language of the designated media; they should be directed to media outlets known to be used by this special public.

Controlled media should be prepared with all the cultural, language, ethnic, age, or other demographic specifications of the target public in mind. Obviously, the organization's Web site will play a crucial role in the program. The Web site can include a great body of information of interest to the target public. Social media can be used to engage a specific group. For example, campaigns promoting new music will usually set up a site on the MySpace.com Web site, and other campaigns may send an e-mail with a link to a blog and ask people to add their comments. As with other publics, there can be no substitute for personal interaction in the effective execution of programs.

Effective Communication

Principles of effective communication are the same for special audiences as they are for most others. Extra care should be taken, however, in the matter of source credibility, which can be enhanced by the selection of a spokesperson from the same demographic group as the targeted audience.

In addition to source credibility, two-way communication and audience participation should also be given extra emphasis in relations with special publics.

Finally, the use of opinion leaders may be highly significant in relations with special publics, especially when the public is an organized ethnic or demographic group. In sum, all aspects of programming for relations with special publics are similar to those of community relations. The special public, in fact, can often be thought of as a community with its own media, leaders, and organizations.

EVALUATION

The process of evaluating communications aimed at special audiences must take into account the program's objectives. Each one should be measured using previously discussed standards and methods.

Evaluation of special publics cases rely generally on the degree of participation by the target audiences and, in most instances, the amount of publicity generated by the program.

SUMMARY

Research for programs that target special audiences focuses on the credibility of the client with a particular special public, along with the need or justification for the program. The audience itself can be analyzed using the same categories applicable to community relations—media, leaders, and organizations. Special audiences can usually be treated as communities, or subcommunities, in their own right.

Objectives for relations with special publics may be impact or output in nature. Impact objectives express desired outcomes, such as augmenting the public's knowledge or influencing its attitudes or behaviors. Without reference to impact, output objectives consist of practitioner efforts to execute the program.

Programming for special publics often uses the significant events of the public's ethnic or cultural past. Along with this, of course, the programming must also address the problems or potential problems of the special group. Although standard controlled and uncontrolled media are used in this form of public relations, there can be no substitute for two-way communication with such audiences. More than others, they need to know that the organization cares enough about them to include a personal touch.

As with other forms of public relations, the special program's stated objectives must be evaluated appropriately. In general, the level of participation by the targeted group and the publicity generated by the program are used as benchmarks of success.

READINGS ON SPECIAL PUBLICS

Bouttilier, Robert. *Targeting Families: Marketing to and Through the New Family*. Ithaca, NY: American Marketing Tools, 1993.

Brier, Noah Rubin. "Coming of Age," American Demographics 26 (November 2004): 16–19.

Gardyn, Rebecca. "Educated Consumers," *American Demographics* 24 (November 2002): 18–19.

Cafasso, ed. "Millennials in the Workplace: Managing Expectations of PR's Next Generation," *Public Relations Strategist* 13 (fall 2007): 38–40.

Carlson, Peter. "Wild Generalization X: In Details, a Hilarious Screed on Turning 40 and Not Loving It," *Washington Post* (April 11, 2006): C02.

Chafetz, Paul K., Helen Holmes, Kim Lande, Elizabeth Childress, and Hilda R. Glazer. "Older Adults and the News Media: Utilization, Opionions, and Preferred Reference Terms," *The Gerontologist* 38 (August 1998): 481–499.

Cook, Fred. "It's a Small World After All: Multiculturalism, Authenticity, Connectedness Among Trends to Watch in Next 50 Years," *Public Relations Strategist* 13 (winter 2007): 30–33.

Daddario, Gina. *Women's Sports and Spectacle: Gendered Television Coverage and the Olympic Games*. Westport, CT: Praeger, 1998.

Edmondson, Brad. "The Minority Majority in 2001," *American Demographics* 18 (October 1996): 16ff.

Ferguson, Robert. *Representing "Race": Ideology, Identity and the Media.* London: Oxford University Press, 1998.

Ford, Rochelle L. "Research Shows Why Race and Ethnicity Matter," *Public Relations Tactics* 13 (March 2006): 6.

Gandy, Oscar H. *Communication and Race: A Structural Perspective.* London: Oxford University Press, 1998.

Gardner, Susan, and Susanna Eng. "What Students Want: Generation Y and the Changing Function of the Academic Library," *Portal: Libraries and the Academy* 15 (July 2005): 405ff.

Gothard, Ann Marie. "Black Newspapers: An Overlooked PR Opportunity," *Public Relations Tactics* 5 (October 1998): 24.

Grunig, Larissa A., Elizabeth Lance Toth, and Linda Childers Hon. *Women in Public Relations: How Gender Influences Practice.* New York: Guilford Publications, 2001.

Jackson, Ronald L. *African American Communication and Identities.* Thousand Oaks, CA: Sage Publications, 2004.

Jandt, Fred E. *Intercultural Communication.* Thousand Oaks, CA: Sage Publications, 2001.

Jones, Mathew, Debra Salmon, and Judy Orme. "Young People's Involvement in a Substance Misuse Communications Campaign," *Drugs: Education, Prevention & Policy* 11 (October 2004): 391–405.

King, Corwin P. "A Diverse Minority Framed by History: Native Americans' Modern Roles and Issues," *Public Relations Strategist* 12 (Summer 2006): 44–45.

Liu, Brooke Fisher. "Communicating with Hispanics About Crises: How Counties Produce and Provide Spanish-Language Disaster Information," *Public Relations Review* (September 2007): 330–333.

Milhouse, Virginia H., Molefi Kete Asante, and Peter O. Nwosu. Trans-cultural Realities. Thousand Oaks, CA: Sage Publications, 2001.

Mitchell, Susan. *Generation X: The Young Adult Market.* Ithaca, NY: New Strategist Publications, 1997.

Montgomery, Kathryn C. *Generation Digital: Politics, Commerce, and Childhood in the Age of the Internet.* Cambridge, MA: MIT Press, 2007.

Morgan, Carol M., and Doran J. Levy. *Segmenting the Mature Market.* New York: Probus, 1994.

Morton, Linda P. "Targeting Hispanic Americans," *Public Relations Quarterly* 47 (fall 2002): 46–48.

Neuliep, Jim. *Intercultural Communication: A Contextual Approach.* Thousand Oaks, CA: Sage Publications, 2006.

Palen, J. John. *The Suburbs.* New York: McGraw-Hill, 1994.

Peterson, Peter G. "Will America Grow Up Before It Grows Old?" *The Atlantic Monthly* 277 (May 1996): 5ff.

Pompper, Donnalyn. "'Difference' in Public Relations Research: A Case for Introducing Critical Race Theory," *Journal of Public Relations Research* 17 (2) (2005): 139–169.

Price, Vincent, Lilach Nir, and Joseph N. Cappella. "Framing Public Discussion of Gay Civil Unions," *Public Opinion Quarterly* 69 (summer 2005): 179–212.

Rabin, Steve. "How to Sell Across Cultures," American Demographics 16 (March 1994): 56ff.

Romaine, Suzanne. *Communicating Gender.* Mahwah, NJ: Erlbaum, 1998.

Samovar, Larry A., and Richard E. Porter. *Intercultural Communication.* Belmont, CA: Wadsworth, 2008.

Solloway, Sylvan. "A Growing Influential Audience: Spanish-Language Broadcast Outreach That Works," *Public Relations Tactics* 14 (June 2007): 18.

Spethmann, Betsy. "Speaking to the Sisterhood," *Promo* (October 1998): 50ff.

Stanfield, John H., II. "Multiethnic Societies and Regions," *American Behavioral Scientist* 40 (September 1996): 8ff.

Svoboda, Sandra A. "Promoting Detroit's African-American Cultural Sites," *Public Relations Tactics* 5 (April 1998): 21.

Sweeney, Katie. "The Merger of Faith and Work," *Public Relations Strategist* 13 (Spring 2007): 6–11.

Ting-Toomey, Stella. *Communicating Across Cultures.* New York: Guilford Publications, 1999.

Vahouny, Karen. "Opportunities for Improvement," *Communication World* 21 (May–June 2004): 32–38.

Wolfe, David B. "Targeting the Mature Mind," *American Demographics* 16 (March 1994): 32ff.

Yun Kim, Young. *Becoming Intercultural.* Thousand Oaks, CA: Sage Publications, 2001.

Ziegler, Dyhana, ed. *Diversity.* Mahwah, NJ: Erlbaum, 1996.

Special Publics Cases

Case 10-1

Some issues demand long-running campaigns that continually inform and educate new generations of women. For 10 years, a campaign to prevent abuse has continually found new avenues to reach teenagers. Exhibit 10-1a is a news release on a public policy issue, Exhibit 10-1b is a fact sheet on the program, and Exhibit 10-1c is a news release on a survey.

Teaching Teens Love Is Not Abuse
Liz Claiborne, Inc. with Ruder Finn, Inc.

SUMMARY

Nearly one in three women suffers from intimate partner abuse, but the level of dating abuse among teens was not widely known. In 2005, Ruder Finn (RF) advised Liz Claiborne Inc. (LCI) to focus their domestic violence campaign on teens. Liz Claiborne sponsored a national survey on teen dating abuse and created the first national curriculum to educate teenagers on this sensitive and controversial issue. The Love Is Not Abuse curriculum has impacted thousands of students and due to high-profile media placements, increased public knowledge of the problem and visibility for Liz Claiborne's long-standing commitment to the many aspects of domestic violence.

SITUATION ANALYSIS

For 10 years, Liz Claiborne's Love Is Not Abuse domestic violence campaign has reached out to different audiences with focused anti-abuse messages with minimal media visibility. In 2005, RF advised Liz Claiborne to focus on a segment of the population that has been typically ignored: teens. Upon initial investigation, it was found that there are little or no legal resources for teens who have been victims of dating violence; there are very few services and programs designed to prevent teen dating violence, and there was minimal data about the levels of dating violence among American teenagers. It was an opportunity for LCI to address a preventable problem by developing a substantive education program for American teenagers. RF suggested the first national online poll on dating abuse, and with the results, RF demonstrated the urgent need for a national program to address this sensitive and controversial issue in schools. RF and Liz Claiborne launched and piloted an unprecedented high school curriculum to educate the teen community, parents, educators, and the media.

RESEARCH

In February 2005, Liz Claiborne commissioned the first national survey on teen relationships to determine the level of and attitudes toward dating abuse among American teenagers. Teenage Research Unlimited (TRU) conducted the online survey polling 683 teens between the ages of 13 and 18 years. Liz Claiborne and RF developed the questionnaire and the results revealed an alarming prevalence of teen dating violence.

Highlights of the survey included:

- One in three teenagers reports knowing a friend or peer who has been hit, punched, kicked, slapped, choked, or physically hurt by their partner.

- Thirteen percent of teenage girls reported being physically hurt or hit in a relationship.

- Eighty percent of teens regard verbal abuse as a "serious issue" for their age group.

This was the first time research of teen dating abuse was so clearly documented. In addition to the primary research results, literature reviews and Internet research were also conducted to identify domestic violence and educational organizations and dating violence prevention programs geared toward teens. Many organizations were subsequently contacted for additional information and materials.

PLANNING

Based on an analysis of the survey results and the secondary research on available programs and data, RF worked with LCI on a plan to collaborate with educational and domestic violence organizations on the development of a teen dating violence curriculum and to mobilize key thought leaders around the issue by forming an advisory board. LCI aimed to develop, pilot, and distribute the first national high school curriculum on teen dating violence and leverage the media to drive more attention to the issue.

Objectives

- To increase awareness of the prevalence of teen dating violence and abuse among teens, and a larger national audience

- To provide information to help prevent future instances of dating violence and abuse in the teen community

- To further demonstrate Liz Claiborne's commitment to the many serious aspects of domestic violence

The Love Is Not Abuse: Teen Dating Violence Prevention curriculum was designed for ninth and tenth grade high school students. The objective for the three-day lesson plan curriculum was to educate teenagers on how to recognize, deal with, and ultimately prevent instances of physical and verbal abuse in relationships. RF worked with LCI to plan media events and opportunities around teaching teens Love Is Not Abuse.

EXECUTION

Liz Claiborne sought to create a curriculum that would be appealing and accessible to teens and educators. RF helped them identify a new approach using a unique blend of lessons designed for health education and/or English language arts classes, drawing on brief engaging literary texts (poetry, short stories) to build awareness of how to make healthy choices in relationships. Coupled with writing assignments and group discussions, the Love Is Not Abuse curriculum would present students with valuable information while allowing them to hone their comprehension and writing skills.

This exciting, new design concept led RF to research organizations with a track record in curriculum development on health and domestic violence organizations with teen expertise to provide content and ongoing resources. A partnership was established with the Education Development Center's Health and Human Development program and Break the Cycle, the only national domestic violence organization for young people, which provided a hotline for teens to turn to if they need help as part of the program. Academics, authors, domestic violence experts, community leaders, and teen survivors of dating violence were invited to join the advisory board.

With its partners and in consultation with their 23 advisory board members, LCI developed the objectives, content, and design of the curriculum, posters, and wallets cards.

In June, the survey results and curriculum were announced at a press conference at the National Press Club in Washington, D.C. RF then organized Liz Claiborne's second "It's Time To Talk Day" on October 11 and arranged with teachers from 20 high schools around the country to launch the curriculum to coincide with the event. As a result, more than 2,000 students learned about teen dating abuse in their classrooms during the month of October. In addition, RF arranged a *Marie Claire* October article about domestic violence and organized the first-ever all-day Talk Radio Row on teen dating abuse and domestic violence for "It's Time To Talk Day." This consisted of back-to-back interviews with 17 talk radio show hosts and 40 prominent guests. RF also coordinated the ringing of the NYSE closing bell with corporate leaders and students from pilot schools in New York.

EVALUATION

Using the new curriculum and survey as a platform, Liz Claiborne's Love Is Not Abuse messages on teen dating and domestic violence reached an estimated 50 million Americans. Through the June press conference, RF conducted outreach to national broadcast outlets, print media outlets targeting education and Washington, D.C., correspondents, and regional outlets where the curriculum was to be piloted. As a result, widespread publicity was generated, including an exclusive Today show segment with additional broadcast coverage on CNN's NewsNight with Aaron Brown and American Morning shows, MSNBC's Live with Lester Holt, BET, Univision, and AP. Reuters and Knight-Ridder/Tribune also ran stories nationwide.

Overall, the Love Is Not Abuse curriculum and campaign was covered by the major wire services and major dailies such as *The Washington Times, Boston Herald, The San Diego Union-Tribune, The Dallas Morning News*, which totaled more than 90 print and online articles and more than 150 television stories.

The Love Is Not Abuse curriculum received endorsements from media partners like *Marie Claire* magazine and RF pioneered a partnership with Talk Radio for "It's Time To Talk Day," which led to the first talk radio row event dedicated to domestic violence.

The compelling nature of the research findings supported Liz Claiborne's announcement of the new curriculum in response to this prevalent problem and sparked the interest of educators, domestic violence organizations, and the media. Due to the initial publicity and heightened awareness of the teen dating violence, LCI was able to double the number of participating schools despite initial hesitation from school officials. With the successful completion of the pilot program and positive feedback from teachers, the Love Is Not Abuse curriculum is being distributed free of charge to high schools nationwide with the potential of curbing future instances of dating violence among American teens.

The 2005 Love Is Not Abuse program has also increased the distribution of the company's domestic violence handbook series by 33 percent and has resulted in more high-profile placements and greater visibility for Liz Claiborne in one year than the previous 10 years of their domestic violence campaign.

EXHIBIT 10-1a News Release On National Campaign

LIZ claiborne inc

PRESS CONTACT:
Natalia Garzon
Tel: (212) 583-2707
Cell: 917-257-9793
garzonn@ruderfinn.com

Parents of Murdered Dating Violence Victim and Champions of the Unprecedented Lindsay Ann Burke Act in Rhode Island Call for all Attorneys General to Mandate Teen Dating Abuse Curricula in Schools Across the Country

National campaign organized by Liz Claiborne Inc. will bring together Jaslene Gonzalez, America's Next Top Model winner, with celebrities and teen dating abuse survivors to enlist thousands of teens to endorse new digital Teen Dating Bill of Rights

New York, NY—September 25, 2007—Ann and Chris Burke, educators and parents of Lindsay Ann Burke who was murdered by her abusive ex-boyfriend, are speaking out publicly to call on Attorneys General across the country to mandate education on teen dating abuse in every high school in their states. Today at "It's Time To Talk Day," a day focused on saving lives by drawing attention to the importance of talking about intimate partner abuse.

Leading domestic violence organizations, including loveisrespect.org, the National Teen Dating Abuse Helpline, the National Domestic Violence Hotline and Safe Horizon, celebrities such as Jaslene Gonzalez and Camille Winbush, several teen survivors of dating abuse, New York City students and teachers will join the Burkes at Liz Claiborne Inc. to highlight the critical need for curricula on teen dating abuse and launch the first digital *Teen Dating Bill of Rights*, an online campaign to end teen dating abuse.

Courtesy Liz Claiborne

E X H I B I T 10-1a   (Continued)

"How many more parents have to lose their children at the hands of an abusive partner? How many more teens have to suffer in an abusive relationship, fearing for their lives and afraid to tell anyone?" asks Ann Burke. "Parents and teens know little about the dynamics of teen dating violence because of the shame and stigma associated with it. We must change that."

After Lindsay's murder in September of 2005, the Burkes worked closely with Rhode Island Attorney General Patrick C. Lynch to create the Lindsay Ann Burke Act, the first legislation to mandate schools teach about teen dating abuse every year from 7th to 12th grade. The legislation also requires teacher training on the issue using curricula, such as *Love is Not Abuse*, a teen dating violence prevention curriculum which was developed by the Education Development Center and sponsored by Liz Claiborne Inc. It is already in more than 1,000 schools across the country and distributed without charge.

"It is clear that all sectors of society must be involved in the campaign to reduce teen dating abuse and break the cycle of intimate partner violence," says Jane Randel, Vice President, Corporate Communications, Liz Claiborne Inc. "This is not just a struggle for advocacy organizations. If we are to have an impact, we need a multi-faceted approach with involvement from the private sector, government, the legal community, educators, non-profit organizations, the media, parents and teens themselves."

"Providing our teenagers with information that enables them to recognize the warning signs of unacceptable behavior – whether insidious or overt, in themselves or others – is a vital first step toward curbing dating violence. Letting teenagers know a support system exists that won't tolerate this type of dangerous abuse is another," said Rhode Island Attorney General Lynch. "In Rhode Island, with the Lindsay Ann Burke Law, we have a new mechanism in place to enhance protections for the segment of our population most vulnerable and at-risk for dating violence. 'It's Time to Talk Day' provides an important forum for putting, and keeping, dating violence in the forefront of our national crime-prevention agenda, and I am proud to be affiliated with it."

Reinforcing the message that teens must take action to stop abuse, courageous teen survivors, 19-year-old Cheryl from California and 18-year-old Kristie from Missouri, are telling their stories and working with Liz Claiborne Inc. to expand the use of the *Love Is Not Abuse* curriculum in their schools. Each young woman has also pledged to sign the new digital *Teen Dating Bill of Rights*.

The digital *Teen Dating Bill of Rights* is being launched today on www.loveisrespect.org, a national teen dating abuse interactive website and helpline created specifically for teens. It is operated by the National Domestic Violence Hotline and was founded by a gift from Liz Claiborne Inc. Since the February 2007 launch of loveisrespect.org, the Helpline has engaged in more than 6,118 telephone and chat contacts.

"We are asking everyone to take action," says, Sheryl Cates, CEO of the National Domestic Violence Hotline. "We hope teens will heed our call to help end teen dating abuse and violence by going to loveisrespect.org and signing the digital dating bill of rights."

Loveisrespect.org is working closely with MySpace to launch the digital *Teen Dating Bill of Rights* with an online video campaign where teens can learn about dating abuse, add their own video statement on how they want to be treated in a dating relationship and encourage their friends to make the pledge.

About "It's Time to Talk Day"

E X H I B I T 10-1a (Continued)

In 2004, Liz Claiborne Inc. designated October 14, 2004 as the first annual "It's Time to Talk Day," a day dedicated to encouraging people to talk about the issue of domestic violence. Since that day, media personalities, government officials, domestic violence advocates, businesses and the public-at-large began to speak openly about domestic violence. Liz Claiborne Inc. has organized "It's Time to Talk Day" every fall since 2004 with key partners, such as *Redbook* and *Seventeen* magazine, to draw national attention to the importance of talking about intimate partner abuse.

Loveisrespect.org, the National Teen Dating Abuse Helpline is a resource that can be accessed by Internet or phone. The Helpline and loveisrespect.org offer real-time one-on-one support from trained advocates. Loveisrespect.org provides resources for teens, parents, friends and family, advocates, government officials, law enforcement officials and the general public. All communication is confidential and anonymous.

Since 1991 Liz Claiborne Inc has been working to end domestic violence. Through its *Love Is Not Abuse* program, the company provides information and tools that men, women, teens and corporate executives can use to learn more about the issue and find out how they can help end this epidemic. http://www.loveisnotabuse.com.

E X H I B I T 10-1b   Fact Sheet

LIZ claiborne inc

LOVE IS NOT ABUSE

Stopping the Violence Before it Happens
1 out of 3 women around the world has been beaten, coerced into sex or otherwise abused during her lifetime.[1] But what is not as widely known is the prevalence of dating abuse among teens—1 in 5 teens who have been in a relationship report being hit, slapped or pushed by a partner.[2]

Over the past 17 years, Liz Claiborne Inc. has been leading efforts to end domestic violence as one of the first major corporations in the U.S. to take a stand on this issue. As pervasive as the issue is, abuse remains one of the most underserved and under funded causes in this country. To date Liz Claiborne Inc. has invested over $8 million in the effort, including the funding of a new National Teen Dating Abuse Helpline. Today, Liz Claiborne Inc.'s *Love Is Not Abuse* initiatives strive to address partner abuse at its root cause and therefore the company has begun a sustained effort to focus on teen dating abuse and violence. With a teen dating abuse prevention curriculum, hand books and innovative research to help teens, teachers, parents, and domestic violence organizations, Liz Claiborne Inc. provides free resources to all members of society— alerting all demographics to the domestic violence epidemic and educating them on what they can do, individually and collectively to curtail abuse.

Generating Awareness on National Domestic Violence Epidemic
Below are some of Liz Claiborne Inc.'s *Love Is Not Abuse* initiatives to raise awareness of the national domestic violence epidemic:

Loveisrespect.org, the National Teen Dating Abuse Helpline:
Loveisrespect.org, the National Teen Dating Abuse Helpline is a national resource for teens that includes a 24-hour telephone helpline (1-866-331-9474 or TTY 1-866-331-8453) and a website (www.loveisrespect.org). The Helpline is designed to help teens prevent and protect themselves from abusive relationships by providing expert advice, peer counseling, information and other support services. The Helpline is operated by the National Domestic Violence Hotline and was established through a gift from Liz Claiborne Inc.

Teen Dating Violence Prevention Curriculum:
Liz Claiborne Inc. partnered with the Education Development Center (EDC) and Break the Cycle to create a teen dating violence prevention curriculum. The curriculum was launched in April 2006 and has been distributed to approximately 3,500 schools and organizations across all 50 states. It includes a teacher's manual with three lesson plans, activities, handouts, wallet cards and a new supplementary video, "Real Teens, Real Stories." Liz Claiborne Inc. is also working with a group of teen survivors and

EXHIBIT 10-1b (Continued)

advocates to educate the public about teen dating abuse as well as to promote the curriculum and other resources to help teens, parents and teachers deal with this issue. The Love Is Not Abuse *curriculum is provided free-of-charge and can be ordered from their website at www.loveisnotabuse.com.*

It's Time to Talk Day:

"It's Time to Talk Day" is dedicated to encouraging people to take one day and talk about the issue of domestic violence. Each year, around the country media personalities, government officials, domestic violence advocates, businesses and the public-at-large come together on this day to speak openly about domestic violence. Since 2004, Liz Claiborne Inc. has organized "It's Time to Talk Day" each fall to draw national attention to the importance of talking about intimate partner abuse. They designed the first-ever Talk Radio Row focusing on domestic violence that featured multiple talk radio hosts doing back-to-back interviews with guests on various domestic violence issues throughout the entire day. Partners have included *Marie Claire, Redbook,* VerizonWireless, *Talkers Magazine* and Talk Radio News. Information on "It's Time to Talk Days" past and present can be found at www.loveisnotabuse.com/itstimetotalk.

Educational Handbooks:

Liz Claiborne Inc. has produced a series of five award-winning educational handbooks, each with valuable information and resources on domestic violence. The content-rich handbooks were authored by experts on the issue of domestic violence and provide direction on opening dialogues about this issue and developing and maintaining healthy relationships. Close to 800,000 handbooks have been distributed since the first one was published in 1998. They can be ordered by calling **1-800-449-STOP (7867)**, or can be downloaded from the company's web site at www.loveisnotabuse.com. The series includes:

- A Parent's Handbook: How to Talk to Your Children About Developing Healthy Relationships (1998)
- A Woman's Handbook: A Practical Guide to Discussing Relationship Abuse (1999)
- What You Need to Know About Dating Violence: A Teen's Handbook (2000)
- A Parent's Guide to Teen Dating Violence: 10 Questions to Start the Conversation (2001)
- Tough Talk: What Boys Need to Know About Relationship Abuse (2004)

Public Service Announcements:

Liz Claiborne Inc. created several public service announcements with celebrities such as Susan Sarandon and Ashley Judd talking about the issue of domestic violence. The PSAs speak directly to the fact that domestic violence can happen to anyone—mothers, sisters, friends—and that anyone can help if they have the resources to do so. In reaching out to men and boys, Liz Claiborne Inc. also created PSAs featuring college football athletes and male recording artists encouraging "inter-gender collaboration," men and women working together to end relationship violence.

E X H I B I T 10-1b   (Continued)

Fundraising Initiatives:
Liz Claiborne Inc.'s fundraising efforts for the *Love Is Not Abuse* campaign have included sales from a series of limited-edition apparel and accessories items. In the recent past, the company has created t-shirts, bags, mugs, watches and jewelry to raise money for both national and local domestic violence partners. Accessories have included a chocolate brown scarf and gloves emblazoned with hearts to signify that love is about respect and not abuse. All profits from sales are donated to the National Domestic Violence Hotline and the Family Violence Prevention Fund.

Network of Partners
Liz Claiborne Inc. partners with leading organizations to strengthen awareness of domestic violence. These partnerships have included:

American School Counselor Association (ASCA):
ASCA supports school counselors' efforts to help students focus on academic, personal/social and career development so they achieve success in school and are prepared to lead fulfilling lives as responsible members of society. ASCA has been working in collaboration with Liz Claiborne Inc. to inform their members about the *Love Is Not Abuse* curriculum and Loveisrespect.org, The National Teen Dating Abuse Helpline. ASCA also encourages their school counselors to teach the curriculum during National Teen Dating Violence Awareness and Prevention Week, which coincides with National School Counselors Week each February. www.schoolcounselors.org

Corporate Alliance to End Partner Violence (CAEPV):
As a member of CAEPV, Liz Claiborne Inc. helped create and publicize a new Web site, www.girlsallowed.org, designed to help girls ages 11-14 identify and avoid unhealthy relationships that could lead to violence (2002). From 2007-2007, Jane Randel, Vice President of Corporate Communications for Liz Claiborne Inc., served as the CAEPV Board President.

Family, Career and Community Leaders of America (FCCLA):
The Ultimate Leadership Experience. FCCLA is a dynamic and effective national student organization that helps young men and women become leaders and address important personal, family, work, and societal issues through Family and Consumer Sciences Education. FCCLA partnered with Liz Claiborne Inc. in April 2006 for the launch of the *Love Is Not Abuse* curriculum to distribute the resource and address teen dating violence in over 1,000 schools in 48 states. www.fcclainc.org

Family Violence Prevention Fund (FVPF):
The FVPF, a San Francisco-based, national non-profit organization focusing on domestic violence prevention, education and public policy reform has been a national philanthropic partner of Liz Claiborne Inc. since 1991. Their expertise and counsel has been invaluable to the company's campaign, and sales of Liz Claiborne Inc.'s fundraising items have raised more than $100,000 for the FVPF. As part of their ongoing collaboration, Liz Claiborne Inc. joined the FVPF in 2004 to introduce the Founding Fathers Workplace Campaign, which aimed to challenge and recruit corporate America to lead by example and demonstrate to employees, customers and business partners that they care about ending violence against women and children.

E X H I B I T 10-1b   (Continued)

National Domestic Violence Hotline (NDVH):
The NDVH has been an ardent supporter of the *Love Is Not Abuse* program. Their expertise on the issue of domestic violence and their respect within the domestic violence movement has been invaluable to the campaign on a local and national level. The new National Teen Dating Abuse Helpline is being operated by NDVH, which is also an ongoing recipient of funds raised through the sale of fundraising items. Additionally, the National Domestic Violence Hotline number is featured on the hangtags of all Liz Claiborne brand apparel and accessories sold in the United States.

Safe Horizon:
The nation's leading nonprofit victim assistance, advocacy, and violence prevention organization, Safe Horizon has been a vital partner for Liz Claiborne Inc.'s *Love Is Not Abuse* campaign and a dedicated supporter of the 2004 initiative to recruit corporate America to join the Founding Father's Workplace Campaign. The company also partners with this organization to present the Liz Claiborne Champion Award at the annual Safe Horizon Champion Awards Luncheon, honoring either victims of abuse who have taken steps to regain their lives and/or those who have helped victims of abuse.

1. Silverman, Jay G., Raj, Anita, and Clements, Karen. "Dating Violence Against Adolescent Girls and Associated Substance Use, Unhealthy Weight Control, Sexual Risk Behavior, Pregnancy, and Suicidality." *Pediatrics*, August 2004.

2. Teenage Research Unlimited, *Teen Relationship Survey* March 2006. Liz Claiborne Inc.

E X H I B I T 10-1c News Release on Survey

LIZ claiborne inc

PRESS CONTACT:
Millicent Fortunoff
Tel: (212) 593-6346
Cell: (917) 306-3841
fortunoffm@ruderfinn.com

Surprising New Research Indicates That Significant Numbers of Children as Young as 11 Are Engaging in Sexual Activity and That Dating Violence and Abuse Are Part of Their Relationships

Findings are part of new national poll that identifies an unexpected prevalence of dating abuse behaviors among the youngest adolescents and uncovers evidence that sexual activity before age 14 is linked to high levels of dating abuse and violence among older teens

Attorney General Patrick C. Lynch, incoming President of the National Association of Attorneys General, urges attorneys general nationwide to join effort to establish curricula on teen dating abuse in schools

Washington, D.C.–February 14, 2008–A new survey released today reports that a surprising number of young adolescents are experiencing significant levels of dating violence and abuse. One in five children between the ages of 11 and 14 (20%) say their friends are victims of dating violence and nearly half of all tweens in relationships say they know friends who are verbally abused. Alarmingly, 40% of the youngest tweens, those between the ages of 11 and 12, report that their friends are victims of verbal abuse in relationships and nearly 1 in 10 (9%) say their friends have had sex.

The survey on Tween and Teen dating relationships conducted by Teenage Research Unlimited (TRU) and commissioned by Liz Claiborne Inc. and the National Teen Dating Abuse Helpline explores how relationships among young adolescents are fueling high levels of dating violence and abuse. The data reveals that early sexual experiences can be a precursor to dating violence and abuse among older teens. For example, among American teens who had sex by age 14, one out of three teens (34%) say they have been physically abused (hit, kicked or choked) by an angry partner compared to 20% of other teens. 69% of teens who had sex before 14 said they had experienced all aspects of dating abuse including verbal, emotional, physical and mental abuse.

Courtesy Liz Claiborne

E X H I B I T 10-1c   (Continued)

"We know that education for tweens and teens helps and is critically important if we are going to break the cycle of abuse and strengthen healthy relationships," says Sheryl Cates, Chief Executive Officer of the National Domestic Violence Hotline, which operates loveisrespect.org, the National Teen Dating Abuse Helpline. "This new data provides important insight into when we need to begin to intervene and how to do it. We need to educate parents, teachers and tweens about a connection between early sexual experimentation and increased levels of teen dating violence and abuse."

In response to the concerns about teen dating violence and abuse across the United States, the incoming president of the National Association of Attorneys General (NAAG), Rhode Island Attorney General Patrick C. Lynch, said that he will introduce a resolution at NAAG's June meeting that will call for the inclusion of curricula on teen dating violence in schools in every state.

The necessity and importance of this education campaign is clear. New survey results show that:

Dating relationships begin much earlier than expected
- Nearly three in four tweens (**72%**) say boyfriend/girlfriend relationships usually begin at age 14 or younger.
- More than one in three 11–12 year olds (**37%**) say they have been in a boyfriend/girlfriend relationship.

    Surprising levels of abusive behavior reported in tween (11-14) dating relationships.

- **62%** of tweens who have been in a relationship say they know friends who have been verbally abused (called stupid, worthless, ugly, etc) by a boyfriend/girlfriend
- Two in five (**41%**) tweens who have been in a relationship know friends who have been called names, put down, or insulted via cellphone, IM, social networking sites (such as MySpace and Facebook), etc.
- One in five 13-14 year olds in relationships (**20%**) say they know friends and peers who have been struck in anger (kicked, hit, slapped, or punched) by a boyfriend or girlfriend
- Only half of all tweens (**51%**) claim to know the warning signs of a bad/hurtful relationship

Significant numbers of teens (15-18) are experiencing emotional and mental abuse and violence in their dating relationships; this is even more prevalent among teens that have had sex by the age of 14.

- Nearly half of teen girls who have been in a relationship (**48%**) say they have been victims of verbal, physical, or sexual abuse by their boyfriends.
- More than one in three teens report that their partners wanted to know where they were (**36%**) and who they were with (**37%**) all the time.
- Among teens who had sex by age 14, it's much higher (58% and 59%, respectively).
- **29%** of teens say their boyfriends/girlfriends call them names and put them down, compared to **58%** of teens who had sex by age 14.
- **22%** of teens say they were pressured to do things they did not want to do, compared to **45%** of teens who had sex by age 14.
- **24%** of teens in a relationship said their boyfriends/girlfriends called them stupid, worthless, and ugly compared to **45%** of teens who had sex by age 14.

E X H I B I T 10-1c   (Continued)

"Currently in my practice I am seeing dozens of young girls who had early sexual experiences and I witnessed directly how it makes these young girls more vulnerable and how it can lead to situations where they will be abused," says Jill Murray, leading psychologist and author of *But He Never Hit Me The Devastating Cost of Non-Physical Abuse to Girls and Women.* "Education for parents, teens, tweens and teachers is an answer to prevent this situation."

In addition, the survey found that parents think they know what is going on, but many don't have any idea. Results show that:

- More than three times as many tweens (**20%**) as parents (**6%**) admit that parents know little or nothing about the tweens' dating relationships.

    - Twice as many tweens report having "hooked up" with a partner (**17%**) as parents reported of their own 11-14 year old child (**8%**).

"Over the past four years Liz Claiborne Inc. has conducted research into the many aspects of teen dating abuse. What makes this current study so disturbing is the clear and unexpected finding that dating abuse and violence begins at such a young age," says Jane Randel, Vice President, Corporate Communications, Liz Claiborne Inc. "We applaud the willingness of Attorney General Lynch to push for the introduction of education about dating abuse in schools across the country. This research shows just how urgently this information is needed."

National Association of Attorneys General Teen Dating Violence and Abuse Campaign

To reduce and prevent teen dating violence and abuse, the incoming president of the National Association of Attorneys General, Rhode Island Attorney General Patrick C. Lynch, will introduce a resolution at NAAG's June meeting in Providence, R.I. to ask that all Attorneys General work to ensure that schools in their states use a dating violence and abuse curriculum. The education campaign is inspired by the Lindsay Ann Burke Act, a law proposed by Attorney General Lynch that became effective in Rhode Island in July 2007. The Lindsay Ann Burke Act, named in the honor of Lindsay Ann Burke, who was murdered after a 2-year struggle in an abusive relationship, requires all school districts in Rhode Island to teach about the signs of dating violence and abuse every year from grades 7-12. Attorney General Lynch and Lindsay's parents, Ann and Christopher Burke, along with Liz Claiborne Inc., made a presentation on this initiative at the National Association of Attorneys General's December 2007 meeting in Park City, Utah.

"We are committed to addressing this issue through education. Abuse and violence in intimate partner relationships not only cause great individual pain, but this destructive behavior breaks down families, communities and our larger society," says Attorney General Lynch. "A curriculum such as Liz Claiborne Inc.'s *Love Is Not Abuse* is an effective way to begin the process of education, prevent abuse and help to save lives."

Liz Claiborne Inc.'s *Love Is Not Abuse* curriculum aims to raise awareness about the problem of dating abuse, recommends resources that provide assistance, such as loveisrespect.org, the National Teen Dating Abuse Helpline, and ultimately, help prevent dating abuse from occurring in the future. The curriculum was piloted around the country in October 2005 and was officially launched in April 2006. As of February 2008, this free curriculum has been distributed to approximately 3,500 schools and organizations across all 50 states.

###

E X H I B I T 10-1c   (Continued)

Survey Methodology
Teenage Research Unlimited (TRU) was commissioned to conduct quantitative research among tweens (ages 11-14), parents of tweens, and teens (ages 15-18) who have been in a relationship about young dating relationships and the presence/absence of sexual activity and abusive behaviors. TRU independently sampled the three groups and fielded a customized 15-minute survey online to each group from January 2-18, 2008. A total of 2,192 interviews (1,043 tweens, 523 parents, and 626 teens) were completed and processed for analysis. The resulting margin of error (at the 95% confidence level) is ±3.0 percentage points for tweens in total, ±3.9 points for parents, and ±4.1 points for teens.

Liz Claiborne Inc.
Since 1991 Liz Claiborne Inc. has been working to end domestic violence. Through its Love Is Not Abuse Program, the company provides information and tools that men, women, children, teens and corporate executives can use to learn more about the issue and find out how they can help end this epidemic. www.loveisnotabuse.com.

National Domestic Violence Hotline
The National Teen Dating Abuse Helpline is a resource that can be accessed by Internet or phone. The Helpline and loveisrespect.org offer real-time one-on-one support from trained advocates. The National Domestic Violence Hotline operates loveisrespect.org, the National Teen Dating Abuse Helpline, from their call center in Austin, Texas. Loveisrespect.org provides resources for teens, parents, friends and family, advocates, government officials, law enforcement officials and the general public. All communication is confidential and anonymous. In the first year of existence, Loveisrespect.org has received 5,455 calls and 3,026 chats with the most common participant identifying themselves as a "victim/survivor." The Helpline is operated by the National Domestic Violence Hotline and was established through a gift from Liz Claiborne Inc.

Case 10-2

What started as a problem in 2005 became a national epidemic by 2008 with the communication campaign taking on even more importance. Reaching those homeowners that faced the greatest challenges in keeping their homes became the thrust of the campaign. Exhibit 10-2a is newspaper advertisement and Exhibit 10-2b is a campaign overview from a program partner.

Bringing Homeowners Back From the Brink

Homeownership Preservation Foundation with Exponent PR

OVERVIEW

Home foreclosures often happen to homeowners who have best of intentions. Life throws a curveball, and they lean too much on credit to buy groceries, gas, and other consumable goods. Soon they find their only asset is a home they don't own. They fall behind on one mortgage payment, convinced they'll get caught up next month, but too proud to ask for help. Then it happens again.

As troubling as this situation seems, the majority of U.S. homeowners teeter one small step away: almost 60 percent live paycheck to paycheck, meaning the next "curveball"—whether a layoff or debilitating injury—could easily result in an unpaid mortgage. Left unchecked, these factors quickly compound, increasing the likelihood a family will be forced out of their home.

In 2005 alone, 847,000 homeowners were stripped of their homes, capping a 50 percent increase in home foreclosures over the past six years. To help combat this emerging crisis, the Homeownership Preservation Foundation developed a toll-free call center (88S-995-HOPE) staffed with counselors ready to help troubled homeowners avoid foreclosure.

Unfortunately, the call center was vastly underutilized; most phones sat silent and those calls that did come in usually came from homeowners too far down the foreclosure road to be helped. All told, the Foundation received 4,800 calls during its first year—reaching only 8 percent of capacity.

The call center provided valuable resources for struggling homeowners, but the Foundation had to constantly fight the pervasive mind-set that there's no way to get above water after missing mortgage payments. Even if they could be convinced the situation could be remedied, Foundation research showed that getting homeowners to come forward was near impossible.

With an emphasis on providing help early and often, the Foundation challenged Exponent Public Relations to raise the flag for homeowners before the critical "point of no return" and flood the call center phones with inquiries.

RESEARCH

The Foundation's primary and secondary research concluded that most homeowners wait until it is too late to save their homes—ignoring or avoiding the problem. All too often, homeowners perceived lenders as adversaries rather than partners in homeownership. A commissioned Harris poll survey of 2,180 homeowner respondents found:

- Fifty percent of homeowners would not call their lender if they were unable to pay their mortgage—subscribing to the myth that lenders would rather take back a house than keep a homeowner in it.

- Nearly 70 percent of homeowner respondents said foreclosure would be a very traumatic experience.

- Respondents would contact a third-party nonprofit for help on three conditions:
    - If it were recommended by a trusted source
    - If services were confidential and free
    - If services were certified by government agencies

Other Research

- Interviews with the Foundation's counselors found that struggling homeowners were rarely lazy or overspenders—they were usually hardworking individuals who had fallen on hard times from a job loss or illness.

- The problems of home foreclosure ripple beyond homeowners and their families: home values drop dramatically near foreclosed homes, and cities lose up to $33,000 per foreclosed home (Apgar-Duda Study, May 2005).

- A single foreclosure can cost its lender up to $58,000 (TowerGroup).

PLANNING

Objectives

- To increase call center usage tenfold; drive 50,000 homeowners to contact 888-995-HOPE or 995HOPE.org in one year.

- To increase awareness of the Foundation's foreclosure prevention counseling.

Strategies

- To create broad-based awareness through a national public service announcement (PSA) campaign.

- To take a grassroots approach to raising awareness with hard-to-reach audiences in major markets with high rates of foreclosure.

- To leverage campaign activities and success with like-minded nonprofits, the mortgage industry, and government organizations.

Target Audiences

- Primary: Overwhelmed homeowners, often dealing with one or more of the big Ds—Death, Divorce, Disability, or Debt. Their mortgage is the last bill they'll skip, but they become more desperate by the day. Target skews female, with a mid-to-lower income, focus in the 20 markets with the highest incidences of foreclosure.

- Secondary: Mortgage lenders and servicers, nonprofit partners, government regulators.

- Gatekeepers: TV and radio station public service directors.

Target Media

- Print and broadcast media in top 20 foreclosure markets.

- National print media.

EXECUTION

The Foundation positioned its hotline as a frontline resource for homeowners in need, educating its audience that many foreclosures can be prevented. Weaving together innovative public service messages with national media relations, the year-long effort broke down the perception that lenders would rather foreclose on a house than keep a homeowner in it.

Strategy 1

Create broad-based awareness through a national PSA campaign. The sooner an at-risk homeowner acknowledges financial difficulties and asks for help, the more options are available to preserve homeownership. Communications were designed to move the homeowner to contact the Foundation sooner rather than later, using the key message: "Debt is more than annoying; it could cost you your home."

- **Broadcast PSA creative:** Television and radio spots personified debt as an annoyance or frustration that will not go away. A key strategy for putting homeowners at ease, humor served to eliminate any confusion between the PSAs and predatory lender commercials, which focus on scare tactics.

- **Broadcast PSA distribution:** PSA distribution included two 15-second and two 30-second TV PSAs to 600 TV stations and four radio PSAs to 1,500 radio stations throughout the United States in January 2006. The TV PSA aired nationally on ESPN during the GMAC Bowl and aired regularly on CNBC. Using humor was critical to making the PSAs standout when viewed by public service directors and station managers—the gatekeepers of PSA placements.

MEDIA RELATIONS

- **Media kits:** Online and hard copy media kits detailed the home foreclosure crisis, introduced the PSAs and featured tips to avoid foreclosure.

- **Media tours:** Media tour featuring former Minneapolis Mayor Sharon Sayles Belton, a Foundation board member, aired on morning news shows in 15 key foreclosure markets. Radio media tour resulted in interviews by 20 radio stations throughout the United States.

- **Matte release:** Distributed two news features, "How to Avoid Foreclosure" and "What to Do if You Have an Adjustable-Rate Mortgage" to local newspapers throughout the United States.

Strategy 2

Take a grassroots approach to raising awareness with hard-to-reach audiences in major markets with high rates of foreclosure. Chicago, Atlanta, Dallas, and Detroit were among the key markets.

Leveraging the Government Megaphone, the governor of Delaware and the mayors of Dallas and Detroit endorsed and promoted the 888-995-HOPE hotline during news conferences, generating publicity to reach homeowners in these crucial markets. The cities of Baltimore, Minneapolis, and Chicago established partnerships with the Foundation to provide counseling through "311" city hotline numbers.

- **Channeling the Message:** In Ohio, the worst state for foreclosure, the Foundation partnered with NeighborWorks, a community revitalization organization, and 15 mortgage lenders to distribute educational materials and spread the word about the Foundation's call center.

- **Bilingual Materials:** Bilingual marketing and media materials and brochures were developed to promote the 888-995-HOPE hotline.

- **Guerrilla Postings:** Using the do-it-yourself feel of "lost pet" posters, Lost Home flyers were placed in convenience stores, hair salons, churches, and on telephone poles. Milk jugs stickers brought the home preservation message to grocery stores and eventually to the dinner table.

Strategy 3

Leverage campaign activities and success with like-minded nonprofits, mortgage industry and government regulators.

- **Nonprofits:** Partnerships with trusted nonprofits such as NeighborWorks America, National Urban League, and military veterans nonprofit USA Cares, promoted the Foundation as a featured resource for financially troubled homeowners.

- **Mortgage Industry:** Press releases, e-newsletters, and an annual report served as the Foundation's ongoing communications tools to reach major mortgage lenders, whose customers the Foundation was counseling.

- **Government Regulators:** The Foundation's executive director was invited to speak at the U.S. Conference of Mayors and the League of Cities Conference, generating awareness and building a sense of urgency to government officials for discussing the home foreclosure crisis.

EVALUATION

Through increased awareness surrounding the call center and its counselors, the Foundation provided thousands of homeowners with the necessary tools to avoid foreclosure.

Objective 1: Increase call center usage tenfold; drive 50,000 homeowners to contact 888-995-HOPE or 995HOPE.org in one year.

- In the first year of the campaign, the Foundation received 28,482 phone calls and 36,788 Web site hits, surpassing the aggressive goal of a tenfold increase. In fact, the 65,300 total contacts represented a 1,360 percent increase from the 4,800 calls and Web hits the previous year.

Objective 2: Increase awareness of the Foundation's foreclosure prevention counseling.

- The TV PSAs have aired 7,000 times on 264 stations, with an audience reach of 184 million. The radio PSAs have aired 42,000 times on stations nationwide with an audience reach of 59 million. Combined, the PSAs aired in 19 of the 20 top foreclosure cities and the ad equivalency totaled $4.1 million.

Campaign efforts aided awareness of HPF rise from zero to one percent just nine months into the year-long campaign among target homeowners (Harris Interactive survey, 2006).

Media Coverage Highlights

The campaign produced 877 editorial placements that generated an audience reach of 184 million that earned media impressions, with placements in *US News & World Report*, *USA Today*, *New York Daily News*, *Newsweek*, *New York Times*, and *The Wall Street Journal*. Coverage reached 19 out of the 20 top foreclosure cities. More than 90 percent of the editorial coverage included the 888-995-HOPE hotline at least once.

E X H I B I T 10-2a Newspaper Advertisement—Doll House

Foreclosure affects more than just you.
It affects your whole family.

A million families will lose their homes this year.
Call today for real help and guidance.
Because nothing is worse than doing nothing.

1-888-995-HOPE

9/07

Courtesy Homeownership Preservation Foundation

E X H I B I T 10-2b   Campaign Overview

---

http://www.foreclosurehelpandhope.org/campaign_overview.html

Preventing Foreclosure: NeighborWorks® America's PSA Campaign

The Issue

Foreclosure is a very serious problem in our country. We estimate that a staggering one million families will face foreclosure this year. Not only does a foreclosure have disastrous financial impact on a family, but it also has harsh consequences for an entire community. Just one or two boarded-up homes can send a residential block into a downward spiral, driving down property values, and leading to increased crime, rundown schools, and flagging economic growth.

Not being able to pay the mortgage can be one of the scariest situations a person faces. Embarrassed about their situation and unsure about what to do, studies show that roughly 50% of delinquent borrowers avoid contact with their lender, hoping the problem will go away. Instead of acting on quality advice, they fall deeper into the hole and increase their chances of foreclosing. If these homeowners could receive solid financial advice and help, tens of thousands of them could avoid foreclosure.

The National PSA Campaign—Reaching at-Risk Homeowners

To reach at-risk homeowners across the country, NeighborWorks America teamed up with the Ad Council to create a national public service advertising campaign. The campaign targets low- and moderate-income families who are having difficulty keeping up with their mortgage payments and encourages them to call The Homeownership Preservation Foundation's Homeowner's HOPE Hotline at 1-888-995-HOPE for confidential financial counseling.

The Hotline provides homeowners with free, unbiased financial advice and counseling, 24 hours a day, 7 days a week, in English and Spanish. The Homeowner's HOPE Hotline connects callers, when appropriate, with their lender or other housing assistance organizations, including NeighborWorks organizations, who can provide face-to-face counseling and additional services.

By highlighting the effects that foreclosure has on the entire family, the PSAs remind homeowners that if they're "not facing their mortgage issues things will only get worse. Call 1-888-995-HOPE now. Because nothing is worse than doing nothing."

The national campaign includes donated TV, radio, newspaper, magazine, web, and outdoor advertising in addition to direct mail and grassroots marketing. Over 190 local nonprofits and municipalities are joining the campaign to promote foreclosure counseling in their communities. Advertising materials are available to all interested communities around the country.

Courtesy Homeownership Preservation Foundation

PART III

Emergency Public Relations

Chapter 11   Emergency Public Relations

11

Emergency Public Relations

In preparation for emergencies, the practitioner should be generally aware of the four aspects of the process model, although its use in this form of public relations will be limited.

RESEARCH

Some research will be helpful in reaching a state of readiness for an emergency. The following three types of research used for other forms of public relations are appropriate.

Client Research

Client research should focus on preparing as many "worst-case" scenarios as possible. What can go wrong? Is the organization's physical plant vulnerable to fire, explosion, or other crises? Is dangerous equipment located on the premises? How will you respond if the organization's president is indicted for fraud? All division heads in the organization should be asked by the director of public relations to prepare a list of potential trouble spots that could erupt in their respective areas. Whenever possible, corrective action should be taken to neutralize these problems before an emergency can occur. Research may also examine the client's reputation and handling of past crises.

Opportunity or Problem Research

Emergency public relations is generically reactive in nature. Some practitioners argue that it is impossible to really get ready for a sweeping disaster. Emergency planning, however, must be proactive in order to be prepared for a proper reactive response to an emergency. Some problems slowly build due to a series of minor events. The public relations staff must monitor trends and detect potential issues to anticipate and prepare for issues that may explode into the public agenda.

Audience Research

The practitioner should make a list of internal and external publics to be immediately notified in case of an emergency. Internal publics would include the chief executive officer and other top organizational officials on a "need-to-know" basis at first. As the emergency progresses, the entire workforce can be notified through existing internal channels of communication. External audiences in an emergency should include, in priority order, law enforcement officials; the next of kin of the injured or dead, notified before the public release of their names; the mass media; government agencies, if appropriate; and trade publications. These internal and external audiences are a suggested starting point. The practitioner needs to be much more specific in creating an emergency contact list designed to notify all concerned parties in a timely fashion.

OBJECTIVES

Because of the exceptional nature of emergencies, objectives for this form of public relations cannot be carefully planned. Nonetheless, some general guidelines are applicable:

1. To provide accurate, timely information to all targeted internal and external audiences

2. To demonstrate concern for the safety of lives

3. To safeguard organizational facilities and assets

4. To maintain a positive image of the organization as a good corporate or community citizen

These guidelines will serve the practitioner well in preparing for the two areas of responsibility involved in programming.

PROGRAMMING

Programming for emergency public relations should focus on two major actions or areas of responsibility: establishing a *public relations emergency headquarters* (PR HQ) and a *media information center* (MIC). Anticipate the necessary resources for a crisis—it may take additional people within the organization or even will require hiring a public relations agency to support expanded operations. Equally important is training these people and running simulations and exercises to practice for the real thing.

The Public Relations Headquarters

The PR HQ will probably be the regular public relations office itself. If more space is needed, other offices may also be designated as part of the PR HQ. This office will be responsible for notification of all internal and external emergency audiences, for preparation of material for the media, and for the establishment of a *public information center* (PIC) to answer inquiries and to control rumors. The director of public relations should remain in the PR HQ to supervise these three functions.

Notification, the first function of the PR HQ, will be the top priority of this office as soon as a crisis occurs. The internal and external audiences were discussed above and will be reviewed in Exhibit 11-a, the "Emergency Public Relations Checklist." Names of the injured or dead should be withheld from public release until the next of kin are notified or for 24 hours, whichever comes first.

E X H I B I T 11-A   Emergency Public Relations Checklist

I.   Public relations emergency headquarters (PR HQ). The PR director stays in the PR department or designated PR HQ and supervises:
   A.   Notification and liaison
      1.   Internal: Notify the CEO and other top officials on immediate "need-to-know" basis.
      2.   External: Notify the media; law enforcement officials; government agencies; and the next of kin of the injured or dead, before public release of names (24-hour rule suggested).
   B.   Preparation of materials for media
      1.   Have company backgrounder, fact sheet, and bios of officers already prepared and on the company Web site.
      2.   Prepare basic news release on crisis as soon as possible (one-hour rule suggested).
         a.   Include all known facts—what happened, how, when, where, who, and how many involved—not why (fault).
         b.   Be certain all information is accurate; never release unconfirmed information.
         c.   Withhold names of victims until the next of kin are notified (or 24 hours, whichever comes first).
         d.   Clear release with senior management, legal department, and personnel department.
         e.   Issue release immediately to local and national mass media, specialized publications, employees by e-mail and phone, community leaders, insurance company, pertinent government agencies by fax and e-mail. Be sure to post the release on the company Web site.
      3.   Issue timely statements to media in ongoing crises.
      4.   Use one-voice principle—information only from official organizational statements.
      5.   Use full-disclosure principle (except admission of fault).
   C.   Public information center (PIC)
      1.   Establish and announce a PIC in the PR HQ.

2. Respond to telephone and e-mail inquiries with accurate information.
3. Provide accurate information to groups where rumors are circulating.
4. Hold meetings with groups as needed to clarify misinformation.
5. Have call center refer all pertinent calls to the PIC.
6. Direct company employees to make no unauthorized statements to media people.
7. Monitor and engage interested online communities (blogs/social networking sites).
8. Use one-voice principle—information only from official organizational statements.
9. Use full-disclosure principle (except admission of fault).

II. Media information center (MIC)
  A. Designate a place for media people to gather, if necessary.
  B. Locate an MIC near the crisis area, but away from the PR HQ. (Media people admitted to disaster site must be escorted by PR personnel.)
  C. Have sole spokesperson on duty day or night at the MIC.
    1. Use one-voice principle—information only from official organizational statements.
    2. Use full-disclosure principle (except admission of fault).

The second function of the PR HQ will be preparation of materials for the media and the public. A company or organizational backgrounder, fact sheet, biographies of major officers, and their captioned photographs should already be prepared and on the organizational Web site. Along with assembling these background materials, the public relations staff should immediately begin the task of preparing its first basic news release/statement on the crisis. A good rule of thumb is that this should be ready for release *no more than one hour* after the occurrence of the emergency. The release should include all known facts, such as what happened, how, when, where, who, and how many were involved. The question of why may be omitted since the organization may run the risk of involving itself in litigation through an admission of fault. This matter should be handled by the legal department. The release should be cleared as quickly as possible with senior management, the legal department, and possibly the personnel department. Then the news release should be issued immediately to local and national mass media, specialized publications, employees, community leaders, and pertinent government agencies. In addition to the first basic release, the PR HQ should issue frequent statements to the media in ongoing crises and should coordinate media interviews with the CEO as warranted.

Through all of these emergency public relations procedures, two principles are recommended: a *one-voice* principle and a *full-disclosure* principle. Above all other considerations, the organization should *speak with one voice*. All employees should be briefed to give information to the media or other concerned parties only from official organizational statements, issued by the PR HQ. The full-disclosure principle refers to giving all known information, with the exception of why the emergency occurred if this might involve admission of fault.

   The third function of the PR HQ is to establish a *PIC*. The responsibilities of the PIC include responding to telephone inquiries with accurate information, providing information to groups to combat rumors, and holding meetings with groups as needed to clarify misinformation. The organization's call center should be briefed in advance to refer all calls in an emergency to the PIC, and the one-voice and full-disclosure principles should be observed at all times in its operation.

The Media Information Center

If media people will be gathering at the site of an emergency or disaster, the director of public relations should set up an *MIC* at some location near the crisis area but away from the PR HQ. Public relations staff members at the PR HQ must be allowed to perform their required tasks without the interruption of news people wanting information. The MIC should, if possible, designate some staff people to escort media representatives if there is a hazardous disaster area. Reporters should not be permitted to wander freely through a dangerous zone, although they usually want unrestricted access to everything. The MIC should be a suitable room, preferably an auditorium if available, where journalists can remain to receive news releases about the emergency. A high-credibility spokesperson and several alternates should be designated in advance and, once chosen, a single spokesperson should be on duty as long as necessary at the MIC to read news releases. Directors of public relations should seldom be designated MIC spokespersons. They should remain at the PR HQ to supervise all operations. The spokesperson, however, should be a high-ranking officer in the organization; otherwise, the organization's credibility could suffer. Needless to say, the one-voice and full-disclosure principles should be stringently applied in the operation of the MIC.

Uncontrolled and Controlled Media

In an emergency situation, most of the communication will be uncontrolled in the form of news releases, interviews with organizational officials, and perhaps photographs, although the media representatives will usually take their own photos.

   Controlled media will be used sparingly, usually as prepared background material or e-mail, voice mail, or in-house bulletins for employees. The organization's Web site can become an important resource in emergency public relations. Ongoing news of the crisis, along with a wealth of other information about the organization, can be posted on the Web site. After the crisis, the Web site can be used to clarify the organization's situation and to provide a record of the course of the crisis itself. Some organizations prepare a special Web site that is "hidden" on the server but can be activated immediately during a crisis. The sites provide additional background material and interactive features to handle exchanges with both the media and the public most affected by the crisis. Engaging the public through social media expands an organization's reach during a crisis. The American Red Cross uses blogs (Wordpress, Blogger), social networks (Facebook, MySpace), social bookmarking sites (del.icio.us), and video-sharing (YouTube) and photo-sharing (Flickr) sites.

Effective Communication

Two-way communication and audience participation may assume greater than usual importance in a crisis. The targeted audiences, especially the media, will want to be involved and interact with the spokesperson as much as possible. But, in general, all the previously discussed principles of communication should be observed.

Programming for emergency public relations, then, concentrates on the two major responsibilities of creating a PR HQ and an MIC (see Exhibit 11-a). Beyond that, customary use of uncontrolled and controlled media and principles of effective communication are appropriate.

EVALUATION

The evaluation of emergency public relations will be less precise than for other forms of the discipline. Since emergencies are unplanned, the PR objectives must be, at best, general and nonquantitative guidelines. In a quiet period well after the organization's recovery from the emergency, it will be appropriate to review the general guidelines previously mentioned and informally assess the PR department's degree of success in meeting them. Such a review should also include analyzing media coverage; tracking complaints from consumers, community, employees, and other relevant publics; holding internal meetings on the crisis plan and its implementation; and assessing damage to the organization's image. Of course, a formal survey of all participants can also be taken. The results may be used for a variety of purposes, possibly including improvement of emergency public relations procedures.

SUMMARY

Although the ROPE (research, objectives, programming, evaluation) process has limited applicability in emergency public relations, it should not be forgotten or discarded.

Research is useful in preparing for emergencies. Worst-case scenarios should be prepared to determine what problems could possibly develop. Although emergency public relations is inherently reactive, planning for such crises should be proactive. Emergency contact lists should be made, including all internal and external individuals, groups, and agencies that are to be notified in a crisis.

Objectives for emergency PR tend to be of an impact nature. They usually concentrate on providing information to important audiences as needed;

safeguarding lives, facilities, and assets; and protecting the credibility of the organization.

Programming should include establishing a PR HQ and, if necessary, an MIC. The functions of the emergency headquarters include notification and liaison and preparation of materials for the media. If reporters will be gathering at the site of a disaster or crisis, an MIC should be established near (but usually not on) the site, and an organizational spokesperson should be designated to be on duty to read statements to the journalists as long as the crisis lasts.

Evaluation for emergency PR is usually less formal than for other types. If objectives have been set before a crisis occurs, each should be appropriately evaluated. If not, the organization should, after the emergency, review its notification functions, its general accessibility and service to the media, and, of course, its media coverage during the event.

READINGS ON EMERGENCY PUBLIC RELATIONS

Adams, William C. "Responding to the Media During a Crisis: It's What You Say and When You Say It," *Public Relations Quarterly* 45 (spring 2000): 26ff.

Alvey, Robert J. "Creating an Effective Crisis Communication Team," *Public Relations Tactics* 12 (December 2005): 12–13.

Barton, Lawrence. *Crisis in Organizations: Managing and Communicating in the Heat of Chaos*, 2d ed. Florence, KY: Thomson Learning, 2000.

Benoit, William L. "Image Repair Discourse and Crisis Communication," *Public Relations Review* 23 (summer 1997): 177–186.

Brown, Lorra M. "VT Tragedy Teaches Students the True Nature of Public Relations," *Public Relations Tactics* 14 (September 2007): 18–19.

Brown, Timothy S. "Powerful Crisis Communications Lessons: PR Lessons Learned from Hurricane Isabel," *Public Relations Quarterly* 48 (winter 2003): 31–35.

Caponigro, Jeffrey R. *The Crisis Counselor.* New York: McGraw-Hill/NTC, 2000.

Chong, Mark. "A Crisis of Epidemic Proportions: What Communication Lessons Can Practitioners Learn From The Singapore SARS Crisis?" *Public Relations Quarterly* 51 (spring 2006) 6–11.

Chyi, Hsiang Iris, and Maxwell McCombs. "Media Salience and the Process of Framing: Coverage of the Columbine School Shootings," *Journalism and Mass Communication Quarterly* 81 (spring 2004): 22–25.

Cobb, Chris. "The Taco Bell E. Coli Outbreak: Calming Public Fears During Food-Borne Illness Scares," *Public Relations Tactics* 14 (February 2007): 11–12.

Coombs, W. Timothy. "An Analytic Framework for Crisis Situations: Better Responses from a Better Understanding of the Situation," *Journal of Public Relations Research* 10 (3) (1998): 177ff.

———. "Crisis Management and Communications," White Paper published by the Institute for Public Relations (December 2007), http://www.instituteforpr.org/ipr_info/crisis_management_and_communications/.

———. "Helping Crisis Managers Protect Reputational Assets," *Communications Quarterly* 16 (November 2002): 165–186.

———. *Ongoing Crisis Communication: Planning, Managing, and Responding*, 2d ed. Thousand Oaks, CA: Sage Publications, 2007.

Dezenhall, Eric and John Weber. *Damage Control*. New York: Penguin Group, 2007.

Duke, Shearlean, and Lynne Masland. "Crisis Communication by the Book," *Public Relations Quarterly* 47 (fall 2002): 30–36.

Fearn-Banks, Kathleen. *Crisis Communications: A Casebook Approach*, 3d ed. Mahwah, NJ: Erlbaum, 2007.

Fearn-Banks, Kathleen, Richard J. Symmes, Mike Murphy, Shayan Amir-Hosseini, et al. "A Snapshot of How Organizations Responded to Tragedy," *Public Relations Tactics* 9 (September 2002): 30–32.

Gallagher, Amanda Hall, Maria Fontenot, and Kris Boyle. "Communicating During Times of Crises: An Analysis of News Releases from the Federal Government Before, During, and After Hurricanes Katrina and Rita," *Public Relations Review* 33 (June 2007): 217–219.

Gaschen, Dennis John. "Crisis—What Crisis? Taking Your Crisis Communications Plan for a Test Drive," *Public Relations Tactics* 10 (May 2003): 12.

Green, Walter G., III. "The Future of Disasters: Interesting Trends for Interesting Times," *Futures Research Quarterly* 20 (fall 2004): 59–68.

Hearit, Keith Michael. *Crisis Management by Apology*. Mahwah, NJ: Erlbaum, 2005.

Hyde, Richard C. "In Crisis Management, Getting the Message Right Is Critical," *Public Relations Strategist* 13 (summer 2007): 32–35.

Kimmel, Allan J. *Rumors and Rumor Control*. Mahwah, NJ: Erlbaum, 2004.

Kruvand, Marjorie. "Two Decades of Crisis Response," *Public Relations Strategist* 8 (fall 2002): 26–27.

Lerbinger, Otto. *The Crisis Manager: Facing Risk and Responsibility*. Mahwah, NJ: Erlbaum, 1997.

Levick, Richard, and Larry Smith. *Stop the Presses: The Crisis and Litigation PR Desk Reference*. Washington, DC: Watershed Press, 2007.

Levy, Ronald N. "Your Coming Crisis: How to Triumph" *Public Relations Quarterly* 51 (2006): 26–28.

Long, Richard K. "Benchmarking as Crisis Planning," *Public Relations Tactics* 7 (February 2000): 10.

Loomis, Lynette M. "Managing Emotions: The Missing Steps in Crisis Communications Planning," *Public Relations Tactics* 15 (March 2008): 13.

Lukaszewski, James E. "Becoming a Crisis Guru: Why Crisis Management Is as Difficult as Ever," *Public Relations Strategist* 13 (summer 2007): 44–45.

———. "Establishing Individual and Corporate Crisis Communication Standards: The Principles and Protocols," *Public Relations Quarterly* 42 (fall 1997), 7ff.

———. *Executive Action Series: Vol. I: War Stories and Crisis Communication Strategies, A Crisis Communication Management Anthology; Vol. II: Crisis Communication Planning Strategies, A Crisis Communication Management Workbook; Vol. IV: Media Relations–Strategies During Emergencies, A Crisis Communication Management Guide*. New York: Public Relations Society of America, 2000.

McLaughlin, Shane. "Sept. 11: Four Views of Crisis Management," *Public Relations Strategist* 8 (winter 2002): 22–29.

Millar, Dan P., and Robert L. Heath, eds. *Responding to Crisis*. Mahwah, NJ: Erlbaum, 2004.

Mitroff, Ian, and Gus Anagnos. *Managing Crises Before They Happen: What Every Executive Needs to Know About Crisis Management*. New York: AMACOM, 2000.

Moore, Aaron J. "Roger Clemens and the Dangers of Misreading the Media," *Public Relations Tactics* 15 (May 2008): 27.

Ogrizek, Michel, and Jean-Michel Guillery. *Communicating in Crisis*. Hawthorne, NY: Aldine de Gruyter, 1999.

Pinsdorf, Marion K. *Communicating When Your Company Is Under Siege: Surviving Public Crisis*, 3d ed. New York: Fordham University Press, 1999.

———. *All Crises Are Global: Managing to Escape Chaos, Communication and Organizational Crisis*. New York: NYU Press, 2004.

Preble, John F. "Integrating the Crisis Management Perspective into the Strategic Management Process," *Journal of Management Studies* 34 (September 1997): 769.

Richards, Barry. "Terrorism and Public Relations," *Public Relations Review* 30 (June 2004): 169–176.

Roach, Thomas. "The NIMBY and Goliath Phenomenon," *Rock Products* 107 (May 2004): 8.

Ropeik, David, and George Gray. *Risk! A Practical Guide for Deciding What's Really Safe and What's Really Dangerous in the World Around You*. New York: Houghton Mifflin, 2002.

Shin, Jae-Hwa, I-Huei Cheng, Yan Jin, and Glen T. Cameron. "Going Head to Head: Content Analysis of High Profile Conflicts as Played Out in the Press," *Public Relations Review* 31 (September 2005): 399–406.

Stateman, Alison. "The Tylenol Tampering Crisis as Examined 25 Years Ago," *Public Relations Tactics* 15 (March 2008): 7.

Surowiecki, James. "In Case of Emergency," *New Yorker* 81 (June 13, 2005): 70.

Sweetser, Kaye D., and Emily Metzgar. "Communicating During Crisis: Use of Blogs as a Relationship Management Tool," *Public Relations Review* 33 (September 2007): 340–342.

Thomas, Glen. "Lessons Learned the Hard Way: Stumbling Through to Better Crisis Communications," *Public Relations Tactics* 15 (March 2008): 12.

Ulmer, Robert Ray, Timothy L. Sellnow, and Matthew Wayne Seeger. *Effective Crisis Communication: Moving From Crisis to Opportunity*. Thousand Oaks, CA: Sage, 2007.

Veil, Shari. "Mayhem in the Magic City: Rebuilding Legitimacy in a Communication Train Wreck," *Public Relations Review* 33 (September 2007): 337–339.

Wiser, Nancy. "After the Storm: PR Efforts Help Quell Public Frustration in Kentucky," *Public Relations Tactics* 11 (January 2004): 11.

Emergency Public Relations Cases

Case 11-1

Hurricane Katrina devastated large areas and produced many communication challenges for government agencies, but pockets of public relations practitioners did an exceptional job, working the communication needs of their organizations. Instead of dwelling on the "big picture" of the storm, this case looks at the emergency communication needs of a campus in the indirect path of the storm. Exhibit 11-1a is a media advisory on the launch of an information center, Exhibit 11-1b is a "Community Outreach" release about distance learning, and Exhibit 11-1c is a media advisory on the availability of satellite images of the storm.

LSU: Managing Crisis Communications Through Hurricane Katrina

Louisiana State University Office of Public Affairs

SUMMARY

On August 29, 2005, Hurricane Katrina slammed into the Louisiana coast, creating the worst natural disaster in the nation's history. Louisiana State University (LSU) found itself in the unprecedented position of serving as a major and central staging ground for state and federal disaster response. The LSU Office of Public Affairs (LSUPA) crisis response communications program focused mainly on (1) effectively communicating key messages to internal and external audiences, (2) managing national and international media's needs as they transmitted critical information to a news-hungry public, and (3) managing community relations, services, and assistance. In all communications, the mission of the overall response effort—serve human needs first—was always foremost.

SITUATION ANALYSIS

LSU, located in Baton Rouge (the nearest major city to New Orleans), acted immediately to offer its facilities and personnel to support large-scale state and federal relief efforts for the thousands of Hurricane Katrina victims who required medical attention after the storm. Athletic facilities were converted into a field hospital and campus buildings offered shelter to relief personnel.

For eight days, the usual activities of the college campus were suspended to help those in need. Thousands of faculty, staff, and students joined the army of volunteers from around the world who were crucial to response efforts. This is the story of how the 30 team members from the LSUPA provided the campus with a single, clear voice in the days following the tragedy.

RESEARCH

- Continuously monitored storm progress and conferred with LSU's Hurricane Center on strike zone probabilities.

- Consulted the LSUPA crisis communications plan, the LSU special needs shelter plan, and referred to the book *When Crisis Strikes on Campus*, edited by Wendy Ann Larson, to identify strategies to use in responding to the disaster.

- Collaborated with PR officials from the Louisiana Department of Health & Hospitals and the Arkansas Department of Health & Human Services to utilize their extensive experience in relation to organizing media credentialing and disaster response.

- Identified key audiences with whom it was important for the LSUPA to share information, including hurricane victims, displaced students, parents of students, media, members of the LSU community, and the general public.

- Attended briefings with the chancellor and his Emergency Operations Response Team, law enforcement officials, state and federal emergency management agencies, and governmental groups to coordinate the ongoing crisis response efforts. The LSUPA continuously kept the lines of communication open in order to assess the effectiveness of the overall communications effort, determine how messages were being received and if changes were required, and solve and clarify problems with regard to issues management.

- Utilized the LSUPA's previously established internal telephone tree and electronic media database to communicate with each other and members of the press, and used the LSU Web site and the toll-free emergency telephone line to disseminate information to the public regarding updates and new information.

PLANNING

Objectives

Managing the Message

- To effectively communicate three key messages throughout the crisis life cycle.

- Victims of the crisis and their human needs are our first priority.

- While adapting to a new mission, the academic mission of research and education should not be forgotten.

- LSU and other universities across the country are in a unique position to assist with recovery efforts due to the inherent resources (intellectual capacity, large facilities, transportation, dining, security, volunteers) within a campus community. LSU's experience can serve as a strategic model for how other universities can assist in times of crisis.

Managing the Media

- To properly manage media-related requests for information and on-site visits, while simultaneously respecting the human need mission and protecting patient confidentiality.

Managing Community Relations

- To successfully distribute accurate information to key audiences and facilitate the call for recovery assistance.

Overall Strategies

- Employed a crisis communication command structure so that critical information and key decisions were filtered down from the LSU Emergency Operations Center (LSUEOC).

- Created a media command center to manage all media issues and requests, as well as to disseminate information.

- Developed several methods for communicating with current and displaced students, parents, faculty and staff, victims of the hurricane, and the general public, including a 24-hour crisis hotline.

- Developed an outreach program to share LSU's campus model for disaster recovery and to impart key lessons learned with other universities and organizations.

EXECUTION

- Held seven media briefings specifically targeted to communicate the three key messages.

- Stationed LSUPA staff members at the LSUEOC, where key decisions were made hourly. An LSUPA representative presented twice daily updates to command officials with regard to the number and nature of the most commonly asked questions from the public Web site developments, and the number of media tours and inquiries.

- Adopted radio communications because traditional methods were ineffective.

- Used broadcast e-mails to inform students, faculty, and staff of class cancellations, resources and volunteers needed, and when normal academic operations would resume.

- Promoted the Katrina Student Relief Fund, created to financially assist displaced college students in Louisiana.

- Communicated the campus model for recovery with the speedy publication of the book *LSU in the Eye of the Storm*, written and illustrated by the LSUPA and printed by the LSU Press.

- Developed an on-demand, customizable PowerPoint presentation titled "LSU: In the Eye of Storm," for university officials to share at conferences, seminars, speaking engagements, and keynote addresses.

Managing the Media

- Organized a media command center where credentials, maps, parking passes, and logistical information were distributed to visiting national and international reporters and television crews.

- Worked with LSU's Offices of Facility Services and Parking, Traffic & Transportation to arrange special staging areas and parking privileges for media crews.

- Set up hourly, guided media tours of the on-campus medical facilities, all the while ensuring patient confidentiality.

- Assigned several team members to answer media phone calls, in order to connect reporters with LSU experts.

- Promoted the scholarly expertise of LSU faculty whose knowledge saved lives during the recovery process.

- Issued more than two dozen press releases and media advisories during the storm crisis period, which began in the days immediately preceding the storm and continued for roughly two weeks.

- Provided HD-quality video footage and still photography of the campus and the converted medical facilities to all media via a variety of formats, including the LSU Web site.

- Provided interim, on-campus facilities for the New Orleans CBS television affiliate and the *New Orleans Times-Picayune*.

Managing Community Relations

- Created a 24-hour manned hotline designed to effectively answer pressing questions from the public and to facilitate the call for volunteers and resources. The call center funneled inquiries to the appropriate units regarding the whereabouts of critically ill patients, evacuation procedures, road closures, social services available, donations, volunteering, enrolling at LSU, and temporary residential assistance.

- Utilized the LSU Web site to provide up-to-date information to the public concerning resources needed, services provided, updates to the academic calendar, and which other universities were accepting displaced students.

EVALUATION

Managing the Message

- Achieved more than 150 media placements in a 2-week period that focused on the 3 key messages. These appeared in outlets such as *The New York Times*, *USA Today*, *Mainichi* (Japan), and CNN.com.

- Returned to educational operations 8 days after the hurricane, while simultaneously operating the human need mission for a total of 21 days.

- Shipped 1,057 *LSU in the Eye of the Storm* books to chancellors and provosts of peer institutions. Nearly 4,000 additional copies were distributed to Louisiana's federal delegation and state legislators, media, national and state agencies, community and social service leaders, and academic colleagues across the country.

- To this date, LSU representatives have presented at more than a dozen separate speaking engagements to share lessons learned with peer institutions and related associations, reaching more than 7,000 participants.

Managing the Media

- More than 50 different LSU experts were cited in various media outlets in the 2 weeks following the storm.

- More than 100 media representatives toured the medical facilities on LSU's campus during a 2-week period.

- More than 200 stories citing LSU experts ran in the first 2 weeks after the storm, in outlets such as the *Washington Post*, the *Christian Science Monitor*, BBC News Online, the *Korea Herald*, and the *Dallas Morning News*.

- More than 30 international, national, and regional news and information broadcasts highlighted the relief efforts at LSU, including the NewsHour with Jim Lehrer, MTV news, ABC's Good Morning America, and NBC's Today Show.

- One-hundred staff members from the New Orleans CBS television affiliate used campus facilities to cover events in New Orleans.

Managing Community Relations

- The 24-hour manned crisis hotline received approximately 6,500 phone calls in a 13-day period.
- The LSU Web site received 2.5 million hits over the course of 3 weeks.
- Information distributed and facilitated through the 24-hour crisis hotline, LSU Web site, and media reports helped to generate 3,000 LSU volunteers; 2,000 nationwide volunteers; thousands of pounds of donated items such as mattresses, blankets, and clothes; and 1,700 volunteer medical personnel who traveled from across the country to treat the 15,000 patients evacuated to LSU. In addition, approximately 2,300 pets passed through the animal evacuation shelter (2,000 animals were reunited with families), 3,200 displaced students applied to LSU, with 2,800 enrolling in 10 days (a 10 percent increase), and more than $1.6 million of direct student aid was raised via the Katrina Student Relief Fund.

EXHIBIT 11-1a Media Advisory

LOUISIANA STATE UNIVERSITY | Baton Rouge, Louisiana

LSUNEWS

SEARCH LSU.EDU
225.578.8654
fax: 225.578.3860

COMMUNICATIONS AND UNIVERSITY RELATIONS | *Public Affairs*   BY CATEGORY ▶   BY DATE ▶

Media Advisory

LSU requests media cooperation, launches 24-hour hurricane information center

08/31/2005 02:04 PM

LSU is playing a crucial role in providing emergency medical services to evacuees from areas devastated by Hurricane Katrina. Given the urgency of the situation and the continuous arrival and departure of emergency vehicles and aircraft, LSU and state emergency officials are requesting complete cooperation from the media in assuring this operation runs smoothly. Michael Ruffner, Vice Chancellor for Communications and University Relations at LSU said, "We are re-allocating our resources so that we can assist state and federal agencies in this massive relief effort, and help coordinate coverage by local, regional and national media. Specifically, we are requesting that all media and private aircraft land at the Baton Rouge Metropolitan Airport, and not on or around the LSU campus." Ruffner added, "Given the large number of students on campus and the large influx of evacuees arriving from storm ravaged areas, public safety at LSU is best served by limiting aircraft landings to those with medical or security missions."

All members of the media planning on covering relief efforts on the LSU campus in Baton Rouge are asked to contact the LSU Office of Public Affairs at 225-578-8654, or via e-mail at urelat1@lsu.edu, to request media credentials. LSU Public Affairs will then assist those credentialed members of the media in coordinating with state and federal emergency units.

In addition, beginning at noon on Wednesday, Aug. 31, LSU will operate a 24-hour Hurricane Information Center through the LSU Office of Public Affairs. Staff will be on hand to coordinate and assist media on campus and take phone calls from media, concerned parents, staff, faculty, students and members of the public concerning relief efforts on the LSU campus in Baton Rouge. There will be a toll-free hotline number, 1-800-516-6444, that will be answered by LSU public affairs representatives 24 hours a day.

–30–

Media Relations
Office of Public Affairs
Baton Rouge, LA 70803
Phone: 225/578-8654
Fax: 225/578-3860

Courtesy Louisiana State University

EXHIBIT 11-1b   Release on Distance Learning

Community Outreach

Displaced college and high school students offered free distance learning option

09/14/2005 03:18 PM

For thousands of college and high school students displaced by Hurricane Katrina, LSU Independent Study offers a classroom-free educational option to complete the fall semester.

LSU will offer enrollment in independent study courses at no cost to those students who were enrolled at one of the colleges or high schools that have canceled fall classes in the affected areas of Louisiana, Mississippi and Alabama.

Students who want to take advantage of the independent study option need to act quickly; LSU is permitting eligible students to enroll for free in up to four college or six high school independent study courses through Sept. 30.

LSU Independent Study offers 80 high school and 150 college credit courses that students can use to continue to make progress on a high school diploma or on a college degree. Unlike traditional classes, these self-paced courses require no classroom meetings, so they are ideal for students who may not be sure where they will be next week or next month. Some courses are available online for students who have computer access; but every independent study course can be completed using the original correspondence course technology: paper, pencil and the postal service.

"As we develop and incorporate new technologies to their best effect, we have been committed to maintaining our print-based courses," said Gail Hawkes, interim director of the Office of Independent Study. "Electricity can go down, cable systems may fail, our Internet site may even go offline for brief periods; but our students can always drop a lesson in a mailbox. And there are some constituencies for whom print-based courses continue to offer the most portability, efficiency and flexibility."

Students do their course work anywhere and send assignments to LSU, where they are graded by a college instructor or high school teacher. Students normally have nine months to complete the assignments and exams in an independent study course, and they can take their exam virtually anywhere under the supervision of a proctor approved by LSU. Textbooks and other required supplies will need to be purchased by the students.

Course work through independent study is generally transferable to a student's home institution. In the case of high school students, the credit is actually given by the student's high school, and pre-approval by a school principal or counselor is required. LSU officials are working with the Louisiana Department of Education to develop agreements that will cover the displaced students who may not be able to contact school staff for approvals.

For more information about the courses that are available, the LSU Independent Study Web site is the best source of information: www.is.lsu.edu. For specific information about special enrollment procedures, consult the Web site. High school students can also call 225-578-3920 or toll-free at 1-800-234-5047. College students should call 225-578-3920 or toll-free at 1-800-234-5046.

–30–

Kristine Calongne/LSU Media Relations/225-578-5985

Courtesy Louisiana State University

E X H I B I T 11-1c   Advisory on Satellite Images

Media Advisory

Hurricane Katrina images, animations available from LSU lab

08/26/2005 04:30 PM

Tracking information, satellite images and animations of Hurricane Katrina are available now from the LSU Earth Scan Lab at www.esl.lsu.edu/quicklinks/hurricanes/2005/KATRINA/.

The LSU Earth Scan Laboratory, part of the Coastal Studies Institute at LSU, is celebrating its 17th year of operation. On its Web site, www.esl.lsu.edu, the lab stores real-time satellite movie loops of current weather, storm motion and ocean currents based on measurements of the GOES-East satellite, as well as historic animations of deadly hurricanes.

The mission of the Earth Scan Laboratory is to support research, education and public service/emergency response with near real-time and archival satellite data, as well as data processing, analysis, interpretation and dissemination. From its central location, the Earth Scan Lab can capture satellite data covering the entire Gulf of Mexico, most of the Western Atlantic, the extreme Eastern Pacific and the land mass from the Hudson Bay to the northernmost part of South America.

For more information, contact lab director Nan Walker at 225-578-5331.

–30–

Courtesy Louisiana State University

Case 11-2

Problems with food safety quickly become banner headlines in newspapers as consumers scramble for answers to potential health problems. Even the hint of problems in one field in one county of one state can tarnish the reputation of growers across the country. Exhibit 11-2a is a release on the background of the E. coli contamination, Exhibit 11-2b is a member alert for a conference call, and Exhibit 11-2c is a media statement.

The 2006 *E. coli* O157:H7 Outbreak in Spinach

United Fresh Produce Association by Amy Philpott

SUMMARY

On Thursday, September 14, 2006, the U.S. Food and Drug Administration (FDA) issued a consumer warning to "not eat bagged fresh spinach at this time." Within 24 hours, the FDA revised its warning to "not eat all spinach or spinach-containing products." These unprecedented warnings to not eat an entire food category created a crisis for the spinach industry, launched the entire fresh produce industry into a new era of food safety, and prompted the United Fresh Produce Association's (UFPA) Board of Directors to unanimously pass a resolution requesting mandatory government oversight based on commodity-based science for all fresh produce, imported and domestic. This case study looks at the crisis communication elements of the outbreak from an industry association perspective.

BACKGROUND

Food safety is a paramount concern of consumers, and the Centers for Disease Control and Prevention (CDC) uses a national tracking system to help identify potential problems. By the end of the "spinach crisis," the CDC had reported that there were a total of 199 persons from 26 states who were infected with the outbreak strain of *E. coli* O157:H7. Airways and newspapers carried banner stories about the outbreak, and grocery store and refrigerator shelves were emptied of any spinach products as the public, government agencies, and the food industry struggled to find answers. Like most crises, uncertainty and the unknown are the great enemies of clear and successful communication that solves a problem.

On September 12, 2006, the first day of an annual, four-day association conference and two days before the FDA announced the outbreak, the United Fresh Fruit & Vegetable Association (UFFVA) and the International Fresh-Cut Produce Association (IFPA) officially merged to form the UFPA. This is significant for several reasons: (1) for the first 24 hours of the outbreak, staff would be operating out of a makeshift office at a hotel, (2) the association's Web content management system and the e-mail exchange server were scheduled to go down over the weekend so that the two membership databases could be merged, and (3) the UFFVA and IFPA Web sites had already been redirected to a landing page that introduced the new association (UFPA) and notified visitors that the site was "under construction." These factors would present communication challenges.

On Wednesday, September 13, a high-profile law firm reported on its Web site that three clients wished to initiate a lawsuit regarding illnesses associated with "bagged baby spinach." At approximately 4:30 p.m. eastern time, the next day, FDA officials notified the UFPA that in two hours the FDA would issue a consumer warning to not eat spinach. By 6:15 p.m. the reporters were calling, and supermarket retailers and foodservice operators were pulling spinach from shelves and off menus. Spinach farmers around the country called harvesting and planting crews and told them not to come to work on Friday. Shipments in transit were stopped throughout the distribution chain, resulting in an entire industry shutdown. At this point, no one knew what the problem was, and intentional tampering with the food chain could not be ruled out.

On Friday, September 15, based on the CDC, FDA, and California State Department of Health joint investigation, one processing company that produced spinach under multiple labels initiated a product recall for fresh spinach products with specific use by dates. On the same day, the FDA advised consumers to "not eat fresh spinach or fresh spinach-containing products until further notice." This caused confusion in the marketplace as consumers began to mistakenly question canned and frozen spinach. On September 29, the FDA issued a notice indicating that spinach from areas other than those implicated in the outbreak could be consumed. The outbreak was officially over. Despite the FDA's September 29 statement and tens of millions of dollars invested in food safety, spinach sales still have not returned to normal even after two years.

CRISIS RESPONSE

The UFPA understood the importance of responding quickly. Within minutes after the initial FDA call, members of the UFPA crisis team met to enact the crisis plan. The work order to modify the e-mail exchange server was cancelled, but the membership databases were already inaccessible, so over the weekend, a backup membership list in Microsoft Excel would be used as a source of e-mail addresses. The team quickly identified key audiences that needed to be reached, including members, consumers, media, industry partners, government officials, and health authorities. Each person on the crisis team focused on a specific audience group and assisted with others when needed. The team conducted a situation analysis and identified key messages for the audiences.

Member communication was an immediate priority, so after the FDA's call on September 14, the UFPA immediately arranged a conference call with three other industry partner associations that share membership with the UFPA. The four groups decided to each send an e-mail to their respective members, notifying them of the impending FDA consumer warning (Exhibit 11-2a). The next day, the UFPA sponsored a joint membership conference call co-hosted by all four industry associations (Exhibit 11-2b). More than 200 industry members joined the call to get the latest updates from scientific and communication staff. Over the weekend, the UFPA sent five e-mail updates to members, and on Monday, select pages on the new association's Web site were functional and dedicated to information about the crisis.

Media communication was equally important. By the time the crisis team assembled at 6:00 a.m. on Friday, reporters from more than 50 different media outlets had contacted the UFPA. Over the first 72 hours, more than 500 media calls came in. Written statements answered some questions, but most reporters wanted fresh quotes and more details, which required phone or on-camera interviews. Amy Philpott, vice president of communications at the UFPA, put into place a triage system in which calls from national media outlets or wire services were returned first in the order of their deadline, then calls from reporters in high-density membership areas, and then others. "The first two days, Our Senior Vice President of Food Safety Dr. James Gorny and I were on the phone with reporters non-stop from 6 a.m. to well past the late night news hour and we still left the office with a list of unreturned calls," said Philpott. Through consistent messaging and broad outreach, news reports picked up two key association messages: The industry was cooperating with officials and committed to protecting public health.

Industry partner communications were critical to presenting a unified industry message to the media and members. Regularly scheduled conference calls enabled the various industry association stakeholders to quickly and accurately coordinate information. During a call among the four primary industry associations, the UFPA proposed that the groups hold a joint press conference that afternoon on Friday, September 15, at the National Press Club in Washington, D.C., so that the industry could get a statement on the evening news before the weekend. The other groups felt equally strongly that the industry should wait until it knew more and possibly hold a press conference on the following Monday or Tuesday. In the end, the UFPA held a press conference on Friday as proposed (Exhibit 11-2c), and the other groups held a joint press conference the following week in Salinas, California. This fundamental difference in crisis management philosophy created tension within the alliance, despite continued collaboration, sharing of information, joint statements, and common message development.

Initially, the messaging framework focused on how the industry was cooperating with federal, state, and local health authorities; the concern for public health; and that only spinach was being investigated—all other leafy greens were not implicated. After the scientific evidence linked the outbreak to spinach, the messaging framework focused on the industry's commitment to determining the specific source of the contamination and working to make sure it would not happen again. Messaging still included assurances that other leafy greens were not involved in the outbreak and were safe to eat. After September 29, the messaging focused on the outbreak being over and on the industry's food safety improvements:

> FDA's confirmation that the outbreak has been tied definitively to spinach from only one food processor clears the way for consumers to once again feel confident that all of the spinach they consume is safe.... And while we continually invest millions of dollars annually to analyze and enhance existing [food safety] systems, we pledge to do more.

The industry partners also communicated jointly with government health officials. The FDA held daily industry briefings by conference call during which industry associations received the latest information on the FDA, CDC, and state investigations followed by a question and answer session. These conference calls ensured that all industry partners were receiving the same information at the same time, which also helped in developing consistent messaging. The UFPA also provided background briefings to members of Congress who need to address constituent calls and concerns.

LESSONS LEARNED

A balance of written and verbal communication was key to effectively communicating among industry groups with government officials and to the industry membership. Although Web-based communication was efficient, in the first few days, it tended to generate more questions and phone calls while the conference calls drastically reduced both. "The biggest advantage of holding the conference calls was that everyone could hear one another's questions and the answers at the same time," said Philpott.

The Internet played a new role in this case. The outbreak was essentially foreshadowed on the Internet the day before the FDA announced it. In the future, it may be that entire outbreaks are unofficially announced on the Internet before science and the government can verify them as a threat to public health. This will no doubt create new communication challenges.

Another lesson to be learned from this case is that risk communication can be especially challenging when it comes to foodborne illness outbreaks. For example, the irony in the spinach case is that only with the benefit of hindsight do we now know that the outbreak was likely over before the FDA issued its first consumer warning. According to Philpott,

(United Fresh Produce Association)

this is because we are always looking in a rear view mirror when it comes to foodborne illness outbreaks. With the current detection and reporting systems, there are roughly two to three weeks between when a person becomes ill and when they are determined to be part of an outbreak. So the information that FDA and CDC give to consumers (and the media) is a reflection of what happened about 15 days ago.

On September 14, when the FDA issued its consumer warning, it did so based on the latest data, which reflected the number of illnesses on or about August 31. On September 29, when the FDA revised its statement and spinach could be sold again in the market, the epidemiological case data showed that the outbreak was over on or about September 15. The illnesses reported after this date represented people who had become ill at least two to three weeks earlier. However, the public perception was that the outbreak was getting worse day by day, when in fact, it was likely already over. No one can fault the health authorities for making the initial announcement based on the information they had, but the inherent delay in the reporting process puts into question the ability to engage in effective risk communication in these situations. The time period between when a person first becomes ill and when he/she is recognized as part of an outbreak must somehow be reduced in order to make risk communication most effective.

Finally, UFPA President Tom Stenzel summarized the most important lesson learned when he said, "Nothing compares with the human impact of the outbreak. Embracing that fact emotionally is what helps drive industry recovery. And although science tells us that there is no such thing as zero risk that is exactly what the produce industry is continuing to strive for in its food safety measures."

REFERENCES

United Fresh Produce Association. September 29, 2006. News Release: "FDA Further Isolates Outbreak; Consumers to Enjoy Spinach Again."

U.S. Food and Drug Administration. September 14, 2006. "FDA Warning on Serious Foodborne *E. Coli* O157:H7 Outbreak." http://www.fda.gov/bbs/topics/NEWS/2006/NEWS01450.html. Accessed on September 14, 2006.

U.S. Food and Drug Administration. September 15, 2006. "FDA Statement on Foodborne *E. Coli* O157:H7 Outbreak in Spinach Update." http://www.fda.gov/bbs/topics/NEWS/2006/NEWS01451.html. Accessed on September 15, 2006.

U.S. Food and Drug Administration. September 29, 2006. "FDA Announces Findings from Investigation of Foodborne *E. Coli* O157:H7 Outbreak in Spinach." http://www.fda.gov/bbs/topics/NEWS/2006/NEWS01474.html. Accessed on September 29, 2006.

E X H I B I T 11-2a Background

United Fresh
PRODUCE ASSOCIATION

1901 Pennsylvania Avenue, NW
Washington, DC 20006
September 14, 2006
Contact: Amy Philpott 202/303-3425
Dr. Jim Gorny 530) 756-8900

Background on Multi-State
E. Coli Outbreak
FDA To Issue Press Release

FDA informed us today of an ongoing investigation of a multi-state outbreak of foodborne illness caused by *E. coli* O157:H7. Preliminary epidemiological evidence suggests that this outbreak may be related to spinach.

The outbreak currently includes one death and about 40 reported cases of illness in Oregon, Wisconsin, Utah, New Mexico, and Minnesota. The appropriate federal and state regulatory authorities are working to determine the source of the outbreak.

FDA indicated it would issue a press release on the issue and we expect consumer publicity on this tonight, over the weekend and into next week.

We are monitoring this story closely, and are fully prepared to address any and all media questions or consumer inquiries that may arise. We have developed talking points which you may find helpful in answering questions should they arise. In addition, please feel free to refer any media calls that you would like us to handle.

Courtesy United Fresh Produce Association

EXHIBIT 11-2b   Member Alert

United Fresh
PRODUCE ASSOCIATION

Member Alert
Joint Alliance, PMA, United Fresh, WGA Industry Information Call

September 15, 2006

Contacts : Amy Philpott, aphilpott@unitedfresh.org
(202) 303-3400 ext. 425
Dr. Jim Gorny, jgorny@unitedfresh.org
(530) 756-8900

Yesterday, The U.S. Food and Drug Administration (FDA) informed the industry and issued a press release regarding an ongoing investigation of a multi-state foodborne illness outbreak caused *by E. coli* O157:H7. In addition, the FDA has advised consumers to not eat bagged spinach.

In order to effectively and efficiently address the industry's concerns and questions, the Food for Farming Alliance, Produce Marketing Association, United Fresh Produce Association, and Western Growers Association held a conference call today to discuss the issue.

You can listen to a recording of the call by dialing 1 888-xxx-xxxx and entering the access code: xxxxxx. The recording will be available until 23:59 on September 16.

Courtesy United Fresh Produce Association

E X H I B I T 11-2c   Statement to the Media

Statement to the Media

United Fresh Produce Association

Washington, D.C.

September 15, 2006, 4:00 pm eastern time

Today at 4:00 p.m. Eastern Time, Tom Stenzel, president & CEO of the United Fresh Produce Association, issued the following statement regarding the multi state *E. coli* outbreak.

The fresh produce industry is extremely concerned that anyone may have become ill from consuming fresh spinach. The illnesses and death that have been reported are a tragedy. The industry is working closely with the FDA and other health authorities to ensure that there is no further risk to the public health. We are also working to determine the potential source of this problem and ensure that this type of outbreak does not occur again.

Media Contact:

Amy Philpott, Vice President, Marketing & Industry Relations

Office 202-303-3400

Courtesy United Fresh Produce Association

Integrated Marketing Communications

12

Integrated Marketing
Communications

Public relations has long been used as a tool for marketing products and services to consumers, but in the past, public relations was segregated or
departmentalized as a function separate from product advertising. Public relations
advertising was strictly defined as advertising used to accomplish public relations
objectives, such as image enhancement, not the sale of products or services.

Since the 1990s, integrated marketing communications (IMC) has become
increasingly more popular in promoting the products and services of corporate
America. IMC simply combines the operations of traditional public relations
with traditional marketing and advertising. One pioneering definition of IMC
is the following:

What is integrated marketing communications? It's a new way of looking at
the whole, where once we only saw parts such as advertising, public relations,
sales promotion, purchasing, employee communications, and so forth. It's rea-
ligning communications to look at it the way the customer sees it—as a flow
of information from indistinguishable sources. Professional communicators have
always been condescendingly amused that consumers called everything "advertising" or "PR." Now they recognize with concern if not chagrin that that's
exactly the point—it is all one thing, at least to the consumer who sees or
hears it.[1]

Like the major forms of public relations discussed in this book, IMC can be
clearly understood using the ROPE process.

RESEARCH

Research for IMC may include investigation of the client, the reason for the program, and the publics or "stakeholders"[2] to be targeted.

Client Research

The usual background information needed for other forms of public relations is also necessary in the research phase of IMC: detailed analysis of the client's product or service, its personnel, financial status, and general reputation in its field. A frequently used tool in marketing is the SWOT analysis. SWOT stands for strengths, weaknesses, opportunities, and threats. To begin, the strengths and weaknesses of the client's products or services in the marketplace versus those of the competition should be honestly appraised. With this analysis in hand, the practitioner should assess opportunities or ways by which the client might best increase the market share of its products or services in competitive situations. Finally, an assessment of external threats, or factors that might work against the client, should be made.[3]

Opportunity or Problem Research

The most obvious reason for any marketing program is to sell the client's merchandise, programs, or services. The traditional product-oriented marketing model focuses on the four Ps: product, price, place, and promotion. This process begins with the underlying assumption that a company decides what product to manufacture; then prices it; distributes it in particular places, locations, or outlets; and finally promotes the product in an essentially one-way mode of communication, usually mass media product advertising.[4]

IMC, on the other hand, begins with the assumption that the needs of the consumers and other stakeholders should come first. This, in turn, calls for an audience-centered, transactional model. Instead of simply selling products, IMC attempts to create *relationships* with consumers and other stakeholders. In addition to striving to get consumers to purchase products, IMC strives to get support and loyalty from consumers and other stakeholders. Often called brand loyalty, these enduring relationships are built on good two-way communication and an understanding of underlying values, needs, and motivations.

Audience Research

IMC audience research, or stakeholder research, consists of using both nonquantitative and quantitative research methods to learn as much as possible about the groups to be targeted for communication. These stakeholder groups include:

Customers

New customers

Old customers

Potential customers

Employees

Management

Nonmanagement

Sales and marketing staff

Customer relations departments

Human resources staff

Individuals staffing phone call centers

Media

Mass

Specialized

Investors

Shareowners and potential shareowners

Financial analysts

Financial press

Suppliers

Competitors

Government regulators

Attitudes, behaviors, media habits, psychographic (value-oriented segmentation), and other demographic data about stakeholders are important research information in IMC.

OBJECTIVES

IMC may use both impact and output objectives.

Impact Objectives

Impact objectives may affect stakeholders by informing them or by modifying their attitudes or behaviors. Examples might include the following:

1. To increase (by 20 percent) the stakeholder's knowledge and awareness of the company's new product (during the next six months)

2. To enhance (by 15 percent) positive attitude formation toward the company's product (during the current year)

3. To increase customer purchases of the client's product (by 50 percent) during the current year

Output Objectives

Output objectives for IMC consist of measurable efforts for the client's program:

1. To increase print advertising in major metropolitan dailies by 10 percent during the sale period
2. To schedule five special events for the client's sales campaign during August

PROGRAMMING

As with the various forms of public relations, IMC may begin with planning the theme and messages. The uniqueness of IMC programming is that it combines the activities of traditional advertising with traditional public relations.

Theme and Messages (consistent, single voice) Advertising

> Print
> Broadcast
>> Radio
>> TV
> Direct Mail
> Telemarketing
> Point-of-purchase
> Specialty advertising

Public Relations

> Uncontrolled
>> Print
>> Broadcast
> Controlled
>> Print
>> Audiovisual
>> Interpersonal
>> Online (Web sites, to include social media sites, search engine optimization, banner ads, e-mail, webinars, and blogs)
>> Action or special events

IMC programming involves a strategic approach. Each public relation component should complement and reinforce marketing efforts. Also, public relations may be more effective with some audiences while direct marketing may work better with other groups. Yet together advertising and public relations form a seamless whole to accomplish essentially marketing goals.

Effective Communication

Since IMC seeks to establish interactive communication between client and stakeholders, the same principles of effective communication apply to it as to public relations. Of special interest to marketing communicators using IMC are the principles of source credibility, two-way communication, and audience participation. IMC is concerned with long-range consumer loyalty, not just the quick, one-shot sale of merchandise. The client's reputation thus becomes a matter of paramount concern. Customer involvement with the client or company is another major hallmark of IMC. Well-established interactive public relations techniques are a decisive advantage in such communication transactions.

EVALUATION

The success of IMC programs should be determined by tracking stated objectives. Impact and output objectives can be measured using the standard tools of public relations programs, as outlined in Chapter 2.

SUMMARY

IMC involves a combination of traditional advertising and public relations practices. The ROPE process is a convenient model for this relatively new field, which brings together separated categories of advertising and public relations into a unified communications campaign.

ENDNOTES

1. Don E. Schultz, Stanley I. Tannenbaum, and Robert F. Lauterborn, *Integrated Marketing Communications* (Chicago: NTC Business Books, 1993), p. xvii.

2. Stakeholders is the preferred term for IMC audiences. See Thomas L. Harris, *Value-Added Public Relations* (Chicago: NTC Business Books, 1998), p. 124, for a concise definition of stakeholders. Also see Tom Duncan and Sandra Moriarty, *Driving Brand Value* (New York: McGraw-Hill, 1997), chap. 4, for a more complete discussion of this concept.

3. For discussions of SWOT, see Harris, *Value-Added Public Relations*, p. 235, and Duncan and Moriarty, *Driving Brand Value*, pp. 149–152.

4. For a discussion of four-Ps theory, see Schultz, Tannenbaum, and Lauterborn, *Integrated Marketing Communications*, pp. 5 and 12.

READINGS ON INTEGRATED MARKETING COMMUNICATIONS

Blakeman, Robyn. *Integrated Marketing Communication: Creative Strategy from Idea to Implementation*. Lanham, MD: Rowman & Littlefield Publishers, 2007.

Debreceny, Peter, and Lisa Cochrane. "Two Disciplines on the Same Road," *Advertising Age* 75 (November 8, 2004): 28.

Eagle, Lynne, and Philip J. Kitchen. "IMC Brand Communications and Corporate Cultures: Client/Advertising Agency Co-Ordination and Cohesion," *European Journal of Marketing* 34 (May–June 2000): 667ff.

Edmondson, Jan. "Come Together: Why Integrated Marketing Works," *Public Relations Tactics* 7 (January 2000): 12.

Elliott, Susan, ed. *Integrated Marketing Communications*. Houston, TX: American Productivity and Quality Center, 1998.

Fernando, Angelo. "Creating Buzz: New Media Tactics Have Changed the PR and Advertising Game," *Communication World* 21 (November–December 2004): 10–11.

Harris, Thomas L. *Value-Added Public Relations*. Chicago: NTC Business Books, 1998.

Henry, Rene A., Jr. *Marketing Public Relations: The Hows That Make It Work*. Ames: Iowa State University Press, 1995.

Heslop, Janet. *The American Marketplace: Demographics and Spending Pattern*, 8th ed. Ithaca, NY: New Strategist Publications, 2007.

"How PR Gives Super Bowl Advertisers More Bang for Their Integrated Marketing Bucks," *PR News* 64 (March 2008).

Hutton, James G. "Defining the Relationship between Public Relations and Marketing: Public Relations' Most Important Challenge," in Heath, Robert L. ed. *Handbook of Public Relations*. Thousand Oaks, CA: Sage, 2004.

Jones, Susan K. *Creative Strategy in Direct Marketing*, 3d ed. Lincolnwood, IL: NTC/Contemporary Publishing, 2005.

Lundstrom, William J., and David Watkins. "Social Cause Dissemination and Feedback Using Multimedia and Internet-Based Techniques: The Case for Equality in Education," *Journal of Public Affairs* 5 (February 2005): 66–70.

Nash, Edward L. *Direct Marketing: Strategy, Planning, Execution*. New York: McGraw-Hill, 2000.

Page, Russell. "Michelin Americas Truck Tires with Jackson-Dawson Integrated Marketing Communications," *Public Relations Tactics* 10 (September 2003): 24.

Percy, Larry. *Strategic Integrated Marketing Communications*. Oxford: Butterworth-Heinemann, 2008.

Pickton, David, and Amanda Broderick. *Integrated Marketing Communications*, 2d ed. Englewood Cliffs, NJ: Prentice-Hall, 2005.

Ratnatunga, Janek, and Michael T. Ewing. "The Brand Capability Value of Integrated Marketing Communication," *Journal of Advertising* 34 (winter 2005): 25–41.

Reid, Mike, Sandra Luxton, and Felix Mavondo. "The Relationship Between Integrated Marketing Communication, Market Orientation and Brand Orientation," *Journal of Advertising* 34 (winter 2005): 11–24.

Ries, Al, and Laura Ries. *The Fall of Advertising and the Rise of PR*. New York: HarperCollins, 2002.

"Rise of New Media and Integrated Marketing Challenge Measurement," *PR News* 63 (February 2007): 1.

Rothenberg, Randall. "Despite All the Talk, Ad and Media Shops Still Aren't Truly Integrated," *Advertising Age* 77 (March 2006): 24–25.

Samli, A. Coskun, and John S. Hill. *Marketing Globally: Planning and Practice*. Lincolnwood, IL: NTC/Contemporary Publishing, 1998.

Schmidt, Jack, and Alan Weber. *Desktop Database Marketing*. Lincolnwood, IL: NTC/Contemporary Publishing, 1998.

Schultz, Don E. "Outdated Approach to Planning Needs Revamping," *Marketing News* 36 (November 11, 2002): 6–7.

Semenik, Richard J. *Promotion and Integrated Marketing Communications*. Cincinnati, OH: South-Western Thomson Learning, 2002.

Sevier, Robert. "Solutions for Marketing Strategies," *University Business* 8 (July 2005): 35–41.

Shimp, Terence A. *Advertising, Promotion, and Other Aspects of Integrated Marketing Communications*, 7th ed. Mason, OH: Thomson/South-Western, 2007.

Stammerjohan, Claire, Charles M. Wood, Yuhmiin Change, and Esther Thorson. "An Empirical Investigation of the Interaction Between Publicity, Advertising, and Previous Brand Attitudes and Knowledge," *Journal of Advertising* 34 (winter 2005): 55–67.

Stevens, Joanna. "Yahoo! PR Events Sing with the Yodel Challenge," *Communication World* 22 (September–October 2005): 40–142.

Swain, William N. "Perceptions of IMC After a Decade of Development: Who's at the Wheel, and How Can We Measure Success?" *Journal of Advertising Research* 44 (March 2004): 46ff.

Thorson, Esther, and Jeri Moore. *Integrated Communication*. Mahwah, NJ: Erlbaum, 1996.

Weiner, Mark. "Marketing PR Revolution," *Communication World* 22 (January–February 2005): 20–25.

"Whatever Happened to Integrated Marketing Communications?" *PR News* 63 (June 2007).

Integrated Marketing Communications Cases

Case 12-1

Women have a tendency to dismiss heart attacks as a man's problem. Changing their attitudes and changing behavior to reduce health risks required a major campaign to convince them that women also were at risk. The "Heart Truth Campaign" started with a fashion week event in 2003 and has blossomed into a multifaceted series of activities that has captured broad national exposure each year since the inaugural campaign. Exhibit 12-1a is the 2003 Red Dress Project announcement, Exhibit 12-1b is an infographic fact sheet, Exhibit 12-1c is an "action plan" target to African American women, and Exhibit 12-1d is a news release on the program's success.

A Fashionable Red Alert Warns Women of The Heart Truth

National Heart, Lung, and Blood Institute, with Ogilvy Public Relations Worldwide

SUMMARY

In 2000, only 34 percent of women knew that their #1 killer is heart disease. Yet, one in three women dies of heart disease, eight times more than breast cancer, and misperceptions about the disease abound—including the belief that it's only a man's disease. This crisis demanded action. The Heart Truth campaign and its Red Dress symbol, created by the National Heart, Lung, and Blood Institute (NHLBI) and Ogilvy Public Relations Worldwide, have sparked a powerful awareness movement within the national women's health community, the media, and corporate America—reaching women nationwide.

Courtesy The National Heart, Lung, and Blood Institute

RESEARCH

The Heart Truth evolved through extensive primary and secondary formative research:

- A comprehensive analysis of mid-life women: demographics, psychographics, geographic and socioeconomic factors, cardiovascular health knowledge, attitudes and behaviors, media preferences

- An NHLBI-conducted literature review of 200+ research articles on cardiovascular health and women

- Eight focus groups in four cities across the country to test creative concepts and messages; and Materials review by the campaign's core government and community organization partners

This research informed a range of elements in the planning process, including target audience selection, message and materials development, channel and activity selection, and partner recruitment.

PLANNING

Objectives

Since its launch, The Heart Truth has continually aimed to:

- Increase awareness that heart disease is the #1 killer of women

- Increase awareness of the risk factors that can lead to heart disease, disability, and death

- Encourage women to talk to their doctors and take action to control these risk factors

Strategic Approach

The Heart Truth primarily targets women ages 40–60 (an age when risk increases), with a secondary target of women ages 18–39. The Heart Truth team prepared an extensive national marketing, media relations, and public service campaign, building relationships with partners who could help reinforce messages at all levels of society. Beyond the communications impact these proven strategies would deliver, we knew that women needed a striking wake-up call to change their thinking—and perhaps even save their lives. The Heart Truth triumphed with its centerpiece creative element, the Red Dress, paired with the tagline: "Heart Disease Doesn't Care What You Wear—It's the #1 Killer of Women." Why a Red Dress? It was proven in focus groups with women to forge a strong emotional link between a woman's focus on her outer self and the need to focus on her inner self—specifically her heart health. Like the pink ribbon for breast cancer, the Red Dress icon gives the cause an unforgettable identity and has proven to be a rallying symbol for partners, media, and women with heart disease.

EXECUTION

To reach women, The Heart Truth campaign has delivered messages through:

- Creative design using compelling photos and stories of real women's struggles with heart disease, which put a face on women's heart disease and provided consistent branding across materials

- Educational and marketing materials—including a 100-page Healthy Heart Handbook for Women and a Speaker's Kit (with a 10-minute video and PowerPoint presentation)—to promote heart health

- A Web site with ideas and materials to help audiences plan Heart Truth events (www.hearttruth.gov)

- National public service advertising (print, radio, and television)

- Partnerships with national nonprofit organizations reinforced at the local level, including WomenHeart, the American Heart Association (AHA), American College of Cardiology, Association of Black Cardiologists, Hadassah, National Black Nurses Association, General Federation of Women's Clubs, the National Association of Latina Leaders, and The Links,Inc.

- Corporate and media partnerships with Mercedes-Benz Fashion Week, IMG Models, Time Inc. Women's Group, GLAMOUR, Wal-Mart, RadioShack, California Pistachio Commission, Swarovski, Inc., Olympus Fashion Week, Johnson & Johnson, Albertsons, Smart Ones, General Mills (Berry Burst Cheerios and 8th Continent Soy Milk brands), Celestial Seasonings, and Minute Maid

Seeking to mobilize an industry intrinsically tied to the target audience, The Heart Truth team forged a groundbreaking collaboration between the federal government and the fashion industry to launch the Red Dress as the national symbol for women and heart disease awareness. The value of the fashion-based partnerships alone—to launch the Red Dress in 2003 and expand campaign messaging through Fashion Week activities during American Heart Month in 2004 and 2005—is conservatively valued at more than $6 million. Programming to advance the Red Dress and campaign messages from February 2003 through March 2005 included:

- A partnership with 7th on Sixth (producers of Fashion Week), IMG and IMG Models, and title sponsor Mercedes-Benz to name women and heart disease awareness as the "cause" for Mercedes-Benz Fashion Week in

February 2003 in New York. Nineteen top fashion designers—from Vera Wang and Donna Karan to Oscar de la Renta and Ralph Lauren—contributed red dresses to a weeklong launch exhibit, and acclaimed jewelry designer Angela Cummings created a Red Dress Pin to launch the symbol

- The participation of one of the most recognizable women in the world—First Lady Laura Bush—to champion the cause and introduce the government's campaign and its symbol under the Bryant Park tents at Fashion Week, including appearances on all of the network morning shows on February 14, 2003, and again in February 2004 and 2005

- Corporate and media partnerships secured by Ogilvy PR subsequent to the February 2003 launch of the Red Dress Project, including Time Inc. Women's Group, GLAMOUR, Wal-Mart, RadioShack, California Pistachio Commission, Swarovski, Inc., Johnson & Johnson, Albertsons, General Mills, and Smart Ones, among others

- A press conference in Washington, D.C., hosted by U.S. Department of Health and Human Services secretary Tommy Thompson, who issued a proclamation declaring "Women's Heart Day"

- Production, placement, and sales of the Red Dress Pin at Wal-Mart in time for Mother's Day 2003 resulting in mainstream media coverage of the pin (*Parade* and *USA Today*)

- GLAMOUR magazine's partnership debut in a 15-page cover-story spread in October 2003, featuring Shania Twain on the cover, an exclusive interview with the First Lady, a foldout of 24 celebrities in red dresses, and a three-year editorial commitment about the issue

- Launch of the LifeWise Heart Truth Pledge program with RadioShack's LifeWise brand of wellness products, encouraging women to make one small change every month to improve their heart health

- Placement of oversized store banners and end cap displays in Albertsons stores nationwide that highlighted the campaign's real women in red and sale of Red Dress Pins and The Heart Truth T-shirts, along with free distribution of 250,000 copies of The Healthy Heart Handbook for Women

- More than 100 local Heart Truth events spearheaded by partners (e.g., health fairs, dances, walks, rallies, celebrity teas, power breakfasts, red dress fashion shows), including 31 Heart Truth Single City Stops across the country; with five community hospital events hosted by Mrs. Bush featuring local heart patients and presentation of campaign messaging to community leaders, local media, and local heart health organizations

- A Heart Truth campaign press event at The White House featuring President and Mrs. Bush declaring February 2004 as American Heart Month and announcing upcoming Heart Truth campaign efforts

- Woman's Day magazine's recognition of the NHLBI/Ogilvy PR Heart Truth team as innovators in women's heart health awareness with an inaugural Red Dress Award presented in February 2004

- The creation of the first annual National Wear Red Day (February 6, 2004) and the same-day debut of the Red Dress Collection 2004 at Olympus Fashion Week with a star-studded fashion show featuring 26 new designs worn by top fashion models and celebrities such as Vanessa Williams and Beverly Johnson, hosted by Patti Hansen

- Implementation of The Heart Truth Road Show in five U.S. cities from March to May 2004 reaching more than 86,000 consumers, exhibiting designer red dresses (including Mrs. Bush's own red Oscar de la Renta suit), and offering free heart health screenings to more than 4,000 individuals

- Adoption of the Red Dress symbol by a full range of campaign partners, including the American Heart Association's introduction of its complementary campaign in February 2004, Go Red for Women

- WomenHeart's expanded cause-marketing program with companies such as CIGNA to launch its Red Bag of Courage in early 2005 with information for patients with heart disease

- Launch of The Heart Truth's Communities of Color initiative at a February 4, 2005, press event in New York featuring First Lady Laura Bush, Duchess of York Sarah Ferguson, Dr. Anne Taylor of the Association of Black Cardiologists, and Dr. Elizabeth G. Nabel, director of NHLBI

- Ongoing development of corporate partner programs to utilize distribution and promotional channels reaching tens of millions of women, including a J&J-sponsored retail FSI (Free-Standing Newspaper Insert) in November 2004, the debut of the first-ever on-pack promotion with 8th Continent in the fall of 2004, the launch of the Berry Burst Cheerios box featuring the Red Dress in February 2005, and Minute Maid packaging featuring the Red Dress symbol through a partnership with WomenHeart

- Debut of the Red Dress Collection 2005 on the second annual National Wear Red Day—February 4, 2005—featuring 26 new designs showcased by celebrities from the arts, sports, and entertainment industries, such as Vanessa Williams, Venus Williams, Paula Abdul, Sheryl Crow, Rosanna Arquette, Phylicia Rashad, Sarah Ferguson, Christie Brinkley, Carly Patterson, and Carmen Dell'Orefice

EVALUATION

The most significant outcome of The Heart Truth is the number of women who are now aware that heart disease is their #1 health threat. An encouraging and steady rise in awareness of heart disease as the leading killer of U.S. women has occurred in recent years. In AHA's 2000 survey, only 34 percent of women spontaneously listed heart disease as women's leading cause of death, a figure that jumped to 57 percent in 2004—less than two years following The Heart Truth launch. As well, 18 months after the Red Dress launch, 25 percent of American women identified the Red Dress as the national symbol for women and heart disease awareness, according to a national survey commissioned in Fall 2004 by Ogilvy PR. This heightened awareness was confirmed again in January 2005 in a survey commissioned by WomenHeart, a founding partner of The Heart Truth.

In addition, The Heart Truth and its Red Dress have amassed impressive process evaluation results:

- Women-targeted and health-focused coverage in major national and local media totals 1,089,242,427 audience impressions (does not include multipliers or pass along rates): Television PSAs garnered nearly 206 million impressions (January–December 2003), radio PSAs gained close to 187 million impressions during their first two months, and airport dioramas currently appear in approximately 22 major airports—often in multiple locations—representing an advertising equivalent of approximately $7 million

  - Color PSA placements in Essence, Parenting, Health, Heart & Soul, BabyTalk, People en Español, and Balance, representing an advertising value close to $500,000 and total impressions of more than 25 million

  - 795,000 Red Dress pins, more than 300,000 copies of the Healthy Heart Handbook, and more than 250,000 Heart Truth brochures (in English and Spanish) distributed

  - More than 20 corporate relationships secured and developed to reach tens of millions of women through promotional programming

  - Four national FSIs—Johnson & Johnson, REACH, General Mills, and Promise—with a combined circulation of 165 million

  - 14.6 million General Mills products feature the Red Dress on packaging

  - Working with partners, The Heart Truth Road Show traveled to five U.S. cities, exhibiting designer red dresses (including Mrs. Bush's) and offering free heart health screenings—more than 86,000 consumers were reached, with nearly 4,000 being screened for heart disease risk factors

  - Core campaign programs, including the Single City Stop program, First Lady events, and health professional conference outreach, resulted in more than 50 events in communities around the country. In addition to these targeted campaign initiatives, organizations and individuals

> executed hundreds of local community events across the country to spread The Heart Truth, including more than 100 events registered in The Heart Truth activity registry

Women's health experts and heart disease thought leaders have acknowledged that the tide is turning in women's awareness of the importance of taking care of their heart. Moreover, these experts believe that The Heart Truth is the engine behind much of this increased attention and awareness.

Of course, there is no greater reward for a public health campaign than proof that it has saved lives. An event in Kansas City, Missouri, featuring remarks by the First Lady, did just that for one woman: "A 54-year-old woman presented to our Emergency Department after being awakened several times during the night with chest discomfort After our wonderful media coverage, the patient confirmed that the surrounding media about the leading cause of death in women and the seriousness of women's heart health prompted her to take personal action—what impact!"

E X H I B I T 12-1a   Red Dress Project

HEART DISEASE IS THE #1 KILLER OF WOMEN

THE RED DRESS PROJECT
**Fashion makes a statement for women and heart disease
at Mercedes-Benz Fashion Week**

*Heart disease is not just a man's disease—it's the #1 killer of women.
The Red Dress Project makes the statement in high fashion introducing the "Red
Dress" as the new symbol for women and heart disease.*

The Heart Truth is a national awareness campaign on women's heart health
sponsored by the National Heart, Lung, and Blood Institute (NHLBI), part of the
National Institutes of Health, U.S. Department of Health and Human Services
(DHHS). The campaign is being conducted in partnership with the American
Heart Association, the Office on Women's Health (DHHS), WomenHeart: the
National Coalition for Women with Heart Disease, and other organizations
committed to women's health.

The primary message driving *The Heart Truth* campaign is: Heart disease is
not just a man's disease—it's the #1 killer of women. The campaign pairs the
message with an arresting visual—the Red Dress—as the national symbol for
women and heart disease.

The Red Dress is the heart of the Red Dress Project debuting at Mercedes-Benz
Fashion Week, February 7-14, 2003, in New York during American Heart
Month. This groundbreaking project, supported by Mercedes-Benz USA and
7ᵗʰ on Sixth (the producers of Mercedes-Benz Fashion Week), launches the red
dress icon to raise awareness of women's risk of heart disease. According to a
national survey conducted in 2000, only a third of women know that heart
disease is the leading cause of death for women.

Why a Red Dress?
The Red Dress has proved to be a positive image to convey heart disease
awareness messages targeted to women. Focus group research across the
country showed that most women:
- Were aware of most major risk factors for heart disease and knew
  about heart-healthy behaviors—but had not adopted a heart-healthy
  lifestyle.

(over)

U.S. DEPARTMENT OF HEALTH AND HUMAN SERVICES ♥ National Institutes of Health ♥ National Heart, Lung, and Blood Institute

Dress illustration adapted from pen design created by Angela Cummings Studio for the Red Dress Project

---

EXHIBIT 12-1a   (Continued)

- Underestimated their personal risk (most thought they had a low to medium personal risk for heart disease even though they had risk factors such as smoking, high blood pressure, and high cholesterol).
- Did not fully understand the devastating impact that heart disease has on one's life and one's family.

The Red Dress Project is designed to build awareness that women are at risk; give a sense of hope that women can reduce their risk, and empower them to do so; and provide a clear call to action coupled with a sense of urgency.

The Red Dress Project

The Red Dress Project of *The Heart Truth* campaign puts the issue of women and heart disease in the national spotlight through a partnership with the Mercedes-Benz Fashion Week and the fashion industry.

Leading fashion designers contributed red dresses from either vintage or current collections to be showcased in the Red Dress Collection at Bryant Park throughout Mercedes-Benz Fashion Week.* A Red Dress pin, specially designed for *The Heart Truth* campaign by leading accessory designer Angela Cummings, will be introduced during Mercedes-Benz Fashion Week.

Mercedes-Benz USA presents the exclusive Mercedes-Benz Fashion Week magma red C320 Sports Coupe to be displayed at Bryant Park. In addition, the display area features an illustration of Angela Lindvall, Cover Girl, wearing a Donna Karan red dress photographed by David LaChapelle. The Red Dress Project of *The Heart Truth* campaign will be unveiled at a media briefing when Mercedes-Benz Fashion Week opens on Friday, February 7.

After Mercedes-Benz Fashion Week, the Red Dress Project will make a stop in Washington, D.C. before heading on a national tour.

For more information about the Red Dress Project, contact Sally McDonough at (202) 452-7815 or by mobile at (571) 259-1481. Photography supporting the Red Dress Project is available at http://www.nhlbi.nih.gov/health/hearttruth/press/press.htm.

*Participating Designers:

Bill Blass	Anne Klein	Badgley Mischka
Chaiken	Calvin Klein	Oscar de la Renta
Diane von Furstenberg	Michael Kors	Vivienne Tam
Carolina Herrera	Ralph Lauren	Carmen Marc Valvo
Tommy Hilfiger	Luca Luca	Vera Wang
Marc Jacobs	Catherine Malandrino	
Donna Karan	Nicole Miller	

EXHIBIT 12-1b Infographic

THE HEART TRUTH IS: HEART DISEASE IS A WOMEN'S ISSUE

Heart Disease is the #1 killer of women, regardless of race or ethnicity. Although significant progress has been made in raising awareness among women about heart disease, from 34 percent to 57 percent in just 4 years, most women fail to make the connection between risk factors, such as high blood pressure and high cholesterol, and their personal risk of developing heart disease. Only 20 percent of women identify heart disease as the greatest health problem facing women today, and awareness levels are lower among African American and Hispanic women. Experts at the National Heart, Lung, and Blood Institute encourage women to talk to their doctors to find out their personal risk for heart disease and how they can take action to lower it. For more information, visit www.hearttruth.gov.

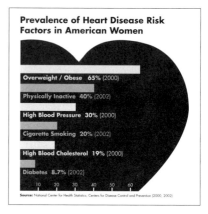

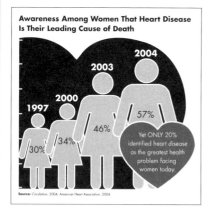

The Heart Truth is a national awareness campaign for women about heart disease sponsored by the National Heart, Lung, and Blood Institute, part of the National Institutes of Health, U.S. Department of Health and Human Services.

To access camera-ready artwork, as well as photography and other creative materials for *The Heart Truth* campaign, visit www.hearttruth.gov. If you have questions, contact media@hearttruth.org.

EXHIBIT 12-1c   Fact Sheet for African American Women

THE HEART TRUTH FOR AFRICAN AMERICAN WOMEN: AN ACTION PLAN

When you hear the term "heart disease," what's your first reaction? Like many women, you may think, "That's a man's disease." But here's *The Heart Truth*: Heart disease is the #1 killer of women in the United States. One in three women dies of heart disease.

For African American women, the risk of heart disease is especially great. Heart disease is more prevalent among black women than white women—as are some of the factors that increase the risk of developing it, including high blood pressure, overweight and obesity, and diabetes.

But there's good news too: You can take action and lower your chance of developing heart disease and its risk factors. In fact, women can lower their heart disease risk by as much as 82 percent just by leading a healthy lifestyle. This fact sheet gives steps you can take to protect your heart health.

WHAT IS HEART DISEASE?
Coronary heart disease is the most common form of heart disease. Often referred to simply as "heart disease," it is a disorder of the blood vessels of the heart that can lead to a heart attack. It is a lifelong condition and will steadily worsen unless you make changes in your daily habits.

Risk Factors for Heart Disease
Lifestyle affects many of the "risk factors" for heart disease. Risk factors are conditions or habits that increase the chances of developing a disease or having it worsen. For heart disease, there are two types—those you can't change and those you can control. The ones you can't change are a family history of early heart disease and age, which for women becomes a risk

factor at 55. That's because, after menopause, women are more likely to get heart disease. Partly, this is because their body no longer produces estrogen. Also, middle age is a time when women tend to develop other heart disease risk factors.

But most of the risk factors can be controlled. Often, all it takes are lifestyle changes; sometimes, medication also is needed. Here's a quick review of these risk factors:

Smoking. About one in five black women smokes. Quit, and just one year later, your heart disease risk will drop by more than half. There's no easy way to quit but making a plan helps. You also can try an organized program or a medication—ask your doctor if either is right for you.

High Blood Pressure. Also called hypertension, high blood pressure increases your risk of heart disease, stroke, and congestive heart failure. Even levels slightly above normal—called "prehypertension"—increase your heart disease risk.

Black women develop high blood pressure earlier in life and have higher average blood pressures compared with white women. About 37 percent of black women have high blood pressure. Hypertension also increases the risk of stroke and congestive heart failure—and black women have high rates of both.

Lower elevated blood pressure by following a heart-healthy eating plan, including limiting your intake of salt and other forms of sodium, getting regular physical activity, maintaining a healthy weight, and, if you drink alcoholic beverages, doing so in moderation (not more than one drink a day). If you have high blood pressure, you also may need to take medication.

U.S. DEPARTMENT OF HEALTH AND HUMAN SERVICES
National Institutes of Health
National Heart, Lung, and Blood Institute

E X H I B I T 12-1c   (Continued)

One good eating plan, shown to lower elevated blood pressure, is called the DASH diet—for a copy of the plan, contact the National Heart, Lung, and Blood Institute (NHLBI) Health Information Center, which is listed in "To Learn More."

High Blood Cholesterol. Nearly half of black women have a total cholesterol that's too high. Excess cholesterol and fat in your blood builds up in the walls of vessels that supply blood to the heart and can lead to blockages. A "lipoprotein profile" tests your levels of the key types of cholesterol—total, LDL ("bad"), and HDL ("good") cholesterol—and triglycerides, a fatty substance in the blood.

Lower cholesterol by following a heart-healthy eating plan, being physically active, maintaining a healthy weight, and, if needed, taking medication.

Overweight/Obesity. Nearly 80 percent of black women are overweight or obese, increasing the risk not only of heart disease but also a host of other conditions, including stroke, gallbladder disease, arthritis, and some cancers. If you're overweight, even a small weight loss will help lower your risk. At the very least, try not to gain more weight.

Lasting weight loss needs a change of lifestyle—adopt a healthy, lower-calorie eating plan and get regular physical activity. Aim to lose no more than $1/2$ to 2 pounds per week.

Physical Inactivity. Fifty-five percent of black women are physically inactive. They do no spare-time physical activity.

Physical activity is crucial for good health, including heart health. Try to do at least 30 minutes of a moderate-intensity activity such as brisk walking on most, and preferably, all days of the week. If you need to, divide the period into shorter ones of at least 10 minutes each.

Diabetes. About 11 million Americans have been diagnosed with diabetes—and another 5.7 million don't know they have it. About two-thirds of those with diabetes die of a heart or blood vessel disease.

The type of diabetes that adults most commonly develop is "type 2." Diabetes can be detected with a blood sugar test. Modest changes in diet and level of physical activity can often prevent or delay the development of diabetes.

QUESTIONS TO ASK YOUR DOCTOR

1. What is my risk for heart disease?

2. What is my blood pressure? What does it mean for me, and what do I need to do about it?

3. What are my cholesterol numbers? (These include total cholesterol, LDL, HDL, and triglycerides, a type of fat found in the blood and food.) What do they mean for me, and what do I need to do about them?

4. What are my "body mass index" (BMI) and waist measurement? Do they mean that I need to lose weight for my health?

5. What is my blood sugar level, and does it mean I'm at risk for diabetes? If so, what do I need to do about it?

6. What other screening tests for heart disease do I need?

7. What can you do to help me quit smoking?

8. How much physical activity do I need to help protect my heart?

9. What's a heart-healthy eating plan for me?

10. How can I tell if I may be having a heart attack? If I think I'm having one, what should I do?

TAKING ACTION

Now that you know *The Heart Truth*, what should you do? Begin by finding out your "risk profile." See the Box above for questions to ask your doctor. Then begin taking the steps to heart health—don't smoke, follow a heart-healthy eating plan, be physically active, and maintain a healthy weight. Start today to keep your heart strong.

TO LEARN MORE

NHLBI Health Information Center
Phone: 301-592-8573
TTY: 240-629-3255
www.hearttruth.gov

American Heart Association
Phone: 1-888-MY HEART
www.americanheart.org/simplesolutions

WomenHeart: the National Coalition for Women with Heart Disease
Phone: 202-728-7199
www.womenheart.org

Office on Women's Health
U.S. Department of Health and Human Services
National Women's Health Information Center
Phone: 1-800-994-WOMAN
TDD: 1-888-220-5446
www.4woman.gov

PAULA, age 45—"In 1991, I went to the ER with chest pains twice in one week...I had emergency surgery. But the damage was done; only 40 percent of my heart muscle functions. I am permanently disabled and had to quit a job I loved."

U.S. DEPARTMENT OF HEALTH AND HUMAN SERVICES
National Institutes of Health
National Heart, Lung, and Blood Institute

NIH Publication No. 03-5066
September 2003

EXHIBIT 12-1d   News Release

U.S. Department of Health and Human Services

NIH News
National Institutes of Health

EMBARGOED FOR RELEASE   Contact: NHLBI Communications (301) 496-4236
February 1, 2008   Email: nhlbi_news@nhlbi.nih.gov

Heart Disease Deaths Continue to Decline in American Women
On National Wear Red Day, Heart Truth campaign continues to raise awareness

New York — Heart disease deaths in American women continued to decline in 2005, and for the first time, have declined six years consecutively, covering the years 2000-2005, according to newly analyzed data announced today by the National Heart, Lung, and Blood Institute (NHLBI) of the National Institutes of Health.

NHLBI experts analyzed preliminary data for 2005, the most recent year for which data are available. The analysis shows that women are living longer and healthier lives, and dying of heart disease at much later ages than in the past years.

In New York City today, *The Heart Truth*—NHLBI's landmark heart health awareness campaign for women—rolls out the red carpet for its Red Dress Collection 2008 Fashion Show —presented by Diet Coke, with national sponsors Johnson & Johnson, Swarovski, and partner Bobbi Brown Cosmetics—at Mercedes-Benz Fashion Week. More than 20 celebrated women will unite with America's top designers on the runway to showcase the annual collection of one-of-a-kind Red Dresses and raise awareness of heart disease in women.

"Nothing draws attention like a little red dress, so this is the Heart Truth's symbol," said First Lady Laura Bush, official national ambassador of *The Heart Truth* campaign. "Across the country, people are rallying around that dress. Women are taking heart disease more seriously. So are their doctors. And every year from 2000 to 2005, heart disease deaths among women decreased."

"This is good progress," Mrs. Bush added. "But we still want more people to know The Heart Truth. Too many women, especially African American women, die of heart disease. More than 80 percent of middle-aged women have at least one risk factor and many of them don't know it."

"Considerable progress continues to be made in the fight against heart disease in women," said Elizabeth G. Nabel, M.D., director of NHLBI.

Courtesy The National Heart, Lung, and Blood Institute

EXHIBIT 12-1d (Continued)

But serious challenges remain—one in four women dies from heart disease. Women of color have higher rates of some risk factors for heart disease and are more likely to die of the disease.

"Unfortunately, many women still do not take heart disease seriously and personally," said Dr. Nabel. "Millions of women still have one or more risk factors for heart disease, dramatically increasing their risk of developing heart disease. In fact, having just one risk factor increases a woman's chance of developing heart disease twofold."

"I am just delighted that for the sixth year on National Wear Red Day, the fashion and entertainment industries will join forces on behalf of *The Heart Truth* to share an urgent message to American women about heart health," said Dr. Nabel. "Although we've helped to dramatically increase awareness among women that heart disease is their leading cause of death, our mission remains to educate women about the seriousness of heart disease and inspire them to take action to reduce their risk."

The Heart Truth effort aims to spread the word that heart disease is largely preventable. In fact, just by leading a healthy lifestyle—such as following a heart healthy eating plan, getting regular physical activity, maintaining a healthy weight, and not smoking—Americans can lower their risk by as much as 82 percent. Risk factors for heart disease include:

- age (55 or older for women);
- a family history of early heart disease;
- high blood pressure;
- high blood cholesterol;
- diabetes;
- smoking;
- being overweight or obese; and
- being physically inactive.

NHLBI's introduction of *The Heart Truth's* Red Dress as the national symbol for women and heart disease awareness in 2002 sparked a national movement that has united partners to promote the common goal of a greater awareness of heart disease and better heart health for all women. The Red Dress is fast becoming one of the most recognizable health symbols in the United States. About half of women recognize the Red Dress as the national symbol for women and heart disease and about half of women are aware that heart disease is the No. 1 killer of women.

Walking in this year's Fashion Show are Hollywood leading ladies, including Allison Janney, Ana Ortiz, Camryn Manheim, Cheryl Hines, Cicely Tyson, Emma Roberts, Heidi Klum, Jenna Fischer, Joss Stone, Leighton Meester, Lisa Rinna, Maria Menounos, Mary Lynn Rajskub, Molly Sims, Rita Moreno, and Sara Ramirez.

Participating designers in the 2008 Collection include Ali Rahimi, Badgley Mischka, Calvin Klein, Carmen Marc Valvo, Catherine Malandrino, Daniel Swarovski, Donna Karan, Marc Jacobs, Marchesa, Michael Kors, Monique L'Huillier, Oscar de la Renta, Rachel Roy, Ralph Lauren, Tracy Reese, and Zac Posen.

Friday, Feb. 1, 2008, is National Wear Red Day when thousands of Americans across the country will wear red to unite in the national movement to give women a

EXHIBIT 12-1d   (Continued)

personal and urgent reminder about their risk for heart disease. The day serves as a reminder to every woman to care for her heart, because heart disease is the #1 killer of women.

About The Heart Truth
The Heart Truth is a national awareness campaign for women about heart disease sponsored by NHLBI, part of the National Institutes of Health, U.S. Department of Health and Human Services.

The Heart Truth's Red Dress reminds women of the need to protect their heart health, and inspires them to take action. NHLBI continues to lead the nation in a landmark heart health awareness movement that is being embraced by millions who share the common goal of greater awareness and better heart health for all women.

The Heart Truth partners include: The Office on Women's Health, Department of Health and Human Services; the American Heart Association; WomenHeart: the National Coalition for Women with Heart Disease, and other organizations committed to the health and well-being of women. To learn more about *The Heart Truth* campaign, visit www.hearttruth.gov.

For additional media information, visit www.hearttruthmedia.com. For downloadable images and photography, please visit www.hearttruth.gov or http://share.hearttruth.com or email your inquiry to media@hearttruth.org.

For additional media information, visit www.hearttruthmedia.com. For downloadable images and photography, please visit www.hearttruth.gov or http://share.hearttruth.com or email your inquiry to media@hearttruth.org.

Please Note: Participants in The Heart Truth's Red Dress Collection 2008 Fashion Show were confirmed at time of release and are subject to change.

Part of the National Institutes of Health, the National Heart, Lung, and Blood Institute plans, conducts, and supports research related to the causes, prevention, diagnosis, and treatment of heart, blood vessel, lung, and blood diseases; and sleep disorders. The Institute also administers national health education campaigns on women and heart disease, healthy weight for children, and other topics. NHLBI press releases and other materials are available online at www.nhlbi.nih.gov.

The National Institutes of Health — The Nation's Medical Research Agency — includes 27 Institutes and Centers and is a component of the U.S. Department of Health and Human Services. It is the primary federal agency for conducting and supporting basic, clinical and translational medical research, and it investigates the causes, treatments, and cures for both common and rare diseases. For more information about NIH and its programs, visit www.nih.gov.

###

Case 12-2

An integrated communication campaign may involve a broad range of media relations, internal communication, community relations events, and advertising/marketing. Exhibit 12-2a shows advertisements for the campaign, Exhibit 12-2b are billboard displays, and Exhibit 12-2c shows media press kit materials.

Thrivent Financial Helps Its Members Thrive in Retirement
Thrivent Financial for Lutherans with OLSON & Company

SITUATION ANALYSIS

How can a fraternal organization whose original charter was to help provide life insurance to immigrants be considered a serious player in today's cutthroat world of financial planning? That was precisely the challenge Thrivent Financial faced. Mainly known as a fraternal organization, its members gave it high marks for integrity, generous spirit, and values, but low scores on product performance and customer service. With more and more members giving business to its competition, Thrivent had to quickly build trust in its financial competence. But given its values-led approach and lack of any new products or services to tout, the challenge was how to do this with little tangible proof to support it.

OLSON, Thrivent's agency of record, knew that it had to give members and prospects a new way to think about Thrivent. To reinvent the organization, the agency developed a two-phased approach to re-brand the organization as a financial institution; and provide tangible proof of Thrivent's financial expertise with a new online retirement planning tool.

Objectives

- Build awareness of Thrivent's financial expertise—specifically retirement planning—with media, Thrivent members, and preretirees.

- Drive traffic and awareness to Thrivent's new online retirement planning tool—ThriveQ.com.

Audience Analysis

Internal

- Thrivent employees in Minneapolis and Appleton, WI
- Thrivent financial representatives

External

- Consumers—Thrivent members/prospects: Lutheran; ages 35–64; HHI S25-75K; some college
- Media—Personal finance reporters at national print and broadcast outlets and in six key markets of Minneapolis/St. Paul, Appleton/Green Bay, Milwaukee, Phoenix, Omaha, and Rochester/Mankato

RESEARCH

Primary

- Conducted pre- and post-campaign research to determine perceptions and awareness of Thrivent's financial planning expertise
- Held focus groups to test campaign messaging

Secondary

- Reviewed competitive marketing materials, Web sites, and previous press coverage

Key Findings

- Members did not have confidence in Thrivent's financial expertise
- Competitors spent up to 38 times more in paid advertising
- PR coverage focused primarily on charitable efforts, not financial expertise

Implication

- We needed to create an innovative, integrated campaign that would be both inspirational and relatable while solidifying Thrivent's financial expertise.

PLANNING

The goal was to position Thrivent Financial as a "Trusted Financial Guide" with a focused campaign from September 2006 to September 2007.

Strategies

Phase I

- Execute a multilayered media mix to surround internal and external audiences
- Position Thrivent as an expert resource with media for "thriving in retirement"

Phase II

- Launch an innovative online retirement planning tool to provide tangible proof of Thrivent's financial expertise
- Create awareness for Thrivent's new online planning tool

EXECUTION/TACTICS

Phase I

Strategy One—Execute a multilayered media mix to surround internal and external audiences.

Thrivent's emphasis on its financial expertise, rather than its fraternal benefits, was a shift in strategy. Before launching the campaign externally, we needed to educate key internal audiences.

- Employees—Showcased the campaign prior to the launch through a lobby display and banner, skyway/elevator window clings, floor graphics, table tents, and brand booklets.
- Financial representatives—Distributed tool kits to 2,500 financial representatives filled with a brand booklet/video, business card holders, posters and window clings, quarter stickers, and bumper stickers. To reach our external audiences, we utilized both nontraditional and traditional paid media tactics to break through the crowded financial services category. Efforts were focused in six key markets, with a national overlay of print advertising.
- Street teams—Produced "branded" quarters and dropped 5,000 coins in high-traffic pedestrian areas throughout Minneapolis/St. Paul. Each quarter featured a sticker with the Thrivent Web site and a short, creative message. The tactic generated media coverage by the FOX and ABC TV affiliates and WCCO-AM.

- Light projections—Projected campaign images on the side of Thrivent's headquarters.

- Airport takeover—Market research revealed that our target had a high propensity to travel. The campaign came to life in the form of ceiling banners, column wraps, and full-sized window clings at the Minneapolis/St. Paul airport.

- Outdoor advertising—Saturated key markets with billboards over a three-month period.

- Print advertising—Created two-page spread ads for *Real Simple, TIME, Money,* and *Life* magazines. Smaller-spaced ads appeared in *The Wall Street Journal* and *USA Today* and key market newspapers.

Strategy Two—Position Thrivent as an expert resource with media for "thriving in retirement."

- "Thriving in Retirement" survey—Conducted the "Thriving in Retirement" survey of 2,500 baby boomers. The survey was unique as it asked questions related to boomers' mind-set as they approach retirement.

- Media teaser mailing—Sent a tropical shirt announcing "There's more to retirement than wearing a tropical shirt" to the top 75 media contacts to inform them that news from Thrivent was forthcoming.

- New York desk-side meetings—Met with reporters at *TIME, PARADE, Redbook,* Bloomberg TV/Radio, *Barron's, Financial Times,* and Ignites.com. A national exclusive was secured with Reuters.

- Media mailing (Mailing I)—Distributed 350 press kits with limited survey results to personal finance reporters at national and key market media. A local exclusive with the *Star Tribune* was secured and *USA Today* featured several key findings in its "Snapshots."

- Media mailing (Mailing II)—The complete survey results were packaged in a full-length report and released in a subsequent mailing, resulting in a second wave of press coverage that included *The Wall Street Journal* and *AARP Magazine.*

- Matte column—Placed release on ARA to secure coverage in C and D market media outlets.

Phase II

Strategy One—Launch an innovative online retirement planning tool to provide tangible proof of Thrivent's financial expertise

- ThriveQ.com—Created a unique online planning tool that allowed visitors to explore their retirement vision. A 20-question quiz provided visitors with his/her "ThriveQ" to help gauge their retirement readiness.

- Third-party partnership—To solidify its financial credibility, Thrivent partnered with Ken Dychtwald and Age Wave, a retirement think tank, to lend expertise in content development.

Strategy Two—Create awareness for Thrivent's new online planning tool.

- Broadcast media relations—Conducted a satellite media tour with Thrivent spokesperson Pam Moret and Dychtwald to announce the launch of ThriveQ.com. A multimedia news release and audio news release complemented the media tour.

- Electronic press kit—Created an electronic press kit to introduce ThriveQ to the media.

- Byline articles—Developed byline articles to be utilized by financial representatives.

- Outdoor advertising—In addition to billboards, the outdoor strategy incorporated a light-rail train wrap and "King-Kong" bus wraps in Minneapolis— one of the most Lutheran-dense markets.

- Airport takeover—The airport domination strategy was extended to Phoenix in Phase II in order to capture the many—"snow birds" on vacation in the winter months.

- Print advertising—New creative to drive consumers to ThriveQ.com was placed in *Real Simple*, *TIME*, *Money*, and *Life* magazines.

- Smaller-space ads ran in *The Wall Street Journal* and *USA Today* and in key market newspapers.

RESULTS

Objective One—Build awareness of Thrivent's financial expertise, specifically retirement planning.

- Earned media impressions surpassed 160 million. Key highlights included Reuters, *USA Today*, *The Wall Street Journal*, *Star Tribune*, *Milwaukee Journal Sentinel*, *AARP Magazine*, and ABC's "Money Minute."

- 1.73 million paid media impressions.

- Post-campaign research revealed Thrivent's brand equity to be at an all-time high with prospects. Those stating that it "has a solid reputation as a financial service company" doubled, while those that believed it "offers a wide range of financial products and services" tripled.

Objective Two—Drive traffic and awareness to Thrivent Financial's new online retirement planning tool, ThriveQ.com.

- Earned media placements featuring ThriveQ totaled nearly 22 million print, broadcast, and online impressions, including hits in Kiplinger's Personal Finance, *Star Tribune*, Orange County Register, "Good News Broadcast" (syndicated nationally), WJBK-TV Detroit, KUSA-TV Denver, and WIBQ-AM Tampa.

- In just six months, the campaign drove unprecedented traffic to ThriveQ.com.

  - Nearly 90,000 site visits

  - Thirty percent completed the quiz

  - Of those, more than one-fifth registered for future ThriveQ and Thrivent correspondence

EXHIBIT 12-2a   Campaign Advertisements

Courtesy Thrivent Financial

E X H I B I T 12-2b   Billboard ADs

Minneapolis Airport Ads

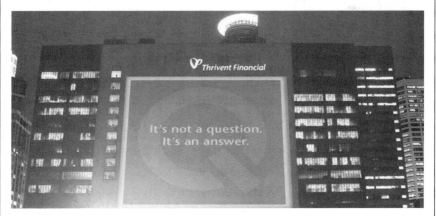

Projection Image on Thrivent Building

Courtesy Thrivent Financial

E X H I B I T 12-2c   News Media Materials

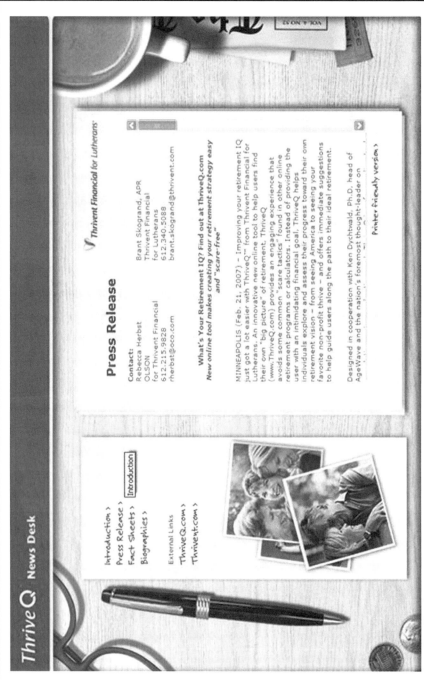

Courtesy Thrivent Financial

Electronic News Desk Press Release

E X H I B I T 12-2c   (Continued)

Press Kit Mailing -"Tropical Shirt"

Case 12-3

Rebranding a city becomes a big challenge, especially when community leaders proposed reinvigorating an "old image." For this campaign, a full range of marketing, special events, and media activities touted the new/old brand identity. Exhibit 12-3a is a kick-off event invitation, and Exhibit 12-3b is a brochure about the initiative.

Rediscovering Kansas City's "Cowtown"

KC Area Development Council (Bayer Animal Health with Fleishman-Hillard, Inc.)

OVERVIEW

Kansas City developed its reputation as a "Cowtown" in 1871 when the Kansas City Stockyards opened for business. More recently, many Kansas Citians felt this distinction limited Kansas City's ability to be known as a leader in science and technology. Instead of building on this reputation, many citizens were trying to shed the city's "Cowtown" image.

In a recent study prepared by noted economist Dr. Richard Seline, animal health and nutrition was identified as a promising sector for life sciences economic development. Joerg Ohle, newly appointed President of Bayer Healthcare, Animal Health, North America Division, recognized an incredible opportunity for growth and revitalization. Ohle committed to making Kansas City's rich history—and reputation as a "Cowtown"—a point of pride for Kansas Citians. A team consisting of Bayer Animal Health, Fleishman-Hillard, Kansas City Area Development Council (KCADC), Greater Kansas City Chamber of Commerce (GKCCC), and the Kansas City Area Life Sciences Institute (KCALSI) led the charge in redefining the "Cowtown" image and branding the Kansas City region as home to animal health and nutrition.

By securing research and communication results, key stakeholders recognized the importance of embracing the animal health industry and became engaged in building economic opportunities. Just one year into the program, local companies already have confidence in the value of the Animal Health Initiative and new animal health companies are beginning to relocate to the Kansas City area.

RESEARCH

Several research elements helped shape the program:

- Regional strengths were assessed during a strategic planning process in a report created by New Economy Strategies. Logical steps were identified to grow the region's economy by focusing resources on realizable technology-driven national or global hubs.

- A review of regional assets called the Asset Profile Report revealed that the animal health industry is one of the fastest growing segments of the United States economy. Furthermore, the report concluded that no region is better suited to capitalize on this growing industry than the Kansas City region.

Primary and secondary research by Brakke Consulting labeled the Kansas City region as the epicenter of animal health and nutrition.

- Companies in Kansas City generate 27 percent of total U.S. animal health sales.

- Kansas City companies generate 30 percent of the global animal health sales.

- Kansas City is home to 4 of the 10 largest global animal health companies.

- Kansas City is home to the world's largest animal health vaccine manufacturer.

CEO Roundtable Discussions—a series of on-site interviews/meetings with Executive Officers of animal health companies to highlight the New Economy Research, the Asset Profile, and Brakke research. Discussions revealed that none of the company executives understood the available economic incentives from branding the region as the place for animal health and nutrition. However, following the briefings, all of the executives realized the initiative's immense value and were willing to participate in the initiative.

While Kansas City has never officially targeted animal health and nutrition companies, research showed that access to quality workforce (a larger pool of highly skilled workforce), access to partnerships across the value chain, increased research support (federal research dollars) to local institutions, and economic incentives were all key factors in attracting companies to the area.

PLANNING

Objectives

1. Brand Kansas City as an animal health and nutrition hub via influencers and media outlets that target community, business, and public affairs leaders.

2. Attract at least one new animal health and nutrition company to the Kansas City region in 2006 and have at least five animal health and nutrition companies in the pipeline in 2007.

3. Showcase Bayer Animal Health as a leader in the Kansas City Animal Health Initiative.

Guiding Strategies

- Market the region as a business location that offers unique benefits to animal health organizations—as "the place to be" if you are in animal health and nutrition (in collaboration with KCADC)

- Create a favorable policy and legislative environment that encourages investments in animal health research and innovation (in collaboration with GKCCC)

- Secure media coverage to reach local, regional, and national corporate and civic decision makers highlighting the animal health and nutrition initiative

- Showcase Bayer Animal Health as the catalyst for building regional partnerships with government, academia, and industry to create economic growth in animal health and nutrition

- Build high-level local and national influencer and third-party support to help spread the word about the initiative

EXECUTION

Tactics

- Developed the "Animal Health Corridor," a region that spans from Manhattan, KS., through Kansas City to Columbia, MO, to attract animal health and nutrition companies to the region. The corridor offers economic incentives for prospective animal health and nutrition companies, works to draw research funds to area institutions, and provides credible visibility to the region. An advisory board of directors—led by Joerg Ohle, and composed of area civic leaders—is responsible for strategy and accountability, while a working group—made up of a Bayer Animal Health representative, a KCALSI member, a KCADC member, and a GKCCC delegate—is charged with plan implementation.

- Launched a comprehensive branding campaign and initiative Web site (www.kcanimalhealth.com) to support recruitment efforts.

- Formed a Kansas City Animal Health Corridor network from ranks of existing regional stakeholders to help garner support for, and increase awareness of, the animal health initiative. Ambassadors acted as advocates and participated in key industry meetings and trade shows and worked to recruit new companies to the region.

- Hosted a "CEO Homecoming Event," reaching out to the regional and national media through roundtable and individual meetings with initiative leadership; press tours; and customized pitching.

- Generated community support for the plan by involving regional civic leaders, government officials, and organizations. Hosted regular meetings and placed follow-up calls to continually involve targeted leaders in the initiative.

EVALUATION

With solid strategies and public relations tactics, this region-wide initiative is attracting national attention. In an effort to brand Kansas City as an animal health hub, the campaign's success was proven by the amount of media coverage generated, enlisted ambassadors, and the increased number of prospective animal health and nutrition companies that have relocated, or are in the pipeline to relocate, to the region.

- The number of prospective companies within the corridor pipeline has greatly exceeded initial expectations of two per year; to date, more than 16 animal health and nutrition companies have expressed interest in relocating to the Kansas City area, a 125 percent increase in one year. (Meets objective 2.)

- There have been more than 80 million confirmed impressions via online, print, television, and radio media. (Meets objective 1.)

- Joerg Ohle's leadership and involvement in the animal health corridor development has created substantial executive visibility. He serves as the Chair of the Animal Health Corridor, Vice Chair of the Task Force for the National Bio and Agro-defense Facility, and several other high-profile positions. Joerg also spoke at GKCCC Economic Forecast breakfast and was the featured speaker at the Governor's Summit and the only speaker invited back for the 2007 summit. (Meets objective 3.)

- Bayer Animal Health is cited as a leader in the animal health initiative in 69 percent of articles about the Animal Health Corridor. An Associated Press story discussing Kansas City as the epicenter for animal health and nutrition reinforced the campaign's momentum. (Meets objective 3.)

- Additional sales and revenue from companies relocating to the Kansas City region fueled the region's economy. Combined, Synbiotics, a leading developer, manufacturer, and marketer of diagnostic products dedicated to the worldwide companion and food animal industries, and IdentiGEN Ltd., a leading provider of DNA-based solutions to the food and agriculture industries in Europe and North America, generated sales of more than $20 million in 2006. Furthermore, Synbiotics invested approximately $3.5 million for equipment in the area. Approximately 47 new jobs were created by these two companies' move to the Kansas City area. IdentiGEN expects to double its employment by 2008 and have a couple of hundred employees within four to five years. Synbiotics plans to build its R&D team here to take advantage of growth opportunities. (Meets objective 2.)

- At the second Annual Governors' Summit in February 2007, Kansas and Missouri State Governors and Kansas City leaders signed a Platform for Action Pact, which officially designated the geographic span of the Animal Health Corridor and committed to growing the region's animal health industry. (Meets objective 1.)

Once trying to shed its image as a "Cowtown," Kansas Citians are now embracing the image as a key economic driver for the region.

The program was delivered on time and on budget. Animal health research studies were conducted from 2003 through 2005, planning sessions took place in late 2004 and 2005, and implementation occurred January 2006 through August 2006.

E X H I B I T 12-3a Kick-off Event Invitation

2600 COMMERCE TOWER
911 MAIN STREET
KANSAS CITY, MO 64105

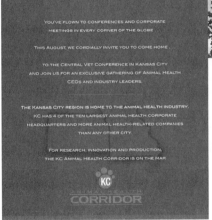

YOU'VE FLOWN TO CONFERENCES AND CORPORATE
MEETINGS IN EVERY CORNER OF THE GLOBE.

THIS AUGUST, WE CORDIALLY INVITE YOU TO COME HOME.

TO THE CENTRAL VET CONFERENCE IN KANSAS CITY
AND JOIN US FOR AN EXCLUSIVE GATHERING OF ANIMAL HEALTH
CEOs AND INDUSTRY LEADERS.

THE KANSAS CITY REGION IS HOME TO THE ANIMAL HEALTH INDUSTRY.
KC HAS 4 OF THE TEN LARGEST ANIMAL HEALTH CORPORATE
HEADQUARTERS AND MORE ANIMAL HEALTH-RELATED COMPANIES
THAN ANY OTHER CITY.

FOR RESEARCH, INNOVATION AND PRODUCTION,
THE KC ANIMAL HEALTH CORRIDOR IS ON THE MAP.

THE STOWERS INSTITUTE
FOR MEDICAL RESEARCH
KANSAS CITY, MISSOURI

MONDAY, AUGUST 28, 2006
5:30 pm   **6:30 pm**
NETWORKING   DINNER AND PROGRAM

FEATURED SPEAKERS:
DR. CHARLES LAMBERT,
DEPUTY UNDER SECRETARY, MARKETING AND REGULATORY PROGRAMS, USDA

RON BRAKKE,
PRESIDENT AND CEO, BRAKKE CONSULTING

SPONSORSHIP OPPORTUNITIES AND SPACES ARE LIMITED
PLEASE CONTACT LYNN PARMAN AT 816.374.5627 · PARMAN@THINKKC.COM

SHUTTLE SERVICE AVAILABLE FROM CVC HOTELS.
FOR MORE DETAILS, PLEASE VISIT THINKKC.COM/HOMECOMING

Courtesy Kansas City Area Development Council

EXHIBIT 12-3b   Brochure

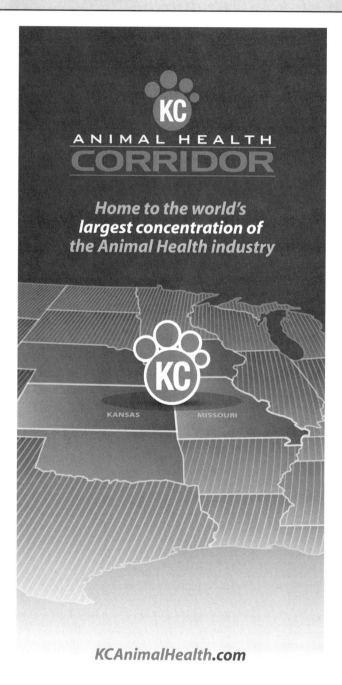

Courtesy Kansas City Area Development Council

EXHIBIT 12-3b   (Continued)

TALENTED WORKFORCE

Kansas City is located within a 300-mile radius of *four of the leading veterinary schools* in the country with over 1,500 students currently enrolled. Kansas City's community colleges and educational institutions offer customized programs such as *veterinary technician training* and *research laboratory training* for the animal health industry.

The KC animal health industry is the largest in the world and growing every day – employing more than 13,000 people.

Additionally, the KC region has a *federally funded, bi-state initiative* focused on creating a competitive, world-class workforce in the high growth/high demand industries of advanced manufacturing, biotechnology and healthcare, all of which are components of the animal health industry.

WORLD-CLASS RESEARCH

Kansas City is within two hours of *Kansas State University's $54 million National Agriculture Biosecurity Center.*

Kansas City is within two hours of the *University of Missouri's $60 million Life Sciences Center* and *the Swine Research Center.* In addition, the university has recently been noted for its work on a USDA Cloned Animal Immune Study.

KC is home to *The Stowers Institute for Medical Research* situated on a 10-acre research campus in the heart of Kansas City, Missouri. The 600,000-square-foot, $300 million facility has a $2 billion endowment. It is one of the most well-funded and highly-regarded research facilities in the world.

The Kansas City Area Life Sciences Institute was formed in 2000 to facilitate collaborative research between scientists at the ten stakeholder institutions with the vision to grow regional life sciences research to $500 million annually by 2010.

Midwest Research Institute provides research and breakthrough developments in National Defense, Health Sciences, Agriculture & Food Safety, Engineering, Environment, Information Technology, Energy, Biological Sciences and Analytical Chemistry.

KCAnimalHealth.com

HISTORICAL FOUNDATION

Thanks to KC's roots and assets within the agriculture sector, KC is home to many prominent national and international associations within the animal health industry including: *American Royal, American Angus Association, American Hereford Association, SouthWestern Association, American International Charolais Association,* and the *U.S. Animal Health Association* which relocated to St. Joseph, Mo. in 2007.

U.S. LIVESTOCK PRODUCED
WITHIN 350 MILES OF KC

45% U.S. HOGS

40% U.S. HOGS

20% U.S. BEEF COWS

The Kansas City region is at the *center of the cattle industry.* Kansas is 2nd and Missouri is 7th in cattle and calves inventory in the United States. Within 350 miles of the KC Corridor, there is more than 45% of the fed cattle in the U.S., more than 40% of U.S. hogs and 20% of U.S. beef cows and calves.

INNOVATIVE INCENTIVES

The state of Kansas recently approved the Kansas Economic Growth Act, which established the *Kansas Biosciences Authority.* It will generate over $500 million in revenue for the development of the bioscience industry over the next 15 years.

The state of Missouri recently approved the *Missouri Quality Jobs Act* that provides a new incentive program for the creation of high-skilled jobs. It offers companies quarterly cash payments of up to five percent of new taxable payroll based upon their new payroll investment.

LOGISTICS ADVANTAGE

Kansas City is located at the crossroads of north–south and east-west trade corridors. It has the *country's largest rail center* based on tonnage, the *largest air cargo facility* for a six-state region, the *nation's third largest trucking center* and *more Foreign Trade Zone space than any other metro in the United States.*

The region consistently ranks in the *top 10 most logistics-friendly cities* in the United States and has an organization, KC SmartPort, solely charged with making it cheaper, faster and more secure for companies to move goods into, from and through the Kansas City area.

LARGEST SINGLE CONCENTRATION

OF ANIMAL HEALTH AND NUTRITION **INTERESTS IN THE WORLD**

The KC Corridor is home to 32 global or U.S. headquarters and has over 125 total companies involved in the industry including: *Bayer HealthCare Animal Health, Fort Dodge Animal Health, Boehringer Ingelheim Vetmedica, Hill's Pet Nutrition, Intervet and many others.* This list represents 5 of the 10 largest global animal health interests and the world's largest animal health generics manufacturer.

KC companies account for *27 percent of total U.S. sales and 34 percent of global sales* in the *$16.8 billion animal health market.* The KC Animal Health Corridor is leading the charge.

34%
of *$16.8 billion in worldwide sales for Animal Health in 2007*

27%
of *$6 billion in U.S. sales for Animal Health in 2007*

13%
of *$45 billion in U.S. sales for Petfood Products in 2007*

The Kansas City region is also home to two nationally-recognized publishers within the animal health industry including: *Vance Publishing,* and *Advanstar Veterinary Healthcare Communications.* These companies publish over 30 leading animal health publications including: *Pork, Dairy Herd Management, DVM, Farm Industry News, Veterinary Economics, Veterinary Forum, Veterinary Medicine, Veterinary Technician, Veterinary Therapeutics* and many others.

SOURCE: BRAKKE CONSULTING, INC.

Appendix I

Questions for Class Discussion and Case Analysis

The following questions can be used in class discussions of each of the cases in this textbook. Students can gain valuable experience by leading class discussions.

RESEARCH

Does the case give adequate background information about the organization itself? What was the major reason for conducting this program? Was the program proactive or reactive? Which audiences were targeted for communication? Should other audiences have also been targeted? How were research data about each audience obtained? Were the data as complete as necessary? Is there anything unusual about the research phase of this case? What are the research strengths and weaknesses of this case?

OBJECTIVES

Categorize this case's objectives. Which are impact objectives? Specify informational, attitudinal, or behavioral. Which are output objectives? Should they have been more quantitative? Should they have used time frames? Were output objectives used when the ultimate goal was really impact? What is your overall assessment of the objectives used in this case?

PRSA Membership Code of Ethics 2000, reprinted with permission from the Public Relations Society of America, New York, NY.

PROGRAMMING

Evaluate the theme (if any) used in this case. Is it short, catchy, memorable, to the point? What major message or messages are communicated in this case? Will the messages resonate with the publics identified by your research phase? Evaluate the central actions or special events in this case. Are they truly worthwhile and newsworthy? Are they "pseudoevents"? Evaluate the types of uncontrolled and controlled media that were used. Were any forms of communication omitted that should have been used? Was adequate use made of interpersonal communication? Did the communication achieve a sense of "grassroots involvement" through interpersonal communication, or was there overreliance on mass media publicity placement or impersonal forms of controlled media? Discuss the use of such communication principles as source credibility, salient information, effective nonverbal and verbal cues, two-way communication, opinion leaders, group influence, selective exposure, and audience participation. How effectively were these principles used? Explain.

EVALUATION

Was each of the case's objectives separately evaluated? Describe the evaluative methods used. How appropriate and effective were these methods? Did the program achieve its stated objectives? Was there a real link between the case's objectives and its evaluation?

OVERALL JUDGMENTS

As a whole, how effective was this public relations program? What are its major strengths and major weaknesses? Explain. What are the major PR lessons or principles to be learned from this case? What, if anything, would you do differently if you were assigned a public relations problem like this one?

Appendix II

PRSA Member Code of Ethics 2000

PREAMBLE

Public Relations Society of America

Member Code of Ethics 2000

- Professional Values
- Principles of Conduct
- Commitment and Compliance

This Code applies to PRSA members. The Code is designed to be a useful guide for PRSA members as they carry out their ethical responsibilities. This document is designed to anticipate and accommodate, by precedent, ethical challenges that may arise. The scenarios outlined in the Code provision are actual examples of misconduct. More will be added as experience with the Code occurs.

The Public Relations Society of America (PRSA) is committed to ethical practices. The level of public trust PRSA members seek, as we serve the public good, means we have taken on a special obligation to operate ethically.

The value of member reputation depends upon the ethical conduct of everyone affiliated with the Public Relations Society of America. Each of us sets an example for each other—as well as other professionals—by our pursuit of excellence with powerful standards of performance, professionalism, and ethical conduct.

Emphasis on enforcement of the Code has been eliminated. But, the PRSA Board of Directors retains the right to bar from membership or expel from the Society any individual who has been or is sanctioned by a government agency or convicted in a court of law of an action that is in violation of this Code.

Ethical practice is the most important obligation of a PRSA member. We view the Member Code of Ethics as a model for other professions, organizations, and professionals.

PRSA MEMBER STATEMENT OF PROFESSIONAL VALUES

This statement presents the core values of PRSA members and, more broadly, of the public relations profession. These values provide the foundation for the Member Code of Ethics and set the industry standard for the professional practice of public relations. These values are the fundamental beliefs that guide our behaviors and decision-making process. We believe our professional values are vital to the integrity of the profession as a whole.

Advocacy

- We serve the public interest by acting as responsible advocates for those we represent.
- We provide a voice in the marketplace of ideas, facts, and viewpoints to aid informed public debate.

Honesty

- We adhere to the highest standards of accuracy and truth in advancing the interests of those we represent and in communicating with the public.

Expertise

- We acquire and responsibly use specialized knowledge and experience.
- We advance the profession through continued professional development, research, and education.
- We build mutual understanding, credibility, and relationships among a wide array of institutions and audiences.

Independence

- We provide objective counsel to those we represent.
- We are accountable for our actions.

Loyalty

- We are faithful to those we represent, while honoring our obligation to serve the public interest.

Fairness

- We deal fairly with clients, employers, competitors, peers, vendors, the media, and the general public.

- We respect all opinions and support the right of free expression.

PRSA CODE PROVISIONS

Free Flow of Information

Core Principle. Protecting and advancing the free flow of accurate and truthful information is essential to serving the public interest and contributing to informed decision making in a democratic society.

Intent
- To maintain the integrity of relationships with the media, government officials, and the public.
- To aid informed decision making.

Guidelines
A member shall:

- Preserve the integrity of the process of communication.

- Be honest and accurate in all communications.

- Act promptly to correct erroneous communications for which the practitioner is responsible.

- Preserve the free flow of unprejudiced information when giving or receiving gifts by ensuring that gifts are nominal, legal, and infrequent.

Examples of Improper Conduct Under This Provision
- A member representing a ski manufacturer gives a pair of expensive racing skis to a sports magazine columnist, to influence the columnist to write favorable articles about the product.

- A member entertains a government official beyond legal limits and/or in violation of government reporting requirements.

Competition

Core Principle. Promoting healthy and fair competition among professionals preserves an ethical climate while fostering a robust business environment.

Intent
- To promote respect and fair competition among public relations professionals.
- To serve the public interest by providing the widest choice of practitioner options.

Guidelines
A member shall:

- Follow ethical hiring practices designed to respect free and open competition without deliberately undermining a competitor.
- Preserve intellectual property rights in the marketplace.

Examples of Improper Conduct Under This Provision
- A member employed by a "client organization" shares helpful information with a counseling firm that is competing with others for the organization's business.
- A member spreads malicious and unfounded rumors about a competitor in order to alienate the competitor's clients and employees in a ploy to recruit people and business.

Disclosure of Information

Core Principle. Open communication fosters informed decision making in a democratic society.

Intent
- To build trust with the public by revealing all information needed for responsible decision making.

Guidelines
A member shall:

- Be honest and accurate in all communications.
- Act promptly to correct erroneous communications for which the member is responsible.
- Investigate the truthfulness and accuracy of information released on behalf of those represented.
- Reveal the sponsors for causes and interests represented.

- Disclose financial interest (such as stock ownership) in a client's organization.
- Avoid deceptive practices.

Examples of Improper Conduct Under This Provision
- Front groups: A member implements "grass roots" campaigns or letter-writing campaigns to legislators on behalf of undisclosed interest groups.
- Lying by omission: A practitioner for a corporation knowingly fails to release financial information, giving a misleading impression of the corporation's performance.
- A member discovers inaccurate information disseminated via a website or media kit and does not correct the information.
- A member deceives the public by employing people to pose as volunteers to speak at public hearings and participate in "grass roots" campaigns.

Safeguarding Confidences

Core Principle. Client trust requires appropriate protection of confidential and private information.

Intent
- To protect the privacy rights of clients, organizations, and individuals by safeguarding confidential information.

Guidelines
A member shall:

- Safeguard the confidences and privacy rights of present, former, and prospective clients and employees.
- Protect privileged, confidential, or insider information gained from a client or organization.
- Immediately advise an appropriate authority if a member discovers that confidential information is being divulged by an employee of a client company or organization.

Examples of Improper Conduct Under This Provision
- A member changes jobs, takes confidential information, and uses that information in the new position to the detriment of the former employer.
- A member intentionally leaks proprietary information to the detriment of some other party.

Conflicts of Interest

Core Principle. Avoiding real, potential, or perceived conflicts of interest builds the trust of clients, employers, and the publics.

Intent
- To earn trust and mutual respect with clients or employers.
- To build trust with the public by avoiding or ending situations that put one's personal or professional interests in conflict with society's interests.

Guidelines
A member shall:

- Act in the best interests of the client or employer, even subordinating the member's personal interests.
- Avoid actions and circumstances that may appear to compromise good business judgment or create a conflict between personal and professional interests.
- Disclose promptly any existing or potential conflict of interest to affected clients or organizations.
- Encourage clients and customers to determine if a conflict exists after notifying all affected parties.

Examples of Improper Conduct Under This Provision
- The member fails to disclose that he or she has a strong financial interest in a client's chief competitor.
- The member represents a "competitor company" or a "conflicting interest" without informing a prospective client.

Enhancing the Profession

Core Principle. Public relations professionals work constantly to strengthen the public's trust in the profession.

Intent
- To build respect and credibility with the public for the profession of public relations.
- To improve, adapt, and expand professional practices.

Guidelines

A member shall:

- Acknowledge that there is an obligation to protect and enhance the profession.

- Keep informed and educated about practices in the profession to ensure ethical conduct.

- Actively pursue personal professional development.

- Decline representation of clients or organizations that urge or require actions contrary to this Code.

- Accurately define what public relations activities can accomplish.

- Counsel subordinates in proper ethical decision making.

- Require that subordinates adhere to the ethical requirements of the Code.

- Report ethical violations, whether committed by PRSA members or not, to the appropriate authority.

Examples of Improper Conduct Under This Provision

- A PRSA member declares publicly that a product the client sells is safe without disclosing evidence to the contrary.

- A member initially assigns some questionable client work to a non-member practitioner to avoid the ethical obligation of PRSA membership.

Resources

Rules and Guidelines. The following PRSA documents, available in The Blue Book, provide detailed rules and guidelines to help guide your professional behavior:

- PRSA Bylaws
- PRSA Administrative Rules
- Member Code of Ethics

If after reviewing them, you still have a question or issue, contact PRSA headquarters as noted below.

Questions. The PRSA is here to help. Whether you have a serious concern or simply need clarification, contact Judy Voss at judy.voss@prsa.org.

Index